Mastering ROS for Robotics Programming

Third Edition

Best practices and troubleshooting solutions
when working with ROS

Lentin Joseph

Jonathan Cacace

BIRMINGHAM—MUMBAI

Mastering ROS for Robotics Programming
Third Edition

Group Product Manager: Wilson D'souza

Publishing Product Manager: Meeta Rajani

Senior Editor: Arun Nadar

Content Development Editor: Yasir Ali Khan

Technical Editor: Shruthi Shetty

Copy Editor: Safis Editing

Project Coordinator: Ajesh Devavaram

Proofreader: Safis Editing

Indexer: Manju Arasan

Production Designer: Alishon Mendonca

First published: December 2015
Second edition: February 2018
Third edition: September 2021

Production reference: 1230821

Published by Packt Publishing Ltd.
Livery Place
35 Livery Street
Birmingham
B3 2PB, UK.

ISBN 978-1-80107-102-4

www.packt.com

We would like to give special thanks to Mr. Franz Pucher for contributing to Chapter 11, Building and Interfacing Differential Drive Mobile Robot Hardware in ROS, of this book.

Contributors

About the authors

Lentin Joseph is an author, roboticist, and robotics entrepreneur from India. He runs a robotics software company called Qbotics Labs in Kochi, Kerala. He has 10 years of experience in the robotics domain, primarily with ROS, OpenCV, and PCL. He has authored other books on ROS, namely *Learning Robotics Using Python*, first and second edition, *Mastering ROS for Robotics Programming*, first and second edition, *ROS Robotics Projects*, first and second edition, and *ROS Learning Path and Robot Operating System for Absolute Beginners*. He pursued his master's in robotics and automation in India and also has worked at the Robotics Institute, CMU, USA. He is also a TEDx speaker.

I would like to dedicate this book to my parents (Jancy Joseph and CG Joseph) and my wife (Aleena Johny).

Jonathan Cacace was born in Naples, Italy, on December 13, 1987. He received a master's degree in computer science from the University of Naples Federico II in 2012 and a Ph.D. degree in robotics in 2016 from the same institution. Currently, he is an assistant professor at the **PRISMA Lab** (**Projects of Robotics for Industry and Services, Mechatronics and Automation Laboratory**) at the University of Naples Federico II, where he is involved in several research projects in the fields of human-robot interaction in industry 4.0 and the autonomous control of UAVs for inspection, maintenance, and robotic manipulation.

I would like to dedicate this book to my family.

About the reviewers

Nick Rotella earned his B.Sc. degree in mechanical engineering from the Cooper Union, followed by his M.Sc. and Ph.D. degrees in computer science from the University of Southern California. As a roboticist, Nick considers himself to be a well-rounded scientist, developer, and engineer. While his Ph.D. thesis focused heavily on model-based motion planning and controls for humanoid robots, he has also worked on autonomous applications in the marine, drone, automotive, mining, and logistics spaces. His experience in controls is based on a deep theoretical understanding of dynamics, estimation, and trajectory generation; Nick has written software at all levels of autonomous system stacks for high-performance controls.

Prateek Nagras is the founder of TechnoYantra (`https://www.technoyantra.com/`), a service-based robotics start-up based in Pune, India.

He is an engineer who studied instrumentation and control engineering at VIT, Pune, and mechatronics with a specialization in robotics at FH Aachen in Germany.

Having gained valuable experience as a robotics engineer in Germany and Austria, he decided to come back to India and started TechnoYantra in December 2019.

TechnoYantra specializes in providing custom robotic solutions to clients in the automobile, health, industrial, and agricultural sectors in the US, Germany, the Netherlands, Saudi Arabia, Singapore, and more.

When Prateek is not building robots, you can find him playing football or watching sports.

Table of Contents

Section 2 – ROS Robot Simulation

3
Working with ROS for 3D Modeling

4
Simulating Robots Using ROS and Gazebo

5
Simulating Robots Using ROS, CoppeliaSim, and Webots

6
Using the ROS MoveIt! and Navigation Stack

7
Exploring the Advanced Capabilities of ROS MoveIt!

8
ROS for Aerial Robots

Section 3 – ROS Robot Hardware Prototyping

9
Interfacing I/O Board Sensors and Actuators to ROS

10

Programming Vision Sensors Using ROS, OpenCV, and PCL

11

Building and Interfacing Differential Drive Mobile Robot Hardware in ROS

Section 4 – Advanced ROS Programming

12

Working with pluginlib, nodelets, and Gazebo Plugins

13

Writing ROS Controllers and Visualization Plugins

14
Using ROS in MATLAB and Simulink

15
ROS for Industrial Robots

16
Troubleshooting and Best Practices in ROS

Other Books You May Enjoy

Index

Preface

The **Robot Operating System** (**ROS**) is a globally used robotics middleware that helps developers to program robotic applications and is currently adopted by robotics companies, research centers, and universities to program advanced robots. *Mastering ROS for Robotics Programming, Third Edition* presents advanced concepts of the ROS framework and is particularly suitable for users who are already familiar with the basic concepts of ROS. However, a brief introduction to the basic ROS concepts is provided in the first chapter in order to help new developers start with the examples in the book.

You will be guided through the creation, the modeling and design, of new robots, as well as simulating and interfacing them with the ROS framework. You will use advanced simulation software to use ROS tools that allow robot navigation, manipulation, and sensor elaboration. Finally, you will learn how to handle important concepts such as ROS low-level controllers, nodelets, and plugins.

You can work with almost all of the examples of the book using only a standard computer without any special hardware requirements. However, additional hardware components will be used in some chapters of the book to discuss how to use ROS with external sensors, actuators, and I/O boards.

The book is organized as follows: after an introduction to the basic concepts of ROS, how to model and simulate a robot is discussed. Gazebo, CoppeliaSim, and the Webots software simulator will be used to control and interact with the modeled robot. These simulators will be used to connect to robots with the MoveIt! and navigation ROS packages. ROS plugins, controllers, and nodelets are then discussed. Finally, the book discusses how to connect MATLAB and Simulink with ROS.

Who this book is for

This book is meant to be used by passionate robotics developers or researchers who want to fully exploit the features of ROS. The book is also good for users who are already familiar with typical robotics applications or who want to start learning how to develop in the world of ROS in an advanced manner, learning how to model, build, and control their robots. Basic knowledge of GNU/Linux and C++ programming is strongly recommended if you want to easily comprehend the contents of the book.

What this book covers

Chapter 1, Introduction to ROS, gives you an understanding of the core underlying concepts of ROS.

Chapter 2, Getting Started with ROS Programming, explains how to work with ROS packages.

Chapter 3, Working with ROS for 3D Modeling, discusses the design of two robots; one is a seven **Degrees of Freedom** (**DOF**) manipulator, and the other is a differential drive robot.

Chapter 4, Simulating Robots Using ROS and Gazebo, discusses the simulation of a seven-DOF arm, differential wheeled robots, and ROS controllers that help control robot joints in Gazebo.

Chapter 5, Simulating Robots Using ROS, CoppeliaSim and Webots, introduces the CoppeliaSim and Webots simulators, showing how to simulate and control different types of robots.

Chapter 6, Using the ROS MoveIt! and Navigation Stack On, covers out-of-the-box functionalities such as robot manipulation and autonomous navigation using ROS MoveIt! and the navigation stack.

Chapter 7, Exploring the Advanced Capabilities of ROS-MoveIt!, discusses the capabilities of MoveIt!, such as collision avoidance, perception using 3D sensors, grasping, picking, and placing. After that, we will see how to interface robotic manipulator hardware with MoveIt!.

Chapter 8, ROS for Aerial Robots, discusses how to simulate and control aerial robots with ROS, considering the particular case of quadcopters.

Chapter 9, Interfacing I/O Boards, Sensors, and Actuators to ROS, discusses interfacing some hardware components, such as sensors and actuators, with ROS. We will look at the interfacing of sensors using I/O boards, such as Arduino or Raspberry Pi, with ROS.

Chapter 10, Programming Vision Sensors Using ROS, OpenCV, and PCL, discusses how to interface various vision sensors with ROS and program them using libraries such as **Open Source Computer Vision (OpenCV)** and **Point Cloud Library (PCL)**.

Chapter 11, Building and Interfacing Differential Drive Mobile Robot Hardware in ROS, helps you to build autonomous mobile robot hardware with differential drive configuration and interface it with ROS. This chapter aims to give you an understanding of building a custom mobile robot and interfacing it with ROS.

Chapter 12, Working with pluginlib, Nodelets, and Gazebo Plugins, shows some of the advanced concepts in ROS, such as ROS `pluginlib`, `nodelets`, and `Gazebo` plugins. We will discuss the functionalities and application of each concept and will practice one example to demonstrate their workings.

Chapter 13, Writing ROS Controllers and Visualization Plugins, shows how to write and run a basic ROS controller. We will also see how to create a plugin for RViz.

Chapter 14, Using ROS in MATLAB and Simulink, discusses how to connect MATLAB and Simulink with ROS.

Chapter 15, ROS for Industrial Robots, helps you understand and install ROS-Industrial packages in ROS. We will see how to develop a MoveIt! IKFast plugin for an industrial robot.

Chapter 16, Troubleshooting and Best Practices in ROS, discusses how to set up a ROS development environment in Eclipse IDE, best practices in ROS, and troubleshooting tips in ROS.

To get the most out of this book

In order to run the examples in this book, you need a standard PC running a Linux OS. Ubuntu 20.04 is the suggested Linux distribution, but Debian 10 is supported as well. The suggested PC configuration requires at least 4 GB of RAM and a modern processor to execute Gazebo simulations and image processing algorithms. You can even work in a virtual environment setup, installing the Linux OS on a virtual machine and using VirtualBox or VMware hosted on a Windows system. The disadvantage of this choice is that more computational power is needed to work with the examples and you could face issues when interfacing ROS with real hardware. The software needed to follow the book is ROS and Noetic Ninjemys. The additional software required is the CoppeliaSim and Webots simulators, Git, MATLAB, and Simulink. Finally, some chapters help you to interface ROS with commercial hardware such as I/O boards (Arduino, ODROID, and Raspberry Pi computers), vision sensors (Intel RealSense), and actuators. These are special hardware components that must be bought to run some examples of the book but are not strictly required to learn ROS.

Download the example code files

You can download the example code files for this book from GitHub at `https://github.com/PacktPublishing/Mastering-ROS-for-Robotics-Programming-Third-edition`. In case there's an update to the code, it will be updated on the existing GitHub repository.

We also have other code bundles from our rich catalogue of books and videos available at `https://github.com/PacktPublishing/`. Check them out!

Code in Action

The Code in Action videos for this book can be viewed at `https://bit.ly/3iYZnGH`.

Download the color images

We also provide a PDF file that has color images of the screenshots/diagrams used in this book. You can download it here: `http://www.packtpub.com/sites/default/files/downloads/9781801071024_ColorImages.pdf`.

Conventions used

There are a number of text conventions used throughout this book.

`Code in text`: Indicates code words in text, database table names, folder names, filenames, file extensions, pathnames, dummy URLs, user input, and Twitter handles. Here is an example: "We are using the `catkin` build system to build ROS packages."

A block of code is set as follows:

```
void number_callback(const std_msgs::Int32::ConstPtr& msg) {
    ROS_INFO("Received [%d]",msg->data);
}
```

When we wish to draw your attention to a particular part of a code block, the relevant lines or items are set in bold:

```
ssh nvidia@nano_ip_adress
password is nano
```

Any command-line input or output is written as follows:

```
$ mkdir css
$ cd css
```

Bold: Indicates a new term, an important word, or words that you see onscreen. For example, words in menus or dialog boxes appear in the text like this. Here is an example: "To create a new simulation, use the top bar menu and select **Wizards | New Project Directory**."

> **Tips or important notes**
> Appear like this.

Get in touch

Feedback from our readers is always welcome.

General feedback: If you have questions about any aspect of this book, mention the book title in the subject of your message and email us at `customercare@packtpub.com`.

Errata: Although we have taken every care to ensure the accuracy of our content, mistakes do happen. If you have found a mistake in this book, we would be grateful if you would report this to us. Please visit `www.packtpub.com/support/errata`, selecting your book, clicking on the Errata Submission Form link, and entering the details.

Piracy: If you come across any illegal copies of our works in any form on the Internet, we would be grateful if you would provide us with the location address or website name. Please contact us at copyright@packt.com with a link to the material.

If you are interested in becoming an author: If there is a topic that you have expertise in and you are interested in either writing or contributing to a book, please visit authors. packtpub.com.

Share Your Thoughts

Once you've read *Mastering ROS for Robotics Programming, Third edition*, we'd love to hear your thoughts! Scan the QR code below to go straight to the Amazon review page for this book and share your feedback.

https://packt.link/r/1-801-07102-0

Your review is important to us and the tech community and will help us make sure we're delivering excellent quality content.

Section 1 – ROS Programming Essentials

This section discusses the fundamental concepts of ROS in detail. You will get a clear and crisp idea of ROS concepts after this section. These concepts are required to be understood in order to work on the chapters covering advanced concepts of ROS.

This section comprises the following chapters:

- *Chapter 1, Introduction to ROS*
- *Chapter 2, Getting Started with ROS Programming*

1
Introduction to ROS

The first two chapters of this book will introduce basic ROS concepts and the ROS package management system in order to approach ROS programming. In this first chapter, we will go through ROS concepts such as the ROS master, the ROS nodes, the ROS parameter server, and ROS messages and services, all while discussing what we need to install ROS and how to get started with the ROS master.

In this chapter, we will cover the following topics:

- Why should we learn ROS?
- Understanding the ROS filesystem level.
- Understanding ROS computation graph level.
- ROS community level.

Technical requirements

To follow this chapter, the only thing you need is a standard computer running Ubuntu 20.04 LTS or a Debian 10 GNU/Linux distribution.

Why should we use ROS?

Robot Operating System (**ROS**) is a flexible framework that provides various tools and libraries for writing robotic software. It offers several powerful features to help developers in tasks such as message passing, distributed computing, code reusing, and implementing state-of-the-art algorithms for robotic applications. The ROS project was started in 2007 by Morgan Quigley and its development continued at Willow Garage, a robotics research lab for developing hardware and open source software for robots. The goal of ROS was to establish a standard way to program robots while offering off-the-shelf software components that can be easily integrated with custom robotic applications. There are many reasons to choose ROS as a programming framework, and some of them are as follows:

- **High-end capabilities**: ROS comes with ready-to-use functionalities. For example, the **Simultaneous Localization and Mapping** (**SLAM**) and **Adaptive Monte Carlo Localization** (**AMCL**) packages in ROS can be used for having autonomous navigation in mobile robots, while the MoveIt package can be used for motion planning for robot manipulators. These capabilities can directly be used in our robot software without any hassle. In several cases, these packages are enough for having core robotics tasks on different platforms. Also, these capabilities are highly configurable; we can fine-tune each one using various parameters.

- **Tons of tools**: The ROS ecosystem is packed with tons of tools for debugging, visualizing, and having a simulation. The tools, such as **rqt_gui**, **RViz**, and **Gazebo**, are some of the strongest open source tools for debugging, visualization, and simulation. A software framework that has this many tools is very rare.

- **Support for high-end sensors and actuators**: ROS allows us to use different device drivers and the interface packages of various sensors and actuators in robotics. Such high-end sensors include 3D LIDAR, laser scanners, depth sensors, actuators, and more. We can interface these components with ROS without any hassle.

- **Inter-platform operability**: The ROS message-passing middleware allows communication between different programs. In ROS, this middleware is known as nodes. These nodes can be programmed in any language that has ROS client libraries. We can write high-haveance nodes in C++ or C and other nodes in Python or Java.

- **Modularity**: One of the issues that can occur in most standalone robotic applications is that if any of the threads of the main code crash, the entire robot application can stop. In ROS, the situation is different; we are writing different nodes for each process, and if one node crashes, the system can still work.

- **Concurrent resource handling**: Handling a hardware resource via more than two processes is always a headache. Imagine that we want to process an image from a camera for face detection and motion detection; we can either write the code as a single entity that can do both, or we can write a single-threaded piece of code for concurrency. If we want to add more than two features to threads, the application behavior will become complex and difficult to debug. But in ROS, we can access devices using ROS topics from the ROS drivers. Any number of ROS nodes can subscribe to the image message from the ROS camera driver, and each node can have different functionalities. This can reduce the complexity in computation and also increase the debugging ability of the entire system.

The ROS community is growing very fast, and there are many users and developers worldwide. Most high-end robotics companies are now porting their software to ROS. This trend is also visible in industrial robotics, in which companies are switching from proprietary robotic applications to ROS.

Now that we know why it is convenient to study ROS, we can start introducing its core concepts. There are mainly three levels in ROS: the filesystem level, the computation graph level, and the community level. We will briefly have a look at each level.

Understanding the ROS filesystem level

ROS is more than a development framework. We can refer to ROS as a meta-OS, since it offers not only tools and libraries but even OS-like functions, such as hardware abstraction, package management, and a developer toolchain. Like a real operating system, ROS files are organized on the hard disk in a particular manner, as depicted in the following diagram:

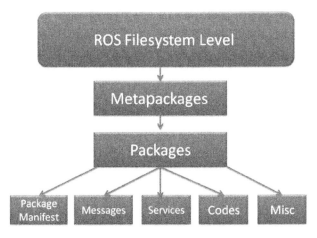

Figure 1.1 – ROS filesystem level

Here are the explanations for each block in the filesystem:

- **Packages**: The ROS packages are a central element of the ROS software. They contain one or more ROS programs (nodes), libraries, configuration files, and so on, which are organized together as a single unit. Packages are the atomic build and release items in the ROS software.

- **Package manifest**: The package manifest file is inside a package and contains information about the package, author, license, dependencies, compilation flags, and so on. The `package.xml` file inside the ROS package is the manifest file of that package.

- **Metapackages**: The term metapackage refers to one or more related packages that can be loosely grouped. In principle, metapackages are virtual packages that don't contain any source code or typical files usually found in packages.

- **Metapackages manifest**: The metapackage manifest is similar to the package manifest, with the difference being that it might include packages inside it as runtime dependencies and declare an `export` tag.

- **Messages** (`.msg`): We can define a custom message inside the `msg` folder inside a package (`my_package/msg/MyMessageType.msg`). The extension of the message file is `.msg`.

- **Services** (`.srv`): The reply and request data types can be defined inside the `srv` folder inside the package (`my_package/srv/MyServiceType.srv`).

- **Repositories**: Most of the ROS packages are maintained using a **Version Control System (VCS)** such as Git, **Subversion (SVN)**, or **Mercurial (hg)**. A set of files placed on a VCS represents a repository.

The following screenshot gives you an idea of the files and folders of a package that we are going to create in the upcoming sections:

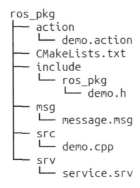

```
ros_pkg
├── action
│   └── demo.action
├── CMakeLists.txt
├── include
│   └── ros_pkg
│       └── demo.h
├── msg
│   └── message.msg
├── src
│   └── demo.cpp
└── srv
    └── service.srv
```

Figure 1.2 – List of files inside the exercise package

The goal of all the files and directories included in a ROS package will be discussed next.

ROS packages

The typical structure of a ROS package is shown here:

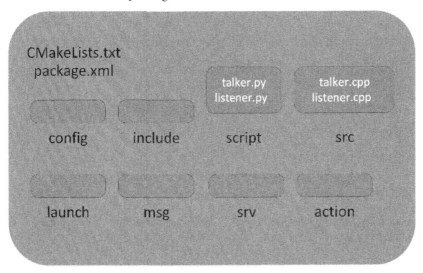

Figure 1.3 – Structure of a typical C++ ROS package

Let's discuss the use of each folder:

- `config`: All configuration files that are used in this ROS package are kept in this folder. This folder is created by the user and it is a common practice to name the folder `config` as this is where we keep the configuration files.

- `include/package_name`: This folder consists of headers and libraries that we need to use inside the package.

- `script`: This folder contains executable Python scripts. In the block diagram, we can see two example scripts.

- `src`: This folder stores the C++ source codes.

- `launch`: This folder contains the launch files that are used to launch one or more ROS nodes.

- `msg`: This folder contains custom message definitions.

- `srv`: This folder contains the services definitions.

- `action`: This folder contains the action files. We will learn more about these kinds of files in the next chapter.

- `package.xml`: This is the package manifest file of this package.

- `CMakeLists.txt`: This file contains the directives to compile the package.

We need to know some commands for creating, modifying, and working with ROS packages. Here are some of the commands we can use to work with ROS packages:

- `catkin_create_pkg`: This command is used to create a new package.

- `rospack`: This command is used to get information about the package in the filesystem.

- `catkin_make`: This command is used to build the packages in the workspace.

- `rosdep`: This command will install the system dependencies required for this package.

To work with packages, ROS provides a bash-like command called `rosbash` (`http://wiki.ros.org/rosbash`), which can be used to navigate and manipulate the ROS package. Here are some of the `rosbash` commands:

- `roscd`: This command is used to change the current directory using a package name, stack name, or a special location. If we give the argument a package name, it will switch to that package folder.

- `roscp`: This command is used to copy a file from a package.

- `rosed`: This command is used to edit a file using the *vim* editor.

- `rosrun`: This command is used to run an executable inside a package.

The definition of `package.xml` in a typical package is shown in the following screenshot:

```xml
<?xml version="1.0"?>
<package>
  <name>hello_world</name>
  <version>0.0.1</version>
  <description>The hello_world package</description>
  <maintainer email="jonathan.cacace@gmail.com">Jonathan Cacace</maintainer>

  <buildtool_depend>catkin</buildtool_depend>
  <build_depend>roscpp</build_depend>
  <build_depend>rospy</build_depend>
  <build_depend>std_msgs</build_depend>

  <run_depend>roscpp</run_depend>
  <run_depend>rospy</run_depend>
  <run_depend>std_msgs</run_depend>

  <export>
  </export>
</package>
```

Figure 1.4 – Structure of package.xml

The `package.xml` file also contains information about the compilation. The `<build_depend></build_depend>` tag includes the packages that are necessary for building the source code of the package. The packages inside the `<run_depend></run_depend>` tags are necessary for running the package node at runtime.

ROS metapackages

Metapackages are specialized packages that require only one file; that is, a `package.xml` file.

Metapackages simply group a set of multiple packages as a single logical package. In the `package.xml` file, the metapackage contains an `export` tag, as shown here:

```
<export>
    <metapackage/>
</export>
```

Also, in metapackages, there are no `<buildtool_depend>` dependencies for `catkin`; there are only `<run_depend>` dependencies, which are the packages that are grouped inside the metapackage.

The ROS navigation stack is a good example of somewhere that contains metapackages. If ROS and its navigation package are installed, we can try using the following command by switching to the `navigation` metapackage folder:

```
roscd navigation
```

Open `package.xml` using your favorite text editor (`gedit`, in the following case):

```
gedit package.xml
```

This is a lengthy file; here is a stripped-down version of it:

```xml
<?xml version="1.0"?>
<package>
    <name>navigation</name>
    <version>1.14.0</version>
    <description>
        A 2D navigation stack that takes in information from odometry, sensor
        streams, and a goal pose and outputs safe velocity commands that are sent
        to a mobile base.
    </description>
    ...
    <url>http://wiki.ros.org/navigation</url>
    ...
    <buildtool_depend>catkin</buildtool_depend>

    <run_depend>amcl</run_depend>
    ...
    <export>
        <metapackage/>
    </export>
</package>
```

Figure 1.5 – Structure of the package.xml metapackage

This file contains several pieces of information about the package, such as a brief description, its dependencies, and the package version.

ROS messages

ROS nodes can write or read data of various types. These different types of data are described using a simplified message description language, also called ROS messages. These data type descriptions can be used to generate source code for the appropriate message type in different target languages.

Even though the ROS framework provides a large set of robotic-specific messages that have already been implemented, developers can define their own message type inside their nodes.

The message definition can consist of two types: `fields` and `constants`. The field is split into field types and field names. The field type is the data type of the transmitting message, while the field name is the name of it.

Here is an example of message definitions:

```
int32 number
string name
float32 speed
```

Here, the first part is the field type and the second is the field name. The field type is the data type, and the field name can be used to access the value from the message. For example, we can use `msg.number` to access the value of the number from the message.

Here is a table showing some of the built-in field types that we can use in our message:

Primitive type	Serialization	C++	Python
bool(1)	Unsigned 8-bit int	uint8_t(2)	bool
int8	Signed 8-bit int	int8_t	int
uint8	Unsigned 8-bit int	uint8_t	int (3)
int16	Signed 16-bit int	int16_t	int
uint16	Unsigned 16-bit int	uint16_t	int
int32	Signed 32-bit int	int32_t	int
uint32	Unsigned 32-bit int	uint32_t	int
int64	Signed 64-bit int	int64_t	long
uint64	Unsigned 64-bit int	uint64_t	long
float32	32-bit IEEE float	float	float
float64	64-bit IEEE float	double	float
string	ascii string(4)	std::string	string
time	secs/nsecs unsigned 32-bit ints	ros::Time	rospy.Time
duration	secs/nsecs signed 32-bit ints	ros::Duration	rospy.Duration

ROS provides a set of complex and more structured message files that are designed to cover a specific application's necessity, such as exchanging common geometrical (geometry_msgs) or sensor (sensor_msgs) information. These messages are composed of different primitive types. A special type of ROS message is called a message header. This header can carry information, such as time, frame of reference or frame_id, and sequence number. Using the header, we will get numbered messages and more clarity about which component is sending the current message. The header information is mainly used to send data such as robot joint transforms. Here is the definition of the header:

```
uint32 seq
time stamp
string frame_id
```

The rosmsg command tool can be used to inspect the message header and the field types. The following command helps view the message header of a particular message:

```
rosmsg show std_msgs/Header
```

This will give you an output like the preceding example's message header. We will look at the rosmsg command and how to work with custom message definitions later in this chapter.

The ROS services

The ROS services are a type of request/response communication between ROS nodes. One node will send a request and wait until it gets a response from the other.

Similar to the message definitions when using the .msg file, we must define the service definition in another file called .srv, which must be kept inside the srv subdirectory of the package.

An example service description format is as follows:

```
#Request message type
string req
---
#Response message type
string res
```

The first section is the message type of the request, which is separated by ---, while the next section contains the message type of the response. In these examples, both `Request` and `Response` are strings.

In the upcoming sections, we will look at how to work with ROS services.

Understanding the ROS computation graph level

Computation in ROS is done using a network of ROS nodes. This computation network is called the computation graph. The main concepts in the computation graph are ROS **nodes**, **master**, **parameter server**, **messages**, **topics**, **services**, and **bags**. Each concept in the graph is contributed to this graph in different ways.

The ROS communication-related packages, including core client libraries, such as `roscpp` and `rospython`, and the implementation of concepts, such as topics, nodes, parameters, and services, are included in a stack called `ros_comm` (`http://wiki.ros.org/ros_comm`).

This stack also consists of tools such as `rostopic`, `rosparam`, `rosservice`, and `rosnode` to introspect the preceding concepts.

The `ros_comm` stack contains the ROS communication middleware packages, and these packages are collectively called the **ROS graph layer**:

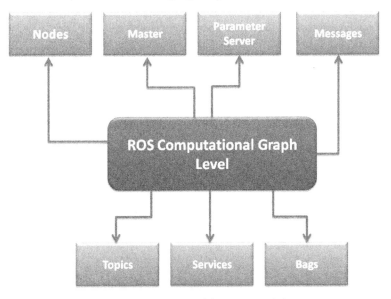

Figure 1.6 – Structure of the ROS graph layer

Some new elements of the ROS graph are as follows:

- **Nodes**: Nodes are the processes that have computation. Each ROS node is written using ROS client libraries. Using client library APIs, we can implement different ROS functionalities, such as the communication methods between nodes, which is particularly useful when the different nodes of our robot must exchange information between them. One of the aims of ROS nodes is to build simple processes rather than a large process with all the desired functionalities. Being simple structures, ROS nodes are easy to debug.

- **Master**: The ROS master provides the name registration and lookup processes for the rest of the nodes. Nodes will not be able to find each other, exchange messages, or invoke services without a ROS master. In a distributed system, we should run the master on one computer; then, the other remote nodes can find each other by communicating with this master.

- **Parameter server**: The parameter server allows you to store data in a central location. All the nodes can access and modify these values. The parameter server is part of the ROS master.

- **Topics**: Each message in ROS is transported using named buses called topics. When a node sends a message through a topic, then we can say the node is publishing a topic. When a node receives a message through a topic, then we can say that the node is subscribing to a topic. The publishing node and subscribing node are not aware of each other's existence. We can even subscribe to a topic that might not have any publisher. In short, the production of information and its consumption are decoupled. Each topic has a unique name, and any node can access this topic and send data through it so long as they have the right message type.

- **Logging**: ROS provides a logging system for storing data, such as sensor data, which can be difficult to collect but is necessary for developing and testing robot algorithms. These are known as bagfiles. Bagfiles are very useful features when we're working with complex robot mechanisms.

The following graph shows how the nodes communicate with each other using topics:

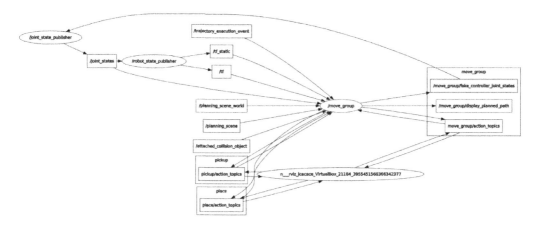

Figure 1.7 – Graph of communication between nodes using topics

As you can see, the topics are represented by rectangles, while the nodes are represented by ellipses. The messages and parameters are not included in this graph. These kinds of graphs can be generated using a tool called `rqt_graph` (http://wiki.ros.org/rqt_graph).

ROS nodes

ROS nodes have computations using ROS client libraries such as `roscpp` and `rospy`.

A robot might contain many nodes; for example, one node processes camera images, one node handles serial data from the robot, one node can be used to compute odometry, and so on.

Using nodes can make the system fault-tolerant. Even if a node crashes, an entire robot system can still work. Nodes also reduce complexity and increase debug-ability compared to monolithic code because each node is handling only a single function.

All running nodes should have a name assigned to help us identify them. For example, `/camera_node` could be the name of a node that is broadcasting camera images.

There is a `rosbash` tool for introspecting ROS nodes. The `rosnode` command can be used to gather information about an ROS node. Here are the usages of `rosnode`:

- `rosnode info [node_name]`: This will print out information about the node.
- `rosnode kill [node_name]`: This will kill a running node.
- `rosnode list`: This will list the running nodes.

- `rosnode machine [machine_name]`: This will list the nodes that are running on a particular machine or a list of machines.

- `rosnode ping`: This will check the connectivity of a node.

- `rosnode cleanup`: This will purge the registration of unreachable nodes.

Next, we will look at some example nodes that use the `roscpp` client and discuss how ROS nodes that use functionalities such ROS topics, service, messages, and actionlib work.

ROS messages

As we discussed earlier, messages are simple data structures that contain field types. ROS messages support standard primitive data types and arrays of primitive types.

We can access a message definition using the following method. For example, to access `std_msgs/msg/String.msg` when we are using the `roscpp` client, we must include `std_msgs/String.h` for the string message definition.

In addition to the `message` data type, ROS uses an MD5 checksum comparison to confirm whether the publisher and subscriber exchange the same message data types.

ROS has a built-in tool called `rosmsg` for gathering information about ROS messages. Here are some parameters that are used along with `rosmsg`:

- `rosmsg show [message_type]`: This shows the message's description.

- `rosmsg list`: This lists all messages.

- `rosmsg md5 [message_type]`: This displays md5sum of a message.

- `rosmsg package [package_name]`: This lists messages in a package.

- `rosmsg packages [package_1] [package_2]`: This lists all packages that contain messages.

Now, let's take a look at ROS topics.

ROS topics

Using topics, the ROS communication is unidirectional. Differently, if we want a direct request/response communication, we need to implement ROS services.

The ROS nodes communicate with topics using a TCP/IP-based transport known as **TCPROS**. This method is the default transport method used in ROS. Another type of communication is **UDPROS**, which has low latency and loose transport and is only suited for teleoperations.

The ROS topic tool can be used to gather information about ROS topics. Here is the syntax of this command:

- `rostopic bw /topic`: This command will display the bandwidth being used by the given topic.
- `rostopic echo /topic`: This command will print the content of the given topic in a human-readable format. Users can use the `-p` option to print data in CSV format.
- `rostopic find /message_type`: This command will find topics using the given message type.
- `rostopic hz /topic`: This command will display the publishing rate of the given topic.
- `rostopic info /topic`: This command will print information about an active topic.
- `rostopic list`: This command will list all the active topics in the ROS system.
- `rostopic pub /topic message_type args`: This command can be used to publish a value to a topic with a message type.
- `rostopic type /topic`: This will display the message type of the given topic.

Now, let's take a look at ROS services.

ROS services

In ROS services, one node acts as a ROS server in which the service client can request the service from the server. If the server completes the service routine, it will send the results to the service client. For example, consider a node that can provide the sum of two numbers that has been received as input while implementing this functionality through an ROS service. The other nodes of our system might request the sum of two numbers via this service. In this situation, topics are used to stream continuous data flows.

The ROS service definition can be accessed by the following method. For example, `my_package/srv/Image.srv` can be accessed by `my_package/Image`.

In ROS services, there is an MD5 `checksum` that checks in the nodes. If the sum is equal, then only the server responds to the client.

There are two ROS tools for gathering information about the ROS service. The first tool is `rossrv`, which is similar to `rosmsg`, and is used to get information about service types. The next command is `rosservice`, which is used to list and query the running ROS services.

Let's explain how to use the `rosservice` tool to gather information about the running services:

- `rosservice call /service args`: This tool will call the service using the given arguments.

- `rosservice find service_type`: This command will find the services of the given service type.

- `rosservice info /services`: This will print information about the given service.

- `rosservice list`: This command will list the active services running on the system.

- `rosservice type /service`: This command will print the service type of a given service.

- `rosservice uri /service`: This tool will print the service's ROSRPC URI.

Now, let's take a look at ROS bagfiles.

ROS bagfiles

The `rosbag` command is used to work with `rosbag` files. A bag file in ROS is used for storing ROS message data that's streamed by topics. The `.bag` extension is used to represent a bag file.

Bag files are created using the `rosbag record` command, which will subscribe to one or more topics and store the message's data in a file as it's received. This file can play the same topics that they are recorded from, and it can remap the existing topics too.

Here are the commands for recording and playing back a bag file:

- `rosbag record [topic_1] [topic_2] -o [bag_name]`: This command will record the given topics into the bag file provided in the command. We can also record all topics using the `-a` argument.

- `rosbag play [bag_name]`: This will play back the existing bag file.

The full, detailed list of commands can be found by using the following command in a Terminal:

```
rosbag play -h
```

There is a GUI tool that we can use to handle how bag files are recorded and played back called rqt_bag. To learn more about rqt_bag, go to https://wiki.ros.org/rqt_bag.

The ROS master

The ROS master is much like a DNS server, in that it associates unique names and IDs to the ROS elements that are active in our system. When any node starts in the ROS system, it will start looking for the ROS master and register the name of the node in it. So, the ROS master has the details of all the nodes currently running on the ROS system. When any of the node's details change, it will generate a callback and update the node with the latest details. These node details are useful for connecting each node.

When a node starts publishing to a topic, the node will give the details of the topic, such as its name and data type, to the ROS master. The ROS master will check whether any other nodes are subscribed to the same topic. If any nodes are subscribed to the same topic, the ROS master will share the node details of the publisher to the subscriber node. After getting the node details, these two nodes will be connected. After connecting to the two nodes, the ROS master has no role in controlling them. We might be able to stop either the publisher node or the subscriber node according to our requirements. If we stop any nodes, they will check in with the ROS master once again. This same method is used for the ROS services.

As we've already stated, the nodes are written using ROS client libraries, such as roscpp and rospy. These clients interact with the ROS master using **XML Remote Procedure Call (XMLRPC)**-based APIs, which act as the backend of the ROS system APIs.

The ROS_MASTER_URI environment variable contains the IP and port of the ROS master. Using this variable, ROS nodes can locate the ROS master. If this variable is wrong, communication between the nodes will not take place. When we use ROS in a single system, we can use the IP of a localhost or the name localhost itself. But in a distributed network, in which computation is done on different physical computers, we should define ROS_MASTER_URI properly; only then will the remote nodes be able to find each other and communicate with each other. We only need one master in a distributed system, and it should run on a computer in which all the other computers can ping it properly to ensure that remote ROS nodes can access the master.

The following diagram shows how the ROS master interacts with publishing and subscribing nodes, with the publisher node publishing a string type topic with a `Hello World` message and the subscriber node subscribing to this topic:

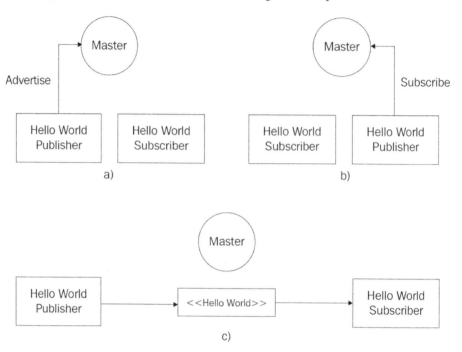

Figure 1.8 – Communication between the ROS master and Hello World publisher and subscriber

When the publisher node starts advertising the `Hello World` message in a particular topic, the ROS master gets the details of the topic and the node. It will check whether any node is subscribing to the same topic. If no nodes are subscribing to the same topic at that time, both nodes will remain unconnected. If the publisher and subscriber nodes run at the same time, the ROS master will exchange the details of the publisher to the subscriber, and they will connect and exchange data through ROS topics.

Using the ROS parameter

When programming a robot, we might have to define robot parameters to tune our control algorithm, such as the robot controller gains P, I, and D of a standard proportional–integral–derivative controller. When the number of parameters increases, we might need to store them as files. In some situations, these parameters must be shared between two or more programs. In this case, ROS provides a parameter server, which is a shared server in which all the ROS nodes can access parameters from this server. A node can read, write, modify, and delete parameter values from the parameter server.

We can store these parameters in a file and load them into the server. The server can store a wide variety of data types and even dictionaries. The programmer can also set the scope of the parameter; that is, whether it can be accessed by only this node or all the nodes.

The parameter server supports the following XMLRPC data types:

- 32-bit integers
- Booleans
- Strings
- Doubles
- ISO8601 dates
- Lists
- Base64-encoded binary data

We can also store dictionaries on the parameter server. If the number of parameters is high, we can use a YAML file to save them. Here is an example of the YAML file parameter definitions:

```
/camera/name : 'nikon'  #string type
/camera/fps : 30      #integer
/camera/exposure : 1.2  #float
/camera/active : true  #boolean
```

The `rosparam` tool is used to get and set the ROS parameter from the command line. The following are the commands for working with ROS parameters:

- `rosparam set [parameter_name] [value]`: This command will set a value in the given parameter.
- `rosparam get [parameter_name]`: This command will retrieve a value from the given parameter.
- `rosparam load [YAML file]`: The ROS parameters can be saved into a YAML file. It can load them into the parameter server using this command.
- `rosparam dump [YAML file]`: This command will dump the existing ROS parameters into a YAML file.
- `rosparam delete [parameter_name]`: This command will delete the given parameter.
- `rosparam list`: This command will list existing parameter names.

These parameters can be changed dynamically when you're executing a node that uses these parameters by using the `dyamic_reconfigure` package (`http://wiki.ros.org/dynamic_reconfigure`).

ROS community level

These are ROS resources that enable a new community in ROS to exchange software and knowledge. The various resources in these communities are as follows:

- **Distributions**: Similar to the Linux distribution, ROS distributions are a collection of versioned metapackages that we can install. The ROS distributions allow us to easily install and collect ROS software. They also maintain consistent versions across a set of software.

- **Repositories**: ROS relies on a federated network of code repositories, where different institutions can develop and release their own robot software components.

- **The ROS Wiki**: The ROS community Wiki is the main forum for documenting information about ROS. Anyone can sign up for an account and contribute their own documentation, provide corrections or updates, write tutorials, and more.

- **Bug ticket system**: If we find a bug in the existing software or need to add a new feature, we can use this resource.

- **Mailing lists**: We can use the ROS-users mailing list to ask questions about ROS software and share program problems with the community.

- **ROS Answers**: This website resource helps us ask questions related to ROS. If we post our doubts on this site, other ROS users can see them and provide solutions.

- **Blog**: The ROS blog updates with news, photos, and videos related to the ROS community (`http://www.ros.org/news`).

Now, let's take a look at prerequisites for starting with ROS.

Prerequisites for starting with ROS

Before getting started with ROS and trying the code in this book, the following prerequisites should be met:

- **Ubuntu 20.04 LTS/Debian 10**: ROS is officially supported by the Ubuntu and Debian operating systems. We prefer to stick with the LTS version of Ubuntu; that is, Ubuntu 20.04.

- **ROS noetic desktop full installation**: Install the full desktop installation of ROS. The version we prefer is ROS Noetic, which is the latest stable version. The following link provides the installation instructions for the latest ROS distribution: `http://wiki.ros.org/noetic/Installation/Ubuntu`. Choose the `ros-noetic-desktop-full` package from the repository list.

Let's see the different versions of ROS framework.

ROS distributions

ROS updates are released with new ROS distributions. A new distribution of ROS is composed of an updated version of its core software and a set of new/updated ROS packages. ROS follows the same release cycle as the Ubuntu Linux distribution: a new version of ROS is released every 6 months. Typically, for each Ubuntu LTS version, an LTS version of ROS is released. **Long Term Support** (**LTS**) and means that the released software will be maintained for a long time (5 years in the case of ROS and Ubuntu):

Distro	Release date	Poster	*Tuturtle*, turtle in tutorial	EOL date
ROS Noetic Ninjemys (Recommended)	May 23rd, 2020			May, 2025 (Focal EOL)
ROS Melodic Morenia	May 23rd, 2018			May, 2023 (Bionic EOL)
ROS Lunar Loggerhead	May 23rd, 2017			May, 2019
ROS Kinetic Kame	May 23rd, 2016			April, 2021 (Xenial EOL)

Figure 1.9 – List of recent ROS releases

The tutorials in this book are based on the latest LTS version of ROS, known as ROS Noetic Ninjemys. It represents the thirteenth ROS distribution release. The list of recent ROS distributions is shown in the preceding image.

Running the ROS master and the ROS parameter server

Before running any ROS nodes, we should start the ROS master and the ROS parameter server. We can start the ROS master and the ROS parameter server by using a single command called `roscore`, which will start the following programs:

- ROS master
- ROS parameter server
- `rosout` logging nodes

The `rosout` node will collect log messages from other ROS nodes and store them in a log file, and will also re-broadcast the collected log message to another topic. The `/rosout` topic is published by ROS nodes using ROS client libraries such as `roscpp` and `rospy`, and this topic is subscribed by the `rosout` node, which rebroadcasts the message in another topic called `/rosout_agg`. This topic contains an aggregate stream of log messages. The `roscore` command should be run as a prerequisite to running any ROS nodes. The following screenshot shows the messages that are printed when we run the `roscore` command in a Terminal.

Use the following command to run `roscore` on a Linux Terminal:

```
roscore
```

After running this command, we will see the following text in the Linux Terminal:

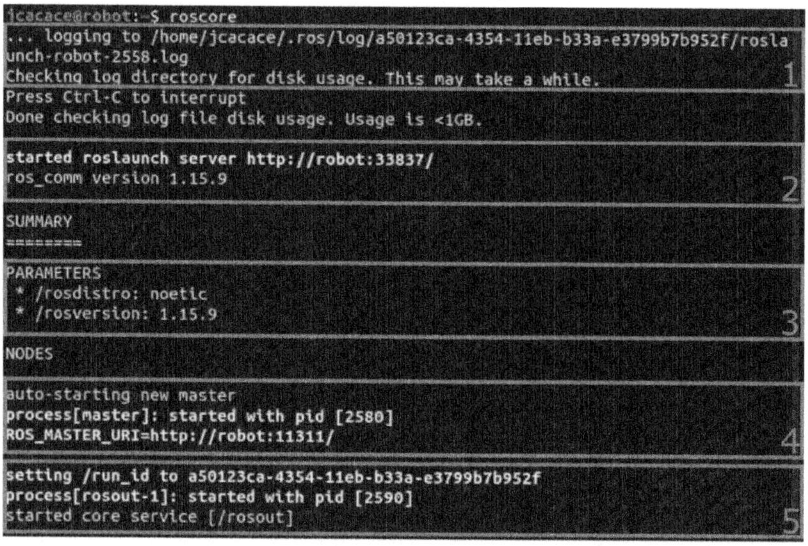

Figure 1.10 – Terminal messages while running the `roscore` command

The following are explanations of each section when executing `roscore` in a Terminal:

- In section **1**, we can see that a log file is created inside the `~/.ros/log` folder for collecting logs from ROS nodes. This file can be used for debugging purposes.

- In section **2**, the command starts a ROS launch file called `roscore.xml`. When a launch file starts, it automatically starts `rosmaster` and the ROS parameter server. The `roslaunch` command is a Python script, which can start `rosmaster` and the ROS parameter server whenever it tries to execute a launch file. This section shows the address of the ROS parameter server within the port.

- In section **3**, we can see parameters such as `rosdistro` and `rosversion` being displayed in the Terminal. These parameters are displayed when it executes `roscore.xml`. We will look at `roscore.xml` in more detail in the next section.

- In section **4**, we can see that the `rosmaster` node is being started with `ROS_MASTER_URI`, which we defined earlier as an environment variable.

- In section **5**, we can see that the `rosout` node is being started, which will start subscribing to the `/rosout` topic and rebroadcasting it to `/rosout_agg`.

The following is the content of `roscore.xml`:

```
<launch>
  <group ns="/">
    <param name="rosversion" command="rosversion roslaunch" />
    <param name="rosdistro" command="rosversion -d" />
    <node pkg="rosout" type="rosout" name="rosout"
respawn="true"/>
  </group>
</launch>
```

When the `roscore` command is executed, initially, the command checks the command-line argument for a new port number for `rosmaster`. If it gets the port number, it will start listening to the new port number; otherwise, it will use the default port. This port number and the `roscore.xml` launch file will be passed to the `roslaunch` system. The `roslaunch` system is implemented in a Python module; it will parse the port number and launch the `roscore.xml` file.

In the `roscore.xml` file, we can see that the ROS parameters and nodes are encapsulated in a group XML tag with a / namespace. The group XML tag indicates that all the nodes inside this tag have the same settings.

The `rosversion` and `rosdistro` parameters store the output of the `rosversionroslaunch` and `rosversion-d` commands using the `command` tag, which is a part of the ROS `param` tag. The `command` tag will execute the command mentioned in it and store the output of the command in these two parameters.

`rosmaster` and the parameter server are executed inside `roslaunch` modules via the `ROS_MASTER_URI` address. This happens inside the `roslaunch` Python module. `ROS_MASTER_URI` is a combination of the IP address and port that `rosmaster` is going to listen to. The port number can be changed according to the given port number in the `roscore` command.

Checking the roscore command's output

Let's check out the ROS topics and ROS parameters that are created after running `roscore`. The following command will list the active topics in the Terminal:

```
rostopic list
```

The list of topics is as follows, as per our discussion of the `rosout` node's subscribe `/rosout` topic. This contains all the log messages from the ROS nodes. `/rosout_agg` will rebroadcast the log messages:

```
/rosout
/rosout_agg
```

The following command lists the parameters that are available when running `roscore`. The following command is used to list the active ROS parameter:

```
rosparam list
```

These parameters are mentioned here; they provide the ROS distribution name, version, the address of the `roslaunch` server, and `run_id`, where `run_id` is a unique ID associated with a particular run of `roscore`:

```
/rosdistro
/roslaunch/uris/host_robot_virtualbox__51189
/rosversion
/run_id
```

The list of ROS services that's generated when running `roscore` can be checked by using the following command:

```
rosservice list
```

The list of services that are running is as follows:

```
/rosout/get_loggers
/rosout/set_logger_level
```

These ROS services are generated for each ROS node, and they are used to set the logging levels.

Summary

ROS is now a trending software framework among roboticists. Gaining knowledge of ROS will be essential in the upcoming years if you are planning to build your career as a robotics engineer. In this chapter, we have gone through the basics of ROS, mainly to refresh you on the concepts if you have already learned about ROS. We discussed the necessity of learning ROS and how it excels among the current robotics software platforms. We went through the basic concepts, such as the ROS master and the parameter server, and provided an explanation of the working of `roscore`. In the next chapter, we will introduce ROS package management and discuss some practical examples of the ROS communication system.

Here are some questions based on what we covered in this chapter.

Questions

- Why should we use ROS?
- What are the basic elements of the ROS framework?
- What are the prerequisites for programming with ROS?
- What is the internal working of `roscore`?

2
Getting Started with ROS Programming

After discussing the basics of the ROS master, the parameter server, and `roscore`, we can now start to create and build a ROS package. In this chapter, we will create different ROS nodes by implementing the ROS communication system. While working with ROS packages, we will also refresh ourselves on the basic concepts of ROS nodes, topics, messages, services, and `actionlib`.

In this chapter, we will cover the following topics:

- Creating a ROS package
- Adding custom message and service files
- Working with ROS services
- Creating launch files
- Applications of topics, services, and actionlib

Technical requirements

To follow this chapter, you will need a standard laptop running Ubuntu 20.04 with ROS Noetic installed. The reference code for this chapter can be downloaded from the following GitHub repository: `https://github.com/PacktPublishing/Mastering-ROS-for-Robotics-Programming-Third-edition.git`. The necessary code is contained in the `Chapter2/mastering_ros_demo_pkg` folder.

You can view this chapter's code in action here: `https://bit.ly/3iXO51W`.

Creating a ROS package

ROS packages are the basic units of ROS programs. We can create a ROS package, build it, and release it to the public. The current distribution of ROS we are using is Noetic Ninjemys. We are using the `catkin` build system to build ROS packages. A build system is responsible for generating `targets` (executable/libraries) from textual source code that can be used by end users. In older distributions, such as Electric and Fuerte, `rosbuild` was the build system. Because of the various flaws of `rosbuild`, `catkin` came into existence. This also allowed us to move the ROS compilation system closer to **Cross Platform Make** (**CMake**). This has a lot of advantages, such as porting the package to another OS, such as Windows. If an OS supports CMake and Python, catkin-based packages can be ported to it.

The first requirement for working with ROS packages is to create a ROS `catkin` workspace. After installing ROS, we can create and build a catkinworkspace called `catkin_ws`:

```
mkdir -p ~/catkin_ws/src
```

To compile this workspace, we should source the ROS environment to get access to ROS functions:

```
source /opt/ros/noetic/setup.bash
```

Switch to the source `src` folder that we created previously:

```
cd ~/catkin_ws/src
```

Initialize a new `catkin` workspace:

```
catkin_init_workspace
```

We can build the workspace even if there are no packages. We can use the following command to switch to the workspace folder:

```
cd ~/catkin_ws
```

The catkin_make command will build the following workspace:

```
catkin_make
```

This command will create a devel and a build directory in your catkin workspace. Different setup files are located inside the devel folder. To add the created ROS workspace to the ROS environment, we should source one of these files. In addition, we can source the setup file of this workspace every time a new bash session starts with the following command:

```
echo "source ~/catkin_ws/devel/setup.bash" >> ~/.bashrc
source ~/.bashrc
```

After setting the catkin workspace, we can create our own package that has sample nodes to demonstrate the working of ROS topics, messages, services, and actionlib. Note that if you haven't set up the workspace correctly, then you won't be able to use any ROS commands. The catkin_create_pkg command is the most convenient way to create a ROS package. This command is used to create our package, in which we are going to create demos of various ROS concepts.

Switch to the catkin workspace's src folder and create the package by using the following command:

```
catkin_create_pkg package_name [dependency1] [dependency2]
```

Source code folder: All ROS packages, either created from scratch or downloaded from other code repositories, must be placed in the src folder of the ROS workspace; otherwise, they won't be recognized by the ROS system and be compiled.

Here is the command for creating the sample ROS package:

```
catkin_create_pkg mastering_ros_demo_pkg roscpp std_msgs
actionlib actionlib_msgs
```

The dependencies in this package are as follows:

- `roscpp`: This is the C++ implementation of ROS. It is a ROS client library that provides APIs to C++ developers to make ROS nodes with ROS topics, services, parameters, and so on. We are including this dependency because we are going to write a ROS C++ node. Any ROS package that uses C++ nodes must add this dependency.

- `std_msgs`: This package contains basic ROS primitive data types, such as integer, float, string, array, and so on. We can directly use these data types in our nodes without defining a new ROS message.

- `actionlib`: The `actionlib` metapackage provides interfaces to create preemptible tasks in ROS nodes. We are creating `actionlib`-based nodes in this package. So, we should include this package to build the ROS nodes.

- `actionlib_msgs`: This package contains standard message definitions needed to interact with the action server and action client.

After package creation, additional dependencies can be added manually by editing the `CMakeLists.txt` and `package.xml` files. We will get the following message if the package has been successfully created:

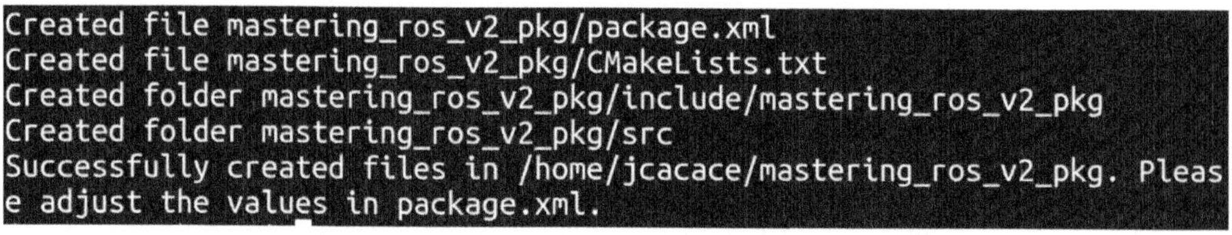

```
Created file mastering_ros_v2_pkg/package.xml
Created file mastering_ros_v2_pkg/CMakeLists.txt
Created folder mastering_ros_v2_pkg/include/mastering_ros_v2_pkg
Created folder mastering_ros_v2_pkg/src
Successfully created files in /home/jcacace/mastering_ros_v2_pkg. Pleas
e adjust the values in package.xml.
```

Figure 2.1 – Terminal messages while creating a ROS package

After creating this package, build the package without adding any nodes by using the `catkin_make` command. This command must be executed from the `catkin` workspace path. The following command shows you how to build our empty ROS package:

```
cd ~/catkin_ws && catkin_make
```

After a successful build, we can start adding nodes to the `src` folder of this package.

The `build` folder in the CMake build files mainly contains the executables of the nodes that are placed inside the `catkin` workspace's `src` folder. The `devel` folder contains a Bash script, header files, and executables in different folders that were generated during the build process. We have seen how to create and compile ROS nodes using `catkin_make`. Let's now discuss how to work with ROS topics.

Working with ROS topics

Topics are used as a communication method between ROS nodes, allowing them to share a continuous stream of information that can be received by other nodes. In this section, we will learn how topics work. We are going to create two ROS nodes for publishing a topic and subscribing to it. Navigate to the `mastering_ros_demo_pkg` folder and join the `/src` subdirectory for the source code. `demo_topic_publisher.cpp` and `demo_topic_subscriber.cpp` are the two sets of code that we are going to discuss.

Creating ROS nodes

The first node we are going to discuss is `demo_topic_publisher.cpp`. This node will publish an integer value on a topic called `/numbers`. Copy the current code into a new package or use this existing file from this book's code repository.

Here is the complete code:

```cpp
#include "ros/ros.h"
#include "std_msgs/Int32.h"
#include <iostream>

int main(int argc, char **argv) {
    ros::init(argc, argv,"demo_topic_publisher");
    ros::NodeHandle node_obj;
    ros::Publisher number_publisher =  node_obj.advertise<std_msgs::Int32>("/numbers", 10);
    ros::Rate loop_rate(10);
    int number_count = 0;
    while ( ros::ok() ) {
        std_msgs::Int32 msg;
        msg.data = number_count;
        ROS_INFO("%d",msg.data);
        number_publisher.publish(msg);
        loop_rate.sleep();
        ++number_count;
    }
    return 0;
}
```

The code starts with the definition of the header files. In particular, `ros/ros.h` is the main header of ROS. If we want to use the `roscpp` client APIs in our code, we should include this header. `std_msgs/Int32.h` is the standard message definition of the integer data type.

Here, we are sending an integer value through a topic. So, we need a message type to handle the integer data. `std_msgs` contains the standard message definition of primitive data types, while `std_msgs/Int32.h` contains the integer message definition. Now, we can initialize a ROS node with a name. It should be noted that the ROS node should be unique:

```
ros::init(argc, argv,"demo_topic_publisher");
```

Next, we need to create a `Nodehandle` object, which is used to communicate with the ROS system. This line is mandatory for all ROS C++ nodes:

```
ros::NodeHandle node_obj;
```

The following line creates a topic publisher and names the topic `"/numbers"` with a message type of `std_msgs::Int32`. The second argument is the buffer size. It indicates how many messages are stored in a buffer if the publisher can't publish data fast enough. This number should be set while considering the message publishing rate. If your program publishes faster than the queue size, some messages will be dropped. The lowest accepted number for the queue size is 1, while 0 means an infinite queue:

```
ros::Publisher number_publisher = node_obj.advertise<std_
msgs::Int32>("/numbers", 10);
```

The following code is used to set the frequency of the main loop of the program and, consequently, the publishing rate in our case:

```
ros::Rate loop_rate(10);
```

This is an infinite `while` loop, and it quits when we press *Ctrl + C*. The `ros::ok()` function returns zero when there is an interrupt. This can terminate this `while` loop:

```
while ( ros::ok() ) {
```

The following lines create an integer ROS message, assigning to it an integer value. Here, `data` is the field name of the `msg` object:

```
std_msgs::Int32 msg;
msg.data = number_count;
```

This will print the message data. These lines are used to log the ROS information and publish the preceding message to the ROS network:

```
ROS_INFO("%d",msg.data);
number_publisher.publish(msg);
```

Finally, this line will provide the necessary delay to achieve a frequency of 10 Hz:

```
loop_rate.sleep();
```

Now that we've discussed the publisher node, we can discuss the subscriber node, which is demo_topic_subscriber.cpp.

Here is the definition of the subscriber node:

```
#include "ros/ros.h"
#include "std_msgs/Int32.h"
#include <iostream>

void number_callback(const std_msgs::Int32::ConstPtr& msg) {
    ROS_INFO("Received [%d]",msg->data);
}

int main(int argc, char **argv) {
    ros::init(argc, argv,"demo_topic_subscriber");
    ros::NodeHandle node_obj;
    ros::Subscriber number_subscriber = node_obj.subscribe("/
numbers",10,number_callback);
    ros::spin();
    return 0;
}
```

Like before, the code starts with the definition of the header files. Then, we develop the callback function, which will execute whenever a ROS message comes to the /numbers topic. Whenever data reaches this topic, the function will call and extract the value and print it to the console:

```
void number_callback(const std_msgs::Int32::ConstPtr& msg) {
    ROS_INFO("Received [%d]",msg->data);
}
```

This is the definition of the subscriber, and here, we are giving the topic name needed to subscribe, the buffer size, and the `callback` function. We are also subscribing to the `/numbers` topic. We looked at the `callback` function in the preceding section:

```
ros::Subscriber number_subscriber = node_obj.subscribe("/
numbers",10,number_callback);
```

This is an infinite loop in which the node will wait in this step. This code will fasten the callbacks whenever data reaches the topic and will terminate only when we press *Ctrl + C*:

```
ros::spin();
```

Now the code is complete. Before we execute it, we need to compile it as discussed in the next section.

Building the nodes

We must edit the `CMakeLists.txt` file in the package to compile and build the source code. Navigate to `mastering_ros_demo_pkg` to view the existing `CMakeLists.txt` file. The following code snippet in this file is responsible for building these two nodes:

```
include_directories(
    include
    ${catkin_INCLUDE_DIRS}
)
#This will create executables of the nodes
add_executable(demo_topic_publisher src/demo_topic_publisher.
cpp)
add_executable(demo_topic_subscriber src/demo_topic_subscriber.
cpp)

#This will link executables to the appropriate libraries
target_link_libraries(demo_topic_publisher ${catkin_LIBRARIES})
target_link_libraries(demo_topic_subscriber ${catkin_
LIBRARIES})
```

We can add the preceding snippet to create a new `CMakeLists.txt` file for compiling the two pieces of code.

The `catkin_make` command is used to build the package. First, let's switch to a workspace:

```
cd ~/catkin_ws
```

Build the ROS workspace, including `mastering_ros_demo_package`, as follows:

```
catkin_make
```

We can either use the preceding command to build the entire workspace or use the `-DCATKIN_WHITELIST_PACKAGES` option. With this option, it is possible to set one or more packages to compile:

```
catkin_make -DCATKIN_WHITELIST_PACKAGES="pkg1,pkg2,..."
```

Note that it is necessary to revert this configuration to compile other packages or the entire workspace. This can be done using the following command:

```
catkin_make -DCATKIN_WHITELIST_PACKAGES=""
```

If the building is done, we can execute the nodes. First, start `roscore`:

```
roscore
```

Now, run both commands in two shells. In the running publisher, run the following command:

```
rosrun mastering_ros_demo_package demo_topic_publisher
```

In the running subscriber, run the following command:

```
rosrun mastering_ros_demo_package demo_topic_subscriber
```

We will see the following output:

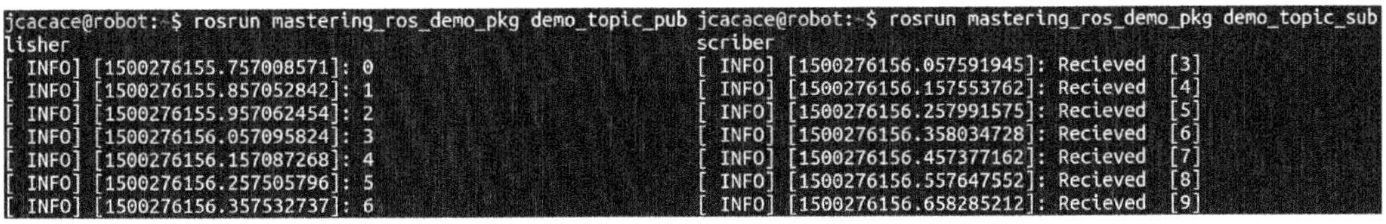

Figure 2.2 – Running the topic publisher and subscriber

The following diagram shows how the nodes communicate with each other. We can see that the demo_topic_publisher node publishes the /numbers topic and then subscribes to the demo_topic_subscriber node:

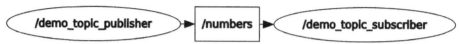

Figure 2.3 – Graph showing the communication between the publisher and subscriber nodes

We can use the rosnode and rostopic tools to debug and understand the working of the two nodes:

- rosnode list: This will list the active nodes.

- rosnode info demo_topic_publisher: This will get information about the publisher node.

- rostopic echo /numbers: This will display the value that's being sent through the /numbers topic.

- rostopic type /numbers: This will print the message type of the /numbers topic.

Now that we've learned how to use standard messages to exchange information between ROS nodes, let's learn how to use custom messages and services.

Adding custom .msg and .srv files

In this section, we will look at how to create custom messages and service definitions in the current package. The message definitions are stored in a .msg file, while the service definitions are stored in a .srv file. These definitions inform ROS about the type of data and the name of the data to be transmitted from a ROS node. When a custom message is added, ROS will convert the definitions into equivalent C++ codes, which we can include in our nodes.

We will start with message definitions. Message definitions must be written in the .msg file and must be kept in the msg folder, which is inside the package. We are going to create a message file called demo_msg.msg with the following definition:

```
string greeting
int32 number
```

So far, we have only worked with standard message definitions. Now, we have created our own definitions, which means we can learn how to use them in our code.

The first step is to edit the package.xml file of the current package and uncomment the <build_depend>message_generation</build_depend> and <exec_depend>message_runtime</exec_depend> lines.

Edit the current CMakeLists.txt file and add the message_generation line, as follows:

```
find_package(catkin REQUIRED COMPONENTS
  roscpp
  rospy
  message_generation
)
```

Uncomment the following line and add the custom message file:

```
add_message_files(
    FILES
    demo_msg.msg
)
## Generate added messages and services with any dependencies
listed here
generate_messages(


)
```

After doing this, we can compile and build the package:

```
cd ~/catkin_ws/
catkin_make
```

To check whether the message has been built properly, we can use the rosmsg command:

```
rosmsg show mastering_ros_demo_pkg/demo_msg
```

If the content shown by the command and the definition are the same, then the procedure ran correctly.

If we want to test the custom message, we can build a publisher and subscriber using the demo_msg_publisher.cpp and demo_msg_subscriber.cpp custom message types, respectively. Navigate to the mastering_ros_demo_pkg folder for these pieces of code.

We can test the message by adding the following lines of code to `CMakeLists.txt`:

```
add_executable(demo_msg_publisher src/demo_msg_publisher.cpp)
add_executable(demo_msg_subscriber src/demo_msg_subscriber.cpp)
```

```
add_dependencies(demo_msg_publisher mastering_ros_demo_pkg_
generate_messages_cpp)
add_dependencies(demo_msg_subscriber mastering_ros_demo_pkg_
generate_messages_cpp)
```

```
target_link_libraries(demo_msg_publisher ${catkin_LIBRARIES})
target_link_libraries(demo_msg_subscriber ${catkin_LIBRARIES})
```

An important difference between this edited `CMakeLists.txt` file and the older one is the dependency specification to the messages generated in `mastering_ros_demo_pkg`. This dependency is specified with the `add_dependencies` instruction. Note that if you forget to include this instruction, the ROS system will start compiling the CPP source code before the message is generated. In this way, a compilation error will be generated since the header files of the custom messages could not be found. Now, we are ready to build the package.

Let's build the package using `catkin_make` and test the node by following these steps:

1. Run `roscore`:

    ```
    roscore
    ```

2. Start the custom message publisher node:

    ```
    rosrun mastering_ros_demo_pkg demo_msg_publisher
    ```

3. Start the custom message subscriber node:

    ```
    rosrun mastering_ros_demo_pkg demo_msg_subscriber
    ```

The publisher node publishes a string along with an integer, while the subscriber node subscribes to the topic and prints its values. The output and graph are as follows:

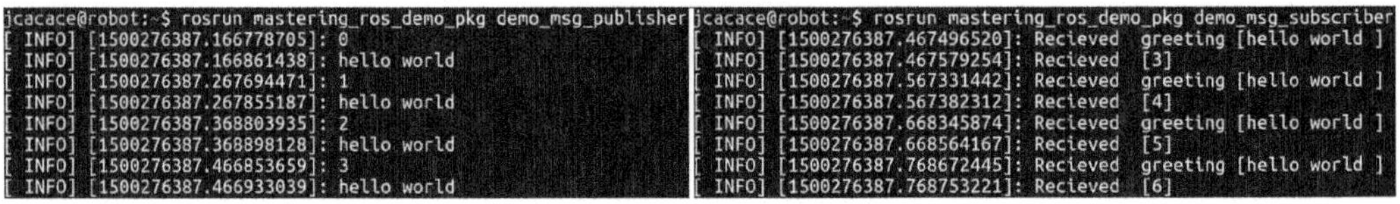

Figure 2.4 – Running the publisher and subscriber using custom message definitions

The topic in which the nodes are communicating is called /demo_msg_topic. Here is the graph view of the two nodes:

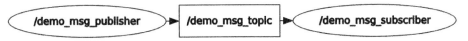

Figure 2.5 – Graph showing the communication between the message publisher and subscriber

Next, we can add .srv files to the package. Create a new folder called srv in the current package folder and add a .srv file called demo_srv.srv. The definition of this file is as follows:

```
string in
---
string out
```

Here, both Request and Response are strings.

Now, we need to uncomment the following lines in package.xml, as we did for the ROS messages:

```
<build_depend>message_generation</build_depend>
<exec_depend>message_runtime</exec_depend>
```

Take CMakeLists.txt and add message_runtime to catkin_package():

```
catkin_package(
    CATKIN_DEPENDS roscpp std_msgs  message_runtime
)
```

We need to follow the same procedure for generating services as we did for the ROS message. Apart from that, we need additional sections to be uncommented, as shown here:

```
## Generate services in the 'srv' folder
add_service_files(
    FILES
    demo_srv.srv
)
```

After making these changes, we can build the package using catkin_make. Then, using the following command, we can verify the procedure:

```
rossrv show mastering_ros_demo_pkg/demo_srv
```

If we see the same content that we defined in the file, we can confirm it is working. The ROS service has been complied and is now available in our ROS workspace. We'll try to use this service in a ROS node in the next section.

Working with ROS services

In this section, we are going to create ROS nodes, which can use the service definition that we defined already. The service nodes we are going to create can send a string message as a request to the server; then, the server node will send another message as a response.

Navigate to `mastering_ros_demo_pkg/src` and find the `demo_service_server.cpp` and `demo_service_client.cpp` nodes.

`demo_service_server.cpp` is the server, and its definition is as follows:

```cpp
#include "ros/ros.h"
#include "mastering_ros_demo_pkg/demo_srv.h"
#include <iostream>
#include <sstream>
using namespace std;


bool demo_service_callback(mastering_ros_demo_pkg::demo_srv::Request &req,
    mastering_ros_demo_pkg::demo_srv::Response &res) {
    ss << "Received Here";
    ROS_INFO("From Client [%s], Server says [%s]",req.in.c_str(),res.out.c_str());
    return true;
}


int main(int argc, char **argv) {
    ros::init(argc, argv, "demo_service_server");
    ros::NodeHandle n;
    ros::ServiceServer service = n.advertiseService("demo_service", demo_service_callback);
    ROS_INFO("Ready to receive from client.");
    ros::spin();
    return 0;
}
```

Let's explain this code. First, we include the header file for defining the service that we want to use in the code:

```
#include "mastering_ros_demo_pkg/demo_srv.h"
```

Here, we included ros/ros.h, which is a mandatory header for a ROS CPP node. The mastering_ros_demo_pkg/demo_srv.h header is a generated header, which contains our service definition, and we can use this in our code.

This is the server callback function that's executed when a request is received on the server. The server can receive the request from clients with a message type of mastering_ros_demo_pkg::demo_srv::Request. It then sends the response with the mastering_ros_demo_pkg::demo_srv::Response message type:

```
bool demo_service_callback(mastering_ros_demo_pkg::demo_
srv::Request &req,
    mastering_ros_demo_pkg::demo_srv::Response &res)
{

std::stringstream ss;
ss << "Received Here";
res.out = ss.str();
```

This creates a service called demo_service, and a callback function is executed when a request comes to this service. The callback function is demo_service_callback, which we saw in the preceding section:

```
ros::ServiceServer service = n.advertiseService("demo_service",
demo_service_callback);
```

Next, let's see how demo_service_client.cpp works. Here is the definition of this code:

```
#include "ros/ros.h"
#include <iostream>
#include "mastering_ros_demo_pkg/demo_srv.h"
#include <iostream>
#include <sstream>
using namespace std;
```

```
int main(int argc, char **argv) {
    ros::init(argc, argv, "demo_service_client");
    ros::NodeHandle n;
    ros::Rate loop_rate(10);
    ros::ServiceClient client = n.serviceClient<mastering_ros_
demo_pkg::demo_srv>("demo_service");
    while (ros::ok()) {
        mastering_ros_demo_pkg::demo_srv srv;
        ss << "Sending from Here";
        srv.request.in = ss.str();
        if (client.call(srv)) {
            ROS_INFO("From Client [%s], Server says [%s]",srv.
request.in.c_str(),srv.response.out.c_str());
        } else {
            ROS_ERROR("Failed to call service");
            return 1;
        }
        ros::spinOnce();
        loop_rate.sleep();
    }
    return 0;
}
```

This line creates a service client that has a message type of mastering_ros_demo_
pkg::demo_srv and communicates with a ROS service named demo_service:

```
ros::ServiceClient client = n.serviceClient<mastering_ros_demo_
pkg::demo_srv>("demo_service");
mastering_ros_demo_pkg::demo_srv srv;
```

Fill the request instance with a string:

```
ss << "Sending from Here";
srv.request.in = ss.str();
if (client.call(srv))
```

If the response is received, then it will print the request and the response:

```
ROS_INFO("From Client [%s], Server says [%s]",srv.request.in.c_
str(),srv.response.out.c_str());
```

Now that we've discussed the two nodes, we can discuss how to build them. The following code is added to CMakeLists.txt to compile and build the two nodes:

```
add_executable(demo_service_server src/demo_service_server.cpp)
add_executable(demo_service_client src/demo_service_client.cpp)

add_dependencies(demo_service_server mastering_ros_demo_pkg_
generate_messages_cpp)
add_dependencies(demo_service_client mastering_ros_demo_pkg_
generate_messages_cpp)

target_link_libraries(demo_service_server ${catkin_LIBRARIES})
target_link_libraries(demo_service_client ${catkin_LIBRARIES})
```

We can execute the following commands to build the code:

```
cd ~/catkin_ws
catkin_make
```

To start the nodes, first, execute roscore and use the following commands:

```
rosrun mastering_ros_demo_pkg demo_service_server
rosrun mastering_ros_demo_pkg demo_service_client
```

The output of these commands is shown in the following screenshot:

Figure 2.6 – Running the ROS service's client and server nodes

We can work with rosservice using the rosservice command:

- rosservice list: This will list the current ROS services.

- rosservice type /demo_service: This will print the message type of /demo_service.

- rosservice info /demo_service: This will print the information of /demo_service.

- rosservice call /service_name service-args: This will call the service server from the command line.

Another important element of ROS is actions. In the next section, we will learn how to use actionlib in a ROS node to create action/server nodes.

Working with ROS actionlib

In ROS services, the user implements a request/reply interaction between two nodes, but if the reply takes too much time or the server has not finished the given work, we have to wait until it completes, which blocks the main application while we wait for the requested action to be terminated. In addition, the calling client can be implemented to monitor the execution of the remote process. In these cases, we should implement our application using actionlib. This is another method in ROS in which we can preempt the running request and start sending another one if the request has not finished on time, as expected. actionlib packages provide a standard way to implement these kinds of preemptive tasks. actionlib is highly used in robot arm navigation and mobile robot navigation. Let's learn how to implement an action server and action client.

Like ROS services, in `actionlib`, we must specify the action specification. The action specification is stored inside the `action` file, and it has an extension of `.action`. This file must be kept inside the `action` folder, which is inside the ROS package. The `action` file has the following parts:

- **Goal**: The action client can send a goal that must be executed by the action server. This is similar to the request in the ROS service. For example, if the joint of a robot needs to be moved from 45 degrees to 90 degrees, the goal here is 90 degrees.

- **Feedback**: When an action client sends a goal to the action server, it will start executing a callback function. Feedback is simply something that tells us of the progress of the current operation inside the callback function. Using the feedback definition, we can get the current progress. In the preceding case, the robot arm joint must move 90 degrees; in this case, the feedback can be the intermediate value between 45 and 90 degrees that the arm is moving in.

- **Result**: After completing the goal, the action server will send a final result, which may either be the computational result or an acknowledgment. In the preceding example, if the joint reaches 90 degrees, then it has achieved the goal and the result can be anything indicating that it has done so.

Now, let's discuss a demo action server and action client. The demo action client will send a number as the goal. When an action server receives this goal, it will count from 0 to the goal number with a step size of 1 and with a 1-second delay. If it completes before the given time, it will send the result; otherwise, the task will be preempted by the client. The feedback here is the progress of counting. The `action` file of this task is as follows and is called `Demo_action.action`:

```
#goal definition
int32 count
---
#result definition
int32 final_count
---
#feedback
int32 current_number
```

Here, the count value is the goal, in which the server has to count from zero to this number. `final_count` is the result, which is the final value after a task has been completed, while `current_number` is the feedback value. This specifies how much progress has been made.

Navigate to `mastering_ros_demo_pkg/src` to find the `demo_action_server.cpp` action server node and the `demo_action_client.cpp` action client node.

Creating the ROS action server

In this section, we will discuss `demo_action_server.cpp`. The action server receives a goal value, which is a number. When the server gets this goal value, it will start counting from zero to this number. When counting is complete, it will successfully finish the action, while if it is preempted before finishing, the action server will look for another goal value.

This code is a bit lengthy, so we will only discuss the important code snippets here.

Let's start with the header files. The first header is the standard action library for implementing an action server node. The second header is generated from the stored action files. It should include accessing our action definition:

```
#include <actionlib/server/simple_action_server.h>
#include "mastering_ros_demo_pkg/Demo_actionAction.h"
```

Create a simple action server instance with our custom action message. Define a class containing the action server definition:

```
class Demo_actionAction {
actionlib::SimpleActionServer<mastering_ros_demo_pkg::Demo_actionAction> as;
```

Create a feedback instance for sending feedback during the operation:

```
mastering_ros_demo_pkg::Demo_actionFeedback feedback;
```

Create a result instance for sending the final result:

```
result:mastering_ros_demo_pkg::Demo_actionResult result;
```

Then, declare an action constructor. By doing this, an action server is created by taking an argument that contains `Nodehandle`, `name`, and `executeCB`, where `executeCB` is the action callback where all the processing is done:

```
Demo_actionAction(std::string name) :
  as(nh_, name, boost::bind(&Demo_actionAction::executeCB,
this, _1), false),
  action_name(name)
```

This line registers a callback when the action is preempted. `preemptCB` is the callback name that's executed when there is a preempt request from the action client:

```
as.registerPreemptCallback(boost::bind(&Demo_
actionAction::preemptCB, this));
```

This is the callback definition that is executed when the action server receives a `goal` value. It will only execute callback functions after checking whether the action server is currently active or whether it has been preempted already:

```
void executeCB(const mastering_ros_demo_pkg::Demo_
actionGoalConstPtr &goal)
{
if(!as.isActive() || as.isPreemptRequested()) return;
```

This loop will execute until the goal value is reached. It will continuously send the current progress as feedback:

```
for(progress = 0 ; progress < goal->count; progress++){
  //Check for ros
  if(!ros::ok()){
  if(!as.isActive() || as.isPreemptRequested()){
         return;
  }
```

If the current value reaches the goal value, then it publishes the result:

```
if(goal->count == progress){
  result.final_count = progress;
  as.setSucceeded(result);
}
```

In `main()`, we must create an instance of `Demo_actionAction`, which will start the action server:

```
Demo_actionAction demo_action_obj(ros::this_node::getName());
```

Now that we've looked at the server, let's learn how to create an action client.

Creating the ROS action client

In this section, we will discuss how an action client works. `demo_action_client.cpp` is the action client node that will send the goal value. This consists of a number, which is the goal it must reach. The client is getting the goal value from the command-line arguments. The first command-line argument of the client is the goal value, while the second is the time of completion for this task.

The goal value will be sent to the server and the client will wait until the given time, in seconds. After waiting, the client will check whether it has completed or not; if it hasn't, the client will preempt the action.

The client code is a bit lengthy, so we will only discuss the important sections of the code here. In `main()`, we create an instance of `Demo_actionAction`, which will start the action server:

```
#include <actionlib/client/simple_action_client.h>
#include <actionlib/client/terminal_state.h>
#include "mastering_ros_demo_pkg/Demo_actionAction.h"
```

In the `main()` function of our ROS node, create an action client instance:

```
int main (int argc, char **argv) {
    ros::init(argc, argv, "demo_action_client");
    if(argc != 3){
        ROS_INFO("%d",argc);
        ROS_WARN("Usage: demo_action_client <goal> <time_to_
preempt_in_sec>");
        return 1;
    }
actionlib::SimpleActionClient<mastering_ros_demo_pkg::Demo_
actionAction> ac("demo_action", true);
 ac.waitForServer();
```

Create an instance of a goal and send the goal value from the first command-line argument:

```
 mastering_ros_demo_pkg::Demo_actionGoal goal;
 goal.count = atoi(argv[1]);
 ac.sendGoal(goal);
 bool finished_before_timeout =
ac.waitForResult(ros::Duration(atoi(argv[2])));
```

If it is not completed, it will preempt the action:

```
ac.cancelGoal();
```

Now, let's take a look at building the ROS action server and client.

Building the ROS action server and client

After creating these two files in the `src` folder, we must edit the `package.xml` and `CMakeLists.txt` files to build the nodes.

The `package.xml` file should contain message generation and runtime packages, similar to the ROS service and messages.

We must include the `Boost` library in `CMakeLists.txt` to build these nodes. Also, we must add the action files that we wrote for this example. We should pass `actionlib`, `actionlib_msgs`, and `message_generation` in `find_package()`:

```
find_package(catkin REQUIRED COMPONENTS
  roscpp
  std_msgs
  actionlib
  actionlib_msgs
  message_generation
)
```

We should also add `Boost` as a system dependency:

```
## System dependencies are found with CMake's conventions
find_package(Boost REQUIRED COMPONENTS system)
## Generate actions in the 'action' folder
 add_action_files(
   FILES
   Demo_action.action
 )
```

Then, we must add `actionlib_msgs` to `generate_messages()`:

```
## Generate added messages and services with any dependencies
listed here
 generate_messages(
   DEPENDENCIES
```

```
  std_msgs
  actionlib_msgs
)
catkin_package(
  CATKIN_DEPENDS roscpp rospy std_msgs actionlib actionlib_msgs
message_runtime
)

include_directories(
  include
  ${catkin_INCLUDE_DIRS}
  ${Boost_INCLUDE_DIRS}
)
```

Finally, we can define the executable that's generated after the compilation of this node, along with its dependencies and linked libraries:

```
##Building action server and action client

add_executable(demo_action_server src/demo_action_server.cpp)
add_executable(demo_action_client src/demo_action_client.cpp)

add_dependencies(demo_action_server mastering_ros_demo_pkg_
generate_messages_cpp)
add_dependencies(demo_action_client mastering_ros_demo_pkg_
generate_messages_cpp)

target_link_libraries(demo_action_server ${catkin_LIBRARIES} )
target_link_libraries(demo_action_client ${catkin_LIBRARIES})
```

After catkin_make, we can run these nodes using the following commands:

1. Run roscore:

    ```
    roscore
    ```

2. Launch the action server node:

    ```
    rosrun mastering_ros_demo_pkg demo_action_server
    ```

3. Launch the action client node:

```
rosrun mastering_ros_demo_pkg demo_action_client 10 1
```

The output of these processes is as follows:

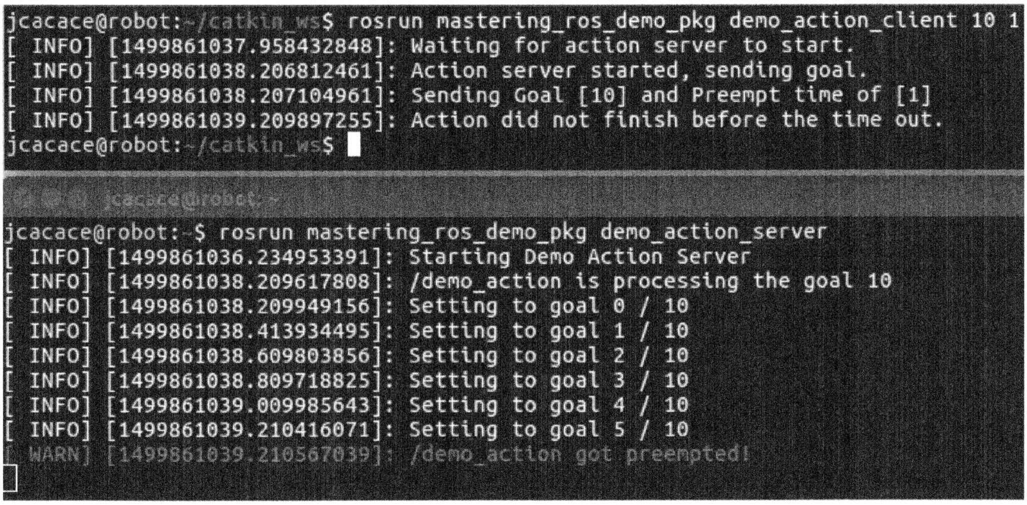

```
jcacace@robot:~/catkin_ws$ rosrun mastering_ros_demo_pkg demo_action_client 10 1
[ INFO] [1499861037.958432848]: Waiting for action server to start.
[ INFO] [1499861038.206812461]: Action server started, sending goal.
[ INFO] [1499861038.207104961]: Sending Goal [10] and Preempt time of [1]
[ INFO] [1499861039.209897255]: Action did not finish before the time out.
jcacace@robot:~/catkin_ws$

jcacace@robot:~$ rosrun mastering_ros_demo_pkg demo_action_server
[ INFO] [1499861036.234953391]: Starting Demo Action Server
[ INFO] [1499861038.209617808]: /demo_action is processing the goal 10
[ INFO] [1499861038.209949156]: Setting to goal 0 / 10
[ INFO] [1499861038.413934495]: Setting to goal 1 / 10
[ INFO] [1499861038.609803856]: Setting to goal 2 / 10
[ INFO] [1499861038.809718825]: Setting to goal 3 / 10
[ INFO] [1499861039.009985643]: Setting to goal 4 / 10
[ INFO] [1499861039.210416071]: Setting to goal 5 / 10
[ WARN] [1499861039.210567039]: /demo_action got preempted!
```

Figure 2.7 – Running the ROS actionlib server and client

Now, let's look at another important feature of ROS: its launch files.

Creating launch files

The launch files in ROS are very useful for launching more than one node. In the preceding examples, we saw a maximum of two ROS nodes, but imagine a scenario in which we have to launch 10 or 20 nodes for a robot. It would be difficult if we had to run each node in a terminal one by one. Instead, we can write all the nodes inside an XML-based file called a launch file and, using a command called **roslaunch**, we parse this file and launch the nodes.

The roslaunch command will automatically start the ROS master and the parameter server. So, in essence, there is no need to start the roscore command and any individual nodes; if we launch the file, all operations will be done in a single command. Note that if you start a node using the roslaunch command, terminating or restarting this command will have the same effect as restarting roscore.

Let's start by creating the launch files. Switch to the package folder and create a new launch file called `demo_topic.launch` to launch two ROS nodes for publishing and subscribing to an integer value. We will keep the launch files in the `launch` folder, which is inside the package:

```
roscd mastering_ros_demo_pkg
mkdir launch
cd launch
gedit demo_topic.launch
```

Paste the following content into the file:

```
<?xml version="1.0" ?>

<launch>
  <node name="publisher_node" pkg="mastering_ros_demo_pkg"
type="demo_topic_publisher" output="screen"/>

  <node name="subscriber_node" pkg="mastering_ros_demo_pkg"
type="demo_topic_subscriber" output="screen"/>
</launch>
```

Let's discuss what is in the code:

```
<?xml version="1.0" ?>
```

This line is useful as it allows text editors to recognize this launch file as a markup language file that enables text highlighting. The `<launch></launch>` tags are the root elements in a `launch` file. All the definitions will be inside these tags.

The `<node>` tag specifies the desired node to launch:

```
<node name="publisher_node" pkg="mastering_ros_demo_pkg"
type="demo_topic_publisher" output="screen"/>
```

The name tag inside `<node>` indicates the name of the node, `pkg` is the name of the package, and `type` is the name of the executable we are going to launch.

After creating the `demo_topic.launch` launch file, we can launch it using the following command:

```
roslaunch mastering_ros_demo_pkg demo_topic.launch
```

Here is the output we will get if the launch is successful:

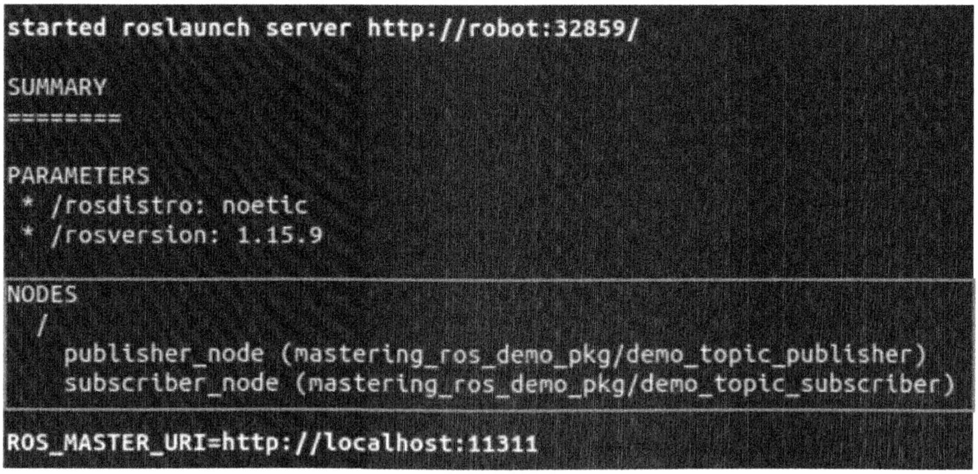

```
started roslaunch server http://robot:32859/

SUMMARY
========

PARAMETERS
 * /rosdistro: noetic
 * /rosversion: 1.15.9

NODES
 /
    publisher_node (mastering_ros_demo_pkg/demo_topic_publisher)
    subscriber_node (mastering_ros_demo_pkg/demo_topic_subscriber)

ROS_MASTER_URI=http://localhost:11311
```

Figure 2.8 – Terminal messages while launching the demo_topic.launch file

We can check the list of nodes by using the following command:

```
rosnode list
```

We can also view the log messages and debug the nodes using a GUI tool called `rqt_console`:

```
rqt_console
```

By doing this, we can see the logs that were generated by the two nodes in this tool, as shown here:

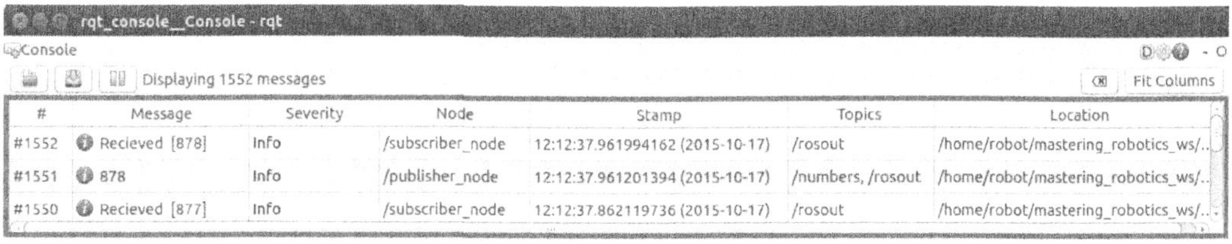

#	Message	Severity	Node	Stamp	Topics	Location
#1552	Recieved [878]	Info	/subscriber_node	12:12:37.961994162 (2015-10-17)	/rosout	/home/robot/mastering_robotics_ws/...
#1551	878	Info	/publisher_node	12:12:37.961201394 (2015-10-17)	/numbers, /rosout	/home/robot/mastering_robotics_ws/...
#1550	Recieved [877]	Info	/subscriber_node	12:12:37.862119736 (2015-10-17)	/rosout	/home/robot/mastering_robotics_ws/...

Figure 2.9 – Logging using the rqt_console tool

In this chapter, we discussed three elements of ROS: topics, the services, and `actionlib`. Each of them can be used in a particular situation. Now, let's discuss how to correctly apply these ROS features.

Applications of topics, services, and actionlib

Topics, services, and `actionlib` are used in different scenarios. We know topics are a unidirectional communication method, services are a bidirectional request/reply kind of communication, and that `actionlib` is a modified form of ROS service in which we can cancel the process that's running on the server as required.

Here are some of the areas where we use these methods:

- **Topics**: Streaming continuous data flows, such as sensor data; for example, we can stream joypad data to teleoperate a robot, publish robot odometry, and publish a video stream from a camera.

- **Services**: Executing procedures that terminate quickly; for example, to save the calibration parameters of sensors, to save a map that's been generated by the robot during its navigation, or to load a parameter file.

- **actionlib**: Executing long and complex actions while managing their feedback; for example, to navigate toward a target or plan a motion path.

The complete source code for this project can be cloned from this book's GitHub repository. The following command will clone the project repository:

```
git clone https://github.com/PacktPublishing/Mastering-ROS-
for-Robotics-Programming-Third-edition.git
```
```
cd Mastering-ROS-for-Robotics-Programming-Third-edition/
Chapter2/
```

After running these commands, you will have a local copy of the source code and also joined the `mastering_ros_demo_pkg` root directory. You can also start compiling and executing the source code contained in this chapter to test ROS's basic functionalities.

Summary

In this chapter, we provided different examples of ROS nodes in which ROS features such as ROS topics, services, and actions were implemented. Such tools are used in every ROS package, both the one already available in the ROS repository and the one created by you. We also discussed how to create and compile ROS packages using custom and standard messages. Usually, different packages use custom messages to handle data generated by their nodes, so it's important to be able to manage custom messages provided by a package.

In the next chapter, we will discuss ROS robot modeling using URDF and `xacro`, and we will design some robot models.

Here are a few questions based on what we covered in this chapter.

Questions

- Which kinds of communication protocols between nodes are supported by ROS?
- What is the difference between the `rosrun` and `roslaunch` commands?
- How do ROS topics and services differ in their operations?
- How do ROS services and `actionlib` differ in their operations?

Section 2 – ROS Robot Simulation

In this section, we will deal with how to simulate a robot using ROS and Gazebo, CoppeliaSim, and Webots. We will see how to model a robot URDF, how to simulate these robots, and how to add high-level features such as navigation, manipulation, and perception.

This section comprises the following chapters:

- *Chapter 3, Working with ROS for 3D Modeling*
- *Chapter 4, Simulating Robots Using ROS and Gazebo*
- *Chapter 5, Simulating Robots Using ROS, CoppeliaSim and Webots*
- *Chapter 6, Using the ROS MoveIt! and Navigation Stack*
- *Chapter 7, Exploring the Advanced Capabilities of ROS MoveIt!*
- *Chapter 8, ROS for Aerial Robots*

3
Working with ROS for 3D Modeling

The first phase of robot manufacturing involves designing and modeling. We can design and model a robot using CAD tools such as Autodesk Fusion 360, SolidWorks, Blender, and many others. One of the main purposes of robot modeling is simulation.

The robotic simulation tool can check for critical flaws in a robot's design and can confirm that the robot will work before it goes to the manufacturing phase.

In this chapter, we are going to discuss the design process of two robots. One is a seven-**Degrees-of-Freedom** (**DOF**) manipulator, and the other is a differential drive robot. In the upcoming chapters, we will look at simulation, learn how to build real hardware, and discuss interfacing with ROS.

If you are planning to create a 3D model of a robot and simulate it using ROS, you will need to learn about some ROS packages that can help in robot designing. Creating a model for our robot in ROS is important for various reasons. For example, you can use this model to simulate and control the robot, visualize it, or use ROS tools to get information regarding the robotic structure and its kinematics.

ROS provides several packages to design and create robot models, such as `urdf`, `kdl_parser`, `robot_state_publisher`, and `collada_urdf`. These packages will help us to create the 3D robot model description with the exact characteristics of the real hardware.

In this chapter, we will cover the following topics:

- ROS packages for robot modeling
- Understanding robot modeling using the **Unified Robot Description Format (URDF)**
- Creating the ROS package for the robot description
- Creating our first URDF model
- Explaining the URDF file
- Visualizing the 3D robot model in RViz
- Adding physical and collision properties to a URDF model
- Understanding robot modeling using **XML Macros (Xacro)**
- Converting xacro to URDF
- Creating the robot description for a seven-DOF robot manipulator
- Explaining the xacro model of the seven-DOF arm
- Creating a robot model for the differential drive mobile robot

Technical requirements

To follow the examples in this chapter, you will need a standard laptop running Ubuntu 20.04 with ROS Noetic installed. The reference code for this chapter can be downloaded from the Git repository at `https://github.com/PacktPublishing/Mastering-ROS-for-Robotics-Programming-Third-edition.git`. The code is contained inside the `Chapter3/mastering_ros_robot_description_pkg/` folder.

You can view this chapter's code in action here: `https://bit.ly/2W5jief`.

ROS packages for robot modeling

ROS provides some good packages that can be used to build 3D robot models. In this section, we will discuss some of the important ROS packages that are commonly used to build and model a robot:

- urdf: The most important ROS package to model a robot is the urdf package. This package contains a C++ parser for the URDF, which is an XML file representing a robot model. Other different components make up urdf, such as the following:

  a. urdf_parser_plugin: This package implements methods to fill the URDF data structures.

  b. urdfdom_headers: This component provides core data structure headers to use the urdf parser.

  c. collada_parser: This package populates data structures by parsing a Collada file.

  d. urdfdom: This component populates data structures by parsing URDF files.

We can define robot models, sensors, and a working environment using URDF. We can also parse them using URDF parsers. We can only describe a robot in URDF that has a tree-like structure in its links, that is, the robot will have rigid links and will be connected using joints. Flexible links can't be represented using URDF. URDF is composed using special XML tags, and we can parse these XML tags using parser programs for further processing. Before working on URDF modeling, let's define some ROS packages that use robot model files:

- joint_state_publisher: This tool is very useful when designing robot models using URDF. This package contains a node called joint_state_publisher, which reads the robot model description, finds all of the joints, and publishes joint values to all of the nonfixed joints. Different sources for the values of each joint are also available. We will discuss this package and its usage in more detail in the upcoming sections.

- joint_state_publisher_gui: This tool is very similar to the joint_state_publisher package. It offers the same functionalities as the joint_state_publisher package and, in addition to this, implements a set of sliders that can be used by the user to interact with each robot joint visualizing the output using RViz. In this case, the source for the joint value is the slider GUI. While designing URDF, the user can verify the rotation and translation of each joint using this tool.

- `kdl_parser`: This package contains a parser tool to build a **Kinematic and Dynamic Library** (**KDL**) tree from the URDF model of the robot. The KDL is a library that is used to solve kinematic and dynamic problems.

- `robot_state_publisher`: This package reads the current robot joint states and publishes the 3D poses of each robot link using the kinematics tree built from the URDF. The 3D pose of the robot is published as the `tf` (transform) ROS. The `tf` ROS publishes the relationship between the coordinate frames of a robot.

- `xacro`: Xacro stands for XML Macros, and we can think to xacro files as URDF files with some add-ons. It contains some add-ons to make the URDF shorter and more readable and can be used to build complex robot descriptions. We can convert `xacro` into URDF at any time using ROS tools. We will learn more about `xacro` and its usage in the upcoming sections.

Now that we have defined the list of packages that are involved in the 3D modeling of a robot, we are ready to analyze our first model using the URDF file format.

Understanding robot modeling using URDF

In the previous section, we listed some important packages that use the `urdf` file format. In this section, we will take a further look at the `URDF` XML tags, which help to model the robot. We need to create a file and write the relationship between each link and joint in the robot and save the file using the `.urdf` extension.

URDF can represent the kinematic and dynamic description of the robot, the visual representation of the robot, and the collision model of the robot.

The following tags are the commonly used URDF tags to compose a URDF robot model:

- `link`: The `link` tag represents the single link of a robot. Using this tag, we can model a robot link and its properties. The modeling includes the size, the shape, and the color; it can even import a 3D mesh to represent the robot link. We can also provide the dynamic properties of the link, such as the inertial matrix and the collision properties.

  The syntax is as follows:

  ```
  <link name="<name of the link>">
  <inertial>..........</inertial>
     <visual> ...........</visual>
       <collision>.........</collision>
  </link>
  ```

The following is a representation of a single link. The **Visual** section represents the real link of the robot, and the area surrounding the real link is the **Collision** section. The **Collision** section encapsulates the real link to detect a collision before hitting the real link:

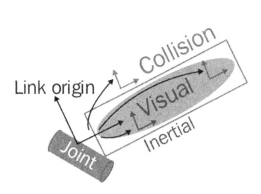

Figure 3.1 – A visualization of the URDF link

- joint: The joint tag represents a robot joint. We can specify the kinematics and dynamics of the joint and set the limits of the joint movement and its velocity. The joint tag supports the different types of joints, such as revolute, continuous, prismatic, fixed, floating, and planar.

The syntax is as follows:

```
<joint name="<name of the joint>">
    <parent link="link1"/>
    <child link="link2"/>

    <calibration .... />
    <dynamics damping ..../>
    <limit effort .... />
</joint>
```

A URDF joint is formed between two links; the first is called the `Parent` link, and the second is called the `Child` link. Note that a single joint can have a single parent and multiple children at the same time. The following is an illustration of a joint and its links:

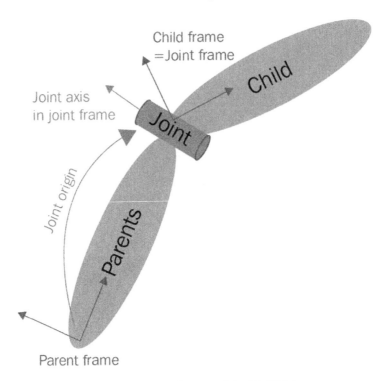

Figure 3.2 – A visualization of the URDF joint

- `robot`: This tag encapsulates the entire robot model that can be represented using URDF. Inside the `robot` tag, we can define the name of the robot, the links, and the joints of the robot.

The syntax is as follows:

```
<robot name="<name of the robot>"
    <link>  ..... </link>
    <link> ...... </link>
    <joint> ....... </joint>
    <joint> ........</joint>
</robot>
```

A robot model consists of connected links and joints. Here is a visualization of the robot model:

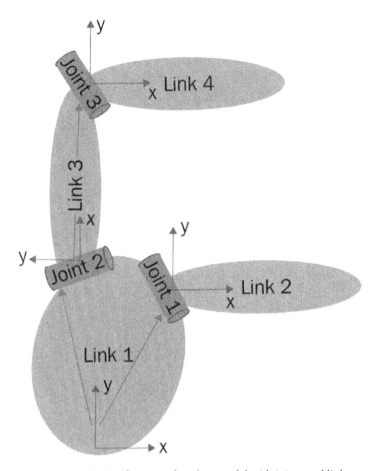

Figure 3.3 – A visualization of a robot model with joints and links

- gazebo: This tag is used when we include the simulation parameters of the **Gazebo** simulator inside the URDF. We can use this tag to include gazebo plugins, gazebo material properties, and more. The following shows an example that uses gazebo tags:

```
<gazebo reference="link_1">
    <material>Gazebo/Black</material>
</gazebo>
```

You can find more URDF tags at http://wiki.ros.org/urdf/XML. We are now ready to use the elements listed earlier to create a new robot from scratch. In the next section, we are going to create a new ROS package containing a description of the different robots.

Creating the ROS package for the robot description

Before creating the URDF file for the robot, let's create an ROS package in the `catkin` workspace so that the robot model keeps using the following command:

```
catkin_create_pkg mastering_ros_robot_description_pkg roscpp tf
geometry_msgs urdf rviz xacro
```

The package mainly depends on the `urdf` and `xacro` packages. If these packages have not been installed on to your system, you can install them using the package manager:

```
sudo apt-get install ros-noetic-urdf
```
```
sudo apt-get install ros-noetic-xacro
```

We can create the `urdf` file of the robot inside this package and create launch files to display the created `urdf` file in RViz. The full package is available in the following Git repository; you can clone the repository for reference to implement this package, or you can get the package from the book's source code:

```
git clone https://github.com/qboticslabs/mastering_ros_3rd_
edition.git
```
```
cd mastering_ros_robot_description_pkg/
```

Before creating the URDF file of this robot, let's create three folders called `urdf`, `meshes`, and `launch` inside the package folder. The `urdf` folder can be used to keep the URDF and xacro files that we are going to create. The `meshes` folder keeps the meshes that we need to include in the `urdf` file, and the `launch` folder keeps the ROS launch files.

Creating our first URDF model

After learning about URDF and its important tags, we can start some basic modeling using URDF. The first robot mechanism that we are going to design is a pan-and-tilt mechanism, as shown in the following diagram.

There are three links and two joints in this mechanism. The base link is static, and all the other links are mounted onto it. The first joint can pan on its axis; the second link is mounted on the first link, and it can tilt on its axis. The two joints in this system are of the revolute type:

Figure 3.4 – A visualization of the pan-and-tilt mechanism in RViz

Let's take a look at the URDF code of this mechanism. Navigate to the `mastering_ros_robot_description_pkg/urdf` directory and open `pan_tilt.urdf`.

We will start by defining the base link of the root model:

```
<?xml version="1.0"?>
<robot name="pan_tilt">
  <link name="base_link">
    <visual>
      <geometry>
      <cylinder length="0.01" radius="0.2"/>
      </geometry>
      <origin rpy="0 0 0" xyz="0 0 0"/>
      <material name="yellow">
        <color rgba="1 1 0 1"/>
      </material>
    </visual>
  </link>
```

Then, we will define the `pan_joint` to connect the `base_link` and the `pan_link`:

```
<joint name="pan_joint" type="revolute">
  <parent link="base_link"/>
  <child link="pan_link"/>
  <origin xyz="0 0 0.1"/>
  <axis xyz="0 0 1" />
</joint>
```

```
<link name="pan_link">
  <visual>
    <geometry>
    <cylinder length="0.4" radius="0.04"/>
    </geometry>
    <origin rpy="0 0 0" xyz="0 0 0.09"/>
    <material name="red">
      <color rgba="0 0 1 1"/>
    </material>
  </visual>
</link>
```

Similarly, we will define the `tilt_joint` to connect the `pan_link` and the `tilt_link`:

```
<joint name="tilt_joint" type="revolute">
  <parent link="pan_link"/>
  <child link="tilt_link"/>
  <origin xyz="0 0 0.2"/>
  <axis xyz="0 1 0" />
</joint>
<link name="tilt_link">
  <visual>
    <geometry>
<cylinder length="0.4" radius="0.04"/>
    </geometry>
    <origin rpy="0 1.5 0" xyz="0 0 0"/>
    <material name="green">
      <color rgba="1 0 0 1"/>
    </material>
  </visual>
</link>
</robot>
```

In the next section, we will analyze the content of this file line by line.

Explaining the URDF file

When we check the code, we can add a <robot> tag at the top of the description. In this way, we inform our system that we are visualizing a markup language file. This also allows the text editor to highlight the keywords of the file:

```
<?xml version="1.0"?>
<robot name="pan_tilt">
```

The <robot> tag defines the name of the robot that we are going to create. Here, we named the robot pan_tilt.

If we check the sections after the <robot> tag definition, we can view the link and joint definitions of the pan-and-tilt mechanism:

```
<link name="base_link">
  <visual>
    <geometry>
    <cylinder length="0.01" radius="0.2"/>
    </geometry>
    <origin rpy="0 0 0" xyz="0 0 0"/>
    <material name="yellow">
      <color rgba="1 1 0 1"/>
    </material>
  </visual>
</link>
```

The preceding code snippet is the base_link definition of the pan-and-tilt mechanism. The <visual> tag describes the visual appearance of the link, which is shown on the robot simulation. We can define the link geometry (cylinder, box, sphere, or mesh) and the material (color and texture) of the link using this tag:

```
<joint name="pan_joint" type="revolute">
  <parent link="base_link"/>
  <child link="pan_link"/>
  <origin xyz="0 0 0.1"/>
  <axis xyz="0 0 1" />
</joint>
```

In the preceding code snippet, we define a joint with a unique name and its joint type. The joint type we used here is `revolute`, and the parent and child links are `base_link` and `pan_link`, respectively. The joint origin is also specified inside this tag.

Save the preceding URDF code as `pan_tilt.urdf` and check whether the `urdf` file contains errors using the following command:

```
check_urdf pan_tilt.urdf
```

To use this command, the `liburdfdom-tools` package must be installed. You can install it using the following command:

```
sudo apt-get install liburdfdom-tools
```

The `check_urdf` command will parse the `urdf` tag and show an error if there is one. If everything is OK, it will output the following:

```
robot name is: pan_tilt
---------- Successfully Parsed XML ---------------
  root Link: base_link has 1 child(ren)
    child(1):  pan_link
      child(1):  tilt_link
```

If we want to view the structure of the robot links and joints graphically, we can use a command tool called `urdf_to_graphiz`:

```
urdf_to_graphiz pan_tilt.urdf
```

This command will generate two files: `pan_tilt.gv` and `pan_tilt.pdf`. We can view the structure of this robot using this command:

```
evince pan_tilt.pdf
```

We will get the following output:

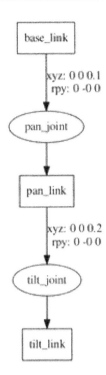

Figure 3.5 – A graph of the joint and links in the pan-and-tilt mechanism

Using the graph visualization helps us to understand the position and the relation of each joint of the robot. However, it is also very useful to visualize the designed model in a 3D viewer. To do this, we can use RViz, as we will discuss in the next section.

Visualizing the 3D robot model in RViz

After designing the URDF, we can view it on RViz. We can create a view_demo. launch launch file and put the following code into the launch folder. Navigate to the mastering_ros_robot_description_pkg/launch directory for the code:

```xml
<?xml version="1.0" ?>
<launch>
  <arg name="model" />
  <param name="robot_description" textfile="$(find mastering_
ros_robot_description_pkg)/urdf/pan_tilt.urdf" />
  <node name="joint_state_publisher_gui" pkg="joint_state_
publisher_gui" type="joint_state_publisher_gui" />
  <node name="robot_state_publisher" pkg="robot_state_
publisher" type="robot_state_publisher" />
```

```
  <node name="rviz" pkg="rviz" type="rviz" args="-d $(find
mastering_ros_robot_description_pkg)/urdf.rviz" required="true"
/>
</launch>
```

We can launch the model using the following command:

```
roslaunch mastering_ros_robot_description_pkg view_demo.launch
```

If everything works correctly, we will get a pan-and-tilt mechanism in RViz, as shown here:

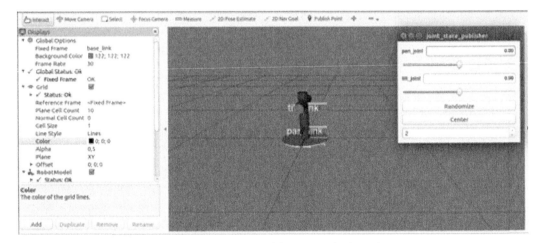

Figure 3.6 – The joint level of the pan-and-tilt mechanism

In the previous version of ROS, the GUI of `joint_state_publisher` was enabled thanks to a ROS parameter called `use_gui`. To start the GUI in the launch file, this parameter had to be set to `true` before starting the `joint_state_publisher` node. In the current version of ROS, launch files should be updated to launch `joint_state_publisher_gui` instead of using `joint_state_publisher` with the `use_gui` parameter.

Interacting with pan-and-tilt joints

We can see that an extra GUI came along with RViz; it contains sliders to control the pan joints and the tilt joints. This GUI is called the **Joint State Publisher Gui node** and belongs to the `joint_state_publisher_gui` package:

```
  <node name="joint_state_publisher_gui" pkg="joint_state_
publisher_gui" type="joint_state_publisher_gui" />
```

We can include this node in the `launch` file using the following statement. The limits of pan-and-tilt should be mentioned inside the `joint` tag:

```
<joint name="pan_joint" type="revolute">
  <parent link="base_link"/>
  <child link="pan_link"/>
  <origin xyz="0 0 0.1"/>
  <axis xyz="0 0 1" />
  <limit effort="300" velocity="0.1" lower="-3.14"
upper="3.14"/>
  <dynamics damping="50" friction="1"/>
</joint>
```

The `<limit>` tag defines the limits of `effort`, `velocity`, and `angle`. In this scenario, `effort` is the maximum force supported by this joint, expressed in Newton; `lower` and `upper` indicate the lower and upper limits of the joint, in radians for the revolute joint and in meters for the prismatic joints. `velocity` is the maximum joint velocity expressed in m/s.

The following screenshot shows the user interface that is used to interact with the robot joints:

Figure 3.7 – The joint level of the pan-and-tilt mechanism

In this user interface, we can use the sliders to set the desired joint values. The basic elements of a `urdf` file have been discussed. In the next section, we will add additional physical elements to our robot model.

Adding physical and collision properties to a URDF model

Before simulating a robot in a robot simulator, such as Gazebo or **CoppeliaSim**, we need to define the robot link's physical properties, such as geometry, color, mass, and inertia, as well as the collision properties of the link.

Good robot simulations can be obtained only if the robot dynamic parameters (for instance, its mass, inertia, and more) are correctly specified in the urdf file. In the following code, we include these parameters as part of the base_link:

```
<link>
......
<collision>
      <geometry>
      <cylinder length="0.03" radius="0.2"/>
      </geometry>
      <origin rpy="0 0 0" xyz="0 0 0"/>
    </collision>

    <inertial>
    <mass value="1"/>
    <inertia ixx="1.0" ixy="0.0" ixz="0.0" iyy="1.0" iyz="0.0"
izz="1.0"/>
      </inertial>
..........
</link>
```

Here, we define the collision geometry as cylinder and the mass as 1 KG, and we also set the inertial matrix of the link.

The collision and inertia parameters are required in each link; otherwise, Gazebo will not load the robot model properly.

We have now seen all the elements of an urdf file. In the next section, we will discuss another file type, that is, the xacro file format.

Understanding robot modeling using xacro

The flexibility of URDF reduces when we work with complex robot models. Some of the main features that URDF is missing include simplicity, reusability, modularity, and programmability.

If someone wants to reuse a URDF block 10 times in their robot description, they can copy and paste the block 10 times. If there is an option to use this code block and make multiple copies with different settings, it will be very useful while creating the robot description.

The URDF is a single file and we can't include other URDF files inside it. This reduces the modular nature of the code. All code should be in a single file, which reduces the code's simplicity.

Also, if there is some programmability, such as adding variables, constants, mathematical expressions, and conditional statements in the description language, it will be more user-friendly.

Robot modeling using **xacro** meets all of these conditions. Some of the main features of xacro are as follows:

- **Simplify URDF**: xacro is a cleaned-up version of URDF. It creates macros inside the robot description and reuses the macros. This can reduce the code length. Also, it can include macros from other files and make the code simpler, more readable, and more modular.

- **Programmability**: The xacro language supports a simple programming statement in its description. There are variables, constants, mathematical expressions, conditional statements, and more that make the description more intelligent and efficient.

We will start by creating the same `pan_tilt` robot that we already made using URDF. The full description of this file can be found in the book's source code. Navigate to `mastering_ros_robot_description_pkg/urdf`, and the filename is `pan_tilt.xacro`. Instead of `.urdf`, we need to use the `.xacro` extension for xacro files.

Here is an explanation of the xacro code:

```
<?xml version="1.0"?>
<robot xmlns:xacro="http://www.ros.org/wiki/xacro" name="pan_tilt">
```

These lines specify a namespace that is needed in all xacro files to parse the xacro file. After specifying the namespace, we need to add the name of the xacro file. In the next section, we will continue our file by including properties.

Using properties

Using xacro, we can declare constants or properties that are the named values inside the xacro file, which can be used anywhere in the code. The main purpose of these constant definitions is that instead of giving hardcoded values on links and joints, we can keep constants, and it will be easier to change these values rather than finding the hardcoded values and then replacing them.

An example of using properties is given here. We declare the length and radius of the base link and the pan link. So, it will be easy to change the dimension here rather than changing the values in each one:

```
<xacro:property name="base_link_length" value="0.01" />
<xacro:property name="base_link_radius" value="0.2" />
<xacro:property name="pan_link_length" value="0.4" />
<xacro:property name="pan_link_radius" value="0.04" />
```

We can use the value of the variable by replacing the hardcoded value with the following definition:

```
<cylinder length="${pan_link_length}"  radius="${pan_link_radius}"/>
```

Here, the old value, "0.4", is replaced with "{pan_link_length}", and "0.04" is replaced with "{pan_link_radius}".

Using the math expression

We can build mathematical expressions inside ${ } using basic operations such as +, -, *, /, unary minus, and parentheses. Exponentiation and modulus are not supported yet. The following is a simple math expression used inside the code:

```
<cylinder length="${pan_link_length}"  radius="${pan_link_radius+0.02}"/>
```

An important element of the xacro file is the macro element. We will discuss how to use a macro in the following section.

Using macros

One of the main features of xacro is that it supports macros. We can use xacro to reduce the length of complex definitions. Here is a `xacro` definition we used in our code to specify inertial values:

```
<xacro:macro name="inertial_matrix" params="mass">
  <inertial>
      <mass value="${mass}" />
         <inertia ixx="0.5" ixy="0.0" ixz="0.0"
         iyy="0.5" iyz="0.0" izz="0.5" />
  </inertial>
</xacro:macro>
```

Here, the macro is named `inertial_matrix`, and its parameter is `mass`. The `mass` parameter can be used inside the inertial definition using `${mass}`. We can include a new inertia block with a single line, as shown here:

```
<xacro:inertial_matrix mass="1"/>
```

Here, the xacro definition improves code readability and reduces the number of lines compared to `urdf`. Next, we will look at how to convert xacro to a URDF file.

Converting xacro to URDF

As already stated, `xacro` files can be converted into `urdf` files every time. After designing the xacro file, we can use the following command to convert it into a URDF file:

```
rosrun xacro pan_tilt.xacro > pan_tilt_generated.urdf
```

We can use the following line in the ROS launch file to convert xacro into URDF and use it as a `robot_description` parameter:

```
<param name="robot_description" command="$(find xacro)/xacro
$(find mastering_ros_robot_description_pkg)/urdf/pan_tilt.
xacro" />
```

We can view the xacro of the pan-and-tilt robot by making a launch file, and it can be launched using the following command:

```
roslaunch mastering_ros_robot_description_pkg view_pan_tilt_
xacro.launch
```

After running this command, we should see the same output of the visualization as the URDF file. Now we are ready to do something more complicated. The pan-and-tilt robot only has two joints and so only two degrees of freedom. In the next section, we will create a robotic manipulator consisting of seven joints.

Creating the robot description for a seven-DOF robot manipulator

Now, we can create some complex robots using URDF and xacro. The first robot we are going to deal with is a seven-DOF robotic arm, which is a serial link manipulator with multiple serial links. The seven-DOF arm is kinematically redundant, which means it has more joints and DOF than required to achieve its goal position and orientation. The advantage of redundant manipulators is that we can have more joint configurations for a desired goal position and orientation. This will improve the flexibility and versatility of the robot's movement and can implement effective collision-free motion in a robotic workspace.

Let's start by creating the seven-DOF arm; the final output model of the robot arm is shown here (the various joints and links in the robot are also marked on the diagram):

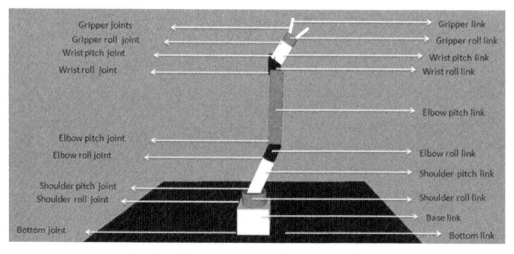

Figure 3.8 – Joints and links of the seven-DOF arm robot

The preceding robot is described using xacro. We can take the actual description file from the cloned repository. We can navigate to the urdf folder inside the cloned package and open the seven_dof_arm.xacro file. We will copy and paste the description to the current package and discuss the major aspects of this robot description. Before we create the robot model file, let's report some specifications of the robotic arm.

Arm specification

In the following list, the characteristics of the seven-DOF arm are reported:

- Degrees of freedom: 7
- Length of the arm: 50 cm
- Reach of the arm: 35 cm
- Number of links: 12
- Number of joints: 11

As you can see, we can define different types of joints. Let's now discuss the type of joints of the seven-DOF arm.

Types of joints

Here is a list of joints containing the name of the joint and its robot type:

Joint number	Joint name	Joint type	Joint limits
1	`bottom_joint`	Fixed	--
2	`shoulder_pan_joint`	Revolute	-150° to 114°
3	`shoulder_pitch_joint`	Revolute	-67° to 109°
4	`elbow_roll_joint`	Revolute	-150° to 41°
5	`elbow_pitch_joint`	Revolute	-92° to 110°
6	`wrist_roll_joint`	Revolute	-150° to 150°
7	`wrist_pitch_joint`	Revolute	92° to 113°
8	`gripper_roll_joint`	Revolute	-150° to 150°
9	`finger_joint1`	Prismatic	0 cm to 3 cm
10	`finger_joint2`	Prismatic	0 cm to 3 cm

As shown in the preceding table, the robot consists of one fixed joint, seven revolute joints, and two prismatic joints for the gripper. We design the xacro of the arm using the preceding specifications. Next, we will explain the xacro arm file.

Explaining the xacro model of the seven-DOF arm

After defining the elements that we must insert in the robot model file, we are now ready to include 10 links and 9 joints (7 for the arm and 2 for the gripper) on this robot, and 2 links and 2 joints on the robot gripper.

Let's start by looking at the xacro definition:

```
<?xml version="1.0"?>
<robot name="seven_dof_arm" xmlns:xacro="http://ros.org/wiki/xacro">
```

Because we are writing a xacro file, we should mention the xacro namespace to parse the file; then, we can start to define the geometric properties of the arm.

Using constants

We use constants inside this xacro to make the robot descriptions shorter and more readable. Here, we define the degree-to-radian conversion factor, the PI value, the length, the height, and the width of each of the links:

```
<property name="deg_to_rad" value="0.01745329251994329577"/>
<property name="M_PI" value="3.14159"/>
<property name="elbow_pitch_len" value="0.22" />
<property name="elbow_pitch_width" value="0.04" />
<property name="elbow_pitch_height" value="0.04" />
```

Next, let's explore the macros that are used to define the same kind of element multiple times.

Using macro

We define macros in this code to avoid repetition and to make the code shorter. Here are the macros we have used in this code:

```
<xacro:macro name="inertial_matrix" params="mass">
    <inertial>
        <mass value="${mass}" />
        <inertia ixx="1.0" ixy="0.0" ixz="0.0" iyy="0.5"
iyz="0.0" izz="1.0" />
    </inertial>
</xacro:macro>
```

This is the definition of the `inertial matrix` macro in which we can use `mass` as a parameter:

```
<xacro:macro name="transmission_block" params="joint_name">
  <transmission name="tran1">
      <type>transmission_interface/SimpleTransmission</type>
      <joint name="${joint_name}">
        <hardwareInterface>PositionJointInterface</
hardwareInterface>
      </joint>
      <actuator name="motor1">
        <hardwareInterface>PositionJointInterface</
hardwareInterface>
        <mechanicalReduction>1</mechanicalReduction>
      </actuator>
  </transmission>
</xacro:macro>
```

In the preceding section of the code, we can view the definition by using the `transmission` tag.

The `transmission` tag relates a joint to an actuator. It defines the type of transmission that we are using in a particular joint along with the type of motor and its parameters. It also defines the type of hardware interface we use when we interface with the ROS controllers.

Including other xacro files

We can extend the capabilities of the robot xacro by including the xacro definition of sensors using the `xacro:include` tag. The following code snippet shows how to include a sensor definition in the robot xacro:

```
<xacro:include filename="$(find mastering_ros_robot_
description_pkg)/urdf/sensors/xtion_pro_live.urdf.xacro"/>
```

Here, we include a xacro definition of the vision sensor called **Asus Xtion pro**; this will be expanded when the xacro file is parsed.

Using `"$(find mastering_ros_robot_description_pkg)/urdf/sensors/xtion_pro_live.urdf.xacro"`, we can access the xacro definition of the sensor, where `find` is used to locate the current `mastering_ros_robot_description_pkg` package.

We will talk more about vision processing in *Chapter 10, Programming Vision Sensors Using ROS, OpenCV, and PCL.*

Using meshes in the link

We can insert a primitive shape inside a link, or we can insert a mesh file using the `mesh` tag. The following example shows how to insert a mesh into the vision sensor:

```
<visual>
   <origin xyz="0 0 0" rpy="0 0 0"/>
   <geometry>
     <mesh filename=        "package://mastering_ros_robot_
description_pkg/meshes/sensors/xtion_pro_live/xtion_pro_live.
dae"/>
   </geometry>
<material name="DarkGrey"/>
</visual>
```

Next, let's take a look at the definition of the gripper of the robotic arm.

Working with the robot gripper

The gripper of the robot is designed for the picking and placing of blocks; the gripper is in the simple linkage category. There are two joints for the gripper, and each joint is prismatic. Here is the `joint` definition of one gripper joint, that is, `finger_joint1`:

```
<joint name="finger_joint1" type="prismatic">
  <parent link="gripper_roll_link"/>
  <child link="gripper_finger_link1"/>
  <origin xyz="0.0 0 0" />
  <axis xyz="0 1 0" />
    <limit effort="100" lower="0" upper="0.03"
 velocity="1.0"/>
    <safety_controller k_position="20"
                       k_velocity="20"
                       soft_lower_limit="${-0.15 }"
                       soft_upper_limit="${ 0.0 }"/>
  <dynamics damping="50" friction="1"/>
 </joint>
```

Here, the first gripper joint is formed by `gripper_roll_link` and `gripper_finger_link1`. Then, we can define the `finger_joint2` to connect the `gripper_roll_link` and `gripper_finger_link2` elements.

The following graph shows how the gripper joints are connected in `gripper_roll_link`:

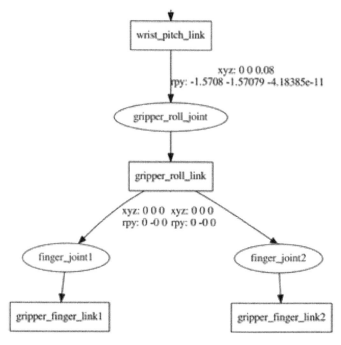

Figure 3.9 – A graph of the end effector section of the seven-DOF arm robot

We are now ready to visualize the arm model using RViz.

Viewing the seven-DOF arm in RViz

Having discussed the robot model, we can now view the designed xacro file in RViz, control each joint using the `joint state publisher` node, and publish the robot state using `robot_state_publisher`.

The preceding task can be performed using a launch file, called `view_arm.launch`, which is inside the `launch` folder of this package:

```xml
<?xml version="1.0" ?>
<launch>
        <arg name="model" />
        <!-- Parsing xacro and setting robot_description
parameter -->
        <param name="robot_description" command="$(find xacro)/
xacro $(find mastering_ros_robot_description_pkg)/urdf/seven_
dof_arm.xacro" />
```

```
    <node name="robot_state_publisher" pkg="robot_state_
publisher" type="robot_state_publisher" />
    <node name="joint_state_publisher_gui" pkg="joint_state_
publisher_gui" type="joint_state_publisher_gui" />
    <!-- Launch visualization in rviz -->
    <node name="rviz" pkg="rviz" type="rviz" args="-d $(find
mastering_ros_robot_description_pkg)/urdf.rviz" required="true"
/>
</launch>
```

Create the following launch file inside the `launch` folder, and build the package using the `catkin_make` command. Launch the `urdf` using the following command:

```
roslaunch mastering_ros_robot_description_pkg view_arm.launch
```

The robot will be displayed on RViz with the `joint_state_publisher` GUI node:

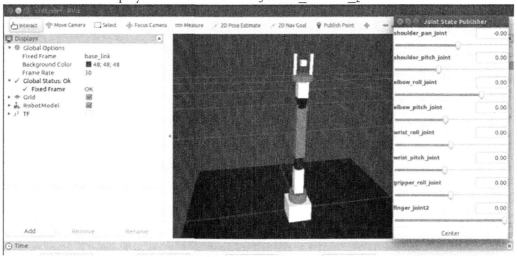

Figure 3.10 – Seven-DOF arm in RViz with joint_state_publisher

We can interact with the joint slider and move the joints of the robot.

Next, we will explore what `joint state publisher` can do.

Understanding joint state publisher

The joint state publisher package is one of the ROS packages that is commonly used to interact with each joint of the robot. The package contains the joint_state_ publisher node, which finds the nonfixed joints from the URDF model and publishes the joint state values of each joint in the sensor_msgs/JointState message format. This package can also be used in conjunction with the robot_state_publisher package to publish the position of all of the joints. Different sources can be used to set the value of each joint. As we have already seen, one way is to use the slider GUI. This way is mainly used for testing. Otherwise, a JointState topic that the node subscribes to can be used.

You can find more about the joint state publisher package at http://wiki. ros.org/joint_state_publisher.

Understanding robot state publisher

The robot state publisher package helps to publish the state of the robot to tf. This package subscribes to joint states of the robot and publishes the 3D pose of each link using the kinematic representation from the URDF model. We can implement the robot state publisher node using the following line inside the launch file:

```
<!-- Starting robot state publish which will publish tf -->
  <node name="robot_state_publisher" pkg="robot_state_
publisher" type="robot_state_publisher" />
```

In the preceding launch file, view_arm.launch, we started this node to publish the tf of the arm. We can visualize the transformation of the robot by clicking on the tf option in RViz, as follows:

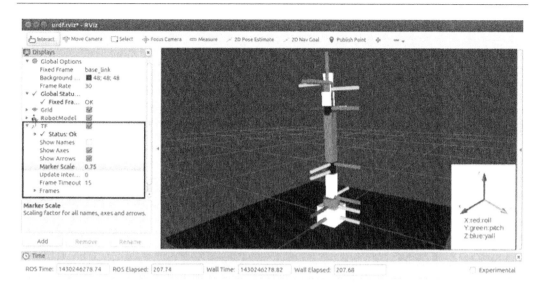

Figure 3.11 – The TF view of the seven-DOF arm in RViz

The `joint_state_publisher` and `robot_state_publisher` packages are installed along with the ROS desktop's installation.

After creating the robot description of the seven-DOF arm, let's discuss how to make a mobile robot with differential wheeled mechanisms.

Creating a robot model for the differential drive mobile robot

A differential wheeled robot will have two wheels connected to opposite sides of the robot chassis, which is supported by one or two caster wheels. The wheels will control the speed of the robot by regulating the velocity of the single wheels. If the two motors are running at the same speed, the wheels will move forward or backward. If one wheel is running slower than the other, the robot will turn to the side of the lower speed. If we want to turn the robot to the left side, we reduce the velocity of the left wheel and vice versa.

There are two supporting wheels, called **caster wheels**, that will support the robot and rotate freely based on the movement of the main wheels.

The URDF model of this robot is present in the cloned ROS package. The final robot model is shown here:

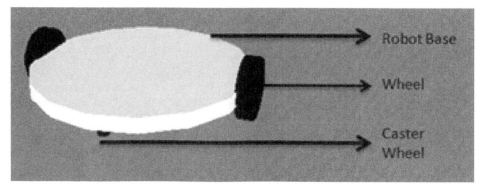

Figure 3.12 – The differential drive mobile robot

The preceding robot has five joints and links. The two main joints connect the wheels to the robot, while the others are fixed joints connecting the caster wheels and the base footprint to the body of the robot.

The preceding robot has five joints and five links. The two main joints connect the wheels with the base of the robot. The other joints are fixed and are used to link the caster wheels and the base footprint of the robot with its base link, respectively. Here is the connection graph of this robot:

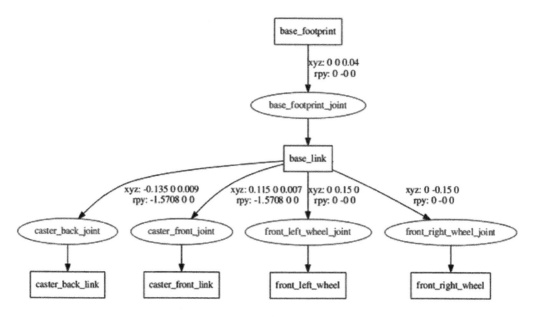

Figure 3.13 – A graphical representation of the links and joints of the differential drive mobile robot

Let's go through the important aspects of code in the URDF file. The URDF file, called `diff_wheeled_robot.xacro`, is placed inside the `urdf` folder of the cloned ROS package.

The first section of the URDF file is given here. The robot is named `differential_wheeled_robot`, and it also includes a URDF file, called `wheel.urdf.xacro`. This xacro file contains the definition of the wheel and its transmission; if we use this xacro file, we can avoid adding two different definitions for the two wheels. We use this xacro definition because the two wheels are identical in shape and size:

```
<?xml version="1.0"?>
<robot name="differential_wheeled_robot" xmlns:xacro="http://
ros.org/wiki/xacro">
  <xacro:include filename="$(find mastering_ros_robot_
description_pkg)/urdf/wheel.urdf.xacro">
```

The definition of a wheel inside wheel.urdf.xacro is given here. We can mention whether the wheel must be placed to the left, right, front, or back. Using this macro, we can create a maximum of four wheels but, for now, we require only two:

```
<xacro:macro name="wheel" params="fb lr parent translateX
translateY flipY"> <!--fb : front, back ; lr: left, right -->
    <link name="${fb}_${lr}_wheel">
```

We also mention the Gazebo parameters required for simulation. The Gazebo parameters associated with a wheel are also mentioned here. We can mention the frictional coefficient and the stiffness coefficient using the `gazebo reference` tag:

```
<gazebo reference="${fb}_${lr}_wheel">
    <mu1 value="1.0"/>
    <mu2 value="1.0"/>
    <kp  value="10000000.0" />
    <kd  value="1.0" />
    <fdir1 value="1 0 0"/>
    <material>Gazebo/Grey</material>
    <turnGravityOff>false</turnGravityOff>
</gazebo>
```

The joints that we define for a wheel are continuous joints because there are no limits in the wheel joint. The `parent link` here is the robot base, and the `child link` is each wheel:

```
<joint name="${fb}_${lr}_wheel_joint" type="continuous">
    <parent link="${parent}"/>
    <child link="${fb}_${lr}_wheel"/>
<origin xyz="${translateX * base_x_origin_to_wheel_origin}
${translateY * base_y_origin_to_wheel_origin} ${base_z_origin_
to_wheel_origin}" rpy="0 0 0" />
    <axis xyz="0 1 0" rpy="0 0 0" />
    <limit effort="100" velocity="100"/>
    <joint_properties damping="0.0" friction="0.0"/>
</joint>
```

We also need to mention the `transmission` tag of each wheel. The macro of the wheel is as follows:

```
    <!-- Transmission is important to link the joints and the
controller -->
    <transmission name="${fb}_${lr}_wheel_joint_trans">
        <type>transmission_interface/SimpleTransmission</type>
        <joint name="${fb}_${lr}_wheel_joint" />
        <actuator name="${fb}_${lr}_wheel_joint_motor">
            <hardwareInterface>EffortJointInterface</
hardwareInterface>
            <mechanicalReduction>1</mechanicalReduction>
        </actuator>
    </transmission>
  </xacro:macro>
</robot>
```

In the `diff_wheeled_robot.xacro` file, we can use the following lines to use the macros defined inside the `wheel.urdf.xacro` file:

```
  <xacro:wheel fb="front" lr="right" parent="base_link"
translateX="0" translateY="0.5" flipY="1"/>
    <xacro:wheel fb="front" lr="left" parent="base_link"
translateX="0" translateY="-0.5" flipY="1"/>
```

Using the preceding lines, we define the wheels on the left and right of the robot base. The robot base is cylindrical, as shown in the preceding figure. The inertia calculating macro is given here. This xacro snippet will use the mass, radius, and height of the cylinder to calculate the inertia using this equation:

```
<!-- Macro for calculating inertia of cylinder -->
<macro name="cylinder_inertia" params="m r h">
  <inertia  ixx="${m*(3*r*r+h*h)/12}" ixy = "0" ixz = "0"
            iyy="${m*(3*r*r+h*h)/12}" iyz = "0"
            izz="${m*r*r/2}" />
</macro>
```

The launch file definition to display this root model in RViz is given here. The launch file is named view_mobile_robot.launch:

```
<launch>
<?xml version="1.0" ?>
    <arg name="model" />
    <!-- Parsing xacro and setting robot_description
parameter -->
    <param name="robot_description" command="$(find xacro)/
xacro $(find mastering_ros_robot_description_pkg)/urdf/diff_
wheeled_robot.xacro" />
    <!-- Starting Joint state publisher node which will
publish the joint values -->
    <node name="joint_state_publisher_gui" pkg="joint_state_
publisher_gui" type="joint_state_publisher_gui" />
    <!-- Starting robot state publish which will publish tf
-->
    <node name="robot_state_publisher" pkg="robot_state_
publisher" type="robot_state_publisher" />
    <!-- Launch visualization in rviz -->
    <node name="rviz" pkg="rviz" type="rviz" args="-d $(find
mastering_ros_robot_description_pkg)/urdf.rviz" required="true"
/>
</launch>
```

The only difference between the arm URDF file is the change in the robot model to load; the other sections are the same.

We can view the mobile robot using the following command:

```
roslaunch mastering_ros_robot_description_pkg view_mobile_
robot.launch
```

An example of the robot in RViz is shown in the following screenshot:

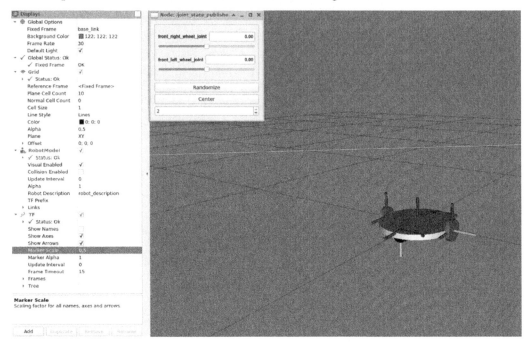

Figure 3.14 – Visualizing the mobile robot in RViz with joint state publisher

Even though you will not be able to really move the robot, you can try to move the wheels of the robot using the slide bars on the user interface of RViz.

Summary

In this chapter, we mainly looked at the importance of robot modeling and how we can model a robot in ROS. We discussed the packages that are used in ROS to model a robotic structure, such as `urdf`, `xacro`, and `joint_state_publisher` and its GUI. We discussed URDF, xacro, and the main URDF tags that we can use. We also created a sample model in URDF and xacro and discussed the differences between the two. Following this, we created a complex robotic manipulator with seven DOF and looked at the usage of the `joint_state_publisher` and `robot_state_publisher` packages. At the end of the chapter, we reviewed the design procedure of a differential drive mobile robot using xacro. In the next chapter, we will take a look at the simulation of these robots using Gazebo.

Questions

1. What are the packages used for robot modeling in ROS?
2. What are the important URDF tags used for robot modeling?
3. What are the reasons for using xacro over URDF?
4. What is the function of the `joint state publisher` and `robot state publisher` packages?
5. What is the function of the `transmission` tag in URDF?

4
Simulating Robots Using ROS and Gazebo

After designing the 3D model of a robot, the next phase is to simulate it. Robot simulation will give you an idea of how robots operate in a virtual environment.

We are going to use the **Gazebo** (`http://www.gazebosim.org/`) simulator to simulate the seven **Degree Of Freedom** (**DOF**) arms and the mobile robot.

Gazebo is a multi-robot simulator for complex indoor and outdoor robotic simulation. We can simulate complex robots, robot sensors, and a variety of 3D objects. Gazebo already has simulation models of popular robots, sensors, and a variety of 3D objects in its repository (`https://bitbucket.org/osrf/gazebo_models/`). We can directly use these models without having to create new ones.

Gazebo is perfectly integrated with ROS thanks to a proper ROS interface, which exposes the complete control of Gazebo in ROS. We can install Gazebo without ROS, but we should install the ROS-Gazebo interface to communicate from ROS to Gazebo.

In this chapter, we will discuss the simulation of seven DOF arms and differential wheeled robots. We will also discuss the ROS controllers that help to control the robot's joints in Gazebo.

We will cover the following topics in this chapter:

- Understanding robotic simulation and Gazebo
- Simulating the model of a robotic arm for Gazebo
- Simulating the robotic arm with a depth sensor
- Moving robot joints using ROS controllers in Gazebo
- Simulating a differential wheeled robot in Gazebo
- Teleoperating a mobile robot in Gazebo

Technical requirements

To follow this chapter, you need a standard laptop running Ubuntu 20.04 with ROS Noetic installed. The reference code for this chapter can be downloaded from the following Git repository: `https://github.com/PacktPublishing/Mastering-ROS-for-Robotics-Programming-Third-edition.git`. The code is contained in the `Chapter4/seven_dof_arm_gazebo` folder.

You can view this chapter's code in action here: `https://bit.ly/2XvBY7o`.

Simulating the robotic arm using Gazebo and ROS

In the previous chapter, we designed a seven DOF arm. In this section, we will simulate the robot in Gazebo using ROS.

Before starting with Gazebo and ROS, we should install the following packages to work with Gazebo and ROS:

```
sudo apt-get install ros-noetic-gazebo-ros-pkgs ros-noetic-
gazebo-msgs ros-noetic-gazebo-plugins ros-noetic-gazebo-ros-
control
```

The default version installed from Noetic ROS packages is **Gazebo 11.x**. The use of each package is as follows:

- `gazebo_ros_pkgs`: This contains wrappers and tools for interfacing ROS with Gazebo.
- `gazebo-msgs`: This contains messages and service data structures for interfacing with Gazebo from ROS.

- `gazebo-plugins`: This contains Gazebo plugins for sensors, actuators, and so on.
- `gazebo-ros-control`: This contains standard controllers to communicate between ROS and Gazebo.

After installation, check whether Gazebo is properly installed using the following commands:

```
roscore & rosrun gazebo_ros gazebo
```

These commands will open the Gazebo GUI. If we have the Gazebo simulator, we can proceed to develop the simulation model of the seven DOF arm for Gazebo.

Creating the robotic arm simulation model for Gazebo

We can create the simulation model for a robotic arm by updating the existing robot description by adding simulation parameters.

We can create the package needed to simulate the robotic arm using the following command:

```
catkin_create_pkg seven_dof_arm_gazebo gazebo_msgs gazebo_
plugins gazebo_ros gazebo_ros_control mastering_ros_robot_
description_pkg
```

Alternatively, the full package is available in the following Git repository; you can clone the repository for a reference to implement this package, or you can get the package from the book's source code:

```
git clone https://github.com/PacktPublishing/Mastering-ROS-for-
Robotics-Programming-Third-edition.git
cd Chapter4/seven_dof_arm_gazebo
```

You can see the complete simulation model of the robot in the `seven_dof_arm.xacro` file, placed in the `mastering_ros_robot_description_pkg/urdf/` folder.

The file is filled with URDF tags, which are necessary for the simulation. We will define the sections of collision, inertial, transmission, joints, links, and Gazebo.

To launch the existing simulation model, we can use the `seven_dof_arm_gazebo` package, which has a launch file called `seven_dof_arm_world.launch`. The file definition is as follows:

```
<launch>
  <!-- these are the arguments you can pass this launch file,
for example paused:=true -->
  <arg name="paused" default="false"/>
  <arg name="use_sim_time" default="true"/>
  <arg name="gui" default="true"/>
  <arg name="headless" default="false"/>
  <arg name="debug" default="false"/>

  <!-- We resume the logic in empty_world.launch -->
  <include file="$(find gazebo_ros)/launch/empty_world.launch">
    <arg name="debug" value="$(arg debug)" />
    <arg name="gui" value="$(arg gui)" />
    <arg name="paused" value="$(arg paused)"/>
    <arg name="use_sim_time" value="$(arg use_sim_time)"/>
    <arg name="headless" value="$(arg headless)"/>
  </include>

  <!-- Load the URDF into the ROS Parameter Server -->
  <param name="robot_description" command="$(find xacro)/xacro
'$(find mastering_ros_robot_description_pkg)/urdf/seven_dof_
arm.xacro'" />

  <!-- Run a python script to the send a service call to
gazebo_ros to spawn a URDF robot -->
  <node name="urdf_spawner" pkg="gazebo_ros" type="spawn_model"
respawn="false" output="screen"
  args="-urdf -model seven_dof_arm -param robot_description"/>
</launch>
```

Launch the following command and check what you get:

```
roslaunch seven_dof_arm_gazebo seven_dof_arm_world.launch
```

You can see the robotic arm in Gazebo, as shown in the following figure; if you get this output without any errors, you are done:

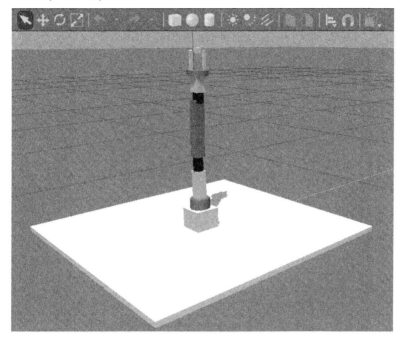

Figure 4.1 – Simulation of a seven DOF arm in Gazebo

In the next section, we will discuss the robot simulation model files in detail.

Adding colors and textures to the Gazebo robot model

We can see in the simulated robot that each link has different colors and textures. The following tags inside the `.xacro` file provide textures and colors to robot links:

```
<gazebo reference="bottom_link">
  <material>Gazebo/White</material>
</gazebo>
<gazebo reference="base_link">
  <material>Gazebo/White</material>
</gazebo>
<gazebo reference="shoulder_pan_link">
  <material>Gazebo/Red</material>
</gazebo>
```

Each `gazebo` tag references a particular link of the robot model.

Adding transmission tags to actuate the model

To actuate the robot using ROS controllers, we should define the `<transmission>` element to link actuators to joints. Here is the macro defined for transmission:

```
<xacro:macro name="transmission_block" params="joint_name">
  <transmission name="tran1">
    <type>transmission_interface/SimpleTransmission</type>
    <joint name="${joint_name}">
                <hardwareInterface>hardware_interface/
PositionJointInterface</hardwareInterface>
    </joint>
    <actuator name="motor1">
      <mechanicalReduction>1</mechanicalReduction>
    </actuator>
  </transmission>
</xacro:macro>
```

Here, `<joint name = "">` is the joint in which we link the actuators, while the `<type>` tag specifies the type of transmission. Currently, the only transmission type supported is `transmission_interface/SimpleTransmission`. Finally, the `<hardwareInterface>` tag is used to define the controller interface to load the position, velocity, or effort interfaces. In the proposed example, a position control hardware interface has been used. The hardware interface is loaded by the `gazebo_ros_control` plugin; we will look at this plugin in the next section.

Adding the gazebo_ros_control plugin

After adding the transmission tags, we should add the `gazebo_ros_control` plugin in the simulation model to parse the transmission tags and assign appropriate hardware interfaces and the control manager. The following code adds the `gazebo_ros_control` plugin to the `.xacro` file:

```
<!-- ros_control plugin -->
<gazebo>
  <plugin name="gazebo_ros_control" filename="libgazebo_ros_
control.so">
    <robotNamespace>/seven_dof_arm</robotNamespace>
  </plugin>
</gazebo>
```

Here, the `<plugin>` element specifies the plugin name to be loaded, which is `libgazebo_ros_control.so`. The `<robotNamespace>` element can be given as the name of the robot; if we are not specifying the name, it will automatically load the name of the robot from the URDF. We can also specify the controller update rate (`<controlPeriod>`), the location of `robot_description` (URDF) on the parameter server (`<robotParam>`), and the type of robot hardware interface (`<robotSimType>`). The default hardware interfaces are `JointStateInterface`, `EffortJointInterface`, and `VelocityJointInterface`.

Adding a 3D vision sensor to Gazebo

In Gazebo, we can simulate the robot's movement and its physics; we can also simulate different kinds of sensors. To build a sensor in Gazebo, we must model its behavior. There are some prebuilt sensor models in Gazebo that can be used directly in our code without writing a new model.

Here, we are adding a 3D vision sensor (commonly known as an **rgb-d** or **depth sensor**) called the **Asus Xtion Pro** model in Gazebo. Different models of depth sensors can be used in robotics. However, except for their performance, they provide the same output format. We will provide additional information about depth and vision sensors in *Chapter 10, Programming Vision Sensors Using ROS, OpenCV, and PCL*.

Regarding the seven DOF arm, the sensor model is already implemented in the `gazebo_ros_pkgs/gazebo_plugins` ROS package, which we have already installed in our ROS system. Each model in Gazebo is implemented as a Gazebo-ROS plugin, which can be loaded by inserting it into the URDF file.

Here is how we include a Gazebo definition and a physical robot model of Xtion Pro in the `seven_dof_arm_with_rgbd.xacro` robot `.xacro` file:

```
<xacro:include filename="$(find mastering_ros_robot_
description_pkg)/urdf/sensors/xtion_pro_live.urdf.xacro"/>
```

Inside `xtion_pro_live.urdf.xacro`, we can see the following lines:

```
<?xml version="1.0"?>
<robot xmlns:xacro="http://ros.org/wiki/xacro">
   <xacro:include filename="$(find mastering_ros_robot_
description_pkg)/urdf/sensors/xtion_pro_live.gazebo.xacro"/>
   ..................
   <xacro:macro name="xtion_pro_live" params="name parent
*origin *optical_origin">
   ..................
```

```
    <link name="${name}_link">
        . . . . . . . . . . . . . . . . . . .
  <visual>
        <origin xyz="0 0 0" rpy="0 0 0"/>
        <geometry>
            <mesh filename="package://mastering_ros_robot_
description_pkg/meshes/sensors/xtion_pro_live/xtion_pro_live.
dae"/>
        </geometry>
        <material name="DarkGrey"/>
    </visual>
    </link>


</robot>
```

Here, we can see it includes another file called xtion_pro_live.gazebo.xacro, which consists of the complete Gazebo definition of Xtion Pro.

We can also see a macro definition named xtion_pro_live, which contains the complete model definition of Xtion Pro, including links and joints:

```
<mesh filename="package://mastering_ros_robot_description_pkg/
meshes/sensors/xtion_pro_live/xtion_pro_live.dae"/>
```

In the macro definition, we are importing a mesh file of the Asus Xtion Pro, which will be shown as the camera link in Gazebo.

In the mastering_ros_robot_description_pkg/urdf/sensors/xtion_pro_live.gazebo.xacro file, we can set the Gazebo-ROS plugin of Xtion Pro. Here, we will define the plugin as a macro with RGB and depth camera support. Here is the plugin definition:

```
        <plugin name="${name}_frame_controller"
filename="libgazebo_ros_openni_kinect.so">
        <alwaysOn>true</alwaysOn>
        <updateRate>6.0</updateRate>
        <cameraName>${name}</cameraName>
        <imageTopicName>rgb/image_raw</imageTopicName>


        </plugin>
```

The plugin filename of Xtion Pro is `libgazebo_ros_openni_kinect.so`, and we can define the plugin parameters, such as the camera name and image topics.

Simulating the robotic arm with Xtion Pro

Now that we have learned about the camera plugin definition in Gazebo, we can launch our complete simulation using the following command:

```
roslaunch seven_dof_arm_gazebo seven_dof_arm_with_rgbd_world.
launch
```

We can see the robot model with a sensor on the top of the arm, as shown here:

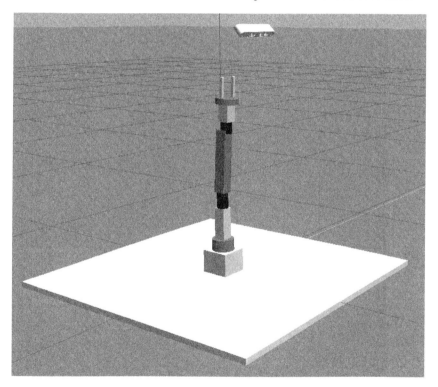

Figure 4.2 – Simulation of a seven DOF arm with Asus Xtion Pro in Gazebo

We can now work with the simulated `rgb-d` sensor as if it were directly plugged into our computer. So, we can check whether it provides the correct image output.

Visualizing the 3D sensor data

After launching the simulation using the preceding command, we can check the topics generated by the sensor plugin:

```
jcacace@robot:-$ rostopic list
/rgbd_camera/depth/image_raw
/rgbd_camera/ir/image_raw
/rgbd_camera/rgb/image_raw
```

Figure 4.3 – rgb-d image topics generated by Gazebo

To see the image data of a 3D vision sensor using a tool called `image_view`, do the following:

- View the RGB raw image:

  ```
  rosrun image_view image:=/rgbd_camera/rgb/image_raw
  ```

- View the IR raw image:

  ```
  rosrun image_view image:=/rgbd_camera/ir/image_raw
  ```

- View the depth image:

  ```
  rosrun image_view image:=/rgbd_camera/depth/image_raw
  ```

Here is the screenshot with all these images:

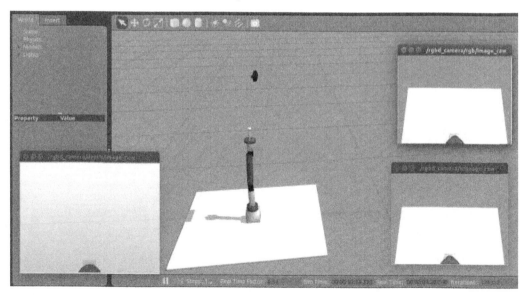

Figure 4.4 – Viewing images of the rgb-d sensor in Gazebo

We can also view the point cloud data of this sensor in RViz.

Launch `rviz` using the following command:

```
rosrun rviz -f /rgbd_camera_optical_frame
```

Add a **PointCloud2** display type and set **Topic** as `/rgbd_camera/depth/points`. We will get a point cloud view as follows:

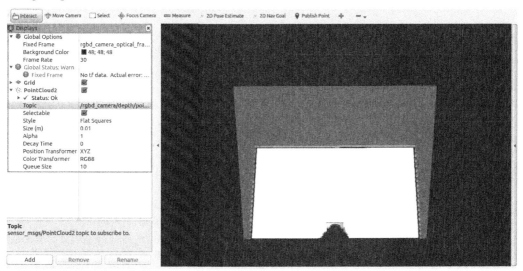

Figure 4.5 – Viewing point cloud data from an rgb-d sensor in rviz

The next step is to control the robot joints to move the simulated robot.

Moving the robot joints using ROS controllers in Gazebo

In this section, we are going to discuss how to move each joint of the robot in Gazebo.

To move each joint, we need to assign an ROS controller. For each joint, we need to attach a controller that is compatible with the hardware interface mentioned inside the `transmission` tags.

An ROS controller mainly consists of a feedback mechanism that can receive a set point and control the output using the feedback from the actuators.

The ROS controller interacts with the hardware using the hardware interface. The main function of the hardware interface is to act as a mediator between ROS controllers and the real or simulated hardware, allocating the resources to control it using the data generated by the ROS controller.

In this robot, we have defined the position controllers, velocity controllers, effort controllers, and so on. The ROS controllers are provided by a set of packages called `ros_control`.

For a proper understanding of how to configure ROS controllers for the arm, we should understand the concepts behind these controllers. In the following section, we will discuss more on the `ros_control` packages, different types of ROS controllers, and how an ROS controller interacts with the Gazebo simulation.

Understanding the ros_control packages

The `ros_control` packages contain the implementation of robot controllers, controller managers, hardware interfaces, different transmission interfaces, and control toolboxes. The `ros_controls` packages are composed of the following individual packages:

- `control_toolbox`: This package contains common modules (PID and Sine) that can be used by all controllers.
- `controller_interface`: This package contains the `interface` base class for the controllers.
- `controller_manager`: This package provides the infrastructure to `load`, `unload`, `start`, and `stop` the controllers.
- `controller_manager_msgs`: This package provides the message and service definition for the controller manager.
- `hardware_interface`: This contains the base class for the hardware interfaces.
- `transmission_interface`: This package contains the interface classes for the `transmission` interface (differential, four-bar linkage, joint state, position, and velocity).

Different types of ROS controllers and hardware interfaces

Let's see the list of ROS packages that contain the standard ROS controllers:

- `joint_position_controller`: This is a simple implementation of the joint position controller.
- `joint_state_controller`: This is a controller to publish joint states.
- `joint_effort_controller`: This is an implementation of the joint effort (force) controller.

The following are some of the commonly used hardware interfaces in ROS:

- `Joint Command Interfaces`: This will send the commands to the hardware.
- `Effort Joint Interface`: This will send the `effort` command.
- `Velocity Joint Interface`: This will send the `velocity` command.
- `Position Joint Interface`: This will send the `position` command.
- `Joint State Interfaces`: This will retrieve the joint states from the actuator's encoder.

Now we can start to interact with the ROS controller in Gazebo.

How the ROS controller interacts with Gazebo

Let's see how an ROS controller interacts with Gazebo. The following figure shows the interconnection of the ROS controller, the robot hardware interface, and the simulator/ real hardware:

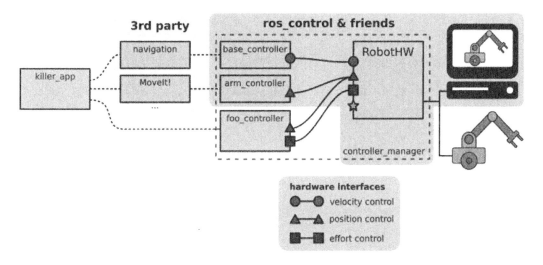

Figure 4.6 – ROS controllers interacting with Gazebo

We can see the third-party tools, the `navigation` and `MoveIt!` packages. These packages can give the goal (set point) to the mobile robot controllers and robotic arm controllers. These controllers can send the position, velocity, or effort to the robot hardware interface.

The hardware interface allocates each resource to the controllers and sends values to each resource. The communications between the robot controllers and robot hardware interfaces are shown in the following diagram:

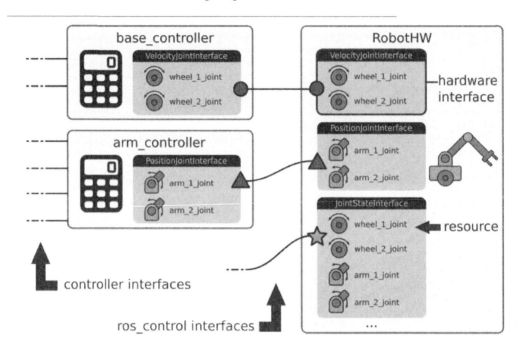

Figure 4.7 – Illustration of ROS controllers and hardware interfaces

The hardware interface is decoupled from the actual hardware and simulation. The values from the hardware interface can be fed to Gazebo for simulation or to the actual hardware itself.

The hardware interface is a software representation of the robot and its abstract hardware. The resource of the hardware interfaces are actuators, joints, and sensors. Some resources are read-only, such as joint states, IMU, and force-torque sensors, and some are read and write compatible, such as position, velocity, and effort joints.

Interfacing the joint state controllers and joint position controllers with the arm

Interfacing robot controllers with each joint is a simple task. The first task is to write a configuration file for two controllers.

The joint state controllers will publish the joint states of the arm and the joint position controllers can receive a goal position for each joint and can move each joint.

We will find the configuration file for the controller at `seven_dof_arm_gazebo_control.yaml` in the `seven_dof_arm_gazebo/config` folder.

Here is the configuration file definition of the joint state controller:

```
seven_dof_arm:
  # Publish all joint states ----------------------------------
  joint_state_controller:
    type: joint_state_controller/JointStateController
    publish_rate: 50
```

As for the position controllers, we need to define a new controller for each joint:

```
  # Position Controllers --------------------------------------
  joint1_position_controller:
    type: position_controllers/JointPositionController
    joint: shoulder_pan_joint
    pid: {p: 100.0, i: 0.01, d: 10.0}
```

We can replicate the previous block of code and configure it for each joint of the robot:

```
  joint2_position_controller:
    type: position_controllers/JointPositionController
    joint: shoulder_pitch_joint
    pid: {p: 100.0, i: 0.01, d: 10.0}
  joint3_position_controller:
    type: position_controllers/JointPositionController
    joint: elbow_roll_joint
    pid: {p: 100.0, i: 0.01, d: 10.0}
  joint4_position_controller:
    type: position_controllers/JointPositionController
    joint: elbow_pitch_joint
    pid: {p: 100.0, i: 0.01, d: 10.0}
  joint5_position_controller:
    type: position_controllers/JointPositionController
    joint: wrist_roll_joint
```

```
      pid: {p: 100.0, i: 0.01, d: 10.0}
  joint6_position_controller:
    type: position_controllers/JointPositionController
    joint: wrist_pitch_joint
    pid: {p: 100.0, i: 0.01, d: 10.0}
  joint7_position_controller:
    type: position_controllers/JointPositionController
    joint: gripper_roll_joint
    pid: {p: 100.0, i: 0.01, d: 10.0}
```

We can see that all the controllers are inside the seven_dof_arm namespace, and the first line represents the joint state controllers, which will publish the joint state of the robot at the rate of 50 Hz.

The remaining controllers are joint position controllers, which are assigned to the first seven joints, and they also define the PID gains.

Launching the ROS controllers with Gazebo

If the controller configuration is ready, we can build a launch file that starts all the controllers along with the Gazebo simulation. Navigate to the seven_dof_arm_gazebo/launch directory and open the seven_dof_arm_gazebo_control.launch file:

```
<launch>
  <!-- Launch Gazebo  -->
  <include file="$(find seven_dof_arm_gazebo)/launch/seven_dof_
arm_world.launch" />


  <!-- Load joint controller configurations from YAML file to
parameter server -->
  <rosparam file="$(find seven_dof_arm_gazebo)/config/seven_
dof_arm_gazebo_control.yaml" command="load"/>


  <!-- load the controllers -->
  <node name="controller_spawner" pkg="controller_manager"
type="spawner" respawn="false"
    output="screen" ns="/seven_dof_arm" args="joint_state_
controller
```

```
            joint1_position_controller
            joint2_position_controller
            joint3_position_controller
            joint4_position_controller
            joint5_position_controller
            joint6_position_controller
            joint7_position_controller"/>


    <!-- convert joint states to TF transforms for rviz, etc -->
    <node name="robot_state_publisher" pkg="robot_state_
publisher" type="robot_state_publisher"
    respawn="false" output="screen">
        <remap from="/joint_states" to="/seven_dof_arm/joint_
states" />
    </node>

</launch>
```

The launch files start the Gazebo simulation of the arm, load the controller configuration, load the joint state controller and joint position controllers, and, finally, run the robot state publisher, which publishes the joint states and **transforms** (**TF**).

Let's check the controller topics generated after running this launch file:

```
roslaunch seven_dof_arm_gazebo seven_dof_arm_gazebo_control.
launch
```

If the command is successful, we will see these messages in the terminal:

```
[ INFO] [1503389354.607765795, 0.155000000]: Loaded gazebo_ros_control.
[INFO] [1503389354.726844, 0.274000]: Controller Spawner: Waiting for service controll
er_manager/switch_controller
[INFO] [1503389354.728599, 0.276000]: Controller Spawner: Waiting for service controll
er_manager/unload_controller
[INFO] [1503389354.730271, 0.277000]: Loading controller: joint_state_controller
[INFO] [1503389354.812192, 0.355000]: Loading controller: joint1_position_controller
[INFO] [1503389354.896451, 0.433000]: Loading controller: joint2_position_controller
[INFO] [1503389354.905462, 0.442000]: Loading controller: joint3_position_controller
[INFO] [1503389354.914256, 0.451000]: Loading controller: joint4_position_controller
[INFO] [1503389354.921049, 0.458000]: Loading controller: joint5_position_controller
[INFO] [1503389354.928891, 0.466000]: Loading controller: joint6_position_controller
[INFO] [1503389354.935862, 0.473000]: Loading controller: joint7_position_controller
[INFO] [1503389354.944609, 0.482000]: Controller Spawner: Loaded controllers: joint_st
ate_controller, joint1_position_controller, joint2_position_controller, joint3_positio
n_controller, joint4_position_controller, joint5_position_controller, joint6_position_
controller, joint7_position_controller
[INFO] [1503389354.947569, 0.485000]: Started controllers: joint_state_controller, joi
nt1_position_controller, joint2_position_controller, joint3_position_controller, joint
4_position_controller, joint5_position_controller, joint6_position_controller, joint7_
position_controller
```

Figure 4.8 – Terminal messages while loading the ROS controllers of the seven DOF arm

Here are the topics generated from the controllers when we run this launch file:

```
/seven_dof_arm/joint1_position_controller/command
/seven_dof_arm/joint2_position_controller/command
/seven_dof_arm/joint3_position_controller/command
/seven_dof_arm/joint4_position_controller/command
/seven_dof_arm/joint5_position_controller/command
/seven_dof_arm/joint6_position_controller/command
/seven_dof_arm/joint7_position_controller/command
```

Figure 4.9 – Position controller command topics generated by the ROS controllers

As you can see from the previous screenshot, a new topic is available for each joint to control its position.

Moving the robot joints

After finishing the preceding topics, we can start commanding each joint into our desired positions.

To move a robot joint in Gazebo, we should publish a desired joint value with the message type std_msgs/Float64 to the joint position controller command topics.

Here is an example of moving the fourth joint to 1.0 radians:

```
rostopic pub /seven_dof_arm/joint4_position_controller/command
std_msgs/Float64 1.0
```

Figure 4.10 – Moving a joint of the arm in Gazebo

We can also view the joint states of the robot by using the following command:

```
rostopic echo /seven_dof_arm/joint_states
```

Now we can control all the joints of the seven DOF arm and, at the same time, we can read their values. In this way, we can implement custom robot control algorithms. In the next section, we will learn how to simulate the differential-drive robot.

Simulating a differential wheeled robot in Gazebo

We have seen the simulation of the robotic arm. In this section, we can set up the simulation for the differential wheeled robot that we designed in the previous chapter.

You will find the `diff_wheeled_robot.xacro` mobile robot description in the `mastering_ros_robot_description_pkg/urdf` folder.

Let's create a launch file to spawn the simulation model in Gazebo. As we did for the robotic arm, we can create an ROS package to launch a Gazebo simulation using the same dependencies of the `seven_dof_arm_gazebo` package. If you have already cloned the code repository, you already have this package, otherwise, clone the entire code from the Git repository, or get the package from the book's source code:

```
git clone https://github.com/PacktPublishing/Mastering-ROS-for-
Robotics-Programming-Third-edition.git
cd Chapter4/seven_dof_arm_gazebo
```

Navigate to the `diff_wheeled_robot_gazebo/launch` directory and take the `diff_wheeled_gazebo.launch` file. Here is the definition of this launch:

```
<launch>

  <!-- these are the arguments you can pass this launch file,
for example paused:=true -->
  <arg name="paused" default="false"/>
  <arg name="use_sim_time" default="true"/>
  <arg name="gui" default="true"/>
  <arg name="headless" default="false"/>
  <arg name="debug" default="false"/>


  <!-- We resume the logic in empty_world.launch -->
  <include file="$(find gazebo_ros)/launch/empty_world.launch">
    <arg name="debug" value="$(arg debug)" />
    <arg name="gui" value="$(arg gui)" />
    <arg name="paused" value="$(arg paused)"/>
    <arg name="use_sim_time" value="$(arg use_sim_time)"/>
    <arg name="headless" value="$(arg headless)"/>
  </include>


  <!-- urdf xml robot description loaded on the Parameter
Server-->
  <param name="robot_description" command="$(find xacro)/xacro
--inorder '$(find mastering_ros_robot_description_pkg)/urdf/
diff_wheeled_robot.xacro'" />


  <!-- Run a python script to the send a service call to
gazebo_ros to spawn a URDF robot -->
  <node name="urdf_spawner" pkg="gazebo_ros" type="spawn_model"
respawn="false" output="screen"
   args="-urdf -model diff_wheeled_robot -param robot_
description"/>


</launch>
```

To launch this file, we can use the following command:

```
roslaunch diff_wheeled_robot_gazebo diff_wheeled_gazebo.launch
```

You will see the following robot model in Gazebo. If you get this model, you have successfully finished the first phase of the simulation:

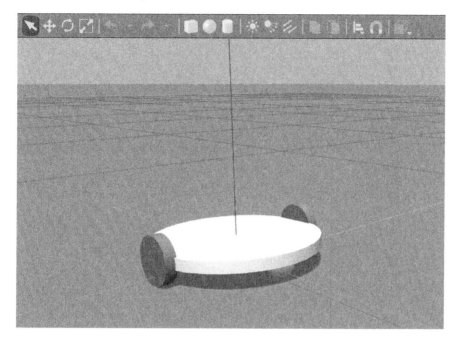

Figure 4.11 – Differential wheeled robot in Gazebo

After this successful simulation, let's add a laser scanner to the robot.

Adding the laser scanner to Gazebo

We add the laser scanner on top of the robot so we can use it to perform high-end operations, such as autonomous navigation or map creation. Here, we should add the following extra code section to `diff_wheeled_robot.xacro` to add the laser scanner to the robot to define the link representing the laser scanner and the joint to connect it to the robot frame:

```
<link name="hokuyo_link">
  <visual>
    <origin xyz="0 0 0" rpy="0 0 0" />
    <geometry>
      <box size="${hokuyo_size} ${hokuyo_size} ${hokuyo_size}"/>
    </geometry>
    <material name="Blue" />
```

```
    </visual>
  </link>
  <joint name="hokuyo_joint" type="fixed">
    <origin xyz="${base_radius - hokuyo_size/2} 0 ${base_
height+hokuyo_size/4}" rpy="0 0 0" />
    <parent link="base_link"/>
    <child link="hokuyo_link" />
  </joint>
```

Then, we need to include Gazebo-specific information to configure the laser scanner plugin:

```
  <gazebo reference="hokuyo_link">
    <material>Gazebo/Blue</material>
    <turnGravityOff>false</turnGravityOff>
    <sensor type="ray" name="head_hokuyo_sensor">
      <pose>${hokuyo_size/2} 0 0 0 0 0</pose>
      <visualize>false</visualize>
      <update_rate>40</update_rate>
      <ray>
        <scan>
          <horizontal>
            <samples>720</samples>
            <resolution>1</resolution>
            <min_angle>-1.570796</min_angle>
            <max_angle>1.570796</max_angle>
          </horizontal>
        </scan>
        <range>
          <min>0.10</min>
          <max>10.0</max>
          <resolution>0.001</resolution>
        </range>
      </ray>
      <plugin name="gazebo_ros_head_hokuyo_controller"
filename="libgazebo_ros_laser.so">
        <topicName>/scan</topicName>
        <frameName>hokuyo_link</frameName>
```

```
      </plugin>
    </sensor>
  </gazebo>
```

In this section, we use the Gazebo ROS plugin file called `libgazebo_ros_laser.so` to simulate the laser scanner. The complete code can be found in the `diff_wheeled_robot_with_laser.xacro` description file in the `mastering_ros_robot_description_pkg/urdf/` directory.

We can view the laser scanner data by adding some objects to the simulation environment. Here, we add some cylinders around the robot and can see the corresponding laser view in the next section of the figure:

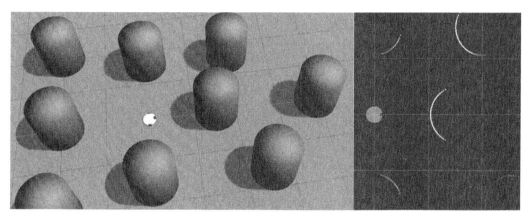

Figure 4.12 – Differential drive robot in between cylinder objects in Gazebo

The laser scanner plugin publishes laser data (`sensor_msgs/LaserScan`) to the `/scan` topic.

Moving the mobile robot in Gazebo

The robot we are working with is a differential robot with two wheels and two caster wheels. The complete characteristics of the robot should be modeled using the Gazebo-ROS plugin. Luckily, the plugin for a basic differential drive function is already implemented.

To get the robot to move in Gazebo, we should add a Gazebo-ROS plugin file called `libgazebo_ros_diff_drive.so`, which will add the differential drive behavior to our robot.

Here is the complete code snippet of the definition of this plugin and its parameters:

```
<!-- Differential drive controller   -->
<gazebo>
    <plugin name="differential_drive_controller"
filename="libgazebo_ros_diff_drive.so">

        <rosDebugLevel>Debug</rosDebugLevel>
        <publishWheelTF>false</publishWheelTF>
        <robotNamespace>/</robotNamespace>
        <publishTf>1</publishTf>
        <publishWheelJointState>false</publishWheelJointState>
        <alwaysOn>true</alwaysOn>
        <updateRate>100.0</updateRate>

        <leftJoint>front_left_wheel_joint</leftJoint>
        <rightJoint>front_right_wheel_joint</rightJoint>

        <wheelSeparation>${2*base_radius}</wheelSeparation>
        <wheelDiameter>${2*wheel_radius}</wheelDiameter>
        <broadcastTF>1</broadcastTF>
        <wheelTorque>30</wheelTorque>
        <wheelAcceleration>1.8</wheelAcceleration>
        <commandTopic>cmd_vel</commandTopic>
        <odometryFrame>odom</odometryFrame>
        <odometryTopic>odom</odometryTopic>
        <robotBaseFrame>base_footprint</robotBaseFrame>


    </plugin>
</gazebo>
```

We can provide parameters such as the wheel joints of the robot (joints should be of a continuous type), wheel separation, wheel diameter, an odometry topic, and so on, using this plugin.

An important parameter that is required to move the robot is the following:

```
<commandTopic>cmd_vel</commandTopic>
```

This parameter is the velocity command topic to the plugin, which is basically a `Twist` message in ROS (`sensor_msgs/Twist`). We can publish the `Twist` message into the `/cmd_vel` topic, and we will see the robot start to move from its position.

Adding joint state publishers to the launch file

After adding the differential drive plugin, we need to join state publishers to the existing launch file, or we can build a new one. You can find the new final launch file, `diff_wheeled_gazebo_full.launch`, in `diff_wheeled_robot_gazebo/launch`.

The launch file contains joint state publishers, which help developers to visualize the `tf` in rviz. Here are the extra lines to be added to this launch file for the joint state publishing:

```
    <node name="joint_state_publisher" pkg="joint_state_
publisher" type="joint_state_publisher" ></node>
    <!-- start robot state publisher -->
    <node pkg="robot_state_publisher" type="robot_state_
publisher" name="robot_state_publisher" output="screen" >
        <param name="publish_frequency" type="double" value="50.0"
/>
    </node>
```

We are now ready to develop our first program to command a robot in an intuitive way. In the next section, we will implement a teleoperation node to move the differential drive robot in the simulation scene.

Adding the ROS teleop node

The ROS teleop node publishes the ROS `Twist` command by taking keyboard inputs. From this node, we can generate both linear and angular velocity, and there is already a standard teleop node implementation available; we can simply reuse the node.

The teleop is implemented in the `diff_wheeled_robot_control` package. The script folder contains the `diff_wheeled_robot_key` node, which is the teleop node. As per usual, you can download this package from the previous Git repository. At this point, you reach this package with the following command:

```
roscd diff_wheeled_robot_control
```

To successfully compile and use this package, you may need to install the `joy_node` package:

```
sudo apt-get install ros-noetic-joy
```

Here is the launch file called `keyboard_teleop.launch` to start the teleop node:

```
<launch>
  <!-- differential_teleop_key already has its own built in
velocity smoother -->
  <node pkg="diff_wheeled_robot_control" type="diff_wheeled_
robot_key" name="diff_wheeled_robot_key"  output="screen">

    <param name="scale_linear" value="0.5" type="double"/>
    <param name="scale_angular" value="1.5" type="double"/>
    <remap from="turtlebot_teleop_keyboard/cmd_vel" to="/cmd_
vel"/>
  </node>
</launch>
```

Let's start moving the robot.

Launch Gazebo with the completed simulation settings using the following command:

```
roslaunch diff_wheeled_robot_gazebo diff_wheeled_gazebo_full.
launch
```

Start the teleop node:

```
roslaunch diff_wheeled_robot_control keyboard_teleop.launch
```

Start RViz to visualize the robot state and laser data:

```
rosrun rviz
```

Add `Fixed Frame: /odom` and `Laser Scan`, set the topic to `/scan` to view the laser scan data, and add the `Robot model element` to view the robot model.

In the teleop terminal, we can use some keys (*U, I, O, J, K, L, M, ",", and "."*) for direction adjustments and other keys (*Q, Z, W, X, E, C, K,* and the spacebar) for speed adjustments. The following figure shows a screenshot demonstrating the robot moving in Gazebo using teleop and its visualization in RViz.

We can add primitive shapes from the Gazebo toolbar to the robot environment, or we can add objects from the online library, which is on the left-side panel:

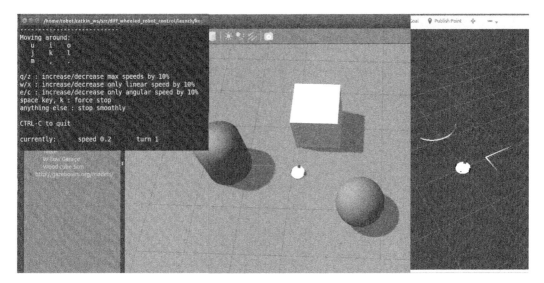

Figure 4.13 – Moving the differential drive robot in Gazebo using teleoperation

The robot will only move when we press the appropriate key inside the teleop node terminal. If this terminal is not active, pressing the key will not move the robot. If everything works well, we can explore the area using the robot and visualize the laser data in RViz.

Questions

1. Why do we perform robotic simulation?
2. How can we add sensors to a Gazebo simulation?
3. What are the different types of ROS controllers and hardware interfaces?
4. How can we move the mobile robot in a Gazebo simulation?

Summary

In this chapter, we were trying to simulate two robots: one was a robotic arm with seven DOF, and the other was a differential wheeled mobile robot. We started with the robotic arm and discussed the additional Gazebo tags needed to launch the robot in Gazebo. We discussed how to add a 3D vision sensor to the simulation. Later, we created a launch file to start Gazebo with a robotic arm and discussed how to add controllers to each joint. We added the controllers and worked with each joint.

Like the robotic arm, we created the URDF for the Gazebo simulation and added the necessary Gazebo-ROS plugin for the laser scanner and differential drive mechanism. After completing the simulation model, we launched the simulation using a custom launch file. Finally, we looked at how to move the robot using the teleop node.

We can learn more about the robotic arm and mobile robots supported by ROS at `http://wiki.ros.org/Robots`.

In the next chapter, we will see how to simulate robots using other robot simulators, namely, **CoppeliaSim** and **Webots**.

5

Simulating Robots Using ROS, CoppeliaSim, and Webots

Having learned how to simulate robots with Gazebo, in this chapter we will discuss how to use the other two powerful robot-simulation software: **CoppeliaSim** (`http://www.coppeliarobotics.com`) and **Webots** (`https://cyberbotics.com/`).

These are multiplatform robotic simulators. CoppeliaSim is developed by *Coppelia Robotics*. It offers many simulation models of popular industrial and mobile robots ready to be used, and different functionalities that can be easily integrated and combined through a dedicated **application programming interface** (**API**). In addition, it can operate with **Robot Operating System** (**ROS**) using a proper communication interface that allows us to control the simulation scene and the robots via topics and services. As with Gazebo, CoppeliaSim can be used as a standalone software, while an external plugin must be installed to work with ROS. As for Webots, it is a free and open source software used to simulate **3D** robots. It is developed by *Cyberbotics Ltd.* and since December 2018 it has been released under a free and open source license.

As with CoppeliaSim, it can be easily interfaced with ROS.

In this chapter, we will learn how to set up these simulators and connect them with the ROS network. We will discuss some initial code to understand how they work with both as standalone software and how they can be used with ROS services and topics.

We will cover the following topics in this chapter:

- Setting up CoppeliaSim with ROS
- Simulating a robotic arm using CoppeliaSim and ROS
- Setting up Webots with ROS
- Writing your first controller
- Writing a **teleoperation (teleop)** node using `webots_ros`

Technical requirements

To follow this chapter, you need a standard laptop running Ubuntu 20.04 with ROS Noetic installed. The reference code for this chapter can be downloaded from the following Git repository: `https://github.com/PacktPublishing/Mastering-ROS-for-Robotics-Programming-Third-edition.git`. The code is contained in the `Chapter5/csim_demo_pkg` and `Chapter5/webost_demo_pkg` folders.

You can view this chapter's code in action here: `https://bit.ly/3AOApje`.

Setting up CoppeliaSim with ROS

Before starting to work with CoppeliaSim, we need to install it on our system and configure our environment to start the communication bridge between ROS and the simulation scene. CoppeliaSim is cross-platform software, available for different operating systems such as Windows, macOS, and Linux. It is developed by *Coppelia Robotics GmbH* and is distributed with both free educational and commercial licenses. Download the latest version of the CoppeliaSim simulator from the *Coppelia Robotics* download page at `http://www.coppeliarobotics.com/downloads.html`, choosing the `edu` version for Linux. In this chapter, we will refer to the `CoppeliaSim 4.2.0` version.

After completing the download, extract the archive. Move to your `download` folder and use the following command:

```
tar vxf CoppeliaSim_Edu_V4_2_0_Ubuntu20_04.tar.xz
```

This version is supported by Ubuntu versions 20.04. It is convenient to rename this folder with something more intuitive, such as this:

```
mv CoppeliaSim_Edu_V4_2_0_Ubuntu20_04 CoppeliaSim
```

To easily access CoppeliaSim resources, it is also convenient to set the `COPPELIASIM_ROOT` environmental variable that points to the `CoppeliaSim` main folder, like this:

```
echo "export COPPELIASIM_ROOT=/path/to/CoppeliaSim/folder >>
~/.bashrc"
```

Here, `/path/to/CoppeliaSim/folder` is the absolute path to the extracted folder.

CoppeliaSim offers the following modes to control simulated robots from external applications:

- **Remote application programming interface** (**API**): The CoppeliaSim remote API is composed of several functions that can be called from external applications developed in C/C++, Python, Lua, or MATLAB. The remote API interacts with CoppeliaSim over the network, using socket communication. You can integrate the remote API in your C++ or Python nodes to connect ROS with the simulation scene. The list of all remote APIs available in CoppeliaSim can be found on the *Coppelia Robotics* website, at `https://www.coppeliarobotics.com/helpFiles/en/remoteApiFunctionsMatlab.htm`. To use the remote API, you must implement both client and server sides, as follows:

  A. **CoppeliaSim client**: The client side resides in the external application. It can be implemented in a ROS node or in a standard program written in one of the supported programming languages.

  B. **CoppeliaSim server**: This side is implemented in CoppeliaSim scripts and allows the simulator to receive external data to interact with the simulation scene.

- `RosInterface`: This is the current interface to enable the communication between ROS and CoppeliaSim. In the past, an **ROS plugin** was used, but this is now deprecated.

In this chapter, we will discuss how to interact with CoppeliaSim using the RosInterface plugin that replicates the remote API functionalities transparently. Using this interface, CoppeliaSim will act as a ROS node that other nodes can communicate with via ROS services, ROS publishers, and ROS subscribers. The interface is implemented by an external library already available in the CoppeliaSim folder. Prior to the setup of the RosInterface plugin, we need to configure the environment to run CoppeliaSim. First, we need to force our operating system to load the Lua and Qt5 shared libraries from the root folder of CoppeliaSim. Lua is a programming language used for different high-level applications, and it is used from CoppeliaSim to program simulated robots directly from its interface.

Now, we are ready to start the simulator. To enable the ROS communication interface, a roscore command should be run on your machine prior to opening the simulator, while to open CoppeliaSim, we can use the following command:

```
cd $COPPELIASIM_ROOT
./coppeliaSim.sh
```

During the startup, all plugins installed in the system will be loaded. In a few words, all the plugins are in the root folder of CoppeliaSim, as shown in the following screenshot:

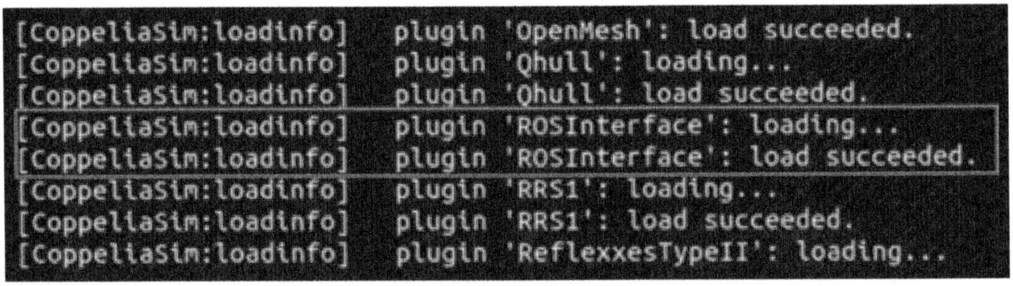

Figure 5.1 – Plugins loading during CoppeliaSim startup

You can check if everything is working properly by listing the nodes running on your system after launching CoppeliaSim, as shown in the following screenshot:

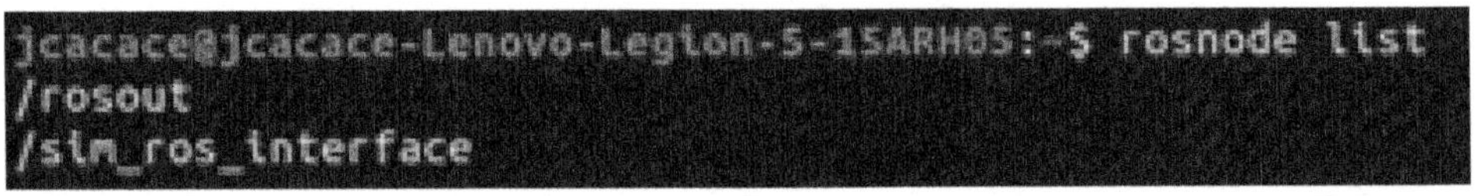

Figure 5.2 – List of active ROS nodes after running CoppeliaSim with the RosInterface plugin

As you can see, the `sim_ros_interface` node has been started with the CoppeliaSim program. To explore the `RosInterface` plugin functionalities, we can have a look at the `plugin_publisher_subscriber.ttt` scene, located in the `csim_demo_pkg/scene` folder of the code provided with this book. To open this scene, use the main drop-down menu and select the **File | Open Scene** option. After opening this scene the simulation windows should appear, as in the following screenshot:

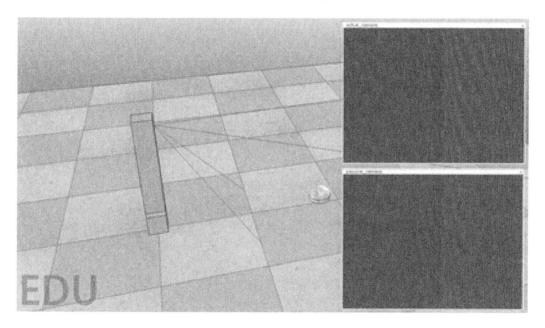

Figure 5.3 – plugin_publisher_subscriber.ttt simulation scene

In this scene, a robot is equipped with two cameras: one active camera acquiring images from the environment and publishing the video stream on a specific topic, and one passive camera that only acquires the video stream from the same topic. We can press the **play** button on the main bar of the CoppeliaSim interface.

After that, the simulation starts; this is what will happen:

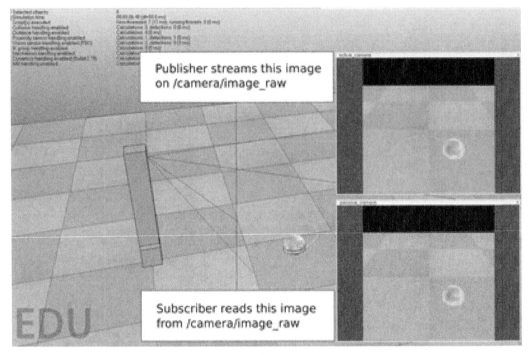

Figure 5.4 – Image publisher and subscriber example

In this simulation, the passive camera displays the image published from the active one, receiving vision data directly from the ROS framework. We can also visualize the video stream published by CoppeliaSim using the image_view package, by running the following command:

```
rosrun image_view image:=/camera/image_raw
```

We can now discuss how to interface CoppeliaSim and ROS using the RosInterface plugin.

Understanding the RosInterface plugin

The RosInterface plugin is part of the CoppeliaSim API framework. Even though the plugin is correctly installed in your system, the load operation will fail if the roscore was not running at that time. In this case, the ROS functions are not able to work properly. To prevent such unexpected behaviors, we will later see how to check if the RosInterface plugin is working properly. Let's discuss how to interact with CoppeliaSim using ROS topics.

Interacting with CoppeliaSim using ROS topics

We will now discuss how to use ROS topics to communicate with CoppeliaSim. This is useful when we want to send information to the objects of the simulation, or retrieve data generated by robot sensors or actuators.

The most common way to program the simulation scene of this simulator is by using *Lua* scripts. Every object of the scene can be associated to a script that is automatically invoked when the simulation starts and is cyclically executed during simulation time.

In the next example, we will create a scene with two objects. One will be programmed to publish integer data from a specific topic while the other one subscribes to this topic, displaying the float data on the CoppeliaSim console.

Use the drop-down menu on the **Scene hierarchy** panel, select the **Add | Dummy** entry. We can create two objects, a dummy_publisher object and a dummy_subscriber object, and associate a script with each of them. Use the right mouse button on the created objects, and select the **Add | Associated child script | Non threaded** entry, as shown in the following screenshot:

Figure 5.5 – Associating a non-threaded script with CoppeliaSim object

Alternatively, we can directly load the simulation scene by opening the demo_publisher_subscriber.ttt file located in the csim_demo_pkg folder of the book source code in the scene directory.

Let's see the content of the script associated with the dummy_publisher object, as follows:

```
function sysCall_init()
    if simROS then
        print("ROS interface correctly loaded")
        pub=simROS.advertise('/number', 'std_msgs/Int32')
    else
        print("<font color='#F00'>ROS interface was not found.
Cannot run.</font>@html")
    end
end

function sysCall_actuation()
    int_data = {}
    int_data['data'] = 13
    simROS.publish(pub, int_data)
end
```

Each *Lua* script linked to CoppeliaSim objects contains the following four sections:

- sysCall_init: This section is only executed the first time that the simulation starts.

- sysCall_actuation: This section is cyclically called at the same frame rate as the simulation. Users can put here the code that controls the actuation of the robot.

- sysCall_sensing: This part will be executed at each simulation step, during the sensing phase of a simulation step.

- sysCall_cleanup: This section is called just before the simulation ends.

As you can see from the previous code snippet, in the initialization part we check if the RosInterface plugin is installed and correctly loaded in the system; if not, an error is displayed. This is done by checking the existence of the simROS object, as shown in the following code snippet:

```
if simROS then
    print("ROS interface correctly loaded")
```

After checking that the ROS plugin has been loaded, we will enable the publisher of the float value, as follows:

```
pub = simROS.advertise('/number', 'std_msgs/Int32')
```

To print messages on the status bar of the simulator, we can use the print function, as follows:

```
print("<font color='#F00'>ROS interface was not found. Cannot
run.</font>@html")
```

This text will be shown if the ROS plugin has not been initialized. The result of the previous line of code is depicted in the following screenshot:

```
[sandboxScript:info]  Simulation started.
ROS interface was not found. Cannot run.
[Plane@childScript:error]  13: attempt to index global 'simROS' (a nil value)
   stack traceback:
      [string "Plane@childScript"]:13: in function <[string "Plane@childScript"]:10>
ROS interface was not found. Cannot run.
```

Figure 5.6 – Error reported in the status bar of CoppeliaSim

Finally, we exploit the cyclic call of the actuation function to continuously stream the int value over the ROS network, as follows:

```
function sysCall_actuation()
    int_data = {}
    int_data['data'] = 13
    simROS.publish(pub, int_data)
end
```

Let's now see the content of the script associated with the dummy_subscriber object, as follows:

```
function sysCall_init()
    if simROS then
        print("ROS interface correctly loaded")
        sub=simROS.subscribe('/number', 'std_msgs/Int32',
'intMessage_callback')
    else
        print("<font color='#F00'>ROS interface was not found.
Cannot run.</font>@html")
```

```
        end
end
function intMessage_callback(msg)
    print ( "data", msg["data"] )
end
```

After checking that the ROS plugin has been loaded, we activate the subscriber of the input number value on the /number topic. The subscribe method of the simROS object expects as parameters the name of the topic, the desired type to stream, and the callback to process the incoming data. The code can be seen in the following snippet:

```
        sub=simROS.subscribe('/number', 'std_msgs/Int32',
'intMessage_callback')
```

Then, we define a callback method to display the data published on the /number topic into the status bar, as follows:

```
function intMessage_callback(msg)
    print ( "data", msg["data"] )
end
```

After starting the simulation, we can see that the float number published by the dummy_ publisher script is correctly received by the dummy_subscriber script. We will now discuss how to use different ROS messages in CoppeliaSim scripts.

Working with ROS messages

To publish a new ROS message in *Lua* scripts, we need to wrap it in a data structure containing the same fields of the original message. The inverse procedure must be done to collect the information published on ROS topics. Let's analyze the work done in the previous example before we move to something more complicated. In the dummy_ publisher example, the goal was to publish integer data on an ROS topic. We can check the structure of an integer message using this ROS command:

```
rosmsg show std_msgs/Int32
int32 data
```

This means that we need to fill the data field of the message structure with the desired value to stream, as we did in the publisher script. The code to do this can be seen here:

```
int_data['data'] = 13
```

Let's now see how to make something more complex, by streaming over ROS an image taken by a camera sensor placed in the simulation scene. Load the `plugin_publisher_subscriber.ttt` simulation scene again and open the script associated with the `active_camera` object. At the start of this script, the handler of the message is retrieved, as follows:

```
visionSensorHandle=sim.getObjectHandle('active_camera')
```

As well as this, the topic publisher is initialized, as follows:

```
pub=simROS.advertise('/camera/image_raw', 'sensor_msgs/Image')
```

Then, the `sysCall_sensing` sensing function is automatically called by the CoppeliaSim executor when a new image is received. Inside it, a `sensor_msgs/Image` data structure must be compiled before publishing the data. Let's see the code.

The `getVisionSensorCharImage` method is used to get the new image and its properties, as illustrated in the following code snippet:

```
function sysCall_sensing()
    local data,w,h=sim.
getVisionSensorCharImage(visionSensorHandle)
```

We now have almost all the elements to configure the image frame, as illustrated in the following code snippet:

```
    d={}
    d['header']={stamp=simROS.getTime(), frame_id="a"}
    d['height']=h
    d['width']=w
    d['encoding']='rgb8'
    d['is_bigendian']=1
    d['step']=w*3
```

And we can stream the data, as follows:

```
    d['data']=data
    simROS.publish(pub,d)
```

Up to now, we have only discussed how to use `RosInterface` to connect ROS and CoppeliaSim. We can use it with the robot model already provided with the simulator. In the next section, we will see how to import our own **Unified Robot Description Format (URDF)** robot model into CoppeliaSim.

Simulating a robotic arm using CoppeliaSim and ROS

In the previous chapter, we used Gazebo to import and simulate the seven-**degrees of freedom** (**DOF**) arm designed in *Chapter 3, Working with ROS for 3D Modeling*. Here, we will do the same thing using CoppeliaSim. The first step to simulate our seven-DOF arm is to import it in the simulation scene. CoppeliaSim allows you to import new robots using URDF files; for this reason, we must convert the xacro model of the arm in a URDF file, saving the generated URDF file in the urdf folder of the csim_demo_pkg package, as follows:

```
rosrun xacro seven_dof_arm.xacro >  /path/to/csim_demo_pkg/
urdf/seven_dof_arm.urdf
```

We can now import the robot model, using the URDF import plugin. Select from the main drop-down menu the **Plugins | URDF import** entry and press the **Import** button, choosing the default import options from the dialog window. Finally, select the desired file to import, and the seven-DOF arm will appear in the scene, as illustrated in the following screenshot:

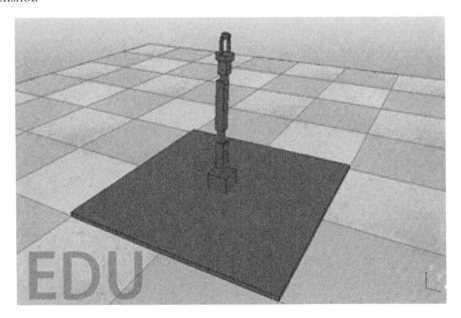

Figure 5.7 – Simulation of seven-DOF arm in CoppeliaSim

All the components of the robot are now imported into the scene, as we can see from the **Scene hierarchy** panel, in which are shown the set of robot joints and links defined in the URDF file.

Even if the robot has been correctly imported, it is not ready to be controlled yet. To actuate the robot, we need to enable all robot motors from the **Joint Dynamic Properties** panel. Until the motor is disabled, it is not possible to move it during the simulation. To enable the motor of a joint, open the **Scene Object Properties** panel, selecting from the main drop-down menu the **Tools | Scene object properties** option. You can also open this dialog with a double-click on an object icon in the scene hierarchy. From this new window, open the **Dynamic properties** dialog and enable the motor and the control loop of the joint, selecting the controller type. By default, the motor is controlled via a **proportional integral derivative (PID)**, as shown in the following screenshot:

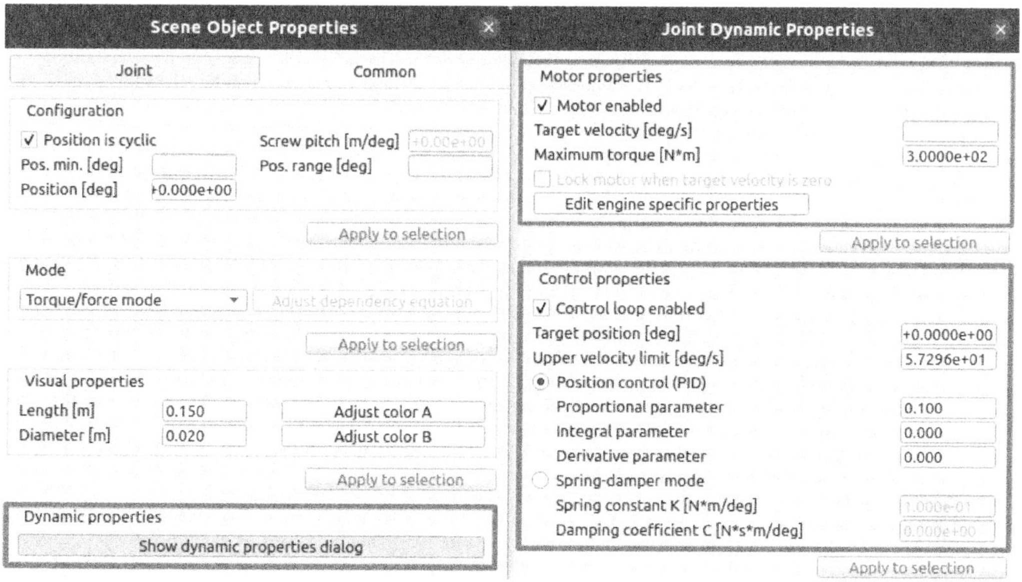

Figure 5.8 – Scene Object Properties and Joint Dynamic Properties dialogs

To increase the performance of the control loop, PID gains should be properly tuned. After enabling motors and control loops for all robot joints, we can check that everything has been configured correctly. Run the simulation and set a target position from the **Scene Object Properties** panel.

Here is an example of moving the fourth joint to 1.0 radians:

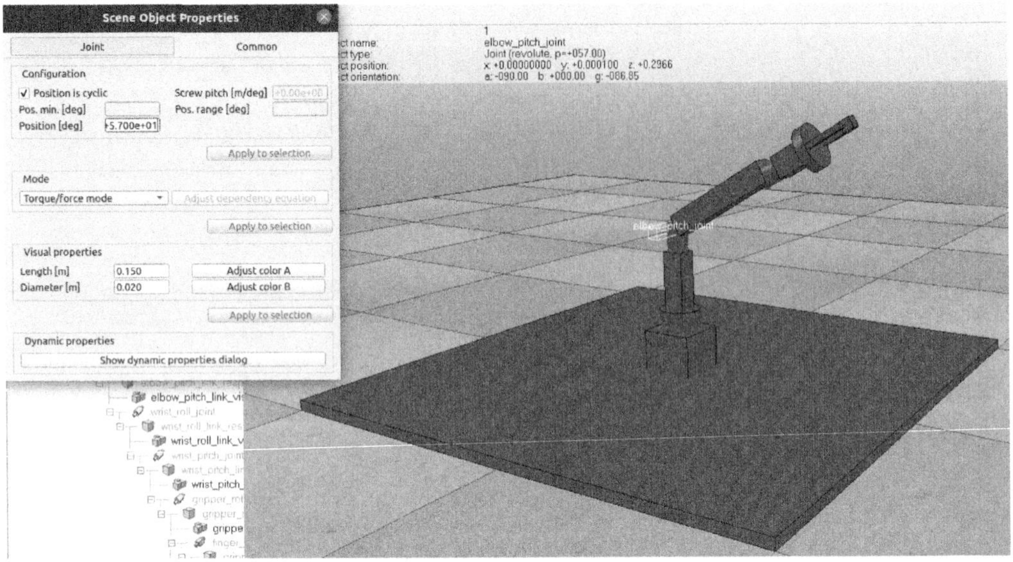

Figure 5.9 – Moving a joint of the arm from CoppeliaSim Scene Object Properties dialog

The robot is now integrated in the simulation scene; however, we cannot control it using ROS. To do this, in the next section we will discuss how to integrate robot controllers with the RosInterface plugin.

Adding the ROS interface to CoppeliaSim joint controllers

In this section, we will learn how to interface the seven-DOF arm with the RosInterface plugin to stream the state of its joints and receive the control input via topics. As already seen in the previous example, select a component of the robot (for example, the base_link_respondable component) and create a *Lua* script that will manage the communication between CoppeliaSim and ROS.

Here is the description script source code.

In the initialization block, we retrieve the handlers of all the joints of the robot, as follows:

```
function sysCall_init()
shoulder_pan_handle=sim.getObjectHandle('shoulder_pan_joint')
    shoulder_pitch_handle=sim.getObjectHandle('shoulder_pitch_
joint')
    elbow_roll_handle=sim.getObjectHandle('elbow_roll_joint')
```

```
elbow_pitch_handle=sim.getObjectHandle('elbow_pitch_joint')
wrist_roll_handle=sim.getObjectHandle('wrist_roll_joint')
wrist_pitch_handle=sim.getObjectHandle('wrist_pitch_joint')
gripper_roll_handle=sim.getObjectHandle('gripper_roll_
joint')
```

Then, we set the publisher of the joint angles, like this:

```
j1_state_pub = simROS.advertise('/csim_demo/seven_dof_arm/
shoulder_pan/state', 'std_msgs/Float32')
```

We must replicate this line for each joint of the model. We need to successfully do the same for the subscribers of the joint commands, as follows:

```
j1_cmd_sub = simROS.subscribe('/csim_demo/seven_dof_arm/
shoulder_pan/cmd', 'std_msgs/Float32', 'j1Cmd_callback')
```

Also, in this case, we must instantiate a new subscriber and a new callback to process the incoming data. For example, to read the joint value published on the ROS topic for a given joint and apply a proper joint command, we will use the following block of code:

```
function j1Cmd_callback( msg )
    sim.setJointTargetPosition( shoulder_pan_handle,
msg['data'] )
end
```

Here, we use the setJointTargetPosition function to change the position of a given joint. The input arguments of such functions are the handler of the joint object and the value to assign. After starting the simulation, we can move a desired joint, such as the elbow_pitch joint, publishing a value using command-line tools, as illustrated in the following code snippet:

```
rostopic pub /csim_demo/seven_dof_arm/elbow_pitch/cmd std_msgs/
Float32 "data: 1.0"
```

At the same time, we can get the position of the joint listening on the state topic, as follows:

```
rostopic echo /csim_demo/seven_dof_arm/elbow_pitch/state
```

This is shown in the following screenshot:

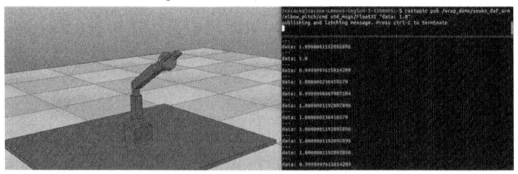

Figure 5.10 – Controlling a seven_dof_arm joint using the RosInterface plugin

We are now ready to implement our control algorithms moving the joints of the seven-DOF arm. With this topic, we conclude the first part of this chapter. In the following section, we continue to discuss robotic simulator software, introducing Webots.

Setting up Webots with ROS

As already done with CoppeliaSim, we need to install Webots on our system before setting it up with ROS. Webots is a multiplatform simulation software supported by Windows, Linux, and macOS. This software was initially developed by the **Swiss Federal Institute of Technology, Lausanne (EPFL)**. Now, it is developed by *Cyberbotics*, and it is released under the free and open source Apache 2 license. Webots provides a complete development environment to model, program, and simulate robots. It has been designed for professional use and it is widely used in industry, education, and research.

You can choose different ways to install the simulator. You can download the .deb package from the Webots web page (http://www.cyberbotics.com/#download) or use the Debian/Ubuntu **Advanced Packaging Tool (APT)** package manager. Assuming that you are running Ubuntu, let's start by authenticating the Cyberbotics repository, as follows:

```
wget -qO- https://cyberbotics.com/Cyberbotics.asc | sudo
apt-key add -
```

Then, you can configure your APT package manager by adding the Cyberbotics repository, as follows:

```
sudo apt-add-repository 'deb https://cyberbotics.com/debian/
binary-amd64/'
sudo apt-get update
```

Then, proceed to the installation of Webots by using the following command:

```
sudo apt-get install webots
```

We are now ready to start Webots using the following command:

```
$ webots
```

After this command, the Webots **user interface** (**UI**) will open. Using the simulation menu on the top of the window you can control the simulation, starting or pausing the simulation or speeding up its execution.

We are now ready to start to simulate robot motion and sensors. Before we discuss how to start programming robots with Webots, we will overview its fundamentals.

Introduction to the Webots simulator

Webots simulations are mainly composed of the following three elements:

- **A world configuration file**: As with Gazebo, the simulation environment is configured by means of a text-based world file with a `.wbt` extension. You can directly create and export world files from the Webots interface. All simulated objects and robots—along with their geometrical shapes and textures, position, and orientation—are described in the world file. Webots already contains some example world files ready to be used. These are contained in the `world` subfolder of Webots. If you installed Webots using APT, such files are contained in the `/usr/local/webots/projects/vehicles/worlds/` folder.

- **Controllers**: Each simulation is handled by one or more controller programs. Controllers can be implemented in different programming languages such as C, C++, Python, or Java. Also, MATLAB scripts are supported. When the simulation starts, the associated controllers start as separate processes. Even in this case, a set of basic controllers are already available in the main directory of Webots; they are placed in the `controllers` subfolder. In this way, Webots already implements different robot functionalities, such as motion functions.

- **Physical plugins**: A set of plugins that can be used to modify the regular physical behavior of the simulation. They can be written in the same languages as those of the controller programs.

The communication bridge between ROS and Webots can be implemented using a proper controller that can be used by any robot of the simulation scene and that acts like a ROS node, providing all the Webots functions as services or topics to other ROS nodes. We will start discussing how to create and program a first simulation scene, before we explore its integration with ROS.

Simulating a mobile robot with Webots

The goal of this section is to create a simulation scene from scratch, containing objects and a mobile wheeled robot. To do this, we need to create a new empty world. We can use the wizard option to create a new simulation scene. This world is already available in the book source code in the `webots_demo_pkg` package. To create a new simulation, use the top-bar menu and select **Wizards | New Project Directory**. An applet will help you to set up everything. Click **Next** to choose a project directory. Insert the path of the folder as you prefer, and choose `mobile_robot` as the folder name. You can also choose a world name; insert `robot_motion_controller.wbt` and be careful to pin the **Add a rectangle area** option. Then, click **Finish** and, after the scene has been loaded, it should appear as depicted in the following screenshot:

Figure 5.11 – Starting scene of Webots

Each object in the scene is organized in a hierarchical way, as the tree shows in the left panel of the UI. At the start, we have the following elements already present:

- `WorldInfo`: This contains a set of simulation parameters, such as fixing the reference frame.

- `Viewpoint`: This defines the main viewpoint camera parameters.

- `TexturedBackground`: This defines the background image of the simulation.

- `TexturedBackgroundlight`: This defines the light associated with the background.

- `RectangleArena`: This represents the floor for our simulation objects.

In Webots, such objects are called nodes. Each node can be customized by setting some properties—for example, by double-clicking on the **RectangleArena** element, we can modify the floor size and the wall's height. We are now ready to add objects to our scene. Select and fold the **RectangleArea** element from the hierarchy panel and click on the + (add) button in the upper panel, as shown in the following screenshot:

Figure 5.12 – Button to add nodes to the Webots scene

Each node of Webots is represented by a `PROTO` file. This is a text file that contains the definition of an object. Webots already contains different `PROTO` models to spawn objects and robots in the simulation scene. After clicking on the + button, choose **PROTO nodes (Webots Projects)** | **objects** | **factory** | **containers** | **WoodenBox (Solid)** to make a big wooden box appear in the simulation. Use the `object` property to modify its size and position. You can also use the mouse to easily move the box, positioning it. Be careful to assign a reasonable mass to the object, since at the start it is 0. Finally, we are ready to import the mobile robot. Exactly like the wooden box, a robot is represented by a `PROTO` element. Webots offers different mobile and industrial robot models. In this section, we will import the `e-puck` mobile robot. This is a small-wheeled, differential-drive educational platform consisting of multiple distance sensors and an onboard camera. Before we add this model or any other model to the environment, you must make sure that the simulation is paused and that the virtual time elapsed is 0 (you can reset the time using the **reset** button). In fact, every time that the world is modified, the virtual time counter on the main toolbar should show **0:00:00:000**. Otherwise, at each save, the position of each object could accumulate errors. Therefore, any modification of the world should be performed after the scene has been reset and saved.

Again, select **RectangleArea** and use the + button, selecting the **(Webots Projects) / robots / gctronic / e-puck / E-puck** PROTO element. Now, position the robot in the scene and save the world. Also, in this case, from the **robot panel** properties, you can configure things such as the sensor parameters (camera resolution, field of view, and similar). You are now ready to start the simulation using the **Start** button. You can also see that this robot is already able to move in the environment avoiding obstacles thanks to its sensors. This is because this robot already implements a *controller* that is called e-puck_avoid_obstacles. You can examine the source code of this controller either by directly opening its source code with a text editor or by using the integrated text editor of Webots. In this latter case, click on the controller in the E-puck node elements and click on **Edit**. The result is shown in the following screenshot:

Figure 5.13 – Controllers editor in Webots

As you can see, this controller is implemented with a C program, so any modifications made to it must be compiled beforehand to make it effective. Now, let's try writing our first controller using Webots.

Writing your first controller

In this section, we will write our first controller for the mobile robot. We have seen how the controllers handle the motion of the robot and its reaction to the sensors. Let's change the controller of the E-puck robot to move some fixed directions. We can choose different programming languages for our controller; however, we will use C++. The goal of the new controller is to command the velocity of the wheels of the robot to show the typical structure of a Webots controller.

The first thing to do is to change the controller associated with our mobile robot. Note that each robot can use only one controller at once. Conversely, we can associate the same controller with different robots. To write our new controller, we must follow these steps:

1. Create a new controller file.

2. Write a new controller.

3. Compile the new controller.

4. Change the default controller of the robot with the new one in the **robot properties** panel.

As already done for the creation of the world, we can use the wizard interface to generate a new controller. Use **Wizards | New Robot Controller**. Using the wizard, you can choose the programming language for the controller and its name. Choose C++ and robot_ motion for its name. Some initial source code will appear in the text editor. Now, you can compile it using the **Build** button.

The code of the controller is listed in the following snippet:

```cpp
#include <webots/Robot.hpp>
#include <webots/Motor.hpp>
#define MAX_SPEED 6.28
//64 Milliseconds
#define TIME_STEP 64
using namespace webots;
int main(int argc, char **argv) {
  Robot *robot = new Robot();
  Motor *leftMotor = robot->getMotor("left wheel motor");
  Motor *rightMotor = robot->getMotor("right wheel motor");
  leftMotor->setPosition(INFINITY);
  rightMotor->setPosition(INFINITY);
  double t=0.0;
```

```
double r_direction=1.0;
while(true)  {
    leftMotor->setVelocity( MAX_SPEED*0.1);
    rightMotor->setVelocity( r_direction*MAX_SPEED*0.1);
    robot->step(TIME_STEP) ;
    t+= TIME_STEP;
    if ( t > 2000 ) {
        r_direction*=-1.0;
    }
    if( t > 4000) {
        r_direction = 1.0;
        t = 0.0;
    }
}
delete robot;
return 0;
}
```

Here is an explanation of the code.

Let's start by including the header files to access the Robot functions and its motors, as follows:

```
#include <webots/Robot.hpp>
#include <webots/Motor.hpp>
```

Then, we define the maximum speed of the wheels, 6.28 radian per second, and the time step representing the sampling time of the simulation. This time is reported in **milliseconds (ms)**. The code is shown here:

```
#define MAX_SPEED 6.28
#define TIME_STEP 64
```

In the `main` function, we have to write the controller procedure. We will start instantiating the `Robot` and the `Motors` objects. For the `Robot` object, its constructor requires the name of the motor. You can get the element's name of the robot from the `PROTO` file describing the robot (right-click on the robot name in the hierarchy panel and then select **View PROTO Source**). The code is illustrated in the following snippet:

```
Robot *robot = new Robot();
Motor *leftMotor = robot->getMotor("left wheel motor");
Motor *rightMotor = robot->getMotor("right wheel motor");
```

To control the robot motor in velocity, we set its position to `INFINITY`, and then we set the desired velocity, as follows:

```
leftMotor->setPosition(INFINITY);
rightMotor->setPosition(INFINITY);
```

The main loop consists of an infinite `while` loop, in which we set the velocity of each motor as 10 percent of the maximum velocity and, for the right motor, a motion direction: `1.0` to move straight forward and `-1.0` to rotate. The code is illustrated in the following snippet:

```
while(true)   {
    leftMotor->setVelocity( MAX_SPEED*0.1);
    rightMotor->setVelocity( r_direction*MAX_SPEED*0.1);
```

We consider the elapsed time to set the control velocity, as follows:

```
t+= TIME_STEP;
```

Finally, to actuate the robot at the end of each iteration, we need to call the `step` function to send the commands to its motors. This function takes as input the time to wait before starting another loop of the controller. This number must be specified in ms. The code is illustrated in the following snippet:

```
robot->step(TIME_STEP) ;
```

We are now ready to compile the controller using the **Build** button and add this controller to the robot. The latter step can be made directly in the hierarchy panel, modifying the controller field and selecting the `robot_motion` controller.

Now, you can start the simulation and see the results of your first Webots controller. In the next section, we will integrate ROS and Webots.

Simulating the robotic arm using Webots and ROS

Webots-ROS integration requires two sides: the ROS side and the Webots side. The ROS side is implemented via the `webots_ros` ROS package, while Webots supports ROS natively thanks to a standard controller that can be added to any robot model. To use Webots with ROS, you need to install the `webots_ros` package. This can be done using APT, as follows:

```
sudo apt-get install ros-noetic-webots-ros
```

Now, we must change the controller previously developed with the one called `ros`, as shown in the following screenshot:

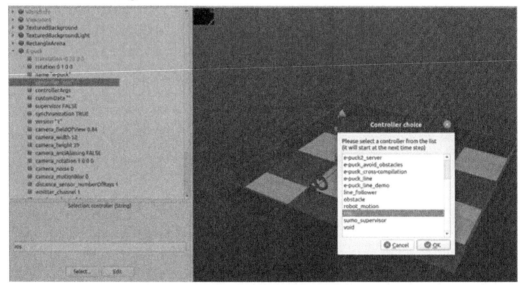

Figure 5.14 – Adding ros controller to the Webots robot

After the simulation starts, we can directly interact with our robot using a set of services implementing Webots functionalities on the ROS network according to the robot's sensors' and actuators' configuration. Of course, a `roscore` must be active in the ROS network, otherwise an error will be displayed in the Webots console. Webots only publishes a topic called `/model_name`. On this topic is published a list of models currently active in the simulation scene. This information is fundamental to use Webots services; in fact, Webots uses a specific syntax to declare its services or topics on the network: `[robot_name]/[device_name]/[service/topic_name]`. This is broken down as follows:

- `[robot_name]`: The name of the robot is followed by the ID of the process.

- `[device_name]`: This field shows you which device it refers to.

- [service/topic_name]: This field is identical or very close to the Webots function it corresponds to.

An example of data published on this topic is shown here:

Figure 5.15 – Model name published by Webots

Now, we can start to use Webots services. The ros controller is very general and can be executed on every robot. Among different sensors, the e-puck robot is endowed with an onboard camera. To stream camera data on the ROS network, the camera must be enabled, and we can use the /camera/enable service. Use the following command-line tools to enable it:

```
rosservice call /e_puck_36112_jcacace_Lenovo_Legion_5_15ARH05/
camera/enable "value: true"
```

At this point, a new topic is published on the ROS network, representing the images taken by the camera. You can see this image using the image_view plugin, as follows:

```
rosrun image_view image:=/e_puck_36112_jcacace_Lenovo_
Legion_5_15ARH05/camera/image
```

Similarly, we can enable and read the other sensors, such as the distance sensors, and we can also set the position, velocity, and torque of the joints of the robot. In our case, we want to set the velocity of the wheels.

As already stated, the integration with ROS requires two sides. On the ROS side, we can implement new nodes using the webots_ros package.

Writing a teleop node using webots_ros

In this section, we will implement a ROS node to directly control the wheels' velocity of the e-puck robot starting from a geometry_msgs::Twist message. To do this, we need to exploit webots_ros as a dependency. Let's create a webots_demo_pkg package, specifying webots_ros as a dependency, as follows:

```
catkin_create_pkg webots_demo_pkg roscpp webots_ros geometry_
msgs
```

The complete source code can be found in the book source code, and it is explained next. Let's start by defining some useful header files implementing the messages needed to use the Webots services, as follows:

```
#include "ros/ros.h"
#include <webots_ros/Int32Stamped.h>
#include <webots_ros/set_float.h>
#include <webots_ros/set_int.h>
#include <webots_ros/robot_get_device_list.h>
#include <std_msgs/String.h>
#include <geometry_msgs/Twist.h>
```

Then, declare some variable to save the data received by the ROS callbacks—the information about the robot modes and the velocity to apply, as follows:

```
static char modelList[10][100];
static int cnt = 0;
static float left_vel = 0.0;
static float right_vel = 0.0;
```

Two callbacks are implemented in this node, one to read the desired linear and angular velocity and to assign the wheels' velocity. The code for this is illustrated in the following snippet:

```
void cmdVelCallback(const geometry_msgs::Twist::ConstPtr &vel)
{
    float wheel_radius = 0.205;
    float axes_length = 0.52;
    left_vel = ( 1/wheel_radius)*(vel->linear.x-axes_
length/2*vel->angular.z);
    right_vel = ( 1/wheel_radius)*(vel->linear.x+axes_
length/2*vel->angular.z);
}
```

The other callback is implemented to read the model name assigned to the e-puck robot, as follows:

```
void modelNameCallback(const std_msgs::String::ConstPtr &name)
{
    cnt++;
    strcpy(modelList[cnt], name->data.c_str());
    ROS_INFO("Model #%d: %s.", cnt, name->data.c_str());
}
```

Finally, we must implement the main function in which we set up everything needed to control the robot. As usual, start initializing the ROS node and the NodeHandle class, as follows:

```
int main(int argc, char** argv ) {
    ros::init(argc, argv, "e_puck_manager");
    ros::NodeHandle n;
    std::string modelName;
```

Then, we must wait for the robot model to be streamed by Webots. Without this information, it will be impossible to use Webots services. The code is illustrated in the following snippet:

```
    ros::Subscriber nameSub = n.subscribe("model_name", 100,
modelNameCallback);
    while (cnt == 0 ) {
      ros::spinOnce();
    }
    modelName = modelList[1];
```

Then, define the subscriber to the /cmd_vel topic, as follows:

```
ros::Subscriber cmdVelSub = n.subscribe("cmd_vel", 1,
cmdVelCallback);
```

As already done in the previous section, to control the velocity wheels of the robots we need to set the wheel position to INFINITY. We can use the proper ROS client, as follows:

```
    webots_ros::set_float wheelSrv;
    wheelSrv.request.value = INFINITY;
```

```
ros::ServiceClient leftWheelPositionClient =
    n.serviceClient<webots_ros::set_float>(modelName + "/left_
wheel_motor/set_position");
    leftWheelPositionClient.call(wheelSrv);
    ros::ServiceClient rightWheelPositionClient =
    n.serviceClient<webots_ros::set_float>(modelName + "/right_
wheel_motor/set_position");
    rightWheelPositionClient.call(wheelSrv);
```

We also set the velocity to 0.0, as follows:

```
wheelSrv.request.value = 0.0;
    ros::ServiceClient leftWheelVelocityClient =
    n.serviceClient<webots_ros::set_float>(modelName + "/left_
wheel_motor/set_velocity");
    leftWheelVelocityClient.call( wheelSrv );
    ros::ServiceClient rightWheelVelocityClient =
    n.serviceClient<webots_ros::set_float>(modelName + "/right_
wheel_motor/set_velocity");
    rightWheelVelocityClient.call( wheelSrv );
```

Finally, in the main loop, the only thing that we must do is to apply the velocities calculated in the geometry_msgs::Twist call, as follows:

```
ros::Rate r(10);
    while(ros::ok()) {
      wheelSrv.request.value = left_vel;
      leftWheelVelocityClient.call( wheelSrv );

      wheelSrv.request.value = right_vel;
      rightWheelVelocityClient.call( wheelSrv );

      r.sleep();
      ros::spinOnce();
    }
    return 0;
}
```

Now, you can use the keyboard teleop node of the `diff_wheeled_robot_control` package developed in the previous chapter to control the mobile robot in Webots with ROS. First, start the simulation, then launch the following nodes:

```
rosrun webots_demo_pkg e_puck_manager
roslaunch diff_wheeled_robot_control keyboard_teleop.launch
```

As already done in the previous chapter, you can use your keyboard to drive the robot in the simulation environment. To conclude this chapter, we will discuss how to start the simulation using a convenient launch file.

Starting Webots with a launch file

In this last section, we will see how to start Webots directly using a launch file. This can be done thanks to a launch file already provided in the `webots_ros` package. To start a desired Webots world we need to include this launch file, setting the `.wbt` file to start, as shown in the `webots_demo_package/launch/e_puck_manager.launch` launch file. This file is shown and described next.

Before we include the `webots_ros` launch file, we set the `no-gui` parameter to `false` to open the UI of Webots, as follows:

```
<launch>
  <arg name="no-gui" default="false" />
  <include file="$(find webots_ros)/launch/webots.launch">
    <arg name="mode" value="realtime"/>
    <arg name="no-gui" value="$(arg no-gui)"/>
```

Here, we set the configuration file representing the world that we want to start—the `e_puck_ros.wbt` world file placed in the `package` directory, as follows:

```
<arg name="world" value="$(find webots_demo_pkg)/scene/mobile_robot/worlds/e_puck_ros.wbt"/>
  </include>
```

Finally, start the `e_puck_manager` node to allow teleop control of the robot, like this:

```
  <node name="e_puck_manager" pkg="webots_demo_pkg" type="e_puck_manager" output="screen" />
```

Be careful of the fact that to use this launch file, we need to set the WEBOTS_HOME environment variable to point to the root folder of Webots. If you have already installed Webots using APT you can set this variable, adding the following line to your .bashrc file:

```
zzecho "export WEBOTS_HOME=/usr/local/webots" >> ~/.bashrc
```

You are now ready to use the launch file to start Webots and the e_puck_manager node.

Summary

In this chapter, we mainly replicated what we have already done in the previous chapter with Gazebo, using other robot simulators: CoppeliaSim and Webots. These are multiplatform simulation software programs that integrate different technologies and are very versatile. Thanks to their intuitive UIs, they might be easier to use for new users.

We mainly simulated two robots, one imported using the URDF file of the seven-DOF arm designed in previous chapters, with the other being a popular differential wheeled robot provided by the Webots simulation models. We learned how to interface and control the robot joints of our model with ROS and how to move a differential-drive mobile robot using topics.

In the next chapter, we will see how to interface the robotic arm with the ROS MoveIt package and the mobile robot with the Navigation stack.

Questions

We should now be able to answer the following questions:

- How do CoppeliaSim and ROS communicate?
- In what way is it possible to control a CoppeliaSim simulation with ROS?
- How can we import new robot models in CoppeliaSim and integrate them with ROS?
- Can Webots be used as standalone software?
- How can ROS and Webots communicate?

6
Using the ROS MoveIt! and Navigation Stack

In the previous chapters, we have been discussing the design and simulation of a robotic arm and a mobile robot. We controlled each joint of the robotic arm in `Gazebo` using the **Robot Operating System** (**ROS**) controller and moved the mobile robot inside `Gazebo` using the `teleop` node.

In this chapter, we are going to address the *motion-planning* problem. Moving a robot by directly controlling its joints manually might be a difficult task, especially if we want to add position or velocity constraints to the robot's motion. Similarly, driving a mobile robot and avoiding obstacles requires the planning of a path. For this reason, we will solve these problems using the ROS **MoveIt!** and **Navigation** stack.

MoveIt! represents a set of packages and tools for doing mobile manipulation in ROS. The official web page (`http://moveit.ros.org/`) contains documentation, a list of robots using MoveIt!, and various examples to demonstrate pick and place, grasping, simple motion planning using **inverse kinematics** (**IK**), and so on.

MoveIt! contains state-of-the-art software for motion planning, manipulation, **three-dimensional** (**3D**) perception, kinematics, collision checking, control, and navigation. Apart from the **command-line interface** (**CLI**), it has some good **graphical user interfaces** (**GUIs**) to configure a new robot in MoveIt!. There is also a **ROS Visualization** (RViz) plugin that enables motion planning from a convenient UI. We will also see how to motion-plan our robot using MoveIt! C++ **application programming interfaces** (**APIs**).

Next is the Navigation stack, another set of powerful tools and libraries to work mainly with mobile robot navigation. The Navigation stack contains ready-to-use navigation algorithms that can be used in mobile robots, especially for differential wheeled robots. Using these stacks, we can make the robot autonomous, and that is the final concept that we are going to see in the Navigation stack.

The first section of this chapter will mainly concentrate on the MoveIt! package, installation, and architecture. After discussing the main concepts of MoveIt!, we will see how to create a MoveIt! package for our robotic arm, which can provide collision-aware path planning to our robot. Using this package, we can perform motion planning (inverse kinematics) in RViz and can interface with Gazebo or a real robot for executing the paths.

After discussing interfacing, we will discuss more about the Navigation stack and see how to perform autonomous navigation using **Simultaneous Localization And Mapping** (**SLAM**) and **Adaptive Monte Carlo Localization** (**Amcl**).

In this chapter, we will discuss the following topics:

- The MoveIt! architecture
- Generating a MoveIt! configuration package using the Setup Assistant tool
- Motion planning of a robot in RViz using the MoveIt! configuration package
- Understanding the ROS Navigation stack
- Building a map using SLAM

Technical requirements

To follow along with this chapter, you need a standard computer running **Ubuntu 20.04** as the operating system, along with ROS Noetic. Additional dependencies will be installed during this chapter.

The reference code for this chapter can be downloaded from the following Git repository: `https://github.com/PacktPublishing/Mastering-ROS-for-Robotics-Programming-Third-edition/tree/main/Chapter6`

You can view this chapter's code in action here: `https://bit.ly/2UxKNN2`.

The MoveIt! architecture

Before using MoveIt! in our ROS system, you have to install it. The installation procedure is very simple and is just a single command. Using the following commands, we install the MoveIt! core, a set of plugins and planners for ROS Noetic:

```
sudo apt-get install ros-noetic-moveit ros-noetic-moveit-
plugins ros-noetic-moveit-planners
```

Let's start with MoveIt! by discussing its architecture. Understanding the architecture of MoveIt! helps to program and interface the robot with MoveIt!. We will quickly go through the architecture and the important concepts of MoveIt!, and start interfacing with and programming our robots.

Here is an overview of the MoveIt! architecture:

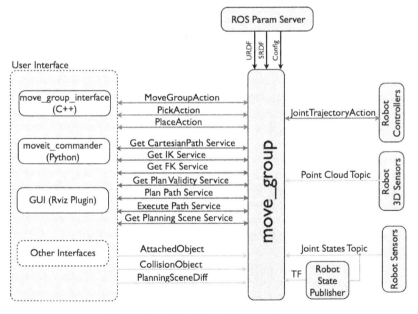

Figure 6.1 – MoveIt! architecture diagram

This diagram is also included in their official web page, at `http://moveit.ros.org/documentation/concepts`.

The move_group node

We can say that `move_group` is the heart of MoveIt!, as this node acts as an integrator of the various components of the robot and delivers actions/services according to the user's needs.

Looking at the architecture, it's clear that the `move_group` node collects robot information such as point cloud, joint state of the robot, and **transforms (TFs)** of the robot in the form of topics and services.

From the parameter server, it collects robot kinematics data, such as the **Unified Robot Description Format (URDF)**, the **Semantic Robot Description Format (SRDF)**, and the configuration files. The SRDF file and the configuration files are generated while we generate a MoveIt! package for our robot. The configuration files contain a parameter file for setting joint limits, perception, kinematics, end effector, and so on. We will see the files when we discuss generating the MoveIt! package for our robot.

After MoveIt! gets all the needed information about the robot and its configuration, we can start commanding the robot from the UIs. We can either use C++ or Python MoveIt! APIs to command the `move_group` node to perform actions such as pick/place, IK, and **forward kinematics (FK)**, among others. Using the RViz motion-planning plugin, we can command the robot from the RViz GUI

Since the `move_group` node is a simple integrator, it does not run any kind of motion-planning algorithms directly but instead connects all the functionalities as plugins. There are plugins for kinematics solvers, motion planning, and so on. We can extend the capabilities through these plugins. After motion planning, the generated trajectory talks to the controllers in the robot using the `FollowJointTrajectoryAction` interface. This is an action interface in which an action server is run on the robot, and `move_node` initiates an action client that talks to this server and executes the trajectory on a real robot or on a robotic simulator.

At the end of our discussion on MoveIt!, we will see how to connect MoveIt! with the RViz GUI to `Gazebo`. The following screenshot shows a robotic arm that is being controlled from RViz and the trajectory being executed inside `Gazebo`:

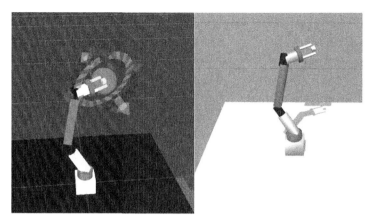

Figure 6.2 – Trajectory from RViz GUI executing in Gazebo

In the next section, we will discuss more about the MoveIt! planning process.

Motion planning using MoveIt!

Assuming that we know the starting pose of the robot, a desired goal pose of the robot, a geometrical description of the robot, and a geometrical description of the world, then motion planning is a technique to find an optimum path that moves the robot gradually from the start pose to the goal pose, while never touching any obstacles in the world and without colliding with the robot links.

In this context, the robot geometry is described via the URDF file. We can also create a description file for the robot environment and use laser or vision sensors of the robot to map its operative space in order to avoid static and dynamic obstacles during the execution of planned paths.

Considering a robotic arm, the motion planner should find a trajectory (consisting of joint spaces of each joint) in which the links of the robot should never collide with the environment, avoid self-collision (collision between two robot links), and not violate the joint limits. MoveIt! can talk to the motion planners through the plugin interface. We can use any supported motion-planner techniques by simply changing the plugin. This method is highly extensible, so we can try our own custom motion planners using this interface.

The `move_group` node talks to the motion planner plugin via the ROS action/server. The default planner library used by MoveIt! is the **Open Motion Planning Library** (**OMPL**). You can find more information on this at `http://ompl.kavrakilab.org/`. To start motion planning, we should send a motion-planning request to the motion planner that specified our planning requirements. The planning requirement may be setting a new goal pose of the end effector, such as performing pick-and-place operations.

We can set additional kinematic constraints for the motion planners. Here are some inbuilt constraints in MoveIt!:

- **Position constraints**: These restrict the position of a link.

- **Orientation constraints**: These restrict the orientation of a link.

- **Visibility constraints**: These restrict a point on a link to be visible in an area (view of a sensor).

- **Joint constraints**: These restrict a joint within its joint limits.

- **User-specified constraints**: Using these constraints, the user can define their own constraints using callback functions.

With the constraints, we can send a motion-planning request, and the planner will generate a suitable trajectory according to the request. The `move_group` node will generate a suitable trajectory from the motion planner that obeys all the constraints. This can be sent to robot joint-trajectory controllers.

Motion-planning request adapters

The motion-planning request adapters help to preprocess the motion-planning request and postprocess the motion-planning response. One use of preprocessing requests is that it helps to correct any violation in the joint states and, for postprocessing, it can convert the path generated by the planner to a time-parameterized trajectory. Here are some default planning request adapters in MoveIt!:

- `FixStartStateBounds`: If a joint state is slightly outside the joint limits, then this adapter can fix the initial joint limits within the limits.

- `FixWorkspaceBounds`: This specifies a workspace for planning with a cube size of 10 m x 10 m x 10 m.

- `FixStartStateCollision`: This adapter samples a new collision-free configuration if the existing joint configuration is in collision. It makes a new configuration by changing the current configuration, by a small factor called `jiggle_factor`.

- `FixStartStatePathConstraints`: This adapter is used when the initial pose of the robot does not obey the path constraints. In this, it finds a near pose that satisfies the path constraints and uses that pose as the initial state.

- `AddTimeParameterization`: This adapter parameterizes the motion plan by applying velocity and acceleration constraints.

To plan motion trajectories, MoveIt! uses a planning scene. Thanks to this scene, information about obstacles and objects can be retrieved.

MoveIt! planning scene

The term *planning scene* is used to represent the world around the robot and store the state of the robot itself. The planning-scene monitor inside move_group maintains the planning-scene representation. The move_group node consists of another section called the world geometry monitor, which builds the world geometry from the sensors of the robot and from the user input.

The planning-scene monitor reads the joint_states topic from the robot, and the sensor information and world geometry from the world geometry monitor. It also receives data from the occupancy map monitor, which uses 3D perception to build a 3D representation of the environment, called an **octomap**.

An octomap can be generated from point clouds that are handled by a point-cloud occupancy map updater plugin and depth images handled by a depth-image occupancy map updater plugin. The following diagram shows an overview of a planning scene from the MoveIt! official wiki (http://moveit.ros.org/documentation/concepts/):

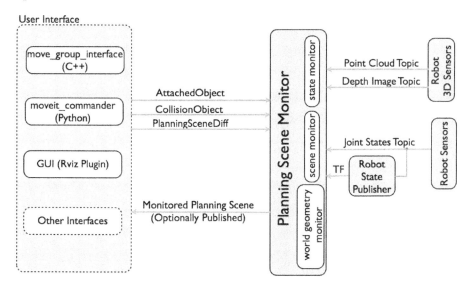

Figure 6.3 – MoveIt! planning-scene overview diagram

Additional elements involved in the MoveIt! planning process regard the possibility of calculating the FK and IK of a manipulator and checking the presence of obstacles along a planned path, as discussed next.

MoveIt! kinematics handling

MoveIt! provides great flexibility to switch IK algorithms using robot plugins. Users can write their own IK solver as a MoveIt! plugin and switch from the default solver plugin whenever required. The default IK solver in MoveIt! is a numerical **Jacobian-based** solver. Compared to analytical solvers, numerical solvers can take time to solve IK. The `IKFast` package can be used to generate C++ code for solving IK using analytical methods, which can be used for different kinds of robot manipulators and performs better if the **degrees of freedom** (**DOF**) is less than `seve`. This C++ code can also be converted into a MoveIt! plugin by using ROS tools. We will look at this procedure in the upcoming chapters.

FK and finding Jacobians are already integrated into the MoveIt! `RobotState` class, so we don't need to use plugins for solving FK.

MoveIt! collision checking

The `CollisionWorld` object inside MoveIt! is used to find collisions inside a planning scene that is using the **Flexible Collision Library** (**FCL**) package as a backend. MoveIt! supports collision checking for different types of objects, such as meshes and primitive shapes such as boxes, cylinders, cones, spheres, and octomaps.

Collision checking is one of the most computationally expensive tasks during motion planning. To reduce this computation, MoveIt! provides a matrix called the **Allowed Collision Matrix** (**ACM**) that contains a binary value corresponding to the need to check for a collision between two pairs of bodies. If the value of the matrix is 1, this means collision of the corresponding pair is not needed. We can set the value to 1 when the bodies are always so far apart that they would never collide with each other. Optimizing ACM can reduce the total computation needed for collision avoidance.

After discussing the basic concepts in MoveIt!, we can now move on to discussing how to interface a robotic arm with MoveIt!. To interface a robot arm with MoveIt!, we need to satisfy the components that we saw in *Figure 6.1*. The move_group node essentially requires parameters such as URDF, SRDF, configuration files, and joint states topics, along with the TF from a robot to start with motion planning.

MoveIt! provides a GUI-based tool called Setup Assistant to generate all these elements. The following section describes the procedure to generate a MoveIt! configuration from the Setup Assistant tool.

Generating a MoveIt! configuration package using the Setup Assistant tool

The **MoveIt! Setup Assistant** tool is a GUI for configuring any robot to MoveIt!. This tool basically generates SRDF, configuration files, launch files, and scripts generated from the robot URDF model, which is required to configure the move_group node.

The SRDF file contains details about the arm joints, end effector joints, virtual joints, and the collision-link pairs that are configured during the MoveIt! configuration process using the Setup Assistant tool.

The configuration file contains details about the kinematic solvers, joint limits, controllers, and so on that are also configured and saved during the configuration process.

Using the generated configuration package of the robot, we can work with motion planning in RViz without the presence of a real robot or simulation interface.

Let's start the configuration wizard, and we can see the step-by-step procedure to build the configuration package of our robotic arm.

Step 1 – Launching the Setup Assistant tool

To start the MoveIt! Setup Assistant tool, we can use the following command:

```
roslaunch moveit_setup_assistant setup_assistant.launch
```

This will bring up a window with two choices: **Create New MoveIt! Configuration Package** or **Edit Existing MoveIt! Configuration Package**. Here, we are creating a new package, so we need to select the first option. If we have a MoveIt! package already, then we can select the second option.

Click on the **Create New MoveIt! Configuration Package** button to display a new screen, as shown next:

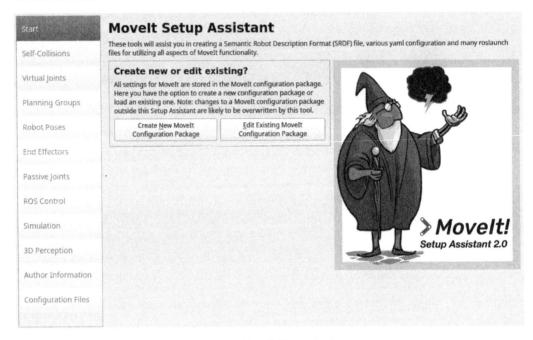

Figure 6.4 – MoveIt! Setup Assistant

In this step, the wizard asks for the URDF model of the new robot. To give the wizard the URDF file, click on the **Browse** button and navigate to `mastering_ros_robot_description_pkg/urdf/seven_dof_arm_with_rgbd.xacro`. Choose this file and press the **Load** button to load the URDF. We can either load a robot model using both the URDF and **XML Macros (Xacro)** files or, if we use Xacro, the tool will convert to URDF internally.

If the robot model is successfully parsed, we can see the robot model in the window, as shown in the following screenshot:

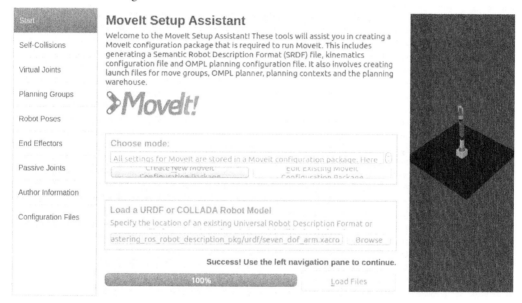

Figure 6.5 – Successfully parsing the robot model in the Setup Assistant tool

The robot is now loaded into the Setup Assistant and we can start to configure MoveIt! for it.

Step 2 – Generating a self-collision matrix

We can now start to navigate all the panels of the window to properly configure our robot. In the **Self-Collisions** tab, MoveIt! searches for a pair of links on the robot that can be safely disabled from the collision checking. These can reduce the processing time. This tool analyzes each link pair and categorizes the links as always in collision, never in collision, in collision in the robot's default position, having adjacent links disabled, and sometimes in collision, and it disables the pair of links that make any kind of collision. The following screenshot shows the **Self-Collisions** window:

Figure 6.6 – Generating a self-collision matrix

The sampling density is the number of random positions to check for self-collision. If the density is large, computation will be high but self-collision will be lower. The default value is 10,000. We can see the disabled pair of links by pressing the **Regenerate Default Collision Matrix** button; it will take a few seconds to list the disabled pair of links.

Step 3 – Adding virtual joints

Virtual joints attach a robot to the world. They are not mandatory for a static robot that does not move. We need virtual joints when the base position of the arm is not fixed— for example, if a robot arm is fixed on a mobile robot, we should define a virtual joint with respect to the odometry frame (odom).

In the case of our robot, we are not creating virtual joints.

Step 4 – Adding planning groups

A planning group is basically a group of joints/links in a robotic arm that plans together to achieve a goal position of a link or the end effector. We must create two planning groups—one for the arm and one for the gripper.

Click on the **Planning Groups** tab on the left side of the screen and click on the **Add Group** button. You will see the following screen, which has the settings of the arm group:

Figure 6.7 – Adding the planning group of the arm

Here, we are setting **Group Name** to arm, and **Kinematic Solver** to kdl_kinematics_plugin/KDLKinematicsPlugin, which is the default numerical IK solver with MoveIt!. We can also choose a default planning algorithm for this group. For example, here, we have chosen the **Rapidly exploring Random Tree** (**RRT**) algorithm. Finally, we can keep the other parameters at their default values while we choose different ways to add elements to a planning group—for example, we could specify the joints of the group, add its links, or directly specify a kinematic chain.

Inside the arm group, we first have to add a kinematic chain, starting from base_link as the first link to grasping_frame.

Add a group called `gripper`—we don't need to have a kinematic solver for the `gripper` group. Inside this group, we can add the joints and links of the gripper. These settings are shown in the following screenshot:

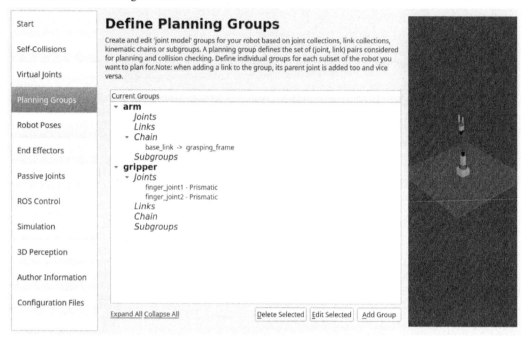

Figure 6.8 – Adding the planning group of the arm and gripper

We can add different planning groups. Each of them can also use only a few joints from our robot and not the whole kinematic chain. In the next step, we will see how to configure some fixed poses for the robot.

Step 5 – Adding the robot poses

In this step, we can add certain fixed poses in the robot configuration—for example, we can assign a home position or a pick/place position in this step. The advantage is that while programming with MoveIt! APIs, we can directly call these poses, which are also called group states. These have many applications in the pick/place and grasping operation. The robot can switch to these fixed poses without any hassle. To add a pose, click the **Add Group** button, and then choose a pose name and a set of joint values for that pose.

Step 6 – Setting up the robot end effector

In this step, we name the robot end effector and assign the end effector group, the parent link, and the parent group.

We can add any number of end effectors to this robot. In our case, it's a gripper designed for pick-and-place operations.

Click on the **Add End Effector** button and name the end effector robot_eef, the right, it must be; the planning group arm, removing the parent group, as illustrated in the following screenshot:

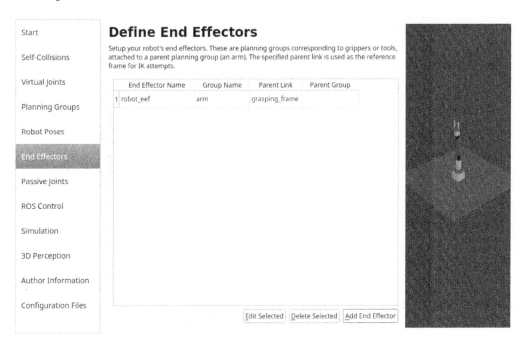

Figure 6.9 – Adding end effectors

The configuration process for MoveIt! basic elements is complete. We have a number of additional steps that we can perform before generating configuration files used to launch MoveIt! to control our robot.

Step 7 – Adding passive joints

In this step, we can specify the passive joints in the robot. Passive joints mean that the joints do not have any actuators. Caster wheels are one example of passive joints. The planner will ignore these kinds of joints during motion planning.

Step 8 – Author information

In this step, the author of the robotic model can add personal information such as their name and email address, required by `catkin` to release the model to the ROS community.

Step 9 – Generating configuration files

We are almost done. We are in the final stage, which is generating configuration files. In this step, the tool will generate a configuration package that contains the file needed to interface MoveIt!.

Click on the **Browse** button to locate a folder to save the configuration file that is going to be generated by the Setup Assistant tool. Here, we can see the files are generated inside a folder called `seven_dof_arm_config`. You can use `add_config` or `_generated` along with the robot name for the configuration package.

Click on the **Generate Package** button, and it will generate the files to the given folder.

If the process is successful, we can click on **Exit Setup Assistant**, which will exit the tool. Note that we skipped some steps to link MoveIt! with the `Gazebo` simulator or with the ROS Control package. We will discuss and implement this link in the rest of the chapter.

The following screenshot shows the generation process:

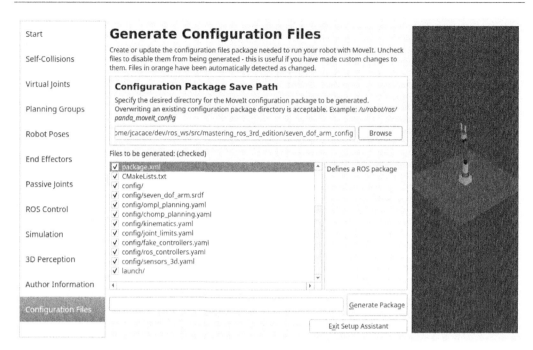

Figure 6.10 – Generating the MoveIt! configuration package

We can directly generate the configuration files in our ROS workspace. In the following section, we are going to work with this package. As usual, the model of the robot created can be obtained from the book's source code.

The configuration of our robot in MoveIt! is now complete. We can now test that everything has been properly configured using RViz, as discussed in the next section.

Motion planning of a robot in RViz using the MoveIt! configuration package

MoveIt! provides an RViz plugin that allows developers to set the planning problem. From this plugin, the desired pose of the manipulator can be set, and a motion trajectory can be generated to test MoveIt! planning capabilities. To launch this plugin along with the robot model, we can directly use the MoveIt! launch files included in the MoveIt! configuration package. This package consists of configuration files and launch files to start motion planning in RViz. There is a demo launch file in the package to explore all the package's functionalities.

Here is the command to invoke the demo launch file:

```
roslaunch seven_dof_arm_config demo.launch
```

If everything works fine, we will get the following screen of RViz being loaded with the `MotionPlanning` plugin provided by MoveIt!:

Figure 6.11 – MoveIt! RViz plugin

As you can see, from this plugin you can configure the planning problem, starting from the definition of the planner. In the next section, we will see how to configure a new planning problem to plan a new motion trajectory.

Using the RViz MotionPlanning plugin

From the preceding figure, we can see that the RViz MotionPlanning plugin is loaded on the left side of the screen. There are several tabs on the **Motion Planning** window, such as **Context**, **Planning**, and so on. The default tab is the **Context** tab, and we can see the default **Planning Library** as OMPL, which is shown in green. This indicates that MoveIt! successfully loaded the motion-planning library. If it is not loaded, we can't perform motion planning.

Next is the **Planning** tab. This is one of the most frequently used tabs, and is used to assign a start state and goal state and to plan and execute a path. Shown next is the GUI of the **Planning** tab:

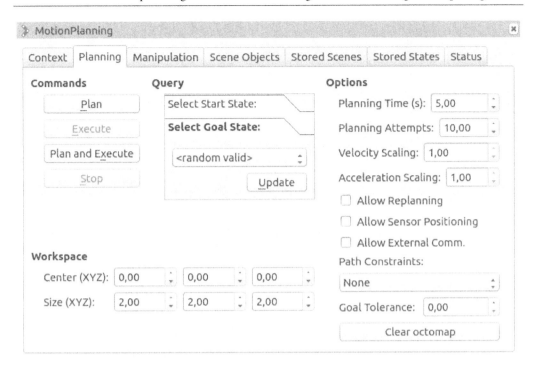

Figure 6.12 – MoveIt! RViz Planning tab

We can assign a start state and goal state to the robot under the **Query** panel. Using the **Plan** button, we can plan the path from the start to the goal state, and if the planning is successful, we can execute it. By default, execution is done on fake controllers. We can change these controllers into trajectory controllers for executing the planned trajectory in Gazebo or a real robot.

We can set the starting and the goal position of the robot end effector by using the interactive marker attached to the arm gripper. We can translate and rotate the marker pose and, if there is a planning solution, we can see an arm in orange. In some situations, the arm will not move even if the end effector marker pose moves, and if the arm does not come to the marker position, we can assume that there is no IK solution in that pose. We may need more DOF to reach there, or there might be some collision between the links.

The following screenshots show a valid goal pose and an invalid goal pose:

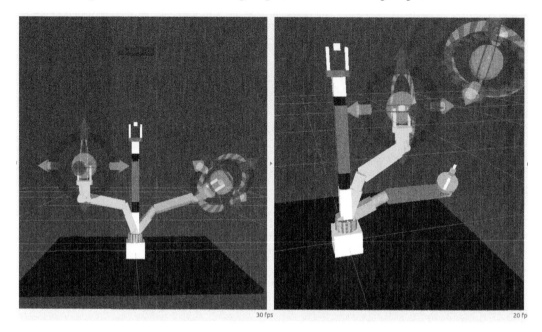

Figure 6.13 – A valid pose and an invalid pose of a robot in RViz

The green arm represents the starting position of the arm, and the orange color represents the goal position. In the first screenshot, if we press the **Plan** button, MoveIt! plans a path from start to goal. In the second screenshot, we can observe two things. First, one of the links of the orange arm is red, which means that the goal pose is in a self-collided state. Secondly, look at the end-effector marker; it is far from the actual end effector, and it has also turned red.

We can also work with some quick motion planning using **random valid** (as seen in *Figure 6.12*) options in the start state and the goal state. If we set the goal state as **random valid** and press the **Update** button, it will generate a random-valid goal pose. Click on the **Plan** button, and we can see the motion planning in operation.

We can customize the RViz visualization using the various options in the MotionPlanning plugin. Shown next are some settings of this plugin:

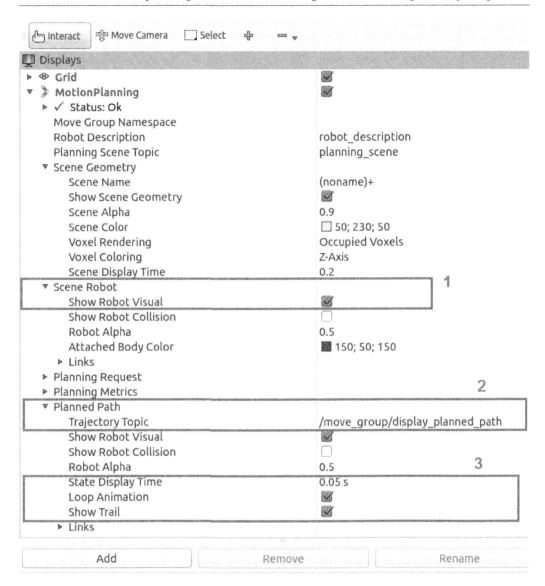

Figure 6.14 – Settings of the MotionPlanning plugin on RViz

The first marked area is **Scene Robot**, which will show the robot model; if it is unchecked, we won't see any robot model. The second marked area is the **Trajectory Topic**, in which RViz gets the visualization trajectory. If we want to animate the motion planning and display the motion trails, we should enable this option.

One of the other sections in the plugin settings is shown in the following screenshot:

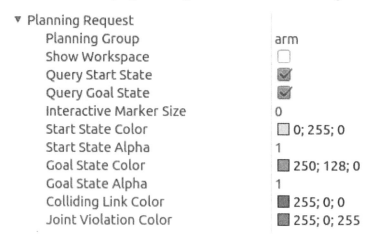

Figure 6.15 – Planning Request setting in MotionPlanning plugin

In the preceding screenshot, we can see the **Query Start State** and the **Query Goal State** options. These options can visualize the start pose and the goal pose of the arm, which we saw in *Figure 6.13*. **Show Workspace** visualizes the cubic workspace (world geometry) around the robot. The visualization can help to debug our motion-planning algorithm and understand the robot motion behavior in detail.

In the next section, we will see how to interface the MoveIt! configuration package to Gazebo. This will execute the trajectory generated by MoveIt! in Gazebo.

Interfacing the MoveIt! configuration package to Gazebo

We have already worked with the Gazebo simulation of this arm and attached controllers to it. For interfacing the arm in MoveIt! to Gazebo, we need a trajectory controller that has the FollowJointTrajectoryAction interface, as we mentioned in *The MoveIt! architecture* section.

Next, we will go through the procedure to interface MoveIt! to Gazebo.

Step 1 – Writing the controller configuration file for MoveIt!

The first step is to create a configuration file for talking with the trajectory controllers in Gazebo from MoveIt!. The controller configuration file called ros_controllers. yaml has to be created inside the config folder of the seven_dof_arm_config package.

Given next is an example of the `ros_controllers.yaml` definition:

```yaml
controller_list:
  - name: seven_dof_arm/seven_dof_arm_joint_controller
    action_ns: follow_joint_trajectory
    type: FollowJointTrajectory
    default: true
    joints:
      - shoulder_pan_joint
      - shoulder_pitch_joint
      - elbow_roll_joint
      - elbow_pitch_joint
      - wrist_roll_joint
      - wrist_pitch_joint
      - gripper_roll_joint

  - name: seven_dof_arm/gripper_controller
    action_ns: follow_joint_trajectory
    type: FollowJointTrajectory
    default: true
    joints:
      - finger_joint1
      - finger_joint2
```

The controller configuration file contains the definition of the two controller interfaces; one is for the arm and the other is for the gripper. The type of action used in the controllers is `FollowJointTrajectory`, and the action namespace is `follow_joint_trajectory`. We have to list the joints in each group. `default: true` indicates that it will use the default controller, which is the primary controller in MoveIt! for communicating with a set of joints.

Step 2 – Creating controller launch files

Next, we have to create a new launch file called `seven_dof_arm_moveit_controller_manager.launch` that can start the trajectory controllers. The name of the file starts with the robot's name, which is added with `_moveit_controller_manager`.

Here is the `seven_dof_arm_config/launch/ seven_dof_arm_moveit_controller_manager.launch` launch file definition:

```
<launch>
<!-- loads moveit_controller_manager on the parameter server
which is taken as argument
if no argument is passed, moveit_simple_controller_manager will
be set -->
<arg name="moveit_controller_manager" default="moveit_simple_
controller_manager/MoveItSimpleControllerManager" />
<param name="moveit_controller_manager" value="$(arg moveit_
controller_manager)"/>
<!-- loads ros_controllers to the param server -->
<rosparam file="$(find seven_dof_arm_config)/config/ros_
controllers.yaml"/>
</launch>
```

This launch file starts the `MoveItSimpleControllerManager` program and loads the joint-trajectory controllers defined inside `controllers.yaml`.

Step 3 – Creating a controller configuration file for Gazebo

After creating MoveIt! configuration files, we have to create a `Gazebo` controller configuration file and a launch file.

Create a new file called `trajectory_control.yaml` that contains a list of the `Gazebo` ROS controllers that need to be loaded along with `Gazebo`.

You will get this file from the `seven_dof_arm_gazebo` package created in *Chapter 4, Simulating Robots Using ROS and Gazebo,* in the `/config` folder.

In the following code snippet, the definition of this file is reported:

```
seven_dof_arm:
  arm_controller:
      type: position_controllers/JointTrajectoryController
      joints:
        - shoulder_pan_joint
        - shoulder_pitch_joint
        - elbow_roll_joint
   - elbow_pitch_joint
        - wrist_roll_joint
```

```
      - wrist_pitch_joint
      - gripper_roll_joint
      constraints:
      goal_time: 0.6
      stopped_velocity_tolerance: 0.05
      shoulder_pan_joint: {trajectory: 0.1, goal: 0.1}
      shoulder_pitch_joint: {trajectory: 0.1, goal: 0.1}
      elbow_roll_joint: {trajectory: 0.1, goal: 0.1}
      elbow_pitch_joint: {trajectory: 0.1, goal: 0.1}
      wrist_roll_joint: {trajectory: 0.1, goal: 0.1}
      wrist_pitch_joint: {trajectory: 0.1, goal: 0.1}
      gripper_roll_joint: {trajectory: 0.1, goal: 0.1}
      stop_trajectory_duration: 0.5
      state_publish_rate:  25
      action_monitor_rate: 10
```

Here, we created a `position_controllers/JointTrajectoryController` configuration, which has an action interface of `FollowJointTrajectory`, for both the arm and the gripper. We also defined the **Proportional-Integral-Derivative (PID)** gain associated with each joint, which can provide a smooth motion.

Step 4 – Creating a launch file for Gazebo trajectory controllers

After creating a configuration file, we can load the controllers along with `Gazebo`. We have to create a launch file that launches `Gazebo`, the trajectory controllers, and the MoveIt! interface in a single command.

The `seven_dof_arm_bringup_moveit.launch` launch file contains the definition to launch all these commands, as illustrated in the following code snippet:

```
<launch>
   <include file="$(find seven_dof_arm_gazebo)/launch/seven_dof_
arm_with_rgbd_world.launch" />
   <rosparam file="$(find seven_dof_arm_gazebo)/config/
trajectory_control.yaml" command="load"/>
   <rosparam file="$(find seven_dof_arm_gazebo)/config/seven_
dof_arm_gazebo_joint_states.yaml" command="load"/>
   <node name="seven_dof_arm_joint_state_spawner"
pkg="controller_manager" type="spawner" respawn="false"
output="screen" ns="/seven_dof_arm" args="joint_state_
```

```
controller arm_controller"/>

  <node name="robot_state_publisher" pkg="robot_state_
publisher" type="robot_state_publisher" respawn="false"
output="screen">

    <remap from="/joint_states" to="/seven_dof_arm/joint_
states" />

  </node>

  <node name="joint_state_publisher" pkg="joint_state_
publisher" type="joint_state_publisher" />

    <remap from="joint_states" to="/seven_dof_arm/joint_
states" />

  <include file="$(find seven_dof_arm_config)/launch/planning_
context.launch">

    <arg name="load_robot_description" value="false" />

  </include>

  <include file="$(find seven_dof_arm_config)/launch/move_
group.launch">

    <arg name="publish_monitored_planning_scene" value="true"
/>

  </include>

  <include file="$(find seven_dof_arm_config)/launch/moveit_
rviz.launch">

    <arg name="rviz_config" value="$(find seven_dof_arm_
config)/launch/moveit.rviz"/>

  </include>

</launch>

</launch>
```

This launch file spawns the robot model in Gazebo, publishes the joint states, attaches the position controller, attaches the trajectory controller, and, finally, launches moveit_ planning_execution.launch inside the MoveIt! package for starting the MoveIt! nodes along with RViz. We may need to load the MotionPlanning plugin in RViz if it is not loaded by default.

We can start motion planning inside RViz and execute in the Gazebo simulation, using the following single command:

```
$ roslaunch seven_dof_arm_gazebo seven_dof_arm_bringup_moveit.
launch
```

Note that before properly launching the planning scene, we should use the following command to install some packages needed by MoveIt! to use ROS controllers:

```
sudo apt-get install ros-noetc-joint-state-controller
ros-noetic-position-controllers ros-noetic-joint-trajectory-
controller
```

After we have installed the preceding packages, we can launch the planning scene. This will launch RViz and Gazebo, and we can do motion planning inside RViz. After motion planning, click on the **Execute** button to send the trajectory to the Gazebo controllers. You should now see a screen like this:

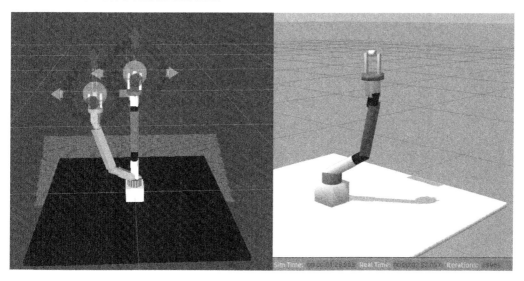

Figure 6.16 – Gazebo trajectory controllers executing the trajectory from MoveIt!

Now, the link between MoveIt! and the simulated (or real) robot is complete. Before we complete the first part of this chapter, let's see how to briefly understand if the MoveIt!-Gazebo connection is working properly.

Step 5 – Debugging the Gazebo-MoveIt! interface

In this section, we will discuss some common issues and debugging techniques in this interface.

If the trajectory is not executing on Gazebo, first list the topics, as follows:

```
rostopic list
```

If the `Gazebo` controllers have been started properly, we will get the following joint-trajectory topics in the list:

```
/seven_dof_arm/gripper_controller/command
/seven_dof_arm/gripper_controller/follow_joint_trajectory/cancel
/seven_dof_arm/gripper_controller/follow_joint_trajectory/feedback
/seven_dof_arm/gripper_controller/follow_joint_trajectory/goal
/seven_dof_arm/gripper_controller/follow_joint_trajectory/result
/seven_dof_arm/gripper_controller/follow_joint_trajectory/status
/seven_dof_arm/gripper_controller/state
/seven_dof_arm/joint_states
/seven_dof_arm/seven_dof_arm_joint_controller/command
/seven_dof_arm/seven_dof_arm_joint_controller/follow_joint_trajectory/cancel
/seven_dof_arm/seven_dof_arm_joint_controller/follow_joint_trajectory/feedback
/seven_dof_arm/seven_dof_arm_joint_controller/follow_joint_trajectory/goal
/seven_dof_arm/seven_dof_arm_joint_controller/follow_joint_trajectory/result
/seven_dof_arm/seven_dof_arm_joint_controller/follow_joint_trajectory/status
/seven_dof_arm/seven_dof_arm_joint_controller/state
/tf
/tf_static
/trajectory_execution_event
```

Figure 6.17 – Topics from the Gazebo-ROS trajectory controllers

We can see `follow_joint_trajectory` for the `gripper` and `arm` groups. If the controllers are not ready, the trajectory will not execute in `Gazebo`.

Also, check the Terminal message while starting the launch file:

```
[1505806707.153599116, 0.343000000]: Added FollowJointTrajectory controller for seven_dof_ar
ller
[1505806707.153740538, 0.343000000]: Returned 2 controllers in list
[1505806707.205783246, 0.347000000]: Trajectory execution is managing controllers
'move_group/ApplyPlanningSceneService'...
'move_group/ClearOctomapService'...
'move_group/MoveGroupCartesianPathService'...
'move_group/MoveGroupExecuteTrajectoryAction'...
'move_group/MoveGroupGetPlanningSceneService'...
'move_group/MoveGroupKinematicsService'...
'move_group/MoveGroupMoveAction'...
'move_group/MoveGroupPickPlaceAction'...
'move_group/MoveGroupPlanService'...
'move_group/MoveGroupQueryPlannersService'...
'move_group/MoveGroupStateValidationService'...                                         1
[1505806835.903571251, 36.978000000]: arm[RRTkConfigDefault]: Starting planning with 1 state
astructure
[1505806835.994742622, 36.997000000]: arm[RRTkConfigDefault]: Created 21 states
[1505806836.036028021, 37.004000000]: arm[RRTkConfigDefault]: Created 38 states
[1505806836.038435520, 37.005000000]: ParallelPlan::solve(): Solution found by one or more t  2
41 seconds
```

Figure 6.18 – The Terminal message showing successful trajectory execution

In *Figure 6.18*, the first section shows that `MoveItSimpleControllerManager` was able to connect with the `Gazebo` controller, and if it couldn't connect to the controller, it shows that it can't connect to the controller. The second section shows a successful motion-planning operation. If the motion planning is not successful, MoveIt! will not send the trajectory to `Gazebo`.

In the next section, we will discuss the ROS Navigation stack and look at the requirements needed to interface the Navigation stack with the `Gazebo` simulation.

Understanding the ROS Navigation stack

The main aim of the ROS Navigation package is to move a robot from the start position to the goal position, without making any collision with the environment. The ROS Navigation package comes with an implementation of several navigation-related algorithms that can easily help implement autonomous navigation in mobile robots.

The user only needs to feed the goal position of the robot and the robot odometry data from sensors such as wheel encoders, **Inertial Measurement Unit (IMU)**, and **Global Positioning System (GPS)**, along with other sensor data streams, such as laser scanner data or 3D point cloud from sensors such as a **Red-Green-Blue Depth (RGB-D)** sensor. The output of the Navigation package will be the velocity commands that will drive the robot to the given goal position.

The Navigation stack contains the implementation of the standard algorithms, such as `SLAM, A *(star), Dijkstra, amcl`, and so on, that can directly be used in our application.

ROS Navigation hardware requirements

The ROS Navigation stack is designed to be generic. There are some hardware requirements that should be satisfied by the robot, and these are outlined in the following list:

- The Navigation package will work better in differential drive and holonomic constraints. Also, the mobile robot should be controlled by sending velocity commands in the form of `x: velocity`, `y: velocity` (linear velocity), and `theta: velocity` (angular velocity).

- The robot should be equipped with a vision (**rgb-d**) or laser sensor to build a map of the environment.

- The Navigation stack will perform better for square- and circular-shaped mobile bases. It will work on an arbitrary shape, but performance is not guaranteed.

The following diagram, taken from the ROS website (`http://wiki.ros.org/navigation/Tutorials/RobotSetup`), shows the basic building blocks of the Navigation stack. We can see the purpose of each block and how to configure the Navigation stack for a custom robot:

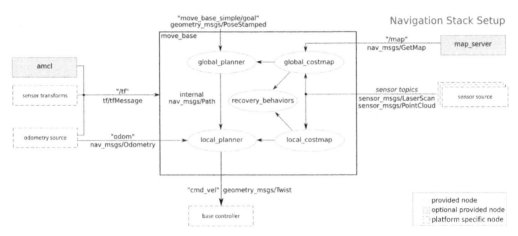

Figure 6.19 – Navigation stack setup diagram

According to the preceding Navigation setup diagram, to configure the Navigation package for a custom robot, we must provide functional blocks that interface with the Navigation stack. The following list provides explanations of all the blocks that are provided as input to the Navigation stack:

- **Odometry source**: Odometry data of a robot gives the robot a position with respect to its starting position. The main odometry sources are wheel encoders, IMU, and 2D/3D cameras (visual odometry). The odom value should publish to the Navigation stack, which has a message type of `nav_msgs/Odometry`. The odom message can hold the position and the velocity of the robot. Odometry data is a mandatory input to the Navigation stack.

- **Sensor source**: We have to provide laser-scan data or point-cloud data to the Navigation stack for mapping the robot environment. This data, along with odometry, combines to build a global and local cost map of the robot. The main sensors used here are laser scanners. The data should be of type `sensor_msgs/LaserScan` or `sensor_msgs/PointCloud`.

- `sensor transforms/tf`: The robot should publish the relationship between the robot coordinate frame using ROS TF.

- `base_controller`: The main function of the base controller is to convert the output of the Navigation stack, which is a twist (`geometry_msgs/Twist`) message, and convert it into corresponding motor velocities of the robot.

The optional tnodes of the Navigation stack are `amcl` and `map_server`, which allow the localization of the robot and help to save/load the robot map.

Working with Navigation packages

Before working with the Navigation stack, we were discussing MoveIt! and the `move_group` node. In the Navigation stack, there is also a node like the `move_group` node, called the `move_base` node. From *Figure 6.19*, it is clear that the `move_base` node takes input from sensors, joint states, the TF, and odometry, which is very similar to the `move_group` node that we saw in MoveIt!.

Let's see more about the `move_base` node.

Understanding the move_base node

The `move_base` node is from a package called `move_base`. The main function of this package is to move a robot from its current position to a goal position, with the help of other navigation nodes. The `move_base` node inside this package links the global planner and the local planner for the path planning, connecting to the `rotate-recovery` package if the robot is stuck in some obstacle and connecting the global `costmap` and the local `costmap` maps to get a map.

The `move_base` node is basically an implementation of `SimpleActionServer`, which takes a goal pose with the message type (`geometry_msgs/PoseStamped`). We can send a goal position to this node using a `SimpleActionClient` node.

The `move_base` node subscribes a navigation goal from a topic called `move_base_simple/goal`, which is the input of the Navigation stack, as shown in the previous diagram.

When this node receives a goal pose, it links to components such as `global_planner`, `local_planner`, `recovery_behavior`, `global_costmap`, and `local_costmap`, generates the output, which is the command velocity (`geometry_msgs/Twist`), and sends it to the base controller to move the robot to achieve the goal pose.

Here is a list of all the packages that are linked by the move_base node:

- global-planner: This package provides libraries and nodes for planning the optimum path from the current position of the robot to the goal position, with respect to the robot map. This package has the implementation of path-finding algorithms—such as A*, Dijkstra, and so on—for finding the shortest path from the current robot position to the goal position.

- local-planner: The main function of this package is to navigate the robot in a section of the global path planned using the global planner. The local planner will take the odometry and sensor reading and send an appropriate velocity command to the robot controller for completing a segment of the global path plan. The base local-planner package is the implementation of the trajectory rollout and dynamic window algorithms.

- rotate-recovery: This package helps the robot to avoid a local obstacle by performing a 360-degree rotation.

- clear-costmap-recovery: This package is also for avoiding a local obstacle by clearing the costmap map by changing the current costmap map used by the Navigation stack to a static map.

- costmap-2D: The main use of this package is to map the robot environment. The robot can only plan a path with respect to a map. In ROS, we create 2D or 3D occupancy grid maps, which is a representation of the environment in a grid of cells. Each cell has a probability value that indicates whether the cell is occupied or not. The costmap-2D package can build a grid map of the environment by subscribing sensor values of the laser scan or point cloud and also the odometry values. There are global cost maps for global navigation and local cost maps for local navigation.

Here are the other packages that are interfaced to the move_base node:

- map-server: The map-server package allows us to save and load the map generated by the costmap-2D package.

- amcl: Amcl is a method to localize the robot in a map. This approach uses a particle filter to track the pose of the robot with respect to the map, with the help of probability theory. In the ROS system, amcl accepts a sensor_msgs/LaserScan message to create a map.

- gmapping: The gmapping package is an implementation of an algorithm called Fast SLAM, which takes the laser scan data and odometry to build a 2D occupancy grid map.

After discussing each functional block of the Navigation stack, let's see how it really works.

Workings of the Navigation stack

In the previous section, we saw the functionalities of each block in the ROS Navigation stack. Let's check how the entire system works. The robot should publish a proper odometry value, TF information, and sensor data from the laser, and have a base controller and map of the surroundings.

If all these requirements are satisfied, we can start working with the Navigation package. The main elements related to the problem of robot navigation are summarized in the following section.

Localizing on the map

The first step the robot is going to perform is to localize itself on the map. The amcl package will help to localize the robot on the map.

Sending a goal and path planning

After getting the current position of the robot, we can send a goal position to the move_base node. The move_base node will send this goal position to a global planner, which will plan a path from the current robot position to the goal position.

This plan is with respect to the global costmap, which is feeding from the map server. The global planner will send this path to the local planner, which executes each segment of the global plan.

The local planner gets the odometry and the sensor value from the move_base node and finds a collision-free local plan for the robot. The local planner is associated with the local costmap, which can monitor the obstacle(s) around the robot.

Collision-recovery behavior

The global and local costmap are tied with the laser scan data. If the robot is stuck somewhere, the Navigation package will trigger the recovery-behavior nodes, such as the clear costmap recovery or rotate recovery nodes.

Sending the command velocity

The local planner generates the command velocity in the form of a twist message that contains linear and angular velocity (`geometry_msgs/Twist`) used by the `move_base` controller. The robot base controller converts the twist message to the equivalent motor speed.

We are now ready to install and configure the ROS Navigation stack for our robot.

Building a map using SLAM

Before to start configuring the Navigation stack, we need to install it. The ROS desktop full installation will not install the ROS Navigation stack. We must install the Navigation stack separately, using the following command:

```
sudo apt-get install ros-noetic-navigation
```

After installing the Navigation package, let's start learning how to build a map of the robot environment. The robot we are using here is the differential wheeled robot that we discussed in the previous chapter. This robot satisfies all three requirements of the Navigation stack.

The ROS `gmapping` package is a wrapper of the open source implementation of SLAM, called `OpenSLAM` (`https://openslam-org.github.io/gmapping.html`). The package contains a node called `slam_gmapping`, which is the implementation of SLAM and helps to create a 2D occupancy grid map from the laser scan data and the mobile robot pose.

The basic hardware requirement for doing SLAM is a laser scanner that is horizontally mounted on the top of the robot, and the robot odometry data. In this robot, we have already satisfied these requirements. We can generate a 2D map of the environment using the `gmapping` package, through the following procedure.

Before operating with `gmapping`, we need to install it using the following command:

```
sudo apt-get install ros-noetic-gmapping
```

After completing the installation, we need to configure `gmapping` for our robot.

Creating a launch file for gmapping

The main task while creating a launch file for the `gmapping` process is to set the parameters for the `slam_gmapping` node and the `move_base` node. The `slam_gmapping` node is the core node inside the ROS `gmapping` package. The `slam_gmapping` node subscribes the laser data (`sensor_msgs/LaserScan`) and the TF data and publishes the occupancy grid map data as output (`nav_msgs/OccupancyGrid`). This node is highly configurable, and we can fine-tune the parameters to improve the mapping accuracy. The parameters are mentioned at `http://wiki.ros.org/gmapping`.

The next node we have to configure is the `move_base` node. The main parameters we need to configure are the global and local `costmap` parameters, the local planner, and the `move_base` parameters. The parameters list is very lengthy. We are representing these parameters in several **YAML Ain't Markup Language (YAML)** files. Each parameter is included in the `param` folder inside the `diff_wheeled_robot_gazebo` package.

The following code is for the `gmapping.launch` file used in this robot. The launch file is placed in the `diff_wheeled_robot_gazebo/launch` folder. The launch file contains a big number of parameters and includes some configuration files. First, we define the topic on which the laser-scanner data will be published, as follows:

```
<launch>
  <arg name="scan_topic" default="scan" />
```

Then, we include the `gmapping` node, as follows:

```
  <node pkg="gmapping" type="slam_gmapping" name="slam_
gmapping" output="screen">
```

An important element of the `gmapping` node is the frames involved in the creation of the map: the base frame, representing the base of the robot, and the `odom` frame, representing the frame in which the position of the robot is calculated considering wheel odometry. The code is illustrated in the following snippet:

```
    <param name="base_frame" value="base_footprint"/>
    <param name="odom_frame"value="odom"/>
```

Then, a set of parameters regulate the behavior of the mapping algorithm. We can classify the parameters in the following classes.

The laser parameters are shown here:

```
<param name="maxUrange" value="6.0"/>
<param name="maxRange" value="8.0"/>
<param name="sigma" value="0.05"/>
<param name="kernelSize" value="1"/>
<param name="lstep" value="0.05"/>
<param name="astep" value="0.05"/>
<param name="iterations" value="5"/>
<param name="lsigma" value="0.075"/>
<param name="ogain" value="3.0"/>
<param name="lskip" value="0"/>
<param name="minimumScore" value="100"/>
<param name="particles" value="80"/>
```

The model parameters are shown here:

```
<param name="srr" value="0.01"/>
<param name="srt" value="0.02"/>
<param name="str" value="0.01"/>
<param name="stt" value="0.02"/>
```

Other parameters related the update of the map are shown here:

```
<param name="linearUpdate" value="0.5"/>
<param name="angularUpdate" value="0.436"/>
<param name="temporalUpdate" value="-1.0"/>
<param name="resampleThreshold" value="0.5"/>
<remap from="scan" to="$(arg scan_topic)"/>
<param name="map_update_interval" value="5.0"/>
```

The initial map dimensions and resolution parameters are shown here:

```
<param name="xmin" value="-1.0"/>
<param name="ymin" value="-1.0"/>
<param name="xmax" value="1.0"/>
<param name="ymax" value="1.0"/>
<param name="delta" value="0.05"/>
```

The likelihood sampling parameters are shown here:

```
<param name="llsamplerange" value="0.01"/>
<param name="llsamplestep" value="0.01"/>
<param name="lasamplerange" value="0.005"/>
<param name="lasamplestep" value="0.005"/>
```

We are now ready to start the mapping node on the differential drive robot.

Running SLAM on the differential drive robot

We can build a ROS package called `diff_wheeled_robot_gazebo` and run the `gmapping.launch` file for building the map. The following code snippets show the commands we need to execute to start the mapping procedure.

Start the robot simulation by using the Willow Garage world (shown in *Figure 6.21*), as follows:

```
roslaunch diff_wheeled_robot_gazebo diff_wheeled_gazebo_full.
launch
```

Start the `gmapping` launch file with the following command:

```
roslaunch diff_wheeled_robot_gazebo gmapping.launch
```

If the `gmapping` launch file is working fine, we will get the following kind of output on the Terminal:

```
[ INFO] [1505810240.049575967, 15.340000000]: Loading from pre-hydro parameter style
[ INFO] [1505810240.168699314, 15.381000000]: Using plugin "static_layer"
[ INFO] [1505810240.384469019, 15.449000000]: Requesting the map...
[ INFO] [1505810240.663457937, 15.552000000]: Resizing costmap to 288 X 608 at 0.050000 m/pix
[ INFO] [1505810240.871384865, 15.650000000]: Received a 288 X 608 map at 0.050000 m/pix
[ INFO] [1505810240.897210021, 15.656000000]: Using plugin "obstacle_layer"
[ INFO] [1505810240.913185546, 15.660000000]:     Subscribed to Topics: scan bump
[ INFO] [1505810241.183408917, 15.714000000]: Using plugin "inflation_layer"
[ INFO] [1505810241.592248141, 15.851000000]: Loading from pre-hydro parameter style
[ INFO] [1505810241.730240828, 15.900000000]: Using plugin "obstacle_layer"
[ INFO] [1505810241.978042290, 16.015000000]:     Subscribed to Topics: scan bump
[ INFO] [1505810242.124180243, 16.057000000]: Using plugin "inflation_layer"
[ INFO] [1505810242.504991688, 16.191000000]: Created local_planner dwa_local_planner/DWAPlannerROS
[ INFO] [1505810242.518319734, 16.198000000]: Sim period is set to 0.20
[ INFO] [1505810244.343111055, 16.967000000]: Recovery behavior will clear layer obstacles
[ INFO] [1505810244.546680028, 17.020000000]: Recovery behavior will clear layer obstacles
[ INFO] [1505810244.697982461, 17.046000000]: odom received!
```

Figure 6.20 – Terminal messages during gmapping process

Start the keyboard teleoperation for manually navigating the robot around the environment. The robot can map its environment only if it covers the entire area. The code is illustrated here:

```
roslaunch diff_wheeled_robot_control keyboard_teleop.launch
```

You can add elements in `Gazebo` directly from the UI—for example, you can add the Willow Garage office in the simulation. This scene is shown in the following screenshot:

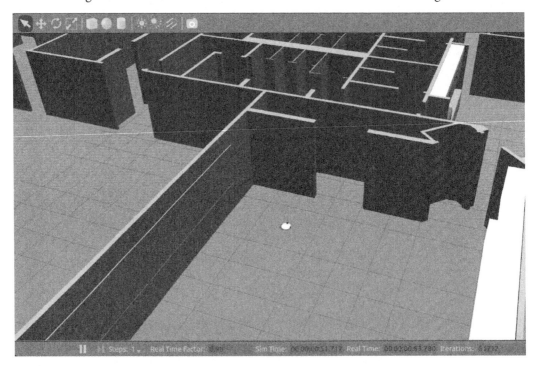

Figure 6.21 – Simulation of the robot using the Willow Garage world

We can launch RViz and add a display type called **Map** and a topic name of /map.

We can start moving the robot inside the world by using keyboard teleoperation, and we can see a map building according to the environment. The following screenshot shows the completed map of the environment shown in RViz:

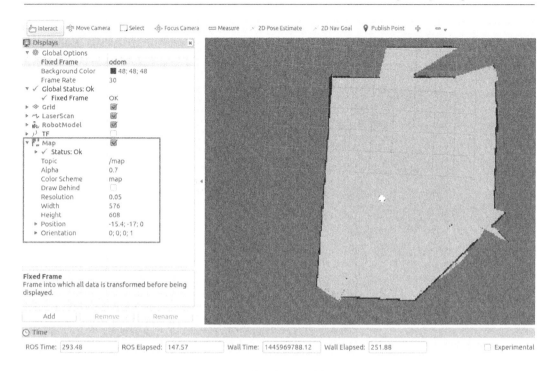

Figure 6.22 – Completed map of the room in RViz

We can save the built map using the following command. This command will listen to the map topic and generate an image containing the whole map. The `map_server` package does this operation:

```
rosrun map_server map_saver -f willo
```

You need to install the map server, as follows:

```
sudo apt-get install ros-noetic-map-server
```

Here, `willo` is the name of the map file. The map file is stored as two files: one is a YAML file that contains the map metadata and the image name, and the other is an image that has the encoded data of the occupancy grid map. Here is a screenshot of the preceding command, running without any errors:

```
jcacace@robot:~$ rosrun map_server map_saver -f willo
[ INFO] [1505810794.895750258]: Waiting for the map
[ INFO] [1505810795.117276658, 21.621000000]: Received a 288 X 608 map @ 0.050 m/pix
[ INFO] [1505810795.119888038, 21.621000000]: Writing map occupancy data to willo.pgm
[ INFO] [1505810795.138065942, 21.632000000]: Writing map occupancy data to willo.yaml
[ INFO] [1505810795.138632329, 21.632000000]: Done
```

Figure 6.23 – Terminal screenshot while saving a map

The saved encoded image of the map is shown next. If the robot gives accurate robot odometry data, we will get this kind of precise map similar to the environment. The accurate map improves the navigation accuracy through efficient path planning:

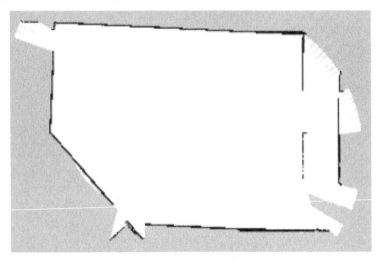

Figure 6.24 – The saved map

The next procedure is to localize and navigate in this static map.

Implementing autonomous navigation using amcl and a static map

The ROS amcl package provides nodes for localizing the robot on a static map. This node subscribes the laser-scan data, laser-scan-based maps, and the TF information from the robot. The amcl node estimates the pose of the robot on the map and publishes its estimated position with respect to the map.

If we create a static map from the laser-scan data, the robot can autonomously navigate from any pose of the map using amcl and the move_base nodes. The first step is to create a launch file for starting the amcl node. The amcl node is highly customizable; we can configure it with a lot of parameters. A list of these parameters is available at the ROS package site (http://wiki.ros.org/amcl).

Creating an amcl launch file

A typical `amcl` launch file is given next. The `amcl` node is configured inside the `amcl.launch.xml` file, which is in the `diff_wheeled_robot_gazebo/launch/include` package. The `move_base` node is also configured separately in the `move_base.launch.xml` file. The map file we created in the `gmapping` process is loaded here, using the `map_server` node, as follows:

```
<arg name="map_file" default="$(find diff_wheeled_robot_
gazebo)/maps/test1.yaml"/>
  <node name="map_server" pkg="map_server" type="map_server"
args="$(arg map_file)" />
  <include file="$(find diff_wheeled_robot_gazebo)/launch/
includes/amcl.launch.xml">

    <arg name="initial_pose_x" value="0"/>
    <arg name="initial_pose_y" value="0"/>
    <arg name="initial_pose_a" value="0"/>

  </include>
```

Then, we include the `move_base` launch file, as follows:

```
  <include file="$(find diff_wheeled_robot_gazebo)/launch/
includes/move_base.launch.xml"/>
</launch>
```

Here is a code snippet taken from `amcl.launch.xml`. This file is a bit lengthy, as we have to configure a lot of parameters for the `amcl` node:

```
<launch>
  <arg name="use_map_topic"   default="false"/>
  <arg name="scan_topic"      default="scan"/>
  <arg name="initial_pose_x" default="0.0"/>
  <arg name="initial_pose_y" default="0.0"/>
  <arg name="initial_pose_a" default="0.0"/>

  <node pkg="amcl" type="amcl" name="amcl">
    <param name="use_map_topic"              value="$(arg use_
map_topic)"/>
    <!-- Publish scans from best pose at a max of 10 Hz -->
```

`<param name="odom_model_type"`	`value="diff"/>`
`<param name="odom_alpha5"`	`value="0.1"/>`
`<param name="gui_publish_rate"`	`value="10.0"/>`
`<param name="laser_max_beams"`	`value="60"/>`
`<param name="laser_max_range"`	`value="12.0"/>`

After creating this launch file, we can start the `amcl` node, using the procedure outlined next.

Start the simulation of the robot in `Gazebo`, as follows:

```
roslaunch diff_wheeled_robot_gazebo diff_wheeled_gazebo_full.
launch
```

Start the `amcl` launch file using the following command:

```
roslaunch diff_wheeled_robot_gazebo amcl.launch
```

If the `amcl` launch file is correctly loaded, the Terminal shows the following message:

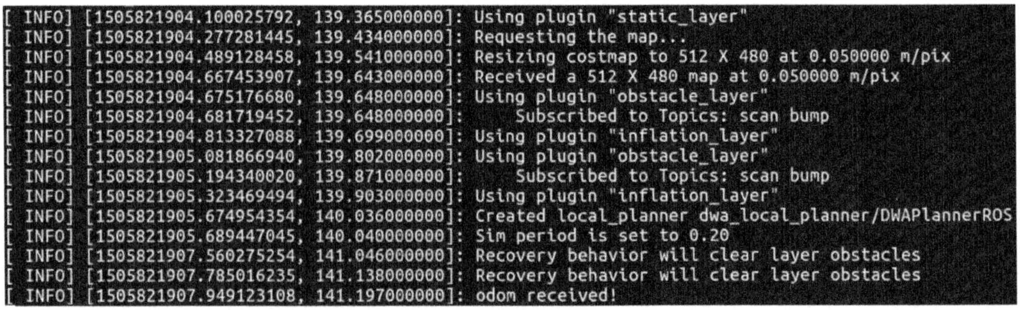

```
[ INFO] [1505821904.100025792, 139.365000000]: Using plugin "static_layer"
[ INFO] [1505821904.277281445, 139.434000000]: Requesting the map...
[ INFO] [1505821904.489128458, 139.541000000]: Resizing costmap to 512 X 480 at 0.050000 m/pix
[ INFO] [1505821904.667453907, 139.643000000]: Received a 512 X 480 map at 0.050000 m/pix
[ INFO] [1505821904.675176680, 139.648000000]: Using plugin "obstacle_layer"
[ INFO] [1505821904.681719452, 139.648000000]:     Subscribed to Topics: scan bump
[ INFO] [1505821904.813327088, 139.699000000]: Using plugin "inflation_layer"
[ INFO] [1505821905.081866940, 139.802000000]: Using plugin "obstacle_layer"
[ INFO] [1505821905.194340020, 139.871000000]:     Subscribed to Topics: scan bump
[ INFO] [1505821905.323469494, 139.903000000]: Using plugin "inflation_layer"
[ INFO] [1505821905.674954354, 140.036000000]: Created local_planner dwa_local_planner/DWAPlannerROS
[ INFO] [1505821905.689447045, 140.040000000]: Sim period is set to 0.20
[ INFO] [1505821907.560275254, 141.046000000]: Recovery behavior will clear layer obstacles
[ INFO] [1505821907.785016235, 141.138000000]: Recovery behavior will clear layer obstacles
[ INFO] [1505821907.949123108, 141.197000000]: odom received!
```

Figure 6.25 – Terminal screenshot while executing amcl

If `amcl` is working fine, we can start commanding the robot to go into a position on the map using RViz, as shown in the following screenshot, in which the arrow indicates the goal position. We have to enable `LaserScan`, `Map`, and `Path` visualizing plugins in RViz for viewing the laser scan, the global/local cost map, and the global/local paths. Using the **2D Nav Goal** button in RViz, we can command the robot to go to the desired position.

The robot will plan a path to that point and give velocity commands to the robot controller to reach that point, as illustrated in the following screenshot:

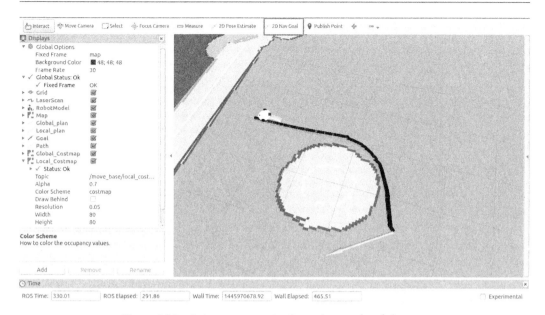

Figure 6.26 – Autonomous navigation using amcl and the map

In the preceding screenshot, we can see that we have placed a random obstacle in the robot's path and that the robot has planned a path to avoid the obstacle.

We can view the amcl particle cloud around the robot by adding a pose array to RViz, and the topic is /particle_cloud. The following screenshot shows the amcl particle cloud around the robot:

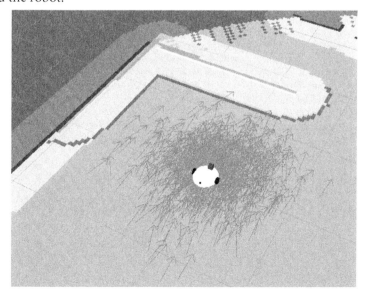

Figure 6.27 – The amcl particle cloud and odometry

Now, the robot is able to localize itself into the map. The shape of the particle cloud gives us information about the quality of the localization. It represents the localization system's uncertainty about the pose of the robot. If the cloud is very spread out, this means that the system is very unsure about the overall pose of the robot. In the previous screenshot, we can see a very condensed cloud that represents a low uncertainty for the localization system.

Summary

This chapter offered a brief overview of MoveIt! and the Navigation stack of ROS and demonstrated its capabilities using `Gazebo` simulation of a robotic arm mobile base. The chapter started with a MoveIt! overview and discussed detailed concepts about MoveIt!. After discussing MoveIt!, we interfaced MoveIt! with `Gazebo`. After interfacing, we executed the trajectory from MoveIt! on `Gazebo`.

The next section was about the ROS Navigation stack. We discussed its concepts and workings as well. After discussing the concepts, we tried to interface our robot in `Gazebo` to the Navigation stack and build a map using SLAM. After this, we performed autonomous navigation using `amcl` and the static map.

In the next chapter, we will discuss `pluginlib`, `nodelets`, and controllers.

Here are few questions based on what we covered in this chapter.

Questions

- What is the main purpose of MoveIt! packages?
- What is the importance of the `move_group` node in MoveIt!?
- What is the purpose of the `move_base` node in the Navigation stack?
- What are the functions of the SLAM and amcl packages?

7
Exploring the Advanced Capabilities of ROS MoveIt!

In the previous chapter, we covered **Robot Operating System** (**ROS**) manipulation and navigation. Similarly, in this chapter, we are going to cover the advanced capabilities of ROS MoveIt!, such as collision avoidance, perception with **three-dimensional** (**3D**) sensors, grasping, picking, and placing. After this, we will see how to interface robotic manipulator hardware with MoveIt!.

These are the main topics discussed in this chapter:

- Motion-planning using the `move_group` C++ interface
- Working with perception using MoveIt! and Gazebo
- Performing object manipulation with MoveIt!
- Understanding DYNAMIXEL ROS servo controllers for robot hardware interfacing
- Interfacing a 7-DOF DYNAMIXEL-based robotic arm with ROS MoveIt!

The first topic that we are going to discuss is how to motion-plan our robot using MoveIt! C++ APIs.

Technical requirements

To follow along with this chapter, you need a standard laptop running **Ubuntu 20.04** with ROS Noetic installed. The reference code for this chapter can be downloaded from the following Git repository: `https://github.com/PacktPublishing/Mastering-ROS-for-Robotics-Programming-Third-edition.git`. The code is contained in the `Chapter7/seven_dof_arm_test` folder.

You can view this chapter's code in action here: `https://bit.ly/3z4179J`.

Motion planning using the move_group C++ interface

In *Chapter 6, Using the ROS MoveIt! and Navigation Stack*, we discussed how to interact with a robot arm and how to plan its path using the **MoveIt! ROS Visualization (RViz) motion planning** plugin. In this section, we will see how to program the robot motion using the `move_group` C++ APIs. Motion planning using RViz can also be done programmatically through the `move_group` C++ APIs.

The first step to start working with C++ APIs is to create another ROS package that has the MoveIt! packages as dependencies. We can create this same package using the following command:

```
catkin_create_pkg seven_dof_arm_test catkin cmake_modules
interactive_markers moveit_core moveit_ros_perception moveit_
ros_planning_interface pluginlib roscpp std_msgs
```

Let's start using the `move_group` API to execute planned trajectories.

Motion planning a random path using MoveIt! C++ APIs

The first example that we are going to see is a random motion plan using MoveIt!. C++ APIs. You will get the code file named `test_random.cpp` from the `src` folder. The code and the description of each line follows. When we execute this node, it will plan a random path and execute it, as illustrated in the following code snippet:

```
#include <moveit/move_group_interface/move_group_interface.h>
int main(int argc, char **argv)
{
  ros::init(argc, argv, "move_group_interface_demo");
  // start a ROS spinning thread
  ros::AsyncSpinner spinner(1);
  spinner.start();
  // this connects to a running instance of the move_group node
  //move_group_interface::MoveGroup group("arm");
  moveit::planning_interface::MoveGroupInterface group("arm");
  // specify that our target will be a random one
  group.setRandomTarget();
  // plan the motion and then move the group to the sampled target
  group.move();
  ros::waitForShutdown();
}
```

To build the source code, we should add the following lines of code to `CMakeLists.txt`. You will get the complete `CMakeLists.txt` file from the existing package itself:

```
add_executable(test_random_node src/test_random.cpp)
add_dependencies(test_random_node seven_dof_arm_test_generate_messages_cpp)
target_link_libraries(test_random_node
${catkin_LIBRARIES})
```

We can build the package using the `catkin_make` command. First, check whether `test_random.cpp` is built properly or not. If the code is built properly, we can start testing the code.

The following command will start the RViz with 7-DOF arm with the motion-planning plugin:

```
roslaunch seven_dof_arm_config demo.launch
```

Move the end effector to check whether everything is working properly in RViz.

Run the C++ node for planning to a random position using the following command:

```
rosrun seven_dof_arm_test test_random_node
```

The output of the RViz is shown next. The arm will select a random position that has valid **inverse kinematics (IK)** and a motion plan from the current position:

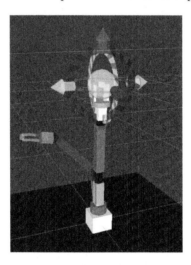

Figure 7.1 – Random motion planning using move_group APIs

In this example, we just try to move the robot with a random, feasible target pose for its end effector. In the next section, we will assign the desired pose to it.

Motion planning a custom path using MoveIt! C++ APIs

We saw random motion planning in the preceding example. In this section, we will check how to command the robot end effector to move to a custom goal position. The following example, test_custom.cpp, will do that job. At the start, we must include MoveIt! header files. The code is illustrated in the following snippet:

```
#include <moveit/move_group_interface/move_group_interface.h>
#include <moveit/planning_scene_interface/planning_scene_interface.h>
```

```cpp
#include <moveit/move_group_interface/move_group_interface.h>
#include <moveit_msgs/DisplayRobotState.h>
#include <moveit_msgs/DisplayTrajectory.h>
#include <moveit_msgs/AttachedCollisionObject.h>
#include <moveit_msgs/CollisionObject.h>
```

Then, we initialize the planning interface and the publishers to visualize the trajectory on MoveIt!, as follows:

```cpp
int main(int argc, char **argv)
{
    //ROS initialization
    ros::init(argc, argv, "move_group_interface_tutorial");
    ros::NodeHandle node_handle;
    ros::AsyncSpinner spinner(1);
    spinner.start();
    sleep(2.0);
    //Move group setup
    moveit::planning_interface::MoveGroupInterface group("arm");
    moveit::planning_interface::PlanningSceneInterface planning_
scene_interface;
    ros::Publisher display_publisher = node_handle.
advertise<moveit_msgs::DisplayTrajectory>("/move_group/display_
planned_path", 1, true);
    moveit_msgs::DisplayTrajectory display_trajectory;
    ROS_INFO("Reference frame: %s",      group.
getEndEffectorLink().c_str());
```

Finally, we set a fixed desired pose for the manipulator target and require the planning and the execution of the generated trajectory, as follows:

```cpp
    //Target pose setup
    geometry_msgs::Pose target_pose1;
    target_pose1.orientation.w = 0.726282;
    target_pose1.orientation.x= 4.04423e-07;
    target_pose1.orientation.y = -0.687396;
    target_pose1.orientation.z = 4.81813e-07;
    target_pose1.position.x = 0.0261186;
    target_pose1.position.y = 4.50972e-07;
```

```
target_pose1.position.z = 0.573659;
group.setPoseTarget(target_pose1);
//Motion planning
moveit::planning_interface::MoveGroupInterface::Plan my_plan;
moveit::planning_interface::MoveItErrorCode success = group.
plan(my_plan);
ROS_INFO("Visualizing plan 1 (pose goal) %s", success.val ?
"":"FAILED");
// Sleep to give Rviz time to visualize the plan.
sleep(5.0);
ros::shutdown();
}
```

Here are the extra lines of code added on for building the source code:

```
add_executable(test_custom_node src/test_custom.cpp)
add_dependencies(test_custom_node seven_dof_arm_test_generate_
messages_cpp)
target_link_libraries(test_custom_node
${catkin_LIBRARIES})
```

Here is the command to execute the custom node:

```
rosrun seven_dof_arm_test test_custom_node
```

The following screenshot shows the result of test_custom_node:

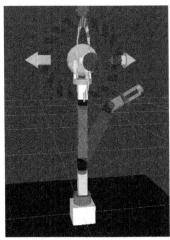

Figure 7.2 – Custom motion planning using MoveIt! C++ APIs

However, in this case, we plan the trajectory in a free space. Motion-planning capabilities are more important when the robot's environment is crowded with obstacles. Let's see in the next section how to add obstacles for collision checking.

Collision checking with a robot arm using MoveIt!

Along with motion planning and the IK solving algorithm, one of the most important tasks done in parallel in MoveIt! is collision checking and its avoidance. MoveIt! can handle both self-collisions and environmental collisions, exploiting the built-in **Flexible Collision Library** (**FCL**) (`http://gamma.cs.unc.edu/FCL/fcl_docs/webpage/generated/index.html`), an open source project that implements various collision-detection-and-avoidance algorithms. MoveIt! takes the power of FCL and handles the collision inside the planning scene using a `collision_detection::CollisionWorld` class. The MoveIt! collision checking includes objects—such as meshes, primitive shapes—such as boxes and cylinders, and octomaps. The OctoMap (`http://octomap.github.io/`) library implements a 3D occupancy grid, called an **octree**, that consists of probabilistic information regarding obstacles in the environment. The MoveIt! package can build an octomap using 3D point-cloud information and can directly feed the **OctoMap** library to FCL library for collision checking.

As with motion planning, collision checking is very computationally intensive. We can fine-tune the collision checking between two bodies—say, a robot link, or with the environment—using a parameter called the **Allowed Collision Matrix** (**ACM**). If the value of a collision between two links is set to 1 in ACM, there will not be any collision checks. We may set this for links that are far from each other. We can optimize the collision-checking process by optimizing this matrix.

Adding a collision object to MoveIt!

We can add a collision object to the MoveIt! planning scene, and we can see how motion planning works. To add a collision object, we can use mesh files, which can directly be imported from the MoveIt! interface and can be added by writing a ROS node using MoveIt! APIs.

We will first discuss how to add a collision object using the ROS node, as follows:

1. In the `add_collision_object.cpp` node, which is inside the `seven_dof_arm_test/src` folder, we are starting a ROS node and creating an object of `moveit::planning_interface::PlanningSceneInterface`, which can access the planning scene of MoveIt! and perform any action on the current scene. We will now add a sleep of 5 seconds to wait for the `planningSceneInterface` object instantiation, as follows:

```
moveit::planning_interface::PlanningSceneInterface
current_scene; 0);
```

2. In the next step, we need to create an instance of the `moveit_msgs::CollisionObject` collision object message. This message is going to be sent to the current planning scene. Here, we are making a collision object message for a cylinder shape, and the message is given as `seven_dof_arm_cylinder`. When we add this object to the planning scene, the name of the object is its **identifier (ID)**, as illustrated in the following code snippet:

```
moveit_msgs::CollisionObject cylinder;
cylinder.id = "seven_dof_arm_cylinder";
```

3. After making the collision-object message, we have to define another message of type `shape_msgs::SolidPrimitive`, which is used to define what kind of primitive shape we are using and its properties. In this example, we are creating a cylinder object, as shown in the following code snippet. We have to define the type of shape, the resizing factor, the width, and the height of the cylinder:

```
shape_msgs::SolidPrimitive primitive;
primitive.type = primitive.CYLINDER;
primitive.dimensions.resize(3);
primitive.dimensions[0] = 0.6;
primitive.dimensions[1] = 0.2;
primitive.dimensions[2] = 0.2;
```

4. After creating a shape message, we have to create a `geometry_msgs::Pose` message to define the pose of this object. We define a pose that may be closer to the robot. We can change the pose after the creation of an object in the planning scene. The code is illustrated in the following snippet:

```
geometry_msgs::Pose;
pose.orientation.w = 1.0;
pose.position.x =   0.0;
pose.position.y = -0.4;
pose.position.z =   -0.4;
```

5. After defining the pose of the collision object, we need to add the defined primitive object and the pose to the cylinder collision object. The operation we need to perform is adding the planning scene, as follows:

```
cylinder.primitives.push_back(primitive);
cylinder.primitive_poses.push_back(pose);
cylinder.operation = cylinder.ADD;
```

6. In the next step, we create a vector called `collision_objects` of type `moveit_msgs::CollisionObject`, inserting the collision object to this vector, like this:

```
std::vector<moveit_msgs::CollisionObject> collision_
objects;
collision_objects.push_back(cylinder);
```

7. We will add the collision object's vector to the current planning scene by using the following line of code. `addCollisionObjects()` inside the `PlanningSceneInterface` class is used to add the object to the planning scene:

```
current_scene.addCollisionObjects(collision_objects);
```

8. Here are the compile and build lines of the code in `CMakeLists.txt`:

```
add_executable(add_collision_object src/add_collision_
object.cpp)
add_dependencies(add_collision_object seven_dof_arm_test_
generate_messages_cpp)
target_link_libraries(add_collision_object
${catkin_LIBRARIES})
```

Let's see how this node works in RViz with the MoveIt! `Motion-Planning` plugin, as follows.

9. We will start the `demo.launch` file inside the `seven_dof_arm_config` package for testing this node:

```
roslaunch seven_dof_arm_config demo.launch
```

10. Then, we add the following collision object:

```
rosrun seven_dof_arm_test add_collision_object
```

When we run the `add_collision_object` node, a green cylinder will pop up, and we can move the collision object, as shown in the following screenshot. When the collision object is successfully added to the planning scene, it will list out in the **Scene Objects** tab. We can click on the object and modify its pose. We can also attach the new model in any links of robots too. There is a **Scale** option to scale down the collision model:

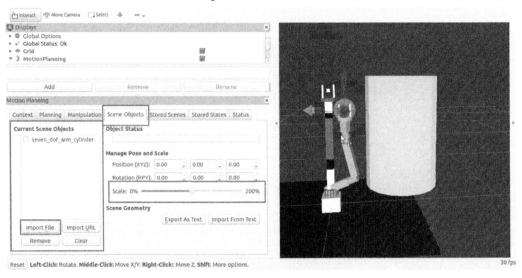

Figure 7.3 – Adding collision objects to RViz using MoveIt! C++ APIs

The RViz `Motion-Planning` plugin also gives an option to import a 3D mesh to the planning scene. Click the **Import File** button for importing the meshes. The following screenshot shows our importing of a cube-mesh **Digital Asset Exchange** (**DAE**) file, which is imported along with the cylinder in the planning scene. We can scale up the collision object using the **Scale** slider, and set the desired pose using the **Manage Pose** option. When we move the arm end effector to any of these collision objects, MoveIt! detects it as a collision. The MoveIt! collision detection can detect environment collision as well as self-collision. Here is a screenshot of a collision with the environment:

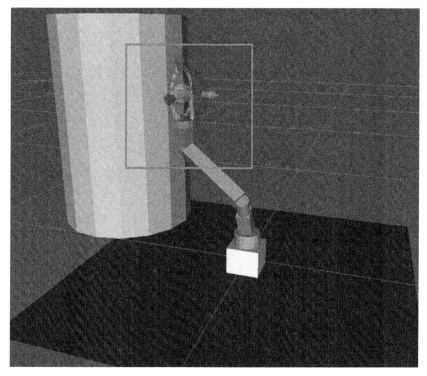

Figure 7.4 – Visualizing collided link

The collided link will turn red when the arm touches the object. In self-collision also, the collided link will turn red. We can change the color setting of the collision in the `Motion-Planning` plugin settings.

Removing a collision object from the planning scene

Removing a collision object from the planning scene is easy. We have to create a `moveit::planning_interface::PlanningSceneInterface` object, as we did in the previous example, along with some delay, as follows:

```
moveit::planning_interface::PlanningSceneInterface current_
scene;
sleep(5.0);
```

Next, we need to create a vector of the string that contains the collision object IDs. Here, our collision object ID is `seven_dof_arm_cylinder`. After pushing the string to this vector, we will call `removeCollisionObjects(object_ids)`, which will remove the collision objects from the planning scene.

The code is illustrated in the following snippet:

```
std::vector<std::string> object_ids;
object_ids.push_back("seven_dof_arm_cylinder");
current_scene.removeCollisionObjects(object_ids);
```

This code is placed in `seven_dof_arm_test/src/remove_collision_object.cpp`.

Attaching a collision object to a robot link

After seeing how to insert and remove objects from the planning scene, we are now going to discuss how to attach and detach objects to the robot's body. This important feature of ROS MoveIt! allows us to perform object manipulation. In fact, after attaching an object to the robot's body, the obstacle avoidance is additionally extended to the grasped object. In this way, the robot will be free to move into its workspace, avoiding obstacles and carrying the object to manipulate. The code we are going to discuss here is the `seven_dof_arm_test/src/attach_detach_objs.cpp` source code. After creating a `moveit::planning_interface::PlanningSceneInterface` object, as shown in the previous examples, we must initialize a `moveit_msgs::AttachedCollisionObject` instance, filling out information about which scene object will be attached to a specific link of the robot's body, as follows:

```
moveit_msgs::AttachedCollisionObject attached_object;
attached_object.link_name = "grasping_frame";
attached_object.object = grasping_object;
current_scene.applyAttachedCollisionObject( attached_object );
```

In this example, the `grasping_object` object attached to the robot link is the one already used in the `add_collision_object.cpp` example. When an object is successfully attached to a robot, its color in the MoveIt! visualization will change from green to purple and will move along with the robot motion. To detach an object from the robot's body, we should invoke the `applyAttachedCollisionObject` function on the desired object to detach modifying its operation from ADD to REMOVE, as illustrated in the following code snippet:

```
grasping_object.operation = grasping_object.REMOVE;
attached_object.link_name = "grasping_frame";
attached_object.object = grasping_object;
```

Let's continue the examples, checking the collisions of the arm with its structure: the self-collisions.

Checking self-collisions using Movelt! APIs

We have seen how to detect collisions in RViz, but what do we have to do if we want to get collision information in our ROS node? In this section, we will discuss how to get the collision information of our robot in ROS code. This example can check self-collisions and environment collisions, and tell which links were collided. The check_collision example is placed in the seven_dof_arm_test/src folder. The following code loads the kinematic model of the robot to the planning scene:

```
robot_model_loader::RobotModelLoader robot_model_loader("robot_
description");
robot_model::RobotModelPtr kinematic_model = robot_model_
loader.getModel();
planning_scene::PlanningScene planning_scene(kinematic_model);
```

To test self-collision in the robot's current state, we can create two instances of the collision_detection::CollisionRequest and collision_detection::CollisionResult classes, named collision_request and collision_result. After creating these objects, pass them to the planning_scene.checkSelfCollision() Movelt! collision-checking function, which can give the collision result in the collision_result object, and we can print the details, which are shown in the following code snippet:

```
planning_scene.checkSelfCollision(collision_request, collision_
result);
ROS_INFO_STREAM("1. Self collision Test: "<< (collision_result.
collision ? "in" : "not in")
<< " self collision");
```

If we want to test collision in a particular group, we can do that by mentioning group_name, as shown in the following code snippet. Here, the group name is arm:

```
collision_request.group_name = "arm";
current_state.setToRandomPositions();
//Previous results should be cleared
collision_result.clear();
planning_scene.checkSelfCollision(collision_request, collision_
result);
ROS_INFO_STREAM("3. Self collision Test(In a group): "<<
(collision_result.collision ? "in" : "not in"));
```

For performing a full collision check, we have to use the following function, called `planning_scene.checkCollision()`. We need to mention the current robot state and the ACM matrix in this function.

Here's the code we'll need to perform full collision checking using this function:

```
collision_detection::AllowedCollisionMatrix acm = planning_
scene.getAllowedCollisionMatrix();
robot_state::RobotState copied_state = planning_scene.
getCurrentState();
planning_scene.checkCollision(collision_request, collision_
result, copied_state, acm);
ROS_INFO_STREAM("6. Full collision Test: "<< (collision_result.
collision ? "in" : "not in")
<< " collision");
```

We can launch the motion-planning demo and run this node using the following command:

```
roslaunch seven_dof_arm_config demo.launch
```

We can run the collision-checking node with this command:

```
rosrun seven_dof_arm_test check_collision
```

You will get a report, such as the one shown in the following screenshot. The robot is now not in collision; if it is in collision, it will send a report of it:

```
[ INFO] [1512837566.744018279]: 1. Self collision Test: not in self collision
[ INFO] [1512837566.744073739]: 2. Self collision Test(Change the state): in
[ INFO] [1512837566.744108096]: 3. Self collision Test(In a group): in
[ INFO] [1512837566.744122925]: 4. Collision points valid
[ INFO] [1512837566.744167799]: 5. Self collision Test: in self collision
[ INFO] [1512837566.744179527]: 6 . Contact between: elbow_pitch_link and wrist_pitch_link
[ INFO] [1512837566.744227589]: 6. Self collision Test after modified ACM: not in self collision
[ INFO] [1512837566.744262790]: 6. Full collision Test: not in collision
```

Figure 7.5 – Collision-checking information messages

Until now, we just used fake execution of motions, without connecting MoveIt! and Gazebo. However, to exploit robot-sensing capabilities, a real robot or a simulation is needed. In the next section, we will discuss how to link the depth sensor of Gazebo simulation with MoveIt!.

Working with perception using MoveIt! and Gazebo

Until now, in MoveIt!, we have worked with an arm only. In this section, we will see how to interface 3D vision-sensor data to MoveIt!. The sensor can be either simulated using Gazebo, or you can directly interface a Re**d-Green-Blue-Depth** (**RGB-D**) sensor, such as Kinect or Intel RealSense, using the `openni_launch` package. Here, we will work using Gazebo simulation. We will add sensors to MoveIt! to create a map of the environment surrounding the robot. The following command will launch the robot arm and the Asus Xtion pro simulation in Gazebo in a world with obstacles:

```
roslaunch seven_dof_arm_gazebo seven_dof_arm_obstacle_world.
launch
```

This command will start the Gazebo scene with arm joint controllers and the Gazebo plugin for the 3D vision sensor. We can add a grasp table and grasp objects to the simulation, as shown in the following screenshot, by simply clicking and dragging them to the workspace. We can create any kind of table or object. The objects shown in the following screenshot are only for demonstration purposes. We can edit the model **Spatial Data File** (**SDF**) file to change the size and shape of the model:

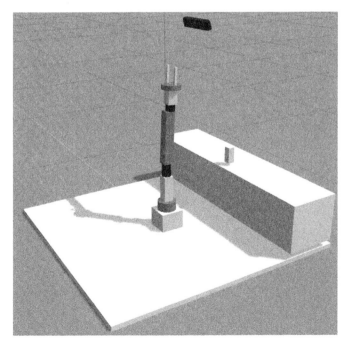

Figure 7.6 – Robot arm with grasp table and object in Gazebo

Check the topics generated after starting the simulation with the following command:

```
rostopic list
```

Make sure that we are getting the RGB-D camera topics, as shown here:

```
/rgbd_camera/depth/camera_info
/rgbd_camera/depth/image_raw
/rgbd_camera/depth/points
/rgbd_camera/ir/camera_info
/rgbd_camera/ir/image_raw
/rgbd_camera/ir/image_raw/compressed
/rgbd_camera/ir/image_raw/compressed/parameter_descriptions
/rgbd_camera/ir/image_raw/compressed/parameter_updates
/rgbd_camera/ir/image_raw/compressedDepth
/rgbd_camera/ir/image_raw/compressedDepth/parameter_descriptions
/rgbd_camera/ir/image_raw/compressedDepth/parameter_updates
/rgbd_camera/ir/image_raw/theora
/rgbd_camera/ir/image_raw/theora/parameter_descriptions
/rgbd_camera/ir/image_raw/theora/parameter_updates
/rgbd_camera/parameter_descriptions
/rgbd_camera/parameter_updates
/rgbd_camera/rgb/camera_info
/rgbd_camera/rgb/image_raw
/rgbd_camera/rgb/image_raw/compressed
/rgbd_camera/rgb/image_raw/compressed/parameter_descriptions
/rgbd_camera/rgb/image_raw/compressed/parameter_updates
/rgbd_camera/rgb/image_raw/compressedDepth
/rgbd_camera/rgb/image_raw/compressedDepth/parameter_descriptions
/rgbd_camera/rgb/image_raw/compressedDepth/parameter_updates
/rgbd_camera/rgb/image_raw/theora
/rgbd_camera/rgb/image_raw/theora/parameter_descriptions
/rgbd_camera/rgb/image_raw/theora/parameter_updates
/rgbd_camera/rgb/points
```

Figure 7.7 – Listing RGB-D sensor topics

We can view the point cloud in RViz using the following command:

```
rosrun rviz rviz -f base_link
```

Now, we can add the PointCloud2 data and the robot model to see the following output:

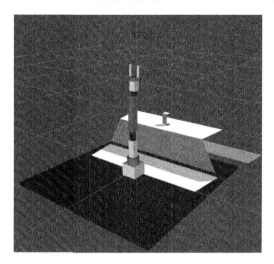

Figure 7.8 ~ Visualizing point-cloud data in RViz

After confirming the point-cloud data from the Gazebo plugins, we have to add some files to the MoveIt! configuration package of this arm—that is, the `seven_dof_arm_config` package, for bringing the point-cloud data from Gazebo to the MoveIt! planning scene.

The robot environment is mapped as an octree representation (`https://en.wikipedia.org/wiki/Octree`), which can be built using a library called **OctoMap**, which we have already seen in the previous section. The OctoMap library is incorporated as a plugin in MoveIt!, called the **Occupancy Map Updater** plugin, which can update an octree from different kinds of sensor inputs, such as point-cloud and depth images from 3D vision sensors. Currently, there are the following plugins for handling 3D data:

- `PointCloudOccupancymap Updater`: This plugin can take input in the form of point clouds (`sensor_msgs/PointCloud2`).

- `DepthImageOccupancymapUpdater`: This plugin can take input in the form of input depth images (`sensor_msgs/Image`).

The first step is to write a configuration file for these plugins. This file contains information about which plugin we are using in this robot and what its properties are. The file exploiting the first plugin is found in the `seven_dof_arm_config/config` folder, called `sensor_3d.yaml`.

The definition of this file is shown in the following code snippet:

```
sensors:
 - sensor_plugin: occupancy_map_monitor/PointCloudOctomapUpdater
```

```
point_cloud_topic: /rgbd_camera/depth/points
max_range: 5
padding_offset: 0.01
padding_scale: 1.0
point_subsample: 1
filtered_cloud_topic: filtered_cloud
```

The explanation of a general parameter is `sensor_plugin`, which is a parameter that specifies the name of the plugin we are using in the robot.

These are the parameters of the given `sensor_plugin` parameter:

- `point_cloud_topic`: This plugin will listen to this topic for point-cloud data.

- `max_range`: This is the distance limit in meters in which points above the range will not be used for processing.

- `padding_offset`: This value will be considered for robot links and attached objects when filtering clouds containing the robot links (self-filtering).

- `padding_scale`: This value will also be considered while self-filtering.

- `point_subsample`: If the update process is slow, points can be subsampled. If we make this value greater than 1, the points will be skipped instead of processed.

- `filtered_cloud_topic`: This is the final filtered cloud topic. We will get the processed point cloud through this topic. It can be used mainly for debugging.

If we are using the `DepthImageOctomapUpdater` plugin, we can have a different configuration file. We are not using this plugin in our example robot, but we can see its usage and properties in the following code snippet:

```
sensors:
 - sensor_plugin: occupancy_map_monitor/
DepthImageOctomapUpdater
   image_topic: /head_mount_kinect/depth_registered/image_raw
   queue_size: 5
   near_clipping_plane_distance: 0.3
   far_clipping_plane_distance: 5.0
   skip_vertical_pixels: 1
   skip_horizontal_pixels: 1
   shadow_threshold: 0.2
   padding_scale: 4.0
```

```
padding_offset: 0.03
filtered_cloud_topic: output_cloud
```

The explanation of a general parameter is `sensor_plugin`, which is a parameter that specifies the name of the plugin we are using in the robot.

These are the parameters of the given `sensor_plugin` parameter:

- `image_topic`: The topic that streams the image.

- `queue_size`: This is the queue size for the depth-image transport subscriber.

- `near_clipping_plane_distance`: This is the minimum valid distance from the sensor.

- `far_clipping_plane_distance`: This is the maximum valid distance from the sensor.

- `skip_vertical_pixels`: This is the number of pixels we have to skip from the top and bottom of the image. If we give a value of 5, it will skip five columns from the first and last pixels of the image.

- `skip_horizontal_pixels`: Skipping pixels in a horizontal direction.

- `shadow_threshold`: In some situations, points can appear below the robot links. This happens because of padding. `shadow_threshold` removes the points with a distance that is greater than the `shadow_threshold` parameter.

After discussing the OctoMap update plugin and its properties, we can now switch to the launch files necessary to initiate this plugin and its parameters. The first file we need to create is inside the `seven_dof_arm_config/launch` folder, with a name of `seven_dof_arm_moveit_sensor_manager.launch`. The definition of this file is shown in the following code snippet. This launch file basically loads the plugin parameters:

```
<launch>
<rosparam command="load" file="$(find seven_dof_arm_config)/
config/sensor_3d.yaml" />
</launch>
```

The next file that we need to edit is the `sensor_manager.launch` file, which is located inside the `launch` folder. The definition of this file is shown in the following code snippet:

```
<launch>
  <!-- This file makes it easy to include the settings for
sensor managers -->
```

```
<!-- Params for the octomap monitor -->
<!--  <param name="octomap_frame" type="string" value="some
frame in which the robot moves" /> -->
  <param name="octomap_resolution" type="double" value="0.015"
/>
  <param name="max_range" type="double" value="5.0" />


  <!-- Load the robot specific sensor manager; this sets the
moveit_sensor_manager ROS parameter -->


  <arg name="moveit_sensor_manager" default="seven_dof_arm" />
  <include file="$(find seven_dof_arm_config)/launch/$(arg
moveit_sensor_manager)_moveit_sensor_manager.launch.xml" />


</launch>
```

The following line of code is commented because it can be used if the robot is mobile. In our case, our robot is static. If it is fixed on a mobile robot, we can give the frame value as odom, or odom_combined of the robot:

```
<param name="octomap_frame" type="string" value="some frame in
which the robot moves" />
```

The following parameter is the resolution of OctoMap, which is visualized in RViz measured in meters. The rays beyond the max_range value will be truncated:

```
  <param name="octomap_resolution" type="double" value="0.015"
/>
  <param name="max_range" type="double" value="5.0" />
```

The interfacing is now complete. We can test the MoveIt! interface and launch Gazebo for perception using the following commands:

```
roslaunch seven_dof_arm_gazebo seven_dof_arm_bringup_obstacle_
moveit.launch
```

Now, RViz has sensor support. We can see the OctoMap in front of the robot in the following screenshot:

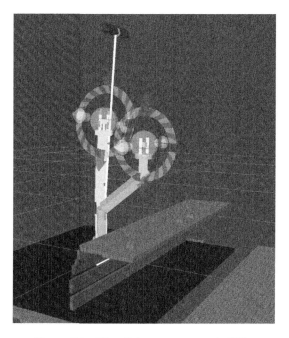

Figure 7.9 – Visualizing an octomap in RViz

The generated OctoMap is continuously updated when new elements appear in the scene and are used in the motion-planning process to generate obstacle-free paths.

However, in the previous examples, we just considered the possibility of safely moving the arm in the working scene. An important feature of the robotic arms is to handle objects. Let's discuss in the next section how to interact with the scene objects in order to manipulate them.

Performing object manipulation with MoveIt!

Manipulating objects is one of the main usages of robotic arms. The capacity to pick up objects and place them in a different location of the robot's workspace is extremely useful, both in industry and research applications. The picking process is also known as *grasping* and represents a complex task because a lot of constraints are required to pick an object up in a proper way. Humans handle grasping operations using their intelligence, but robots need rules for it. One of the constraints in grasping is the approaching force; the end effector should adjust the grasping force for picking the object but not make any deformation on the object while grasping. In addition, a grasping pose is needed to pick an object in the best way and should be calculated considering its shape and its pose. In this section, we will interact with the scene object of MoveIt! to simulate pick-and-place operations.

Working with a robot pick-and-place task using MoveIt!

We can pick and place objects in various ways. One is by using pre-defined sequences of joint values; in this case, we put the object in a known position, and move the robot toward that by providing direct joint values or **forward kinematics** (**FK**). Another pick-and-place method is to use IK without any visual feedback. In this case, we command the robot to move in a cartesian position with respect to the robot base frame, and by solving IK. In this way, the robot can reach that position and pick up that object. One more method is to use external sensors, such as vision ones, to calculate the pick-and-place positions; in this case, a vision sensor is used to identify the object's location, and the arm goes to that position by solving to pick the object. Of course, the use of vision sensors requires the development of robust algorithms to perform object recognition and tracking and calculate the best grasping pose to pick that object. But in this section, we want to demonstrate a pick-and-place sequence, by defining the approaching and grasping position to pick the object and place it on another location of its workspace. We can work with this example along with Gazebo, or simply use the MoveIt! demo interface. The complete source code of this example is reported in the `seven_dor_arm_test/src/pick_place.cpp` file. As we have already seen, we should first initialize the planning scene, as follows:

```
ros::init(argc, argv, "seven_dof_arm_planner");
ros::NodeHandle node_handle;
ros::AsyncSpinner spinner(1);
spinner.start();
moveit::planning_interface::MoveGroupInterface group("arm");
moveit::planning_interface::PlanningSceneInterface planning_
scene_interface;
sleep(2);
moveit::planning_interface::MoveGroupInterface::Plan my_plan;
const robot_state::JointModelGroup *joint_model_group =
group.getCurrentState()->getJointModelGroup("arm");
```

Then, we must create the working environment of the robot. In this context, we manually create two objects: a plane and a grasping object. Our goal is to pick the grasping object from its initial position and to transport it to another position. Let's start creating collision objects, as follows:

```
moveit::planning_interface::PlanningSceneInterface current_
scene;
geometry_msgs::Pose;
```

```
shape_msgs::SolidPrimitive primitive;
primitive.type = primitive.BOX;
primitive.dimensions.resize(3);
primitive.dimensions[0] = 0.03;
primitive.dimensions[1] = 0.03;
primitive.dimensions[2] = 0.08;
moveit_msgs::CollisionObject grasping_object;
```

Then, we create a grasping object, as follows:

```
grasping_object.id = "grasping_object";
pose.orientation.w = 1.0;
pose.position.y =  0.0;
pose.position.x =  0.33;
pose.position.z =  0.35;
grasping_object.primitives.push_back(primitive);
grasping_object.primitive_poses.push_back(pose);
grasping_object.operation = grasping_object.ADD;
grasping_object.header.frame_id = "base_link";
primitive.dimensions[0] = 0.3;
primitive.dimensions[1] = 0.5;
primitive.dimensions[2] = 0.32;
```

Next, we create a surface, like this:

```
moveit_msgs::CollisionObject grasping_table;
grasping_table.id = "grasping_table";
pose.orientation.w = 1.0;
pose.position.y =  0.0;
pose.position.x =  0.46;
pose.position.z =  0.15;
grasping_table.primitives.push_back(primitive);
grasping_table.primitive_poses.push_back(pose);
grasping_table.operation = grasping_object.ADD;
grasping_table.header.frame_id = "base_link";
```

Finally, we add the collision objects to the planning scene, like this:

```
std::vector<moveit_msgs::CollisionObject> collision_objects;
collision_objects.push_back(grasping_object);
collision_objects.push_back(grasping_table);
current_scene.addCollisionObjects(collision_objects);
```

Now that the planning scene is properly configured, we can request the motion of the robot toward a preconfigured position of the workspace to bring its end effector close to the object and pick it up, as follows:

```
geometry_msgs::Pose target_pose;
target_pose.orientation.x = 0;
target_pose.orientation.y = 0;
target_pose.orientation.z = 0;
target_pose.orientation.w = 1;
target_pose.position.y = 0.0;
target_pose.position.x = 0.28;
target_pose.position.z = 0.35;
group.setPoseTarget(target_pose);
group.move();
sleep(2);
target_pose.position.y = 0.0;
target_pose.position.x = 0.34;
target_pose.position.z = 0.35;
group.setPoseTarget(target_pose);
group.move();
```

If the grasping succeeded, we could attach the object to the end effector of the robot to place it in another location of the workspace, as illustrated in the following code snippet:

```
moveit_msgs::AttachedCollisionObject att_coll_object;
att_coll_object.object.id = "grasping_object";
att_coll_object.link_name = "gripper_finger_link1";
att_coll_object.object.operation = att_coll_object.object.ADD;
planning_scene_interface.applyAttachedCollisionObject(att_coll_
object);
target_pose.position.y = 0.0;
target_pose.position.x = 0.34;
```

```
target_pose.position.z = 0.4;
group.setPoseTarget(target_pose);
group.move();
//---
target_pose.orientation.x = -1;
target_pose.orientation.y = 0;
target_pose.orientation.z = 0;
target_pose.orientation.w = 0;
target_pose.position.y = -0.1;
target_pose.position.x = 0.34;
target_pose.position.z = 0.35;
group.setPoseTarget(target_pose);
group.move();
```

Finally, we must remove the object from the robot's gripper, as follows:

```
grasping_object.operation = grasping_object.REMOVE;
attached_object.link_name = "grasping_frame";
attached_object.object = grasping_object;
current_scene.applyAttachedCollisionObject( attached_object );
```

To run this example, launch the MoveIt! demo by running the following command:

```
roslaunch seven_dof_arm_config demo.launch
```

Run the pick-and-place program by executing the following command:

```
rosrun seven_dof_arm_test pick_place
```

Here is a screenshot of the grasping process:

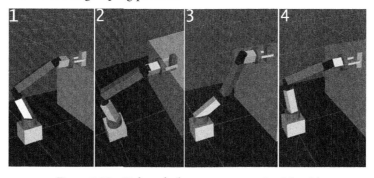

Figure 7.10 – Pick-and-place sequences using MoveIt!

The various steps in the grasping process are explained next:

- In the first step, we can see a green block, which is the object that is going to be grasped by the robot gripper. We have created this object inside the planning scene using the `pick_and_place` node. In the first part of the node, the end effector of the robot is approaching the object.

- After approaching the object, a valid trajectory to grasp the object is generated. After the grasping is completed, the green block will be attached to the robot's gripper and it will change its color to purple.

- After picking up the block, the robot will transport it to another place in the workspace, before placing it on the working table. If there is a valid IK in the place pose, the gripper holds the object in the planned trajectory.

- Finally, the object is placed on the table and detached from the robot's gripper.

Another way to perform the pick-and-place tasks is by using actions provided by MoveIt!. After launching MoveIt!, two action servers start, as detailed here:

- `pickup`: This action accepts a `moveit_msgs::PickupGoal` message in which we mainly must specify the target object to grasp, and a list of possible grasping configurations. These configurations are filled in a `moveit_msgs::Grasp` message in which we have to set the complete position of the joints of the robot during the approaching and grasping actions, and the position of the end effector during the picking.

- `place`: This action is used to place an object onto a surface. It accepts a `moveit_msgs::PlaceGoal` message to specify a list of possible objects, positioning the configuration.

Using MoveIt! actions assures the success of safe and complete pick-and-place tasks, but a lot of pre-planned information is required, making them difficult to use in advanced complex and dynamic robotic applications.

Pick-and-place actions in Gazebo and real robots

The grasping sequence executed in the MoveIt! demo uses fake controllers. We can send the trajectory to the actual robot or Gazebo. In Gazebo, we can launch the grasping world to perform this action.

In real hardware, the only difference is that we need to create joint-trajectory controllers for the arm. One of the commonly used hardware controllers is the **DYNAMIXEL controller**. We will learn more about DYNAMIXEL controllers in the next section.

Understanding DYNAMIXEL ROS servo controllers for robot hardware interfacing

Till now, we have learned about MoveIt! interfacing using Gazebo simulation. In this section, we will see how to replace Gazebo and put a real robot interface to MoveIt!. Let's discuss DYNAMIXEL servos and the ROS controllers.

DYNAMIXEL servos

DYNAMIXEL servos are smart, high-performance networked actuators for high-end robotics applications. These servos are manufactured by a Korean company called *ROBOTIS* (`http://en.robotis.com/`). These servos are very popular among robotics enthusiasts because they can provide excellent position and torque control, as well as a variety of feedback, such as position, speed, temperature, voltage, and so on. One of their useful features is that they can be networked in a daisy-chain manner. This feature is very useful in multi-joint systems, such as robotic arms, humanoid robots, robotic snakes, and others. The servos can be directly connected to PCs using a **Universal Serial Bus** (**USB**) to DYNAMIXEL controller, which is provided by ROBOTIS. This controller has a USB interface, and when it is plugged into the PC, it acts as a virtual **communication** (**COM**) port. We can send data to this port, and internally it will convert the *RS 232* protocol to **transistor-transistor logic** (**TTL**), and in *RS 485* standards. The DYNAMIXEL servo can be powered and then connected to the USB-to-DYNAMIXEL controller to start working with it. DYNAMIXEL servos support both TTL and *RS 485*-level standards. The following screenshot shows a DYNAMIXEL servo called **MX-106** and a **USB-to-DYNAMIXEL** controller:

DYNAMIXEL Servo   USB-to-DYNAMIXEL

Figure 7.11 – DYNAMIXEL servo and USB-to-DYNAMIXEL controller

There are different series of DYNAMIXEL servos available on the market. Some of the series are MX—28, 64, and 106; RX—28, 64, 106; and so on. The following diagram shows how to connect DYNAMIXEL motors to a PC using the USB port:

USB PORT

USB2DYNAMIXEL   Power line

Figure 7.12 – DYNAMIXEL servos connected to a PC using a USB-to-DYNAMIXEL controller

Multiple DYNAMIXEL devices can be connected in a sequence (or a daisy chain), as shown in the preceding figure. Each DYNAMIXEL has a firmware setting inside its controller. We can assign the ID of servos, the joint limits, the position limits, the position commands, the **Proportional Integral Derivative** (**PID**) values, the voltage limits, and so on inside the controller. There are ROS drivers and controllers for DYNAMIXEL, which are available at `http://wiki.ros.org/dynamixel_motor`.

DYNAMIXEL-ROS interface

The ROS stack for interfacing the DYNAMIXEL motor is named `dynamixel_motor`. This stack contains an interface for DYNAMIXEL motors, such as MX-28, MX64, MX-106, RX-28, RX64, EX106, AX-12, and AX-18. The stack consists of the following packages:

- `dynamixel_driver`: This package is the driver package of DYNAMIXEL, which can do low-level **input/output** (**I/O**) communication with DYNAMIXEL from the PC. This driver has a hardware interface for the previously mentioned series of servos and can do the read/write operations for DYNAMIXEL through this package. This package is used by high-level packages, such as `dynamixel_controllers`. There are only a few cases when the user directly interacts with this package.

- `dynamixel_controllers`: This is a higher-level package that works using the `dynamixel_motor` package. Using this package, we can create a ROS controller for each DYNAMIXEL joint of the robot. The package contains a configurable node, services, and spawner script to start, stop, and restart one or more controller plugins. In each controller, we can set the speed and the torque. Each DYNAMIXEL controller can be configured using the ROS parameters or can be loaded by a YAML file. The `dynamixel_controllers` package supports position, torque, and trajectory controllers.

- `dynamixel_msgs`: These are message definitions that are used inside the `dynamixel_motor` stack.

Dynamixel servo motors can be used to build real robotic arms with multiple **degrees of freedom (DOF)**, as discussed in the next section.

Interfacing a 7-DOF DYNAMIXEL-based robotic arm with ROS MoveIt!

In this section, we will discuss a 7-DOF robot manipulator called **COOL arm-5000**, which is manufactured by a company called *ASIMOV Robotics* (`http://asimovrobotics.com/`) and is shown in the following screenshot. The robot is built using DYNAMIXEL servos. We will see how to interface a DYNAMIXEL-based robotic arm to ROS using `dynamixel_controllers`:

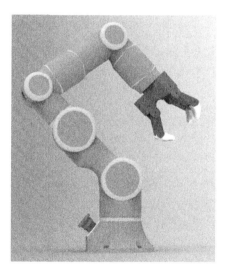

Figure 7.13 – COOL robotic arm

COOL arm robots are fully compatible with ROS and MoveIt! and are mainly used in education and research. Here are the details of the arms:

- **DOF**: 7 DOF

- **Types of actuators**: DYNAMIXEL MX-64 and MX-28

- **List of joints**: Shoulder roll, shoulder pitch, elbow roll, elbow pitch, wrist yaw, wrist pitch, and wrist roll

- **Payload**: 5 **kilograms (kg)**

- **Reach**: 1 **meter (m)**
- **Work volume**: 2.09 m³
- **Repeatability**: +/- 0.05 **millimeters (mm)**
- **Gripper** with three fingers

Creating a controller package for a COOL arm robot

The first step is to create a controller package for a COOL arm for interfacing with ROS. The COOL arm controller package is available for download along with the book code. Before we create the package, we should install the dynamixel_controllers package, as follows:

```
sudo apt-get install ros-kinetic-dynamixel-controllers
```

The following command will create a controller package with the necessary dependencies. The important dependency of this package is the dynamixel_controllers package:

```
catkin_create_pkg cool5000_controller roscpp rospy dynamixel_
controller std_msgs sensor_msgs
```

The next step is to create a configuration file for each joint. The configuration file is called cool5000.yaml and contains a definition of each controller's name, its type, and its parameters. We can see this file in the cool5000_controller/config folder. We have to create parameters for the seven joints in this arm. Here is a snippet of this configuration file:

```
joint1_controller:
    controller:
        package: dynamixel_controllers
        module: joint_position_controller
        type: JointPositionController
    joint_name: joint1
    joint_speed: 0.1
    motor:
        id: 0
        init: 2048
        min: 320
        max: 3823
joint2_controller:
```

```
controller:
    package: dynamixel_controllers
    module: joint_position_controller
    type: JointPositionController
joint_name: joint2
joint_speed: 0.1
motor:
    id: 1
    init: 2048
    min: 957
    max: 3106
```

The controller configuration file mentions the joint name, package of the controller, controller type, joint speed, motor ID, initial position, and minimum and maximum limits of the joint. We can connect as many motors as we want and can create controller parameters by including them in the configuration file. The next configuration file to create is a `joint_trajectory controller` configuration file. MoveIt! can only interface if the robot has the `FollowJointTrajectory` action server. The `cool5000_trajectory_controller.yaml` file is put in the `cool5000_controller/config` folder, and its definition is given in the following code snippet:

```
cool5000_trajectory_controller:
    controller:
        package: dynamixel_controllers
        module: joint_trajectory_action_controller
        type: JointTrajectoryActionController
    joint_trajectory_action_node:
        min_velocity: 0.0
        constraints:
            goal_time: 0.01
```

After creating the `JointTrajectory` controller, we need to create a `joint_state_aggregator` node for combining and publishing the joint states of the robotic arm. You can find this node, named `joint_state_aggregator.cpp`, from the `cool5000_controller/src` folder. The function of this node is to subscribe controller states of each controller with a message type of `dynamixel::JointState` and combine each message of the controller with the `sensor_msgs::JointState` messages and publish them in the `/joint_states` topic. This message will be the aggregate of the joint states of all the DYNAMIXEL controllers. The definition of `joint_state_aggregator.launch`, which runs the `joint_state_aggregator` node with its parameters, is shown in the following code snippet. It is placed in the `cool5000_controller/launch` folder:

```
<launch>
    <node name="joint_state_aggregator" pkg="cool5000_
controller" type="joint_state_aggregator" output="screen">
    <rosparam>
            rate: 50
        controllers:
                - joint1_controller
                - joint2_controller
                - joint3_controller
                - joint4_controller
                - joint5_controller
                - joint6_controller
                - joint7_controller
                - gripper_controller
        </rosparam>
    </node>
</launch>
```

We can launch the entire controller using the `cool5000_controller.launch` file, which is inside the `launch` folder. The code inside this launch file will start communication between the PC and the DYNAMIXEL servos and will also start the controller manager. The controller manager parameters are serial port, baud rate, servo ID range, and update rate. The code is illustrated in the following snippet:

```
<launch>

    <!-- Start the Dynamixel motor manager to control all
cool5000 servos -->

    <node name="dynamixel_manager" pkg="dynamixel_controllers"
type="controller_manager.py" required="true" output="screen">
        <rosparam>
            namespace: dxl_manager
            serial_ports:
                dynamixel_port:
                    port_name: "/dev/ttyUSB0"
                    baud_rate: 1000000
                    min_motor_id: 0
                    max_motor_id: 6
                    update_rate: 20
        </rosparam>
    </node>
```

In the next step, it should launch the controller spawner by reading the controller configuration file, as follows:

```
    <!-- Load joint controller configuration from YAML file
to parameter server -->
  <rosparam file="$(find cool5000_controller)/config/cool5000.
yaml" command="load"/>

    <!-- Start all  Cool Arm joint controllers -->
    <node name="controller_spawner" pkg="dynamixel_controllers"
type="controller_spawner.py"
        args="--manager=dxl_manager
            --port dynamixel_port
            joint1_controller
```

```
                        joint2_controller
                     joint3_controller
                     joint4_controller
                     joint5_controller
                     joint6_controller
              joint7_controller
                     gripper_controller"
           output="screen"/>
```

In the next section of the code, it will launch the `JointTrajectory` controller from the controller configuration file, as follows:

```
    <!-- Start the cool5000 arm trajectory controller -->
      <rosparam file="$(find cool5000_controller)/config/
cool5000_trajectory_controller.yaml" command="load"/>
      <node name="controller_spawner_meta" pkg="dynamixel_
controllers" type="controller_spawner.py"
      args="--manager=dxl_manager
           --type=meta
           cool5000_trajectory_controller
           joint1_controller
           joint2_controller
           joint3_controller
           joint4_controller
           joint5_controller
           joint6_controller"
           output="screen"/>
```

The following section will launch the `joint_state_aggregator` node and the robot description from the `cool5000_description` package, as follows:

```
    <!-- Publish combined joint info -->
    <include file="$(find cool5000_controller)/launch/joint_
state_aggregator.launch" />

    <param name="robot_description" command="$(find xacro)/xacro.
py '$(find cool5000_description)/robots/cool5000.xacro'" />
    <node name="joint_state_publisher" pkg="joint_state_
publisher" type="joint_state_publisher" output="screen">
```

```
    <rosparam param="source_list">[joint_states]</rosparam>
    <rosparam param="use_gui">FALSE</rosparam>
  </node>
```

That's it for the COOL arm controller package. Next, we need to set up the `cool5000_moveit_config` controller configuration inside the MoveIt! configuration package of the COOL arm.

MoveIt! configuration of the COOL arm

The first step is to configure the `controllers.yaml` file, which is inside the `cool5000_moveit_config/config` folder. The definition of this file is shown in the following code snippet. For now, we are only focusing on moving the arm, and not on handling the gripper control. So, the configuration only contains the `arm` group joints:

```
controller_list:
  - name: cool5000_trajectory_controller
    action_ns: follow_joint_trajectory
    type: FollowJointTrajectory
    default: true
    joints:
      - joint1
      - joint2
      - joint3
      - joint4
      - joint5
      - joint6
      - joint7
```

Here is the definition of the `cool5000_description_moveit_controller_manager.launch.xml` file inside `cool5000_moveit_config/launch`:

```
<launch>
<!--
  Set the param that trajectory_execution_manager needs to find
the controller plugin
-->
<arg name="moveit_controller_manager" default="MoveIt_simple_controller_manager/MoveItSimpleControllerManager"/>
```

```
<param name="MoveIt_controller_manager" value="$(arg MoveIt_
controller_manager)"/>
```

```
<!-- load controller_list -->
```

```
<rosparam file="$(find cool5000_moveit_config)/config/
controllers.yaml"/>
</launch>
```

After configuring MoveIt!, we can start working on the arm. Apply a proper power supply to the arm and connect it to your PC or to the USB of the DYNAMIXEL servo. We will see a serial device generated; this may be either /dev/ttyUSB0, or /dev/ttyACM0. According to the device, change the port name inside the controller launch file.

Start the cool5000 arm controller using the following command:

```
roslaunch cool5000_controller cool5000_controller.launch
```

Start the RViz demo and start path planning. If we press the **Execute** button, the trajectory will execute on the hardware arm, as follows:

```
roslaunch cool5000_moveit_config 5k.launch
```

A random pose (which is shown in RViz) and the COOL arm is shown in the following screenshot:

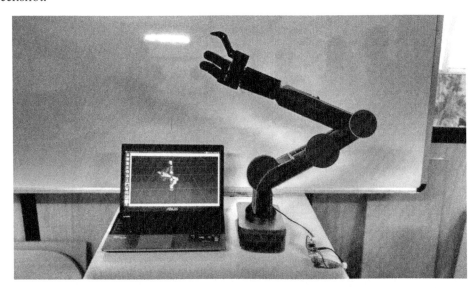

Figure 7.14 – COOL-Arm-5000 prototype with MoveIt! visualization

To summarize, MoveIt! represents a fundamental tool to solve robotic manipulation tasks, in the case of both research and industrial applications. In particular, MoveIt! can be easily integrated with real hardware from companies such as Kuka, ABB, or Universal Robot, as discussed in *Chapter 15, ROS for Industrial Robots*.

Summary

In this chapter, we explored some advanced features of MoveIt!, showing how to write C++ code to control simulated and real robotic manipulators. The chapter started with a discussion on collision checking using MoveIt!. We saw how to add a collision object using MoveIt! APIs, and saw the direct importing of mesh to the planning scene. We discussed a ROS node to check collision using MoveIt! APIs. After learning about collisions, we moved to perception using MoveIt!. We connected the simulated point-cloud data to MoveIt! and created an octomap in MoveIt!. After discussing these aspects, we switched to hardware interfacing of MoveIt! using DYNAMIXEL servos and its ROS controllers. In the end, we saw a real robotic arm called COOL arm and its interfacing to MoveIt!, which was completely built using DYNAMIXEL controllers. In the next chapter, we will discuss another kind of robotic platform, aerial robots, and how to integrate and program them using ROS.

Here are few questions based on what we covered in this chapter.

Questions

1. What is the role of the FCL library in MoveIt!?
2. How does MoveIt! build an octomap of the environment?
3. How could a robot avoid obstacles after grasping an object?
4. What are the main features of DYNAMIXEL servos?

8
ROS for Aerial Robots

In previous chapters, we have considered only ground-based and industrial robots. In the last decade, a new kind of system has become very popular – flying robots, also known as **Unmanned Aerial Vehicles** (**UAVs**). Nowadays, UAVs are constructed in different shapes and dimensions. In the main, they can be divided into fixed-wing (these being airplane-like vehicles) and rotary-wing (these being vehicles with multiple vertical axis rotors). Modern UAVs are equipped with onboard computers and sensors that make them real autonomous robots, able to perform different tasks, such as autonomous navigation. Using ROS makes it possible to read a UAV's sensors and send commands to the aerial platform. In addition to the real-life devices, it is also possible to use Gazebo to simulate the hardware and the sensors of different kinds of aerial systems.

This chapter is divided into two sections. First, we will discuss the basic components of aerial robots and one of the most common autopilots: the Pixhawk board. We will also learn how we can interact with it using ROS and the Px4 flight control stack. In the second part of the chapter, we will focus on the simulation of the rotors of a UAV, modeling the dynamics of the robot and its propellers.

In this chapter, we will cover the following topics:

- Using aerial robots
- Using the Px4 flight control stack
- PC/autopilot communication
- Writing a ROS-Px4 application
- Using the RotorS simulation framework

Technical requirements

To follow along with this chapter, you will need a standard laptop running Ubuntu 20.04 with ROS Noetic installed. The reference code for this chapter can be downloaded from the following Git repository: `https://github.com/PacktPublishing/Mastering-ROS-for-Robotics-Programming-Third-edition.git`. The code is contained inside the `Chapter8/px4_ros_ctrl` and `Chapter8/iris_model` folders.

You can view this chapter's code in action here: `https://bit.ly/3svXX9L`.

Using aerial robots

At present, flying vehicles are very popular. Even in their primary configuration where they are controlled by a *radio controller*, some flying vehicles can be considered as robots that respond to their environment in order to stay in the air. Such vehicles can use external sensors to estimate their state and pose, thus allowing them to fly autonomously. Of course, providing a flying robot with autonomy is more complicated than doing the same for a ground robot because of several reasons, listed here:

- **Stabilization**: A flying robot must be able to adjust its pose to hold its position and orientation relative to the environment. Inertial sensors are not enough to accomplish this task, since they are not able to estimate position divergence caused by external disturbances (like wind or *ground airflow*), or the possible errors generated due to an *inertial measurement unit* sensor.

- **Low computation resources**: Compared to a ground robot, flight platforms have payload problems. For this reason, only small and light hardware must be used. Therefore, small companion computers must be used.

- **Debugging problems**: During the development of *sensor fusion* and control strategies, debugging is not an easy task. Problems related to wrong reference frames or control gain can cause the aerial platform to fall. This can cause damage to the robot and nearby people.

- **Communication with a ground station**: Communication between the UAV *companion PC* and a ground station typically relies on low power and slow communication protocols in order to cope with the distance between the robot and the ground PC.

Another problem with these robots is that the *controller* of the robot is implemented on an integrated embedded board. This is called the autopilot and, in some cases, the motion performance of the robots strictly depends on the autopilot. Over the next few sections, we will discuss the basic UAV hardware sensors and their respective autopilot functions. Then, we will learn how to simulate a real flying robot by interfacing it with ROS.

UAV hardware

The core of a UAV is the autopilot. This is responsible for the onboard sensors' initialization and interfacing. Additionally, it is the *autopilot* that receives the input to properly control the actuators of the UAV (its propellers). Different platform configurations exist for UAVs. The most common one is the *quadrotor*. This has four motors and can be actuated with a cross (X) or plus (+) configuration. Also, in their coaxial versions, *quadrotors* have two lines of motors. Every axis of the quadrotor has two motors and propellors installed coaxially, giving it eight in total. The same is true for *hexacopters* and *octocopters*. However, control strategies do not directly depend on the airframe configuration, because the *autopilot* directly translates the control data into motor input.

The main sensor of the autopilot is the **Inertial Measurement Unit (IMU)**. This module is used to calculate the attitude, altitude, and direction of flight. It typically includes the following:

- A **gyroscope** that determines the attitude of the craft, including its pitch and roll. This indicates the rotational motion of the craft.

- An **accelerometer** that determines the rate of change of velocity of the craft with respect to the three axes.

- An **altimeter** or barometer that determines the altitude of the craft above ground. At low altitudes, a down-looking sonar sensor may be used to determine altitudes of up to several meters.

- A **magnetometer** serves as a compass to indicate the craft's direction by using the Earth's magnetic field as a reference.

The inertial sensor combines these sensors to measure and display the complete information relating to the flight characteristics of the quadrotor. Typically, this unit will measure the acceleration and orientation of the flying craft in all three dimensions. These sensors allow indoor and outdoor flight. However, they suffer from slight errors that may accumulate during flight. Another important sensor for any UAV is the **Global Positioning System** (**GPS**). This sensor allows the robot to estimate the *global position* of itself in terms of latitude and longitude, permitting the robot to stabilize its position. However, this sensor can only be used outdoors. For this reason, other techniques based on vision or **LiDAR** sensors must be used in indoor environments. Now that we have examined the basic elements of an *autopilot*, let's discuss one of the most common open source autopilots used on aerial robots – the Pixhawk autopilot.

Pixhawk autopilot

Among the different open source autopilots that exist on the market, the **Pixhawk** autopilot has proven to be a very popular board. It has been released in multiple different versions and with multiple different hardware capabilities. One such board is shown in the following figure, along with its digital input/output signals:

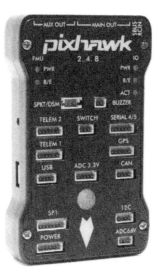

Figure 8.1 – Pixhawk v1 autopilot board

This board has multiple input and output connectors for interfacing with external sensors or connecting the autopilot to the companion PC, using **USB-serial** communication.

This board can be programmed from scratch, exactly like an **Arduino** board. Additionally, the autopilot controller code is open source and can be modified to apply changes and custom behavior to the UAV. Two main control stacks are suitable for this autopilot:

- **ArduCopter**: `https://ardupilot.org/`
- **PX4**: `https://px4.io/`

There is not a big difference in terms of performance between these two software stacks. The main differences lie in the license and the community supporting the development of the control code. Each supports a different set of vehicles (also ground and underwater vehicles) with different airframes.

In this chapter, we mainly consider the PX4 control stack. PX4 consists of two main layers:

- The **flight stack**: This is the implementation of the flight control system.
- The **middleware**: This is a general layer that can support any type of autonomous robot, providing internal/external communications and hardware integration.

The PX4 control stack supports different *airframes*, and all share the same code. The flight stack is a collection of *guidance*, *navigation*, and *control algorithms* for autonomous vehicles. It includes controllers for fixed-wing, multirotor, and **Vertical TakeOff and Landing** (**VTOL**) airframes, as well as estimators for attitude and position. Note that, even if we do not have the real aerial platform and the autopilot, we can modify, compile, and run the code installed on the autopilot by connecting it to the ROS Gazebo simulator.

In the next section, we will install the PX4 flight stack in our system and then discuss how to simulate and program the autopilot code on our laptop. However, while we will discuss a brief overview of the firmware control code, we will not attempt any modification to the autopilot source code.

Using the PX4 flight control stack

PX4 firmware allows developers to directly simulate the code running on the autopilot board on your Linux system. Additionally, it is possible to modify the autopilot source code and reload the new version on the Pixhawk board. To install the firmware on your system, you will firstly need to download it. Even though it is not mandatory, linking this with the ROS will conveniently place it in your ROS workspace. To download the autopilot code, enter your ROS workspace and use the following command:

```
git clone https://github.com/PX4/PX4-Autopilot.git --recursive
```

This repository contains all the necessary files to run the PX4 firmware on a ROS-Gazebo simulation, using different UAV quadrotors equipped with a camera, a depth camera, a laser scanner, and so on. Simulation represents a quick, easy, and *safe* way to test changes to PX4 code before attempting to fly in the real world. It is also a good way to start flying with PX4 when you have not yet got a vehicle to experiment with.

Note that we used the `--recursive` option in the `clone` command to download all the submodules included in the main repository. This means that some parts of the autopilot source code are stored in other, external repositories that are linked by the main one. The `clone` command may take several minutes. Note that, after the `clone` command is completed, a new directory called `PX4-Autopilot` has been created. This folder contains all the files necessary to modify and upload the firmware on the embedded controller (the autopilot) and to simulate source code on different simulators. To link all the necessary elements, the firmware directory is recognized as a ROS package, even though it is not compiled as such. In addition, the name of this package is px4. Note that the name of the directory doesn't necessarily represent the name of the ROS package. So, after you have cloned this directory into your ROS workspace, you can join the firmware folder with the following command:

```
roscd px4
```

You are now ready to compile this package and start the simulation. Before doing this, you need to install the following set of dependencies:

```
sudo apt install python3-pip
pip3 install --user empy
pip3 install --user toml
pip3 install --user numpy
pip3 install --user packaging
sudo apt-get install libgstreamer-plugins-base1.0-dev
pip3 install --user jinja2
```

To allow ROS/**Flight Control Unit** (**FCU**) communication, you should install the `mavros` package:

```
sudo apt-get install ros-noeitc-mavros ros-noeitc-mavros-msgs
```

Now you can install the geographic dataset:

```
sudo /opt/ros/noetic/lib/mavros/install_geographiclib_datasets.
sh
```

Finally, you can run the following command to compile it:

```
roscd px4 && make px4_sitl_default
```

In this case, we used the `make` command with a specific target. This is the **Software in the Loop** (**SITL**) target. This allows us to simulate the firmware source code. As already stated, a simulator allows the PX4 flight code to control a computer-modeled vehicle in a simulated world. After we have launched the simulation, we can interact with this vehicle just as we might with a real vehicle, using ground station software such as **QGroundControl**, an offboard API, or a radio controller gamepad. Different simulators are supported. The complete list can be found at the following link: `https://docs.px4.io/master/en/simulation/`. However, we will use Gazebo. To launch the PX4 control code with Gazebo, run the following command from the root directory of the firmware source:

```
make px4_sitl_default gazebo
```

This command will start a new Gazebo scene with a 3DR IRIS quadrotor, as shown in the following figure:

Figure 8.2 – 3DR IRIS quadrotor simulated in Gazebo with the PX4 control stack

Note that this is the standalone version of Gazebo, so there is no link with the ROS yet. You can also choose other targets to be compiled. For example, to compile the firmware for the real Pixhawk, you can use the following command:

```
make px4_fmu-v2_default
```

You can interact with the simulator in different ways. The simplest method is by using a ground control station program such as **QGroundControl**. Using this software, you can take off and land your simulated UAV, and move it around the environment. Using this interface, you can also set some parameters to configure the behavior of the autopilot and tune the controller gains.

The following commands must be used to start QGroundControl:

```
sudo usermod -a -G dialout $USER
sudo apt-get remove modemmanager -y
sudo apt install gstreamer1.0-plugins-bad gstreamer1.0-libav
gstreamer1.0-gl -y
```

Now download the QGroundControl app, as follows:

```
wget https://s3-us-west-2.amazonaws.com/qgroundcontrol/latest/
QGroundControl.AppImage
chmod +x QGroundControl.AppImage
```

Finally, start the PX4 simulation (as seen previously) and launch the QGroundControl software:

```
./QGroundControl.AppImage
```

The user interface will be displayed, as depicted in the following figure:

Figure 8.3 – QGroundControl user interface

Note that you will use the same method if you start up a real autopilot connected (wired or wireless) to your laptop. Before we proceed with connecting the PX4 control stack to ROS, we will briefly discuss the PX4 software architecture.

PX4 firmware architecture

Even though we will not modify the default firmware of the PX4 control stack, it is important to understand how it is organized. The whole system architecture is depicted in the following figure:

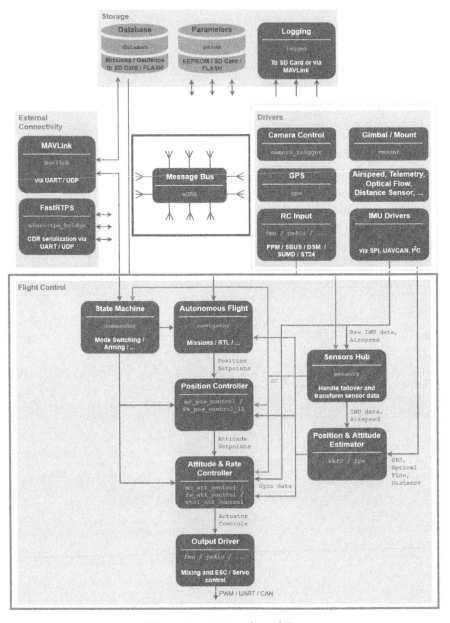

Figure 8.4 – PX4 stack modules

The source code of the controller is split into self-contained modules/programs (shown in monospace in *Figure 8.4*). Each building block corresponds to exactly one module. The modules can be found in the source folder of the firmware's main directory. Like ROS, PX4 software modules communicate with each other through a publish/subscribe message bus named uORB. The use of the publish/subscribe protocol means the following:

- The system is reactive – it is asynchronous and will update instantly when new data is available. All operations and communication are fully parallelized.

- A system component can consume data from anywhere in a thread-safe fashion. The flight stack is a collection of guidance, navigation, and control algorithms for autonomous drones. It includes controllers for fixed-wing, multirotor, and UAV airframes, as well as estimators for attitude and position.

In particular, the main modules of the PX4 software architecture are as follows:

- An **estimator**: This takes one or more sensor inputs, combines them, and computes a vehicle state (for example, the attitude from *IMU* sensor data).

- A **controller**: This is a component that takes a *setpoint* and measurement, or estimated state (process variable), as input. Its goal is to adjust the value of the process variable so that it matches the *setpoint*. The output is a correction to eventually reach that setpoint. For example, the position controller takes position setpoints as inputs, the process variable is the current estimated position, and the output takes the form of an *attitude* and *thrust setpoint* that moves the vehicle toward the desired position.

- A **mixer**: This takes motion commands (such as *turn right*) and translates them into individual motor commands while ensuring that some limits are not exceeded. This translation is specific for a vehicle type and depends on various factors, such as the motor arrangements with respect to the center of gravity, or the vehicle's rotational inertia.

As already stated, all the module source codes are placed in the PX4-Autopilot/ src folder. Conversely, everything related to the ROS and Gazebo is confined to the PX4-Autopilot/Tools/sitl_gazebo folder. We are now ready to link the PX4 control stack with ROS.

PX4 SITL

The px4 package already contains useful sources and launch files that can be used to simulate a UAV in the Gazebo ROS framework. The integration of Gazebo ROS with the PX4 control stack is possible thanks to a communication protocol used by a huge number of aerial vehicles. This communication protocol is called mavlink. In this context, the communication between the simulation and the control software is shown in the following figure:

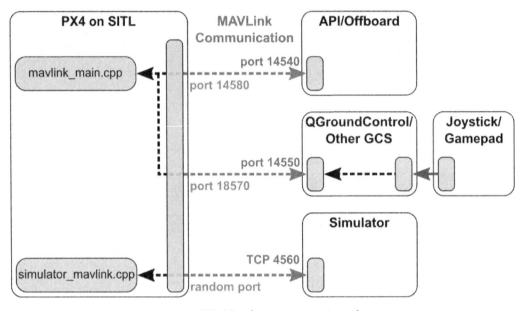

Figure 8.5 – PX4/Gazebo communication schema

The control stack communicates with the simulation scene to receive the sensor data while sending the actuator values to the simulated robot. At the same time, it sends onboard information (UAV attitude, position, GPS, and so on) to an **offboard** program or a **ground control station**. Before providing more information on the communication protocol, let's now try to start a simulation embedded into the ROS framework. As before, we will use the SITL tool from the PX4 firmware stack. After compiling the stack in the previous section, we now just need to load a configuration file and then start a launch file. The package already contains all the configuration and launch files needed to start ROS and the communication bridge with the PX4 controller. Before discussing what is going on behind the scenes, let's start by loading the configuration files. First, navigate to the px4 directory:

```
roscd px4
```

Then, load the configuration files:

```
source Tools/setup_gazebo.bash $(pwd) $(pwd)/build/px4_sitl_
default
export ROS_PACKAGE_PATH=$ROS_PACKAGE_PATH:$(pwd)
export ROS_PACKAGE_PATH=$ROS_PACKAGE_PATH:$(pwd)/Tools/sitl_
gazebo
```

It would be convenient to add these lines to your `.bashrc` file. Now, launch the simulation:

```
roslaunch px4 mavros_posix_sitl.launch
```

Nothing is changed with respect to the previous execution. A set of ROS topics and services are now available. These can get information from the drone and control its actions. You can use the `rostopic list` command to see all the topics. For example, if you are interested in the attitude of the UAV, you can view the `/mavros/imu/data` topic. But what is `mavros`? **mavros** establishes the communication between ROS and the PX4 software. In the next section, we will discuss this communication bridge.

PC/autopilot communication

To send and receive information from the aerial platform (simulated or real), we can use the following two modes:

- **Ground station**: High-level software that can be connected to the autopilot to send commands such as take off and land or relay waypoint navigation information.

- **API**: Programming an API allows developers to manage the behavior of the robot.

In both cases, the communication is managed by the MAVLink protocol. **Micro Air Vehicle Link (MAVLink)**and is a protocol for communicating with small, unmanned vehicles. It is designed as a header-only message-marshaling library. It is used mostly for communication between a **Ground Control Station (GCS)** and unmanned vehicles, and in the intercommunication of the subsystem of the vehicle. A packet *datagram* example is shown in the following figure:

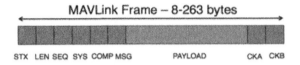

Byte Index	Content	Value	Explanation
0	Packet start sign	v1.0: 0xFE (v0.9: 0x55)	Indicates the start of a new packet.
1	Payload length	0 - 255	Indicates length of the following payload.
2	Packet sequence	0 - 255	Each component counts up his send sequence. Allows to detect packet loss
3	System ID	1 - 255	ID of the SENDING system. Allows to differentiate different MAVs on the same network.
4	Component ID	0 - 255	ID of the SENDING component. Allows to differentiate different components of the same system, e.g. the IMU and the autopilot.
5	Message ID	0 - 255	ID of the message - the id defines what the payload "means" and how it should be correctly decoded.
6 to (n+6)	Data	(0 - 255) bytes	Data of the message, depends on the message id.
(n+7) to (n+8)	Checksum (low byte, high byte)	ITU X.25/SAE AS-4 hash, **excluding packet start sign, so bytes 1..(n+6)** Note: The checksum also includes MAVLINK_CRC_EXTRA (Number computed from message fields. Protects the packet from decoding a different version of the same packet but with different variables).

Figure 8.6 – MAVLink protocol

Messages are no more than 263 bytes. The sender always fills in the `System ID` and `Component ID` fields so that the receiver knows where the packet came from. The system ID is a unique ID for each vehicle or ground station. Ground stations normally use a high system ID such as `255`, while vehicles default to using `1`. The component ID for the ground station or flight controller is normally `1`. The `Message ID` field can be seen in `common.xml` and `ardupilot.xml`, next to the message name. For example, the *HEARTBEAT* message ID is `0`. Finally, the data portion of the message holds the individual field values that are being sent. Currently, the latest version of MAVLink is 2.0 and this is compatible with the first version of the protocol. This means that if a device understands MAVLink2 messages, then it certainly understands MAVLink1 messages. As for the transport protocol, MAVLink is based on serial communication. Therefore, messages from the board can be read implementing a classical serial communication based on **User Datagram Protocol (UDP)**.

To summarize, MAVLink provides the standard communication protocol to get data from UAVs and send commands to them. Like many other control stacks, PX4 uses the MAVLink communication framework for interfacing with a **Ground Control Station (GCS)** or an onboard PC. Examples of MAVLink messages generated by the UAV include the following:

- **Global position**: The output of the fixed GPS of the UAV
- **Local position**: The Cartesian position of the UAV, generated via the *global position* and other local sensors
- **Attitude**: Information about the attitude of the UAV

As for the commands accepted by the UAV, there are the following:

- **Take off**: To take off in a specified *global position* and at a certain altitude.
- **Setpoint**: A position to reach. Such a position can be specified in different ways: local, global, position, and velocity setpoints are acceptable.
- **Flight mode**: The desired flight mode. The flight mode determines the way in which the robot responds to user input and controls vehicle movement.

The different modes can include position control, attitude control, and `OFFBOARD` mode. When using `OFFBOARD` mode, the vehicle obeys a position, velocity, or attitude setpoint provided over MAVLink. In this context, the setpoint may be provided by a companion computer (usually connected via a serial cable or Wi-Fi). As usual, we do not need to implement the MAVLink protocol from scratch. We can use a wrapper of this library made in ROS, called `mavros`.

The mavros ROS package

To develop the MAVLink protocol from scratch using MAVLink libraries is not required. Instead, we can rely on the ROS wrapper called `mavros`. This package provides a communication driver for various autopilots, based on the MAVLink communication protocol. It also provides a UDP MAVLink bridge for control stations or companion PCs. `mavros` is an extensible package – the main node can be extended by plugins. To install `mavros`, use the following command:

```
sudo apt-get install ros-noetic-mavros ros-noetic-mavros-msgs
ros-noetic-mavros-extras
```

As you can see, we also installed some extra packages from `mavros`. This package provides additional nodes and plugins not included in `mavros`. It can be executed with a set of launch and configuration files. Let's try to configure `mavros` for the PX4 control stack. We have different parameters to configure how `mavros` runs, as follows:

- `fcu_url`: This defines the address point of the serial communication. This can be defined as a local network connection or as the address of the serial communication device. For example, for a real board connected via USB to our PC, it will be something like `/dev/ttyACM0:57600`. In this context, the physical device address is `/dev/ttyACM0`, while the communication UDP port is `57600`.

- `pluginlists_yaml`: This is the `yaml` configuration file that defines the list of plugins to start with `mavros`. Each plugin publishes and listens to a particular topic or service.

- `config_yaml`: The configuration of each plugin started with the `mavros` node. Examples of these files are installed in your system as part of the `apt` package installation.

We are now ready to create our first ROS package to control the motion of a simulated UAV.

Writing a ROS-PX4 application

Let's now create a new package in which we will store all the source and launch files needed to send and receive data from the simulated UAV using ROS. Enter your ROS source workspace and use the following command:

```
catkin_create_project px4_ros_ctrl roscpp mavros_msgs
geometry_msgs
```

As you can see, this package depends from the `mavros_msgs`. This will be used to retrieve data from the UAV. Here, we will discuss the ROS node that controls the vehicle. The complete code can be found in the book source code and it is contained into the `src/px4_ctrl_example.cpp` source file.

To achieve our goal, we need to perform the following operations:

1. Arm the quadrotor. Arming the vehicle allows the motors to start spinning. This can be done using `mavros` through ROS services. The `/mavros/cmd/arming` service can be used.

2. Switch to `OFFBOARD` mode. After that, the motors should start to spin and we can send input to the UAV. To accept external commands, you must enable `OFFBOARD` mode. Even in this case, we can use a ROS service: `/mavros/set_mode`.

3. Send the desired position. We can require the UAV to reach a new position just publishing on the `/mavros/setpoint_position/local` topic.

4. Land. We can use `/mavros/cmd/land` to have the UAV land.

Let's inspect the code. As usual, we start by including the header files. Along with the common ROS header files, we include a set of the header files to use `mavros` messages:

```
#include "ros/ros.h"
#include "geometry_msgs/PoseStamped.h"
```

We use the `State` message to get information on the autopilot state, the `CommandBool` and `CommandTOL` messages to require actions of the robot, and the `SetMode` command to change the operating mode of the UAV (for example, external control, position control mode, and so on):

```
#include "mavros_msgs/State.h"
#include "mavros_msgs/CommandBool.h"
#include "mavros_msgs/SetMode.h"
#include "mavros_msgs/CommandTOL.h"
```

Then, we declare the mavros_msgs::State data used to store information about that state of the UAV, provided by the autopilot. This message contains different information. For example, if the autopilot is properly connected and armed (the vehicle is fully powered and its motors may be turning).

```
mavros_msgs::State mav_state;
```

Finally, we declare the callback for this message.

```
void mavros_state_cb( mavros_msgs::State mstate) {
```

```
    mav_state = mstate;
}
int main(int argc, char** argv ) {
    ros::init(argc, argv, "px4_ctrl_example");
    ros::NodeHandle nh;
```

We will use a ROS service that accepts a `CommandBool` message type. The service name is `/mavros/cmd/arming`. Similarly, we can change the operation mode and require the UAV to land using the `/mavros/set_mode` and `/mavros/cmd/land` services:

```
    ros::ServiceClient arming_client =
nh.serviceClient<mavros_msgs::CommandBool>("mavros/cmd/
arming");
    ros::ServiceClient set_mode_client =
nh.serviceClient<mavros_msgs::SetMode>("mavros/set_mode");
    ros::ServiceClient land_client =
nh.serviceClient<mavros_msgs::CommandTOL>("/mavros/cmd/land");
Then, we subscribe to the state message and publish the
position command using the /mavros/state and /mavros/setpoint_
position/local topics.
    ros::Subscriber mavros_state_sub =        nh.subscribe( "/
mavros/state", 1, mavros_state_cb);
    ros::Publisher         local_pos_pub =
nh.advertise<geometry_msgs::PoseStamped>("mavros/setpoint_
position/local", 1);
```

We are ready to change the operation mode of the robot. To send control data from an external computer, `OFFBOARD` mode must be selected. For this reason, we use the `custom_mode` field of the `SetMode` message, filling it with the `"OFFBOARD"` string. Then, we call the client, as follows:

```
    mavros_msgs::SetMode offb_set_mode;
    offb_set_mode.request.custom_mode = "OFFBOARD";
    if( set_mode_client.call(offb_set_mode) && offb_set_mode.
response.mode_sent){
        ROS_INFO("Manual mode enabled");
    }
```

Now, we are ready to arm the system. In this case, we set the value field of the
CommandBool message to true (to disarm, set the value to false):

```
mavros_msgs::CommandBool arm_cmd;
arm_cmd.request.value = true;
if( arming_client.call(arm_cmd) && arm_cmd.response.success){
    ROS_INFO("Ready to be armed");
}
```

Then, we wait until the system is correctly armed before continuing:

```
while(!mav_state.armed ) {
    usleep(0.1*1e6);
ros::spinOnce();
}
ROS_INFO("Vehicle armed");
```

We set the desired position to reach using geometry_msgs::PoseStamped:

```
geometry_msgs::PoseStamped pose;
pose.pose.position.x = 1;
pose.pose.position.y = 0;
pose.pose.position.z = 2;
```

In the main loop of this program, we simply send the desired point, then wait for
20 seconds until the UAV reaches the point. Note that the autopilot requires that, in
OFFBOARD mode, the desired control input is continuously streamed. Otherwise, a
watchdog implemented on the autopilot will enable the **Return-to-Land** (**RTL**) safety
control mode:

```
ros::Rate r(10);
float t = 0.0;
while( ros::ok() && (t < 20.0) ) {
    local_pos_pub.publish(pose);
    t += (1.0/10.0);
    r.sleep();
    ros::spinOnce();
}
```

Finally, we use the land service to bring the UAV back to the ground:

```
mavros_msgs::CommandTOL land_srv;
land_client.call( land_srv );
return 0;
}
```

We are now ready to launch this node. First, we must start the Gazebo simulation and the `mavros` node. We can start the controller node.

To launch the simulator, you can use the `px4_ros.launch` file included in the `px4_ros_ctrl` package. Part of this file will be discussed shortly. We start by initializing some parameters, such as the position of the robot in the simulation scene:

```
<launch>
        <arg name="x" default="0"/>
        <arg name="y" default="0"/>
        <arg name="z" default="0"/>
        <arg name="R" default="0"/>
        <arg name="P" default="0"/>
        <arg name="Y" default="0"/>
```

Other parameters are closely related to the PX4 control stack. In particular, the attitude and pose estimation algorithm used by the autopilot and the robot model must be specified. By default, the extended Kalman filter (`ekf`) is selected, while the vehicle represents the robot model. The PX4 contains several models of multirotors and is stored in the `PX4-Autopilot/Tools/sitl_gazebo/models/` folder in the form of `.sdf` files:

```
<arg name="est" default="ekf2"/>
        <arg name="vehicle" default="iris"/>
        <arg name="sdf" default="$(find mavlink_sitl_gazebo)/
models/$(arg vehicle)/$(arg vehicle).sdf"/>
```

The vehicle and the estimator declared as ROS arguments are also used to set the following variable environments:

```
        <env name="PX4_SIM_MODEL" value="$(arg vehicle)" />
        <env name="PX4_ESTIMATOR" value="$(arg est)" />
```

Then, the Gazebo ROS parameters are set:

```
<arg name="gui" default="true"/>
<arg name="debug" default="false"/>
<arg name="verbose" default="false"/>
<arg name="paused" default="false"/>
<arg name="respawn_gazebo" default="false"/>
```

We can choose whether or not to start the node in interactive mode. In the former case, we can use an interactive sheet to send a command to the autopilot, such as to take off, land, or reboot the autopilot code:

```
<arg name="interactive" default="true"/>
    <arg unless="$(arg interactive)" name="px4_command_arg1"
value="-d"/>
    <arg         if="$(arg interactive)" name="px4_command_
arg1" value=""/>
```

Finally, we are ready to start the SITL node of the px4 package. This node is responsible for simulating the real functionalities of the PX4 control stack, such as the state estimation, the motion actions (such as takeoff or waypoint navigation), and all the safety layers. If we don't start this node, we will only simulate a multirotor:

```
<node name="sitl" pkg="px4" type="px4" output="screen"
    args="$(find px4)/build/px4_sitl_default/etc -s etc/init.d-
posix/rcS $(arg px4_command_arg1)" required="true"/>
```

Then, the model is spawned in the simulation scene:

```
<node name="$(anon vehicle_spawn)" pkg="gazebo_ros"
type="spawn_model" output="screen" args="-sdf -file $(arg sdf)
-model $(arg vehicle) -x $(arg x) -y $(arg y) -z $(arg z) -R
$(arg R) -P $(arg P) -Y $(arg Y)"/>
```

Finally, we need to start `mavros` in order to exchange data with the aerial platform. `mavros` is launched with a set of launch and configuration files. For this reason, we include the `px4.launch` file of the same ROS package. The contents of this file will be discussed later. It is important to define the `fcu_url` element – the address of the **flight control unit**. In this case, we refer to the IP and port of the computer where the simulation is running:

```
<arg name="fcu_url" default="udp://:14540@localhost:14557"/>
<arg name="respawn_mavros" default="false"/>


        <include file="$(find px4_ros_ctrl)/launch/px4.launch">
            <arg name="fcu_url" value="$(arg fcu_url)"/>
        </include>
```

The content of the `px4.launch` file is reported in the following. Here we launch the `mavros` node, including two YAML configuration files, as follows:

- The `pluginlists_yaml` configuration file specifies which `mavros` plugin must be loaded through the definition of a whitelist and a blacklist.
- The `config_yaml` configuration file allows you to configure the loaded plugin.

In this example, we will use the default configuration file:

```
<include file="$(find mavros)/launch/node.launch">
        <arg name="pluginlists_yaml" value="$(find mavros)/
launch/px4_pluginlists.yaml" />
        <arg name="config_yaml" value="$(find mavros)/launch/
px4_config.yaml" />
 </include>
```

In this example, we used the default configuration file.

After seen the content of the launch file, we can start the `px4` control node using the following commands:

```
roslaunch px4_ros_ctrl px4_ros.launch
rosrun px4_ros_ctrl px4_ctrl_example
```

Typically, robots are commanded using a continuous stream of positions that precisely pilot the robot under certain velocity or acceleration constraints. This is the principle of trajectory planning. In the next sections, we will discuss how to send a trajectory to the robot autopilot.

Writing a trajectory streamer

In the previous example, we published a point to reach, and the UAV attempted to reach it using its maximum acceleration and velocity. However, we may want to stream a trajectory so as to better control the velocity profile of the robot's motion. In that case, we would need to use the `mavros_msgs::PositionTarget` message instead of the simple `geometry_msgs::PoseStamped` message. Using `PositionTarget`, we can specify both the position and velocity of the UAV. The definition of this message is as follows.

The first field is the header:

```
std_msgs/Header header
```

Now we can choose the coordinate frame. The coordinate frame is defined by a set of constants already provided by the message definition. We will discuss the reference frame in the next section of this chapter. Note that only FRAME_LOCAL_NED and FRAME_BODY_NED are supported:

```
uint8 coordinate_frame
uint8 FRAME_LOCAL_NED = 1
uint8 FRAME_LOCAL_OFFSET_NED = 7
uint8 FRAME_BODY_NED = 8
uint8 FRAME_BODY_OFFSET_NED = 9
```

Now, we can set a bit mask that will help us to define a few elements of the control message. For example, we might decide to stream only the velocity, or the position, of the UAV. We can also set it to ignore the rotation around the z axis:

```
uint16 type_mask
uint16 IGNORE_PX = 1
uint16 IGNORE_PY = 2
uint16 IGNORE_PZ = 4
uint16 IGNORE_VX = 8
uint16 IGNORE_VY = 16
uint16 IGNORE_VZ = 32
uint16 IGNORE_AFX = 64
uint16 IGNORE_AFY = 128
uint16 IGNORE_AFZ = 256
uint16 FORCE = 512     uint16 IGNORE_YAW = 1024
uint16 IGNORE_YAW_RATE = 2048
```

Finally, we can set the position, the velocity, and the acceleration for the three Cartesian axes, as well as the position and the velocity of the UAV yaw:

```
geometry_msgs/Point position
geometry_msgs/Vector3 velocity
geometry_msgs/Vector3 acceleration_or_force
float32 yaw
float32 yaw_rate
```

For example, if we want to stream just the position, ignoring the velocity and the acceleration data, we should include the following code in our ROS node:

```
mavros_msgs::PositionTarget ptarget;
    ptarget.coordinate_frame = mavros_
msgs::PositionTarget::FRAME_LOCAL_NED;
    ptarget.type_mask =
    mavros_msgs::PositionTarget::IGNORE_VX |
    mavros_msgs::PositionTarget::IGNORE_VY |
    mavros_msgs::PositionTarget::IGNORE_VZ |
    mavros_msgs::PositionTarget::IGNORE_AFX |
    mavros_msgs::PositionTarget::IGNORE_AFY |
    mavros_msgs::PositionTarget::IGNORE_AFZ |
    mavros_msgs::PositionTarget::FORCE |
    mavros_msgs::PositionTarget::IGNORE_YAW_RATE;
```

This source code used the local NED as a coordinate frame. The coordinate frame specifies how to locate a point (or an object) in the world or the simulation environment. For this reason, understanding the coordinate frame is important for both the localization of the UAV and for sending correct motion commands. The PX4 autopilot internally has only one reference frame, called the **North, East, Down** (**NED**) frame. This means that the x of the robot is positive along the ahead direction, the y in the right direction and finally, the z is downward. Meanwhile, the default reference frame used by ROS and Gazebo for global positioning is ENU (*right, ahead, upward*). For this reason, when using the mavros package, everything sent to the autopilot must be in the ENU frame. Everything received by mavros will therefore also be in the ENU frame. This information is particularly important when we want to externally estimate the position of the UAV, for example, by using SLAM algorithms. Note that, in the previous message, we are able to specify the command in the body frame as well (using the FRAME_BODY_NED constant). In this case, the target position will be interpreted based on the rotation of the UAV.

External pose estimation for PX4

UAVs need to know their position in a fixed coordinate frame (the world frame) in order to stabilize during flight. Inertial sensors, such as IMU, are not accurate enough to accomplish this task. For this reason, external sensors such as GPS, LiDAR, or cameras are used. The typical control loop of a UAV is shown in the following figure:

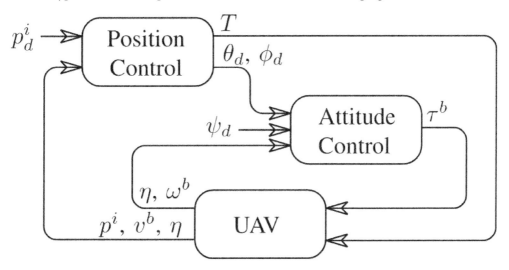

Figure 8.7 – PX4 control loop

In the **position control loop** (the outer loop), the current position of the UAV is needed. When available, this information is directly retrieved via **GPS**. However, in some cases – for example, when you fly in indoor spaces – GPS cannot be used. In these cases, the position of the robot must be estimated to allow for the stabilization and position control of the aerial robot. External sensors can be used to estimate the pose of the UAV. In particular, **Optitrack** and **Vicon** systems are very popular in this field. These systems offer high-performance optical tracking (including motion capture software and high-speed tracking cameras). In short, these systems act as very high-precision and super-fast GPS. In addition, the UAV must be able to estimate its pose using onboard sensors, such as standard cameras, depth cameras, or **LiDARs**. In this context, SLAM algorithms are suitable for this purpose. In recent years, many sensors have been deployed to the market that can reconstruct their pose using FPGA devices to speed up the computation process. This is the case with the Intel **Realsense t265** tracking camera.

Refer to the following URL for information about this particular camera: `https://www.intelrealsense.com/tracking-camera-t265`. The PX4 control stack can be configured to accept an estimated position from a companion PC. This can be configured using PX4 parameters and `mavros` plugins. To enable external pose estimation, the `vision_pose_estimate` plugin can be used to configure the following parameters. Open `QGroundControl` and set the following parameters:

- `EKF2_AID_MASK`: From here you can select the list of the external estimation sources. To use the external pose, select `vision_position_fusion` and `vision_yaw_fusion`.

- `EKF2_HGT_MODE`: You must select the vision source to estimate the height of the UAV.

We can now stream the desired position on the `/mavros/vision_pose/` topic using the `geometry_msgs::PoseStamped` message type in the ENU reference frame. Be aware that the system only checks the data that is streamed, and not the data that is reported in the correct reference frame.

Simulating UAVs using the PX4 stack involves multiple elements. In the first part of this chapter, we focused on the connection between the autopilot code and Gazebo. The question now is: how effectively can Gazebo simulate the sensors and dynamics of a UAV? This question is answered thanks to a set of Gazebo plugins implemented by RotorS. We will discuss all this in the next section.

Using the RotorS simulation framework

In the previous section, we discussed how to simulate flight controller unit code using Gazebo ROS. However, in some cases, we might be interested in simulating only UAV dynamics with basic sensors (such as IMU, GPS, and so on) and propellers. This is the goal of the RotorS simulator. This simulator provides a set of configuration files and models shaped as ROS packages in order to simulate different types of UAVs. Besides the standard models, RotorS allows developers to configure new multirotor systems from scratch. In short, this ROS package implements both sensors and mechanisms in the form of Gazebo plugins that can be mounted on the multirotor. In this section, we will install RotorS on our ROS. Later, we will create a new multirotor model containing four rotors.

Installing RotorS

Let's start by installing RotorS on our system. To accomplish this step, you should install the following dependencies:

```
sudo apt-get install ros-noetic-joy ros-noetic-octomap-
ros ros-noetic-mavlink protobuf-compiler libgoogle-glog-dev
ros-noetic-control-toolbox
```

Now, clone the RotorS repository in your ROS workspace:

```
roscd && cd ../src
git clone https://github.com/ethz-asl/rotors_simulator.git
```

Then, compile the workspace using the `catkin_make` command.

If the compilation ends without any errors occurring, then you are ready to launch the simulator using one of the models provided by RotorS. Additionally, this package implements a UAV controller to command its position in the simulated world. For example, to simulate the model of a hexacopter, you can use the following command:

```
roslaunch rotors_gazebo mav_hovering_example.launch mav_
name:=firefly world_name:=basic
```

The `mav_hovering_exmaple.launch` file is explained in the following code snippet. First, the UAV type is defined using `mav_name`. In this case, we selected the one called `firefly`:

```
<launch>
  <arg name="mav_name" default="firefly"/>
```

Then, we set the environmental variables to add the configuration files used to launch the simulation to Gazebo. In particular, GAZEBO_MODEL_PATH contains the list of directories where Gazebo will search for models, while GAZEBO_RESOURCE_PATH contains the list of directories for other resources, such as world and media files:

```
  <env name="GAZEBO_MODEL_PATH" value="${GAZEBO_MODEL_
PATH}:$(find rotors_gazebo)/models"/>
  <env name="GAZEBO_RESOURCE_PATH" value="${GAZEBO_RESOURCE_
PATH}:$(find rotors_gazebo)/models"/>
```

Then, we can start Gazebo:

```
<include file="$(find gazebo_ros)/launch/empty_world.launch">
    <arg name="world_name" value="$(find rotors_gazebo)/
worlds/$(arg world_name).world" />
    <arg name="debug" value="$(arg debug)" />
    <arg name="paused" value="$(arg paused)" />
    <arg name="gui" value="$(arg gui)" />
    <arg name="verbose" value="$(arg verbose)"/>
</include>
```

Based on the UAV type, a set of launch files are included. The following one is to spawn the model in the Gazebo simulator:

```
<group ns="$(arg mav_name)">
    <include file="$(find rotors_gazebo)/launch/spawn_mav.
launch">
    <arg name="mav_name" value="$(arg mav_name)" />
    <arg name="model" value="$(find rotors_description)/urdf/
mav_generic_odometry_sensor.gazebo" />
    <arg name="enable_logging" value="$(arg enable_logging)"
/>
    <arg name="enable_ground_truth" value="$(arg enable_
ground_truth)" />
    <arg name="log_file" value="$(arg log_file)"/>
</include>
```

Now, the robot is ready to be controlled. So, the next step is to run the controller node that generates the velocity for each propeller of the UAV. Again, this is a node provided in the set of RotorS packages, `lee_position_controller_node`:

```
    <node name="lee_position_controller_node" pkg="rotors_
control" type="lee_position_controller_node" output="screen">
    <rosparam command="load" file="$(find rotors_gazebo)/
resource/lee_controller_$(arg mav_name).yaml" />
    <rosparam command="load" file="$(find rotors_gazebo)/
resource/$(arg mav_name).yaml" />
    <remap from="odometry" to="odometry_sensor1/odometry" />
</node>
```

Finally, the `hovering_example` node is used to control the robot. The goal of this node is to publish a setpoint using `geometry_msgs::Pose` data:

```
<node name="hovering_example" pkg="rotors_gazebo"
type="hovering_example" output="screen"/>
```

The `hovering_example` node can be switched with your node to drive the robot into the simulated environment. To summarize, relying on RotorS to simulate and control UAVs with ROS is easier than using the PX4 SITL and ROS. With RotorS, you can send commands directly to the vehicle. However, autonomous navigation routines must first be implemented. Before we continue by showing how we can define a new multirotor model, let's inspect the elements of RotorS and discuss the contents of its packages.

RotorS packages

The RotorS simulator is divided into different packages, as shown in the following figure:

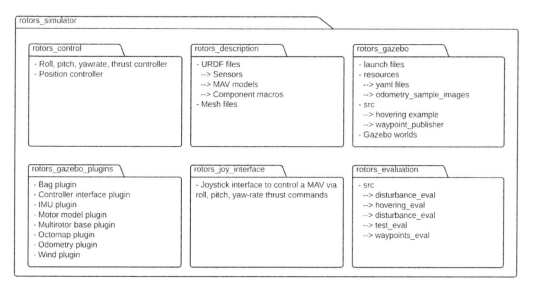

Figure 8.8 – RotorS simulator's packages

The main elements of RotorS are detailed in the following list:

- `rotors_description`: The `rotors_description` package contains the `xacro` files and the 3D models of the components involved in the simulation (sensors, UAV frames, and so on).

- `rotors_control`: This package contains a set of low-level controllers for the UAV that generate the propeller's velocities based on the desired position input.

- `rotors_gazebo_plugins`: This package contains a set of Gazebo plugins that are used to simulate the UAV sensors and propellers. All the models will include the following plugins:

  IMU plugin: This simulates the inertial sensor.

  Motor model plugin: This simulates the dynamics of the motors mounted on the UAV.

  Multirotor base plugin: This plugin calculates and applies the forces and torques to the base link of the UAV, based on motor speeds.

  Odometry plugin: This plugin simulates an odometry sensor in order to stream the UAV position and orientation.

  Rotors Gazebo-ROS interface: This plugin represents the communication layer between the RotorS ROS messages and the Gazebo simulation scene. If you fail to load this plugin, you cannot use any ROS topic to command the robot. In addition, only one instance of this plugin may be loaded. For this reason, it's convenient to load this plugin in the Gazebo world file.

- `rotors_gazebo`: This package contains the launch file to start the different models in the Gazebo simulator.

The combination of the elements included in the RotorS packages allows you to create new robots, or modify the ones already implemented, adding sensors or changing their dynamic parameters (such as the robot mass or inertia).

To understand how these plugins works, let's try to start the `firefly` robot by inspecting the available ROS topics:

```
roslaunch rotors_gazebo mav_hovering_example.launch mav_
name:=firefly world_name:=basic
rostopic list
```

The following salient topics are active in the ROS network:

- `/firefly/command/motor_speed`: This is the only input of the system and represents the velocity of each propeller of the UAV. The message type is part of a `mav_msgs` package (`http://wiki.ros.org/mav_msgs`). This topic accepts a `mav_msgs::Actuator` message, whose definition is as follows:

```
std_msgs/Header header
  uint32 seq
  time stamp
```

```
    string frame_id
  float64[] angles
  float64[] angular_velocities
  float64[] normalized
```

In this context, we are interested in `angular_velocities`. This is a vector whose size depends on the number of motors of the robot. In this case, we have a vector of six elements.

- `/firefly/odometry_sensor1/odometry`: This topic is published by the odometry plugin and represents the estimated position, orientation, and velocity of the UAV. This topic streams a `nav_msgs/Odometry` message.

- `/firefly/motor_speed/${num_motor}`: This topic is published by a plugin modeling the motors. It can be used to debug.

- `/firefly/imu`: This topic is published by the IMU plugin and represents the attitude of the UAV.

Note that all the topics start with the name of the UAV because this is the namespace set in the variables of the launch file. Now that we have discussed the main components, in the next section, let's find out how to define a new UAV model.

Creating a new UAV model

The RotorS simulator possesses several UAV models with different configurations. However, you can add new robot models with the desired number of motors, placed anywhere on the robot base frame. To import a new model in the RotorS framework, we need to define the `xacro` file containing all the joints, links, and sensors of the multirotor. The `rotors_description` package contains a set of `xacro` files for implementing different macros to simplify creating the UAV. In particular, the following `xacro` files will be included in our robot:

- The `multirotor_base.xacro` file represents the main element of the UAV. It sets `base_link` for the robot.

- The `component_snippets.xacro` file contains the macros for several simulation-related components (sensors, motors, and so on).

We will refer to these files to create our new model. Let's now try to create a model for the IRIS robot. The first step is to create a new ROS package, that depends from the `rotors_description` package, in which is located the `xacro` file that was listed previously:

```
catkin_create_pkg iris_model roscpp rotors_description mav_msgs
```

Now, we must create the `urdf` directory. Let's create two `xacro` files inside this directory, the `iris.xacro` and `iris_base.xacro` files. Note that we will use the other resources from other RotorS packages (such as CAD models, additional macro files, as well as others). For this reason, our new package will depend on the `rotors_description` package.

Let's start from the `iris_base.xacro` file. To begin, we define the robot name as follows:

```
<?xml version="1.0"?>
<robot name="iris" xmlns:xacro="http://ros.org/wiki/xacro">
```

Then, we include two additional `xacro` files – one containing an important macro (the `component_snippets.xacro` file) and another containing the main frame of the multirotor (called the `iris.xacro` file):

```
  <xacro:include filename="$(find rotors_description)/urdf/
component_snippets.xacro" />
  <xacro:include filename="$(find iris_model)/urdf/iris.xacro"
/>
```

Finally, we include two sensors: the `imu` sensor. This uses the `default_imu` macro, as defined in the `component_snippets.xacro` file, and the odometry sensor:

```
    <xacro:default_imu namespace="${namespace}" parent_
link="${namespace}/base_link" />
```

The odometry plugin must be configured with parameters including the following:

- The namespace of the robot that is specified in the launch file and is required to properly link the sensor to the base link of the robot:

```
<xacro:odometry_plugin_macro
    namespace="${namespace}"
    odometry_sensor_suffix="1"
    parent_link="${namespace}/base_link"
```

- The topic on which the data is streamed (position, velocity):

```
    pose_topic="odometry_sensor1/pose"
  pose_with_covariance_topic="odometry_sensor1/pose_
with_covariance"
    position_topic="odometry_sensor1/position"
    transform_topic="odometry_sensor1/transform"
    odometry_topic="odometry_sensor1/odometry"
    parent_frame_id="world"
    child_frame_id="${namespace}/odometry_sensor1"
```

- Possible noise. This is used to inject odometry measurement errors in order to have more realistic simulations:

```
    mass_odometry_sensor="0.00001"
    measurement_divisor="1"
    measurement_delay="0"
    unknown_delay="0.0"
    noise_normal_position="0 0 0"
    noise_normal_quaternion=»0 0 0»
    noise_normal_linear_velocity=»0 0 0»
    noise_normal_angular_velocity=»0 0 0»
    noise_uniform_position=»0 0 0»
    noise_uniform_quaternion=»0 0 0»
    noise_uniform_linear_velocity=»0 0 0»
    noise_uniform_angular_velocity=»0 0 0»
    enable_odometry_map=»false»
    odometry_map=»»
    image_scale=»»>
    <inertia ixx=»0.00001» ixy=»0.0» ixz=»0.0»
```

```
iyy=»0.00001» iyz=»0.0» izz=»0.00001» /> <!-- [kg m^2]
[kg m^2] [kg m^2] [kg m^2] [kg m^2] [kg m^2] -->
        <origin xyz=»0.0 0.0 0.0» rpy=»0.0 0.0 0.0» />
    </xacro:odometry_plugin_macro>
</robot>
```

We can now define the `iris.xacro` file. This file could be very long, since it contains the definition of each propeller of the robot, as well as the other sensors. The first part of the file also contains the definition of some parameters. We can choose to slow down the rotation velocity of the propellers in the simulation view, and we can set the **CAD** file to use as the robot frame:

```
<?xml version="1.0"?>
<robot name="iris" xmlns:xacro="http://ros.org/wiki/xacro">
  <!-- Properties -->
  <xacro:property name="namespace" value="$(arg namespace)" />
  <xacro:property name="rotor_velocity_slowdown_sim" value="10"
/>
  <xacro:property name="use_mesh_file" value="true" />
  <xacro:property name="mesh_file" value="package://rotors_
description/meshes/iris.dae" />
```

Now, some UAV specific parameters must be defined, such as its mass, inertia, length of its arm, and so on. In addition, the dynamic of the rotors is also modeled considering some constants such as the motor and moment constants. Such parameters depend on the motor mode:

```
  <xacro:property name="mass" value="1.5" />
  <xacro:property name="body_width" value="0.47" />
  <xacro:property name="body_height" value="0.11" />
  <xacro:property name="mass_rotor" value="0.005" />
  <xacro:property name="arm_length_front_x" value="0.13" />
  <xacro:property name="arm_length_back_x" value="0.13" />
  <xacro:property name="arm_length_front_y" value="0.22" />
  <xacro:property name="arm_length_back_y" value="0.2" />
  <xacro:property name="rotor_offset_top" value="0.023" />
  <xacro:property name="radius_rotor" value="0.1" />
  <xacro:property name="motor_constant" value="8.54858e-06" />
  <xacro:property name="moment_constant" value="0.016" />
```

```
<xacro:property name="time_constant_up" value="0.0125" />
<xacro:property name="time_constant_down" value="0.025" />
<xacro:property name="max_rot_velocity" value="838" />
<xacro:property name="rotor_drag_coefficient"
value="8.06428e-05" />
<xacro:property name="rolling_moment_coefficient"
value="0.000001" />
```

Some property blocks can now be defined to specify the body and rotor inertias:

```
<!-- Property Blocks -->
<xacro:property name="body_inertia">
    <inertia ixx="0.0347563" ixy="0.0" ixz="0.0"
iyy="0.0458929" iyz="0.0" izz="0.0977" /> <!-- [kg.m^2] [kg.
m^2] [kg.m^2] [kg.m^2] [kg.m^2] [kg.m^2] -->
</xacro:property>
<xacro:property name="rotor_inertia">
    <xacro:box_inertia x="${radius_rotor}" y="0.015"
z="0.003" mass="${mass_rotor*rotor_velocity_slowdown_sim}" />
</xacro:property>
```

Now, we include another `xacro` file, used to instantiate the main part of the multirotor. After including this file, we will have access to the `mulitror_base_macro` macro block that is filled according to the size of the platform and the mesh file used in the simulation scene:

```
<xacro:include filename="$(find rotors_description)/urdf/
multirotor_base.xacro" />
<!-- Instantiate multirotor_base_macro once -->
<xacro:multirotor_base_macro
    robot_namespace="${namespace}"
    mass="${mass}"
    body_width="${body_width}"
    body_height="${body_height}"
    use_mesh_file="${use_mesh_file}"
    mesh_file="${mesh_file}"
    >
    <xacro:insert_block name="body_inertia" />
</xacro:multirotor_base_macro>
```

In the rest of the file, we simply instantiate the motors of the UAV. We are modeling a quadrotor, so we will include four different motors. We are free to configure the parameters of each rotor using the following parameters:

- **Direction**: This parameter represents the rotation direction of the propeller. It can be set as cw: clockwise or ccw: counterclockwise.

- **Motor number**: This is the ID of the rotor. All the motors must have a unique ID.

- **Origin block**: This block is fundamental to correctly create the UAV model because it represents the position of the motor with respect to the center of the UAV.

Note that the value of some of these parameters, such as the rotation direction or the motor and moment constants, will depend on the controller that you wish to develop. In the following block, we instantiate motor 0. To do this, we use the vertical_rotor macro defined in the multirotor_base.xacro file:

```
<xacro:vertical_rotor
    robot_namespace="${namespace}"
    suffix="front_right"
    direction="ccw"
    motor_constant="${motor_constant}"
    moment_constant=»${moment_constant}»
    parent=»${namespace}/base_link»
    mass_rotor=»${mass_rotor}»
    radius_rotor=»${radius_rotor}»
    time_constant_up=»${time_constant_up}»
    time_constant_down=»${time_constant_down}»
    max_rot_velocity=»${max_rot_velocity}»
    motor_number=»0»
    rotor_drag_coefficient=»${rotor_drag_coefficient}»
    rolling_moment_coefficient=»${rolling_moment_
coefficient}»
    color=»Blue»
    use_own_mesh=»false»
mesh=»»>
    <origin xyz=»${arm_length_front_x} -${arm_length_front_y}
${rotor_offset_top}» rpy=»0 0 0» />
    <xacro:insert_block name=»rotor_inertia» />
</xacro:vertical_rotor>
```

Then we add motor 1, rotating counterclockwise:

```
<xacro:vertical_rotor
    robot_namespace="${namespace}"
    suffix="back_left"
    direction="ccw"
    motor_constant="${motor_constant}"
    moment_constant="${moment_constant}"
    parent="${namespace}/base_link"
    mass_rotor="${mass_rotor}"
    radius_rotor="${radius_rotor}"
    time_constant_up="${time_constant_up}"
    time_constant_down="${time_constant_down}"
    max_rot_velocity="${max_rot_velocity}"
    motor_number="1"
    rotor_drag_coefficient="${rotor_drag_coefficient}"
                            rolling_moment_
coefficient="${rolling_moment_coefficient}"
    color="Red"
    use_own_mesh="false"
    mesh="">
    <origin xyz="-${arm_length_back_x} ${arm_length_back_y}
${rotor_offset_top}" rpy="0 0 0" />
    <xacro:insert_block name="rotor_inertia" />
</xacro:vertical_rotor>
```

Then we add motor 2, rotating clockwise:

```
<xacro:vertical_rotor robot_namespace="${namespace}"
    suffix="front_left"
    direction="cw"
    motor_constant="${motor_constant}"
    moment_constant=»${moment_constant}»
    parent=»${namespace}/base_link»
    mass_rotor=»${mass_rotor}»
    radius_rotor=»${radius_rotor}»
    time_constant_up=»${time_constant_up}»
    time_constant_down=»${time_constant_down}»
```

```
      max_rot_velocity=»${max_rot_velocity}»
      motor_number=»2»
      rotor_drag_coefficient=»${rotor_drag_coefficient}»
      rolling_moment_coefficient=»${rolling_moment_
coefficient}»
      color=»Blue»
      use_own_mesh=»false»
      mesh=»»>
      <origin xyz=»${arm_length_front_x} ${arm_length_front_y}
${rotor_offset_top}» rpy=»0 0 0» />
      <xacro:insert_block name=»rotor_inertia» />
   </xacro:vertical_rotor>
```

And finally, we add the last motor with ID equal to 3 and rotating in a clockwise direction:

```
   <xacro:vertical_rotor robot_namespace="${namespace}"
      suffix="back_right"
      direction="cw"
      motor_constant="${motor_constant}"
      moment_constant="${moment_constant}"
      parent="${namespace}/base_link"
      mass_rotor="${mass_rotor}"
      radius_rotor="${radius_rotor}"
      time_constant_up="${time_constant_up}"
      time_constant_down="${time_constant_down}"
      max_rot_velocity="${max_rot_velocity}"
      motor_number="3"
      rotor_drag_coefficient="${rotor_drag_coefficient}"
      rolling_moment_coefficient="${rolling_moment_
coefficient}"
      color="Red"
      use_own_mesh="false"
      mesh="">
      <origin xyz="-${arm_length_back_x} -${arm_length_back_y}
${rotor_offset_top}" rpy="0 0 0" />
      <xacro:insert_block name="rotor_inertia" />
   </xacro:vertical_rotor>
</robot>
```

Now we have defined the UAV model. To start the simulation with this new UAV, we need to create a Gazebo world file and a launch file. Let's start by defining a Gazebo world file in the `iris_model` package. Let's create a `world` directory in the `iris_model` package and then create an `empty.world` file:

```
roscd iris_model
mkdir world && cd world
touch empty.world
```

The content of this file is as follows. As usual, we include some models to define the ground and the environmental light, as follows:

```
<?xml version="1.0" ?>
<sdf version="1.4">
  <world name="default">
      <include>
      <uri>model://ground_plane</uri>
      </include>
      <include>
      <uri>model://sun</uri>
      </include>
```

Then, we have to include the RotorS Gazebo-ROS interface plugin in order to control the robot motors using the ROS topic and retrieve sensor information from the Gazebo scene:

```
<plugin name="ros_interface_plugin" filename="librotors_gazebo_
ros_interface_plugin.so"/>
```

As already stated, typically UAVs work using **GPS** localization. For this reason, it may be convenient to add a spherical coordinates reference system that converts the planar coordinates (x, y, and z) into spherical ones (latitude, longitude, and altitude). We can also add the latitude and longitude origins, as follows:

```
      <spherical_coordinates>
          <surface_model>EARTH_WGS84</surface_model>
          <latitude_deg>47.3667</latitude_deg>
          <longitude_deg>8.5500</longitude_deg>
          <elevation>500.0</elevation>
            <heading_deg>0</heading_deg>
          </spherical_coordinates>
```

Finally, we include the dynamic solver, as follows:

```
<physics type='ode'>
 <ode>
 <solver>
        <type>quick</type>
        <iters>1000</iters>
        <sor>1.3</sor>
    </solver>
    <constraints>
        <cfm>0</cfm>
        <erp>0.2</erp>
            <contact_max_correcting_vel>100</contact_
max_correcting_vel>
            <contact_surface_layer>0.001</contact_surface_
layer>
    </constraints>
    </ode>
    <max_step_size>0.01</max_step_size>
    <real_time_factor>1</real_time_factor>
    <real_time_update_rate>100</real_time_update_rate>
    <gravity>0 0 -9.8</gravity>
    </physics>
  </world>
</sdf>
```

The last step before starting the simulation is to write a proper launch file to launch the previously created world and spawn the IRIS model inside it. Let's create a launch file in the `iris_model/launch` directory. The file is very similar to the `mav_hovering_example` program that was previously discussed. There are two main differences. The first is the world file to load. This is defined using the `world_name` argument, in which we load the world file located in the `iris_model` folder, as follows:

```
<arg name="world_name" value="$(find iris_model)/worlds/
empty.world" />
```

The second is the model to load, in which we refer to the `iris_base.xacro` file, as follows:

```
<arg name="model" value="$(find iris_model)/urdf/iris_base.
xacro" />
```

To start the simulation, use the following command:

```
roslaunch iris_model spawn_iris.launch
```

We are now ready to control the robot motors. We will discuss this in detail in the next section.

Interacting with RotorS motor models

In this section, we will create a ROS node to interact with the motors of the IRIS UAV model we previously developed. Let's create a source file called `motor_example.cpp` in the `src` folder of the `iris_model` package. The content of this file is discussed in the following section.

First, we include the `mav_msgs::Actuators` header to send the commands to the UAV, as follows:

```
#include "ros/ros.h"
#include "mav_msgs/Actuators.h"
using namespace std;
```

In the `main` function, we define the publisher to the `/iris/gazebo/command/motor_speed` topic, as follows:

```
int main(int argc, char ** argv ) {
    ros::init(argc, argv, "motor_example");
    ros::NodeHandle nh;
    ros::Publisher actuators_pub;
    actuators_pub = nh.advertise<mav_msgs::Actuators>("/iris/
gazebo/command/motor_speed", 1);
    ros::Rate r(10);
```

The goal of this code is to require a rotation of 800 rad/s from each motor, moving one motor at a time. We now resize the `angular_velocities` field of the actuators message to consider all four motors of the UAV, as follows:

```
mav_msgs::Actuators m;
m.angular_velocities.resize(4);
while(ros::ok()) {
   for(int i=0; i<4; i++) {
    for(int j=0; j<4; j++) {
            if( i!=j) m.angular_velocities[j] = 0.0;
            else m.angular_velocities[i] = 800;
        }
```

Finally, we publish the actuator message, as follows:

```
        actuators_pub.publish(m);
        ros::spinOnce();
        sleep(1);
    }
 }
    return 0;
}
```

After compiling this code, we can test whether the motors run correctly.

Let's launch the Gazebo simulation:

```
roslaunch iris_model spawn_iris.launch
```

Then, we can send input to the robot motors:

```
rosrun iris_model motor_example
```

You can now see in the Gazebo scene that the motors will rotate in sequence, and you can program your controller to regulate the velocity of the four rotors in order to stabilize and move the robot in the simulated world.

Summary

This chapter introduced the concept of aerial robots and discussed their main elements. We also described one of the most famous autopilot boards used to develop custom applications with UAV – the Pixhawk control board running the PX4 autopilot. After we learned how to use real multirotor platforms and integrate them with ROS, we then went on to discuss two simulation modalities. It is very important to simulate the effect of control algorithms before running them on a real UAV. This is in order to prevent damage to the robot and nearby people.

In the next chapter, we will discuss how to interface microcontroller boards and actuators with ROS.

Here are some questions based on what we learned in this chapter.

Questions

- What is an aerial robot?
- What is the main element of an aerial robot?
- What is the PX4 control stack?
- What are the main differences between PX4 SITL and RotorS simulations?

Section 3 – ROS Robot Hardware Prototyping

In this section, we will deal with the hardware prototyping of a robot. We will look at robot sensor interfacing, embedded board interfacing, and finally, how to build an actual differential robot using ROS.

This section comprises the following chapters:

- *Chapter 9, Interfacing I/O Boards, Sensors, and Actuators to ROS*
- *Chapter 10, Programming Vision Sensors Using ROS, OpenCV, and PCL*
- *Chapter 11, Building and Interfacing Differential Drive Mobile Robot Hardware in ROS*

9
Interfacing I/O Board Sensors and Actuators to ROS

In the previous chapters, we discussed different kinds of plugin frameworks that are used in ROS. In this chapter, we are going to discuss the interfacing of some hardware components, such as sensors and actuators, to ROS. We will look at the interfacing of sensors using I/O boards such as **Arduino**, **Teensy**, **Raspberry Pi 4**, **Jetson Nano**, and **Odroid-XU4** to ROS, and we will discuss interfacing smart actuators, such as DYNAMIXEL, to ROS. The following is the detailed list of topics that we are going to cover in this chapter:

- Understanding the Arduino-ROS interface
- What is the the Arduino-ROS interface packages?
- Interfacing a non-Arduino board to ROS
- Interfacing DYNAMIXEL actuators to ROS

Technical requirements:

The reference code for this chapter can be downloaded from the following Git repository: `https://github.com/PacktPublishing/Mastering-ROS-for-Robotics-Programming-Third-edition/tree/main/Chapter9`

You can view this chapter's code in action here: `https://bit.ly/3k3RM9f`.

Understanding the Arduino-ROS interface

Let's see what Arduino is first. Arduino is one of the most popular open source development boards on the market. The ease of programming and the cost-effectiveness of the hardware have made Arduino a big success. Most of the Arduino boards are powered by Atmel microcontrollers, which are available from 8 bit to 32 bit, with clock speeds from 8 MHz to 84 MHz. Arduino can be used for the quick prototyping of robots. The main applications of Arduino in robotics are interfacing sensors and actuators, used for communicating with PCs to receive high-level commands and to send sensor values to PCs using the UART protocol.

There are different varieties of Arduino available on the market. Selecting one board for our purpose will be dependent on the nature of our robotic application. Let's see some boards that we can use for beginner, intermediate, and high-end users:

Beginner: Arduino UNO

Intermediate: Arduino Mega

Advanced: Arduino DUE

Figure 9.1 – Different versions of the Arduino board

In the following table, we will look at each Arduino board specification in brief and see where it can be deployed:

Boards	Arduino UNO	Arduino Mega 2560	Arduino Due
Processor	ATmega328P	ATmega2560	ATSAM3X8E
Operating/Input Voltage	5V / 7-12 V	5V/ 7 - 12 V	3.3V / 7 - 12 V
CPU Speed	16 MHz	16 MHz	84 MHz
Analog In/Out	6/0	16/0	12/2
Digital IO/PWM	14/6	54/15	54/12
EEPROM[KB]	1	4	-
SRAM [KB]	2	8	96
Flash [KB]	32	256	512
USB	Regular	Regular	2 Micro
UART	1	4	4
Application	Basic robotics and sensor interfacing	Intermediate robotic application	High-end robotics application

Figure 9.2 – Comparison of different Arduino boards

Let's look at how to interface Arduino to ROS.

What is the Arduino-ROS interface?

Most of the communication between PCs and I/O boards in robots will be through the UART protocol. When the devices communicate with each other, there should be some program on both sides that can translate the serial commands from each of the devices. We can implement our logic to receive and transmit the data from the board to the PC and vice versa. The interfacing code can be different in each I/O board because there are no standard libraries to do this communication.

The Arduino-ROS interface is a standard way of communicating between Arduino boards and a PC. Currently, this interface is exclusive to Arduino boards and boards supported by the Arduino IDE. Some of the examples of those boards are OpenCR (https://robots.ros.org/opencr/) and Teensy (https://www.pjrc.com/teensy/). For other boards, we may need to write a custom ROS interface. Tutorials are provided on the rosserial tutorial page: http://wiki.ros.org/rosserial_client/Tutorials. You can find the list of boards supporting the rosserial protocol at the following link: http://wiki.ros.org/rosserial.

In the next section, detailed information about the rosserial package in ROS is provided.

Understanding the rosserial package in ROS

The `rosserial` package is a set of standardized communication protocols implemented for communication between ROS and character devices, such as serial ports and sockets, and vice versa. The `rosserial` protocol can convert the standard ROS message and service data types to equivalent embedded device data types. It also implements multi-topic support by multiplexing the serial data from a character device (`https://askubuntu.com/questions/1021394/what-is-a-character-device`). The serial data is sent as data packets by adding a header and tail bytes on the packet. The packet representation is shown next:

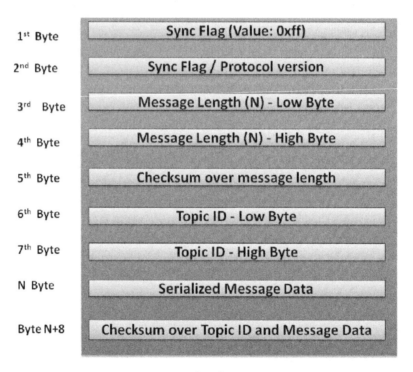

Figure 9.3 – rosserial packet representation

The function of each byte follows:

- **Sync Flag**: This is the first byte of the packet, which is always `0xff`.

- **Sync Flag/Protocol version**: This byte was `0xff` on ROS Groovy and after that, it is set to `0xfe`.

- **Message Length**: This is the length of the packet.

- **Checksum over message length**: This is the checksum of packet length for finding packet corruption.

- **Topic ID**: This is the ID allocated for each topic; the range `0-100` is allocated for system-related functionalities.

- **Serialized Message Data**: This is the data associated with each topic.

- **Checksum over Topic ID and Message Data**: This is the checksum for the topic and its serial data for finding the packet, `corruption`.

The checksum of packet length is computed using the following equation:

Checksum = 255 - ((Topic ID Low Byte + Topic ID High Byte + ... data byte values) % 256)

The ROS client libraries, such as `roscpp`, `rospy`, and `roslisp`, enable us to develop ROS nodes from different programming languages. There is a client library available in ROS that helps us to develop a ROS node from an embedded device, such as Arduino and embedded Linux-based boards, which is called the `rosserial_client` library. Using the `rosserial_client` library, we can develop the ROS nodes from Arduino and other embedded board platforms. The following is the list of `rosserial_client` libraries for each of these platforms:

- `rosserial_arduino`: This `rosserial_client` works on Arduino platforms, such as Arduino UNO, Leonardo, Mega, and the Due series for advanced robotic projects.

- `rosserial_embeddedlinux`: This client supports embedded Linux platforms, such as VEXPro, Chumby alarm clock, WRT54GL router, and so on.

- `rosserial_windows`: This is a client for the Windows platform.

- `rosserial_mbed`: The client library for the Mbed platform.

- `rosserial_tivac`: The client library for TI's LaunchPad boards, TM4C123GXL and TM4C1294XL.

- `ros-teensy`: The client library for the Teensy platform.

On the PC side, we need some other ROS nodes to decode the serial message and convert it to exact topics from the `rosserial_client` libraries. The following packages help in decoding the serial data:

- `rosserial_python`: This is the recommended PC-side node for handling serial data from a device. The receiving node is completely written in Python.

- `rosserial_server`: This is a C++ implementation of `rosserial` on the PC side. There are fewer inbuilt functionalities compared to `rosserial_python`, but it can be used for high-performance applications.

We are mainly focusing on running ROS nodes from Arduino. First, we will see how to set up the `rosserial` package on our PC, and then discuss how to set up the `rosserial_arduino` client in the Arduino IDE.

Installing rosserial packages on Ubuntu 20.04

To enable ROS in the Arduino IDE on Ubuntu 20.04, we must install `rosserial` ROS packages and then set up the Arduino-ROS client library to communicate with the ROS environment. We can install the `rosserial` packages on Ubuntu using the following commands:

1. Install the `rosserial` package binaries, using the `apt` package manager:

    ```
    sudo apt install ros-noetic-rosserial ros-noetic-
    rosserial-arduino ros-noetic-rosserial-python
    ```

2. To install the rosserial_client library called ros_lib in Arduino, we must download the latest Arduino IDE for Linux 32/64 bit.

    One of the easiest options to install Arduino IDE is using arduino snap tool(`https://snapcraft.io/arduino`). You can use the following command to install Arduino IDE using the snap app store:

    sudo snap install arduino

    You can find the Arduino IDE by searching 'arduino' in the Unity Dash Search box in Ubuntu.

    If we want to download the latest binaries, we can use the following link to download the Arduino IDE: `https://www.arduino.cc/en/main/software`. In this book, we are using Arduino IDE 1.8.x, you can download it from following link `https://www.arduino.cc/en/main/OldSoftwareReleases`.

    Here, we download the Linux 64-bit version and copy the Arduino IDE folder to the Ubuntu desktop. Arduino requires Java runtime support to run it. If it is not installed, we can install it using the following command:

    ```
    sudo apt install default-jre
    ```

3. After installing the Java runtime, we can switch the `arduino` folder using the following command. The *x* is your Arduino IDE version:

    ```
    cd ~/Desktop/arduino-1.8.x-linux64/
    ```

4. Start Arduino, using the following command:

```
./arduino
```

Shown next is the Arduino IDE window:

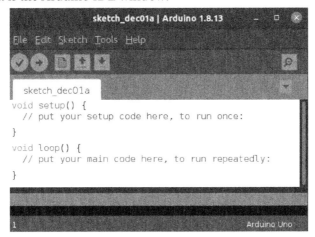

Figure 9.4 – The Arduino IDE

5. Go to **File** | **Preference** to configure the sketchbook folder of Arduino. The Arduino IDE stores sketches in this location. We created a folder called `Arduino1` in the user's `home` folder and set this folder as the **Sketchbook location**:

Sketchbook location:

| /home/robot/Arduino1 | Browse |

Editor language: System Default   ▼   (requires restart of Arduino)

Editor font size: 12

Show verbose output during: ☐ compilation   ☐ upload

Compiler warnings: None   ▼

☐ Display line numbers
☐ Enable Code Folding
☑ Verify code after upload
☐ Use external editor
☑ Check for updates on startup
☑ Update sketch files to new extension on save (.pde -> .ino)
☑ Save when verifying or uploading

Additional Boards Manager URLs: [   ]   🖿

More preferences can be edited directly in the file
/home/robot/.arduino15/preferences.txt
(edit only when Arduino is not running)

OK   Cancel

Figure 9.5 – Preferences in the Arduino IDE

We will see a folder called `libraries` inside the `Arduino1` folder.

6. Go to the Arduino IDE menu, **Sketch | Include Library | Manage Libraries** and search for `rosserial,` as shown in the following screenshot:

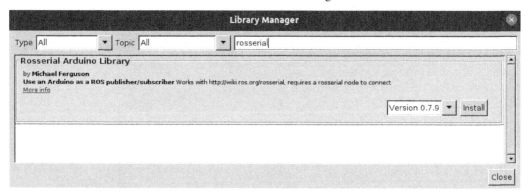

Figure 9.6 – Arduino Library Manager

Install the `rosserial` library you are seeing in the **Library Manager**. You have now installed the Arduino ROS library in the `Arduino1` folder and now you can start implementing a ROS node inside an Arduino board.

There is an alternate way to install the Arduino ROS library, which is given here: `http://wiki.ros.org/rosserial_arduino/Tutorials/Arduino%20 IDE%20Setup`

These ROS messages and services will convert into the Arduino C/C++ code equivalent, as shown next:

- Conversion of ROS messages:

```
ros_package_name/msg/Test.msg  --> ros_package_name::Test
```

- Conversion of ROS services:

```
ros_package_name/srv/Foo.srv  --> ros_package_name::Foo
```

For example, if we include `#include <std_msgs/UInt16.h>`, we can instantiate the `std_msgs::UInt16` number.

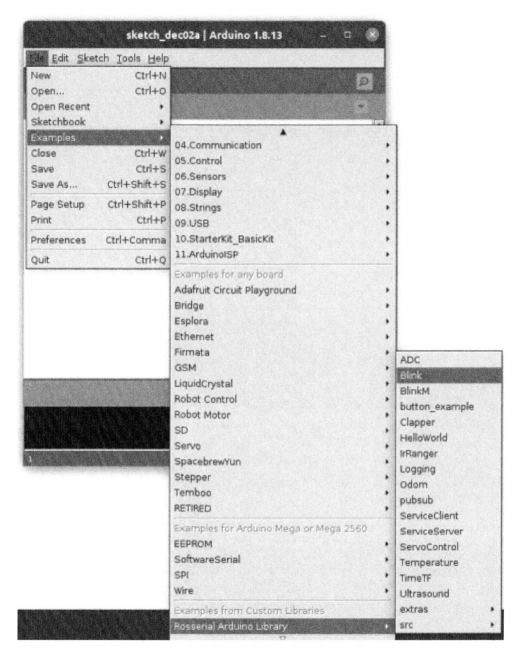

Figure 9.7 – Rosserial_Arduino library examples

We can take any example and make sure that it is building properly to ensure that the `rosserial_arduino` package APIs are working fine. The APIs required for building ROS Arduino nodes are discussed next.

Understanding ROS node APIs in Arduino

The following is the basic structure of the ROS Arduino node. We can see the function of each line of code:

```
#include <ros.h>


ros::NodeHandle nh;

void setup() {
  nh.initNode();
}

void loop() {
  nh.spinOnce();
}
```

The creation of NodeHandle in Arduino is done using the following line of code:

```
ros::NodeHandle nh;
```

Note that Nodehandle should be declared before the setup() function, which will give a global scope to the NodeHandle instance called nh. The initialization of this node is done inside the setup() function:

```
nh.initNode();
```

The Arduino setup() function will execute only once when the device starts. Note that we can only create one node from a serial device.

Inside the loop() function, we have to use the following line of code to execute the ROS callback once:

```
nh.spinOnce();
```

We can create the Subscriber and Publisher objects in Arduino, like the other ROS client libraries. The following are the procedures for defining the subscriber and the publisher.

Here is how we define a Subscriber object in Arduino:

```
ros::Subscriber<std_msgs::String> sub("talker", callback);
```

Here, we define a subscriber that is subscribing a `String` message. The callback is the callback function that is executing when a `String` message is available on the talker topic. Given next is an example callback for handling the `string` data:

```
std_msgs::String str_msg;


ros::Publisher chatter("chatter", &amp;str_msg);


void callback ( const std_msgs::String&amp; msg){
  str_msg.data = msg.data;


  chatter.publish( &amp;str_msg );


}
```

Note that the `callback()`, `Subscriber`, and `Publisher` definitions will be above the `setup()` function for getting the global scope. Here, we are receiving `String` data, using `const std_msgs::String&amp; msg`.

The following code shows how to define a `Publisher` object in Arduino:

```
ros::Publisher chatter("chatter", &amp;str_msg);
```

This next code shows how we publish the string message:

```
chatter.publish( &amp;str_msg );
```

After defining the publisher and the subscriber, we have to initiate this inside the `setup()` function, using the following lines of code:

```
nh.advertise(chatter);
nh.subscribe(sub);
```

There are ROS APIs for logging from Arduino. The following are the different logging APIs supported:

```
nh.logdebug("Debug Statement");
nh.loginfo("Program info");
nh.logwarn("Warnings.);
nh.logerror("Errors..");
nh.logfatal("Fatalities!");
```

We can retrieve the current ROS time in Arduino using ROS built-in functions, such as `Time` and `Duration`:

- The function to retrieve current ROS time is as follows:

```
ros::Time begin = nh.now();
```

- The function for converting the ROS time to seconds is as follows:

```
double secs = nh.now().toSec();
```

- The function for creating a duration in seconds is as follows:

```
ros::Duration ten_seconds(10, 0);
```

In this section, we have seen important functions in the ROS-Arduino library. In the next section, we will see how to use these functions to implement different applications.

ROS-Arduino Publisher and Subscriber example

The first example using the Arduino and ROS interface is a chatter and talker interface. Users can send a `String` message to the `talker` topic and Arduino will publish the same message in a `chatter` topic. The following ROS node is implemented for Arduino, and we will discuss this example in detail:

```
#include <ros.h>
#include <std_msgs/String.h>

//Creating Nodehandle
ros::NodeHandle  nh;

//Declaring String variable
std_msgs::String str_msg;

//Defining Publisher
ros::Publisher chatter("chatter", &str_msg);
//Defining callback
void callback ( const std_msgs::String& msg){

  str_msg.data = msg.data;
  chatter.publish( &str_msg );
```

```
}

//Defining Subscriber
ros::Subscriber<std_msgs::String> sub("talker", callback);


void setup()
{
  //Initializing node
  nh.initNode();
  //Start advertising and subscribing
  nh.advertise(chatter);
  nh.subscribe(sub);
}

void loop()
{
  nh.spinOnce();
  delay(3);
}
```

We can compile the preceding code and upload it to the Arduino board. Before compiling the code, select the desired Arduino board that we are using for this example and the device serial port of the Arduino IDE.

Go to **Tools | Boards** to select your current Arduino board and **Tools | Port** to select the device port name of the board. We are using **Arduino Mega** for these examples.

After compiling and uploading the code, we can start the ROS serial client nodes in the PC that connects Arduino and the PC, using the following command:

Start `roscore` in a new terminal:

```
roscore
```

Now we can start the `rosserial` Python client:

```
rosrun rosserial_python serial_node.py /dev/ttyACM0
```

In this case, we are running `serial_node.py` on port `/dev/ttyACM0`. We can search for the port name listing the contents of the `/dev` directory. Note that, to use this port, root permissions are needed. In this case, we could change the permissions using the following command to read and write data on the desired port:

```
sudo chmod 666 /dev/ttyACM0
```

We are using the `rosserial_python` node here as the ROS bridging node. We have to mention the device name and baud rate as arguments. The default baud rate of this communication is `57600`. We can change the baud rate according to our application and the usage of `serial_node.py` inside the `rosserial_python` package is given at `http://wiki.ros.org/rosserial_python`. If the communication between the ROS node and the Arduino node is correct, we will get the following message:

```
[INFO] [WallTime: 1438880620.972231] ROS Serial Python Node
[INFO] [WallTime: 1438880620.982245] Connecting to /dev/ttyACM0 at 57600 baud
[INFO] [WallTime: 1438880623.117417] Note: publish buffer size is 512 bytes
[INFO] [WallTime: 1438880623.118587] Setup publisher on chatter [std_msgs/String
]
[INFO] [WallTime: 1438880623.132048] Note: subscribe buffer size is 512 bytes
[INFO] [WallTime: 1438880623.132745] Setup subscriber on talker [std_msgs/String
```

Figure 9.8 – Running the rosserial_python node

When `serial_node.py` starts running from the PC, it will send some serial data packets called query packets to get the number of topics, the topic names, and the types of topics that are received from the Arduino node. We have already seen the structure of serial packets that are being used for Arduino ROS communication. Given next is the structure of a query packet that is sent from `serial_node.py` to Arduino:

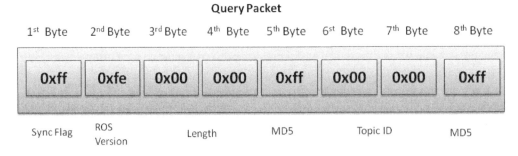

Figure 9.9 – Structure of the query packet

The query topic contains fields such as **Sync Flag**, **ROS Version**, the length of the message, the MD5 sum, **Topic ID**, and so on. When the query packet is received on the Arduino, it will reply with a topic info message that contains the topic name, type, length, topic data, and so on. The following is a typical response packet from Arduino:

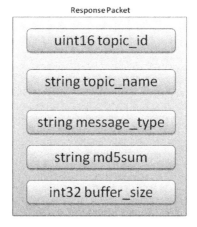

Figure 9.10 – Structure of the response packet

If there is no response for the query packet, it will send it again. The synchronization in communication is based on ROS time.

From *Figure 9.11*, we can see that when we run `serial_node.py`, the buffer size allocated for publishing and subscribe is 512 bytes. The buffer allocation is dependent on the amount of RAM available on each microcontroller that we are working with. The following is a table showing the buffer allocation of each Arduino controller. We can override these settings by changing the `BUFFER_SIZE` macro inside `ros.h`.

AVR model	Buffer Size	Publisher/Subscribers
ATMEGA 168	150 bytes	6/6
ATMEGA 328P	280 bytes	25/25
All others	512 bytes	25/25

Figure 9.11 – Structure of the response packet

There are also some limitations in the `float64` data type of ROS in Arduino. It will truncate to 32 bit. Also, when we use string data types, use the unsigned `char` pointer to save memory.

After running `serial_node.py`, we will get the list of ROS topics using the following command:

```
rostopic list
```

We can see that topics such as `chatter` and `talker` are being generated. We can simply publish a message to the `talker` topic using the following command:

```
rostopic pub -r 5 talker std_msgs/String "Hello World"
```

It will publish the "Hello World" message with a rate of 5.

We can echo the chatter topic, and we will get the same message as we published:

```
rostopic echo /chatter
```

We have seen a basic publisher-subscriber setup in this section. In the next section, we will see how to blink an LED using a push button and using ROS topics.

Arduino-ROS example – blinking an LED with a push button

In this example, we can interface the LED and push button to Arduino and control them using ROS. When the push button is pressed, the Arduino node sends a True value to a topic called pushed, and at the same time, it switches on the LED, which is on the Arduino board.

The following shows the circuit for this example:

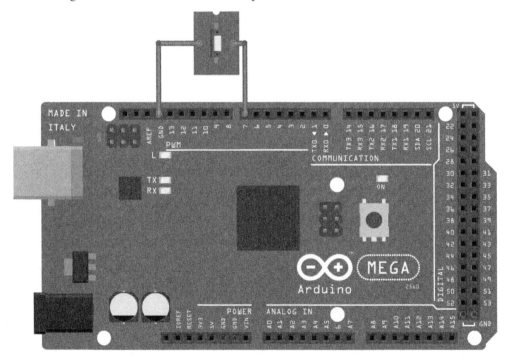

Figure 9.12 – Interfacing the push button to Arduino

Here is the Arduino-ROS code snippet for blinking an LED and handling a push-button event in Arduino.

We have to define a Boolean message for publishing the state of the push button. To publish the push button state, we also create a publisher called `pushed`. So, once the button is pressed, the state will be published in the `pushed` topic:

```
std_msgs::Bool pushed_msg;
ros::Publisher pub_button("pushed", &amp;pushed_msg);
```

Initialize the publisher object and assign Arduino pins for the LED and interfacing the button. The LED pin is configured as output and the button pin is configured as input:

```
   nh.advertise(pub_button);
   pinMode(led_pin, OUTPUT);
   pinMode(button_pin, INPUT);
```

To handle the input signal through the push button pin, we have to enable the internal pull-up resistor. We can enable it by writing a `HIGH` value to the pin that is connected to the push button:

```
   digitalWrite(button_pin, HIGH);
```

The value from the push button pin can be read using `digitalRead()`. The value will be inverted and stored in a variable to get the initial value:

```
   last_reading = ! digitalRead(button_pin);
```

In the main loop of the code, we are checking the debouncing of the button first (`https://www.arduino.cc/en/Tutorial/BuiltInExamples/Debounce`) and if the button value is stable, it will switch on the LED and publish the button state to the `pushed` topic:

```
void loop()
{

  bool reading = ! digitalRead(button_pin);

  if (last_reading!= reading){
      last_debounce_time = millis();
      published = false;
  }
  if ( !published &amp;&amp; (millis() - last_debounce_time)   >
debounce_delay) {
```

```
    digitalWrite(led_pin, reading);
    pushed_msg.data = reading;
    pub_button.publish(&amp;pushed_msg);
    published = true;
}
    last_reading = reading;
  nh.spinOnce();
}
```

The preceding code handles the key debouncing and changes the button state only after the button release. The preceding code can be uploaded to Arduino and interfaced to ROS, using the following commands:

1. Start `roscore`:

    ```
    roscore
    ```

2. Start `serial_node.py`:

    ```
    rosrun roserial_python serial_node.py /dev/ttyACM0
    ```

3. We can see the button press event by echoing the topic pushed:

    ```
    rostopic echo pushed
    ```

We will get the following values when a button is pressed:

Figure 9.13 – Output of Arduino pushing the button

We have seen how to interface a push button to blink an LED using ROS topics. Now we will see how to interface an accelerometer in Arduino and publish the data as ROS topics.

Arduino-ROS example – Accelerometer ADXL 335

In this example, we will interface the Accelerometer ADXL 335 to the Arduino Mega through ADC pins and plot the values using the ROS tool called `rqt_plot`.

The following diagram shows the circuit of the connection between the ADLX 335 and Arduino:

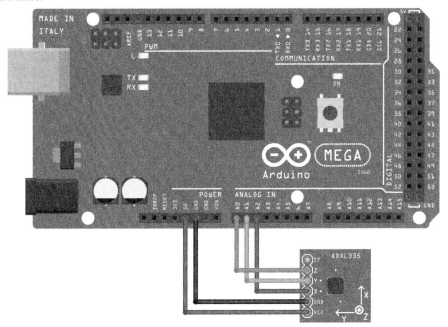

Figure 9.14 – Interfacing Arduino – ADXL 335

The ADLX 335 is an analog accelerometer. We can simply connect to the ADC port and read the digital value. The following is the code snippet and an explanation of the embedded code to interface the ADLX 335 with the Arduino ADC.

The `rosserial_arduino` package has an `Adc` message type, which can be used for this application. We create an `Adc` message variable and create a ROS publisher to start to publish the `Adc` values:

```
ros::NodeHandle nh;
rosserial_arduino::Adc adc_msg;
ros::Publisher pub("adc", &amp;adc_msg);
```

We average the analog reading to eliminate some of the noise:

```
int averageAnalog(int pin){
  int v=0;
```

```
for(int i=0; i<4; i++) v+= analogRead(pin);
return v/4;
}
```

Inside the `loop()` method, we can insert the ADC values of *X*, *Y*, and *Z* axes to the ADC message and publish them in a topic called `/adc`. We can plot the values using the `rqt_plot` tool:

```
void loop()
{
    adc_msg.adc0 = averageAnalog(xpin);
    adc_msg.adc1 = averageAnalog(ypin);
    adc_msg.adc2 = averageAnalog(zpin);
    pub.publish(&amp;adc_msg);
    nh.spinOnce();
    delay(10);
}
```

The following is the command to plot the three axes values in a single plot:

```
rqt_plot adc/adc0 adc/adc1 adc/adc2
```

Next is a screenshot of the plot of the three channels of ADC:

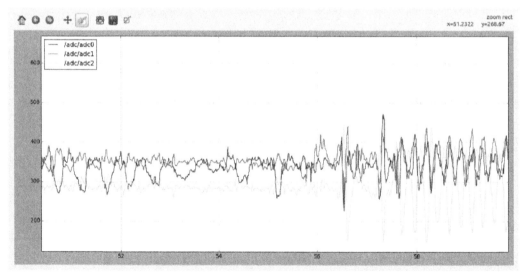

Figure 9.15 – Plotting ADXL 335 values using rqt_plot

We have seen how to interface an accelerometer to Arduino and how to publish the values as ROS topics. In the next section, we will see how to interface an ultrasonic distance sensor with Arduino and publish the value as a ROS topic.

Arduino-ROS example – ultrasonic distance sensor

One of the useful types of sensors in robots is range sensors. One of the cheapest ranges of sensors is the ultrasonic distance sensor. The ultrasonic sensor has two pins for handling input and output, called `Echo` and `Trigger`. We are using the HC-SR04 ultrasonic distance sensor, which is shown in the following diagram:

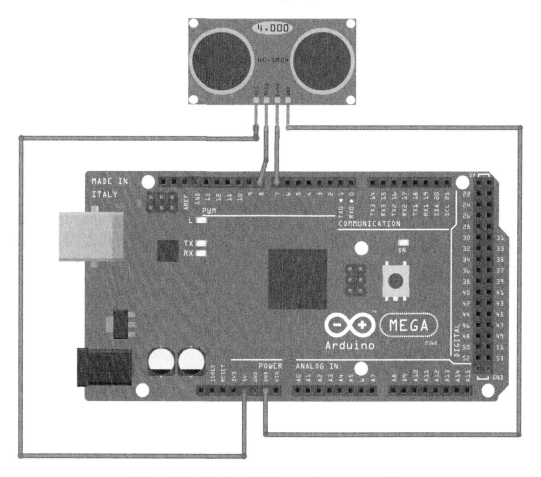

Figure 9.16 – Plotting ADXL 335 values using rqt_plot

The ultrasonic sound sensor contains two sections: one is the transmitter and the other is the receiver. The ultrasonic distance sensor works like this: when a trigger pulse with a short duration is applied to the trigger pin of the ultrasonic sensors, the ultrasonic transmitter sends the sound signals to the robot environment. The sound signal sent from the transmitter hits some obstacles and is reflected in the sensor. The reflected sound waves are collected by the ultrasonic receiver, generating an output signal that has a relation to the time required to receive the reflected sound signals.

Equations to find distance using the ultrasonic range sensor

The following are the equations used to compute the distance from an ultrasonic range sensor to an obstacle:

*Distance = Speed * Time/2*

Speed of sound at sea level = 343 m/s or 34,300 cm/s

*Thus, Distance = 17,150 * Time (unit cm)*

We can compute the distance to the obstacle using the pulse duration of the output. The following is the code to work with the ultrasonic sound sensor and send a value through the ultrasound topic using the range message definition in ROS.

We can use the ROS `sensor_msgs/Range` message definition to handle the ultrasonic sensor data. We have included the following header to get this ROS message:

```
#include <sensor_msgs/Range.h>
```

Create the `Range` ROS message type and publish it in the `ultrasound` topic:

```
sensor_msgs::Range range_msg;
ros::Publisher pub_range( "/ultrasound", &amp;range_msg);
```

We can fill the range message with values that are not going to change. For example, the frame ID, field of view, and the minimum and maximum range can be filled in this message in the `setup()` function:

```
void setup() {

  range_msg.radiation_type = sensor_msgs::Range::ULTRASOUND;
  range_msg.header.frame_id =  frameid;
  range_msg.field_of_view = 0.1;  // fake
  range_msg.min_range = 0.0;
  range_msg.max_range = 60;
```

```
  pinMode(trigPin, OUTPUT);
  pinMode(echoPin, INPUT);

}
```

The following function will return the distance of the object from the ultrasonic sensor:

```
float getRange_Ultrasound(){

 int val = 0;
 for(int i=0; i<4; i++) {
digitalWrite(trigPin, LOW);
 delayMicroseconds(2);
 digitalWrite(trigPin, HIGH);
 delayMicroseconds(10);
 digitalWrite(trigPin, LOW);
 duration = pulseIn(echoPin, HIGH);

 //Calculate the distance (in cm) based on the speed of sound.
  val += duration;
 }
 return val / 232.8 ;

}
```

In the `loop()` method, the range value is published every 50 milliseconds, the time required to stabilize the sensor:

```
void loop() {
   if ( millis() >= range_time ){
    int r =0;

   range_msg.range = getRange_Ultrasound();
   range_msg.header.stamp = nh.now();
   pub_range.publish(&amp;range_msg);
   range_time =  millis() + 50;
 }
```

```
    nh.spinOnce();

  delay(50);
}
```

We can plot the distance value using the following commands:

- Start `roscore`:

  ```
  roscore
  ```

- Start `serial_node.py`:

  ```
  rosrun rosserial_python serial_node.py /dev/ttyACM0
  ```

- Plot values using `rqt_plot`:

  ```
  rqt_plot /ultrasound
  ```

As seen in the following screenshot, the centerline indicates the current distance (`range`) from the sensor. The upper line is the `max_range` and the line below is the `min_range`.

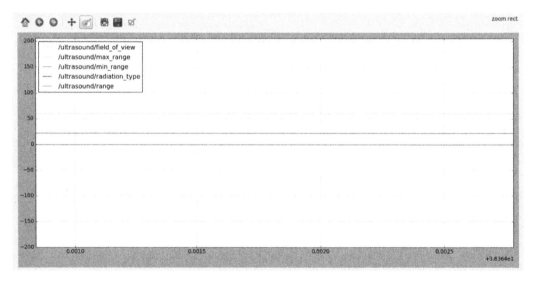

Figure 9.17 – Plotting the ultrasonic sound sensor distance value

We have seen how to interface an ultrasonic distance sensor to Arduino and publish the range values in a ROS topic. In the next section, we will see how to generate odometry data from Arduino and publish it as a ROS topic.

Arduino-ROS example – odometry data publisher

In this example, we will see how to send an odom message from an Arduino node to a PC. This example can be used in a robot for computing odom and sending it to the ROS navigation stack as the input. The motor encoders can be used for computing odom and can transmit to a PC. In this example, we will see how to send odom for a robot that is moving in a circle, without taking the motor encoder values.

The following will create a transform broadcaster object to publish the transform between the base_link and odom frame:

```
geometry_msgs::TransformStamped t;
tf::TransformBroadcaster broadcaster;
```

We will initialize the TF broadcaster in the setup() function:

```
void setup()
{
  nh.initNode();
  broadcaster.init(nh);
}
```

Generate an odom value X, Y, and theta using the circle equation:

```
void loop()
{
  double dx = 0.2;
  double dtheta = 0.18;

  x += cos(theta)*dx*0.1;
  y += sin(theta)*dx*0.1;
  theta += dtheta*0.1;

  if(theta > 3.14)
    theta=-3.14;
```

Publish the current odom values as a transform between base_link and odom:

```
  t.header.frame_id = odom;
  t.child_frame_id = base_link;
```

```
t.transform.translation.x = x;
t.transform.translation.y = y;

t.transform.rotation = tf::createQuaternionFromYaw(theta);
t.header.stamp = nh.now();

broadcaster.sendTransform(t);
nh.spinOnce();

delay(10);
}
```

After uploading the code, run `roscore` and `rosserial_node.py`. We can view `tf` and `odom` in RViz. Open RViz and view `tf`, as shown next. We will see the `odom` pointer moving in a circle on RViz, as follows:

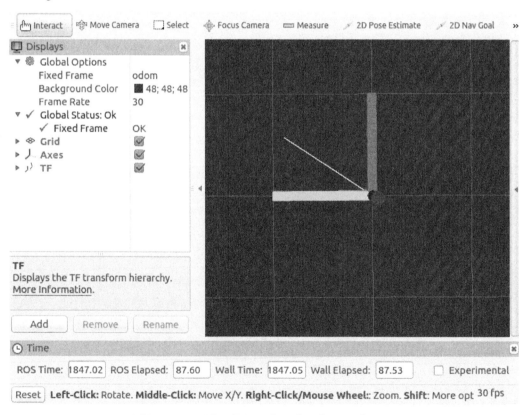

Figure 9.18 – Visualizing odom data from Arduino

We have seen how to generate odometry data from Arduino and publish the values as a ROS topic. In the next section, we will see how to interface different Arduino-like boards to ROS.

Interfacing non-Arduino boards to ROS

Arduino boards are commonly used boards in robots, but what happens if we want a board that is more powerful than Arduino? In such a case, we may want to write a custom driver for the board, which can convert the serial messages into topics. The following link helps you to guide writing a custom driver for the new board: `http://wiki.ros.org/action/fullsearch/rosserial_client/Tutorials/Adding%20Support%20for%20New%20Hardware`.

Setting up the Odroid-C4, Raspberry Pi 4, and Jetson Nano for installing ROS

The Odroid-C4 and Raspberry Pi 4 are single-board computers that have a low form factor, the size of a credit card. These single board computers can be installed in robots and we can install ROS on them.

A comparison of the main specifications of Odroid-C4, Raspberry Pi 4, and Jetson Nano is shown next:

Device	Odroid-XU4	Raspberry Pi 4	Jetson Nano
CPU	2.0 GHz quad-core ARM Cortex-A55 CPU from Amlogic	1.5 GHz quad-core ARM Cortex A72-64-bit CPU from Broadcom	quad-core ARM A57 @ 1.43 GHz
GPU	Mali-G31 GPU	VideoCore IV	128-core Maxwell
Memory	4 GB	2 GB, 4 GB or 8 GB	2GB, 4 GB 64-bit LPDDR4 25.6 GB/s
Storage	SD card slot or eMMC module	SD card slot	SD card slot
Connectivity	4 x USB 3.0, 1 x Micro USB 2.0 (OTG), HDMI 2.0, Gigabit Ethernet	2 x USB 3.0, 2 x micro-HDMI, Ethernet, 3.5 mm audio jack	4x USB 3.0, USB 2.0, Micro-B, HDMI and display port, Gigabit Ethernet
OS	Android, Ubuntu/Linux	Raspbian, Ubuntu/Linux, Windows 10, Android	Ubuntu
Connectors	GPIO, SPI, I2C, ADC, PWM	Camera interface (CSI), Display interface (DSI), GPIO, SPI, I2C, JTAG	GPIO, I2C, I2S, SPI, UART
Price	$50	$35, $55, $75	$54, $99

Figure 9.19 – Comparison of boards

The following is a photograph of the Odroid-C4 board:

Figure 9.20 – Odroid-C4 board

The Odroid board is manufactured by a company called **Hard Kernel**. The official web page of the Odroid-C4 board is at `https://www.hardkernel.com/shop/odroid-c4/`.

Odroid-C4 is one of the latest boards of the Odroid family. There are cheaper and lower-performance boards as well, such as Odroid-C1+ and C2. All these boards support ROS. One of the popular single-board computers is the Raspberry Pi. Raspberry Pi boards are manufactured by the **Raspberry Pi Foundation**, which is based in the UK (visit `https://www.raspberrypi.org`).

The following is a photograph of the Raspberry Pi 4 board:

Figure 9.21 – The Raspberry Pi 4 board

We can install Ubuntu and Android on Odroid. There are also unofficial distributions of Linux, such as Debian mini, Kali Linux, Arch Linux, and Fedora, and support libraries such as ROS, OpenCV, PCL, and so on. To get ROS on Odroid, we can either install a fresh Ubuntu version 20.04 and install ROS manually like a standard desktop PC, or directly download the unofficial Ubuntu distribution for Odroid with ROS already installed.

Figure 9.22 – The Jetson Nano board

NVIDIA Jetson Nano is one of the popular and affordable ARM-based SBCs from NVIDIA. There are two variants from Jetson Nano, one 2 GB and one 4 GB. Compared with the other two boards, Nano has a great advantage to do GPU-based computing for deep learning applications.

An image for Ubuntu 20.04 for Odroid boards can be downloaded from `https://wiki.odroid.com/odroid-c4/odroid-c4`. You can download the Ubuntu MATE desktop version or Ubuntu minimal images board from `https://wiki.odroid.com/odroid-c4/os_images/ubuntu`.

A list of the other operating systems supported on Odroid-C4 is given on the wiki page mentioned previously.

Raspberry Pi 4 official OS images are given at `https://www.raspberrypi.org/software/`. The official OS supported by the Raspberry Pi Foundation is the Raspberry Pi OS (previously called Raspbian). There is an unofficial Ubuntu MATE distribution that is also available for Raspberry Pi 4 here: `https://ubuntu-mate.org/ports/raspberry-pi/`.

There are 32- and 64-bit versions of the OS for the Raspberry Pi. The 64-bit version performs well compared to the 32-bit OS.

From my personal experience, both the Ubuntu and Raspbian OSes will work fine. I prefer Ubuntu MATE for robots compared to the Raspberry Pi OS. The reason is that Ubuntu has the latest software packages and there is not much difference in the OS if you are working with Ubuntu 20.04 on your desktop.

In Jetson Nano, we can install customized Ubuntu version 18.04 with NVIDIA drivers. You can find the installation instructions at the following link: `https://developer.nvidia.com/embedded/learn/getting-started-jetson`.

You can find the Getting Started guide for each board at the preceding URL. You can click and there is a provision to download and set up the Nano board.

Installing an OS image to the Odroid-C4, Raspberry Pi 4, and Jetson Nano

We can download the Ubuntu image for Odroid and the Ubuntu image for the Raspberry Pi 4 and can install them on a micro SD card, preferably 32 GB. Format the micro SD card in the FAT32 filesystem, or we can use the SD card adapter or the USB memory card reader for connecting to a PC.

We can either install the OS in Windows or Linux. The procedure for installing the OS on these boards follows.

Installing the OS image from Windows/Linux/Mac

In Windows/Linux/Mac, there is a tool called **balenaEtcher**, which is designed to flash the OS to an SD card. This tool will work if you are planning to flash any OS image to the Odroid or Raspberry Pi. You can download the tool from `https://www.balena.io/etcher/`.

Run **balenaEtcher** after installing it from the preceding link. Select the downloaded image, select the target memory card drive, and write the image to the drive.

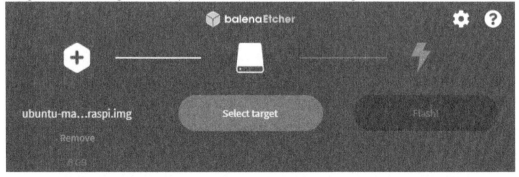

Figure 9.23 – balenaEtcher imager for Raspberry Pi/Odroid/Jetson Nano

After completing this wizard, we can put the micro SD card in the Odroid/Raspberry Pi and boot up the OS.

Installing ROS on the Raspberry Pi 4/Odroid/Nano

If you are working with Ubuntu 20.04 on the Raspberry Pi/Odroid, you can follow the official ROS Noetic installation procedure to install ROS: `http://wiki.ros.org/noetic/Installation/Ubuntu`.

If you are working with the *Raspberry Pi OS*, the following tutorial will help you to install ROS:

```
http://wiki.ros.org/noetic/Installation/Debian
```

```
https://varhowto.com/install-ros-noetic-raspberry-pi-4/
```

Connecting to the Odroid-C4, Raspberry Pi 4, and Jetson Nano from a PC

We can work with the Odroid-XU4, Raspberry Pi 4, and Nano by connecting to the HDMI display port and connecting the keyboard and mouse to the USB like a normal PC. This is the simplest way of working with these boards.

In most projects, the boards will be placed on the robot, so we can't connect the display and the keyboards to them. There are several methods for connecting these boards to a PC. It would be good if we could connect these boards to the internet too. The following methods can connect the internet to these boards, and at the same time, we can remotely connect via the SSH protocol:

- **Remote connection using a Wi-Fi router and Wi-Fi dongle through SSH**: In this method, we need a Wi-Fi router with internet connectivity and a Wi-Fi dongle on the board to get Wi-Fi support. Both the PC and board will connect to the same Wi-Fi network, so each will have an IP address and can communicate using that address.

- **Direct connection using an Ethernet hotspot**: We can share the internet connection and communicate using SSH via `Dnsmasq`, a free software DNS forwarder and DHCP server using few system resources in Linux. Using this tool, we can tether the Wi-Fi internet connection of the laptop to the Ethernet and we can connect the board to the Ethernet port of the PC. This kind of communication can be used for robots that are static in operation. If you are working with Windows, you can think about buying an application called **Connectify Hotspot** (`https://www.connectify.me/`), which can be used to do the same job as `Dnsmasq`. You can easily create an Ethernet hotspot in Windows.

The first method is very easy to configure; it's connecting two PCs on the same network using SSH. You can install `openssh-server` on both systems and both will be ready to connect using the `ssh` command using its IP address.

You can install `openssh-server` using the following command:

```
sudo apt install openssh-server
```

After installing `ssh-server` on both systems, you can try to connect to any computer using the following commands:

- From PC: Connecting to the Odroid:

```
ssh odroid@odroid_ip_address
password is odroid
```

- From PC: Connecting to the Raspberry Pi:

```
ssh pi@rpi_ip_adress
password is raspberry
```

The IP address of each device can be found using the `ifconfig` command in Linux. In Windows, it's `ipconfig`. In order to get the username, you can run the `whoami` command.

The second method is a direct connection from the board to the laptop through the Ethernet cable. This method can be used when the robot is not moving. In this method, the board and the laptop can communicate via SSH at the same time and can share internet access too. The advantage of this method is, because it is wired, we will get more bandwidth from the remote connection compared to the Wi-Fi connection. We are using this method in this chapter for working with ROS.

Configuring an Ethernet hotspot

The procedure for creating an Ethernet hotspot in Ubuntu and sharing Wi-Fi internet through this connection follows.

Go to **Edit Connections...** in the network settings and click on **Add** to add a new connection, as shown next:

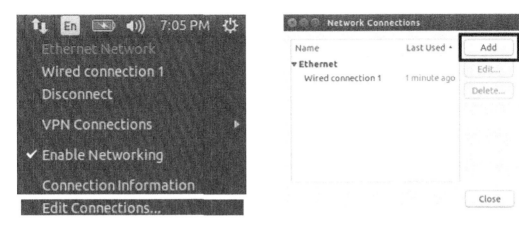

Figure 9.24 – Configuring a network connection in Ubuntu

Create an **Ethernet** connection and in the **IPv4** setting, change the method to **Shared to other computers**, and set the connection name as **Share**, as shown next:

Figure 9.25 – Creating a new connection for sharing through the Ethernet

Plug in the micro SD card, power up the desired board, and connect the Ethernet port from the board to the PC using a LAN cable. When the board boots up, we will see that the shared network is automatically connected to the board network.

We can communicate with the board using the following commands:

- Odroid:

```
ssh odroid@ip_address
password is odroid
```

- Raspberry Pi 4:

```
ssh pi@ip_adress
password is raspberry
```

- Jetson Nano:

```
ssh nvidia@nano_ip_adress
password is nano
```

After doing SSH into the board, we can launch `roscore` and most of the ROS commands on the board like our PC. We will look at two examples using these boards. One is for blinking an LED, and the other is for handling a push button. The library we will use to handle the GPIO pins of the Odroid and Raspberry Pi is called **WiringPi**. The official WiringPi is deprecated so we are going to use the unofficial WiringPi library. For Jetson Nano GPIO handling, NVIDIA provides the jetson-gpio library (`https://github.com/NVIDIA/jetson-gpio`).

The Odroid and Raspberry Pi have the same pin layout and most of the Raspberry Pi GPIO libraries are ported to Odroid, which will make the programming easier. One of the libraries we are using in this chapter for GPIO programming is WiringPi. WiringPi is based on C++ APIs, which can access the board GPIO using C++ APIs.

In the following sections, we will look at the instructions for installing WiringPi on the Odroid and Raspberry 2.

Installing WiringPi on the Odroid-C4

The following procedure can be used to install WiringPi on the Odroid-C4. This is a customized version of WiringPi, which can't be used with the Raspberry Pi 4:

```
git clone https://github.com/hardkernel/wiringPi.git
cd wiringPi
sudo ./build
```

The Odroid-C4 has 40 pins placed as shown in the following diagram:

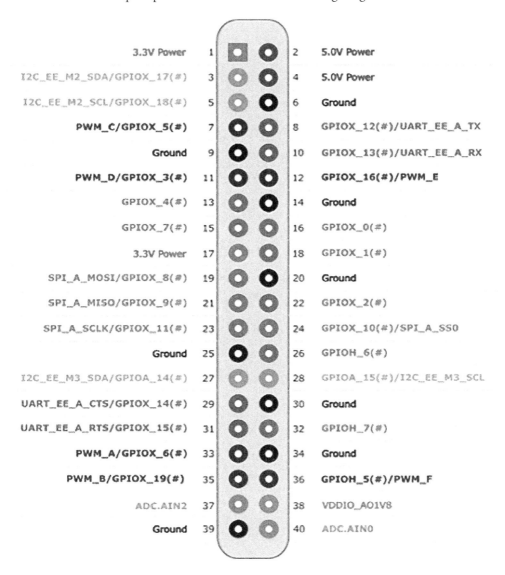

Figure 9.26 – Pinout of the Odroid-C4

We have seen the installation and pinout diagram of the WiringPi library on the Odroid-C4. In the next section, we will see how to install WiringPi on the Raspberry Pi 4.

Installing WiringPi on the Raspberry Pi 4

The following procedure can be used to install WiringPi on the Raspberry Pi 4:

```
git clone https://github.com/WiringPi/WiringPi.git
cd WiringPi
sudo ./build
```

The pinout of the Raspberry Pi 4 and WiringPi is shown next:

P1: The Main GPIO connector							
WiringPi Pin	BCM GPIO	Name	Header		Name	BCM GPIO	WiringPi Pin
		3.3v	1	2	5v		
8	Rv1:0 - Rv2:2	SDA	3	4	5v		
9	Rv1:1 - Rv2:3	SCL	5	6	0v		
7	4	GPIO7	7	8		14	15
		0v	9	10		15	16
0	17	GPIO0	11	12	GPIO1	18	1
2	Rv1:21 - Rv2:27	GPIO2	13	14	0v		
3	22	GPIO3	15	16	GPIO4	23	4
		3.3v	17	18	GPIO5	24	5
12	10	MOSI	19	20	0v		
13	9	MISO	21	22	GPIO6	25	6
14	11	SCLK	23	24	CE0	8	10
		0v	25	26	CE1	7	11

P5: Secondary GPIO connector (Rev. 2 Pi only)							
WiringPi Pin	BCM GPIO	Name	Header		Name	BCM GPIO	WiringPi Pin
		5v	1	2	3.3v		
17	28	GPIO8	3	4	GPIO9	29	18
19	30	GPIO10	5	6	GPIO11	31	20
		0v	7	8	0v		

Figure 9.27 – Pinout of the Raspberry Pi 4

The following are the ROS examples for the Raspberry Pi 4.

Blinking the LED using ROS on the Raspberry Pi 4

This is a basic LED example that can blink the LED connected to the first pin of WiringPi, which is the twelfth pin on the board. The LED cathode is connected to the GND pin and the twelfth pin as an anode. The following diagram shows the circuit of the Raspberry Pi with an LED:

Figure 9.28 – Blinking an LED using the Raspberry Pi 4

We can create the example ROS package, using the following command:

```
catkin_create_pkg ros_wiring_example roscpp std_msgs
```

You will get the existing package from the `ros_wiring_examples` folder.

Create a `src` folder and create the following code, called `blink.cpp`, inside the `src` folder:

```
#include "ros/ros.h"
#include "std_msgs/Bool.h"
#include <iostream>
```

```cpp
//Wiring Pi header
#include "wiringPi.h"

//Wiring PI first pin

#define LED 1

//Callback to blink the LED according to the topic value
void blink_callback(const std_msgs::Bool::ConstPtr&amp; msg)
{

  if(msg->data == 1){
   digitalWrite (LED, HIGH) ;
   ROS_INFO("LED ON");
   }
  if(msg->data == 0){
    digitalWrite (LED, LOW) ;
   ROS_INFO("LED OFF");
     }
}
int main(int argc, char** argv)
{
   ros::init(argc, argv,"blink_led");
   ROS_INFO("Started Raspberry Blink Node");
    //Setting WiringPi
   wiringPiSetup ();  //Setting LED pin as output
   pinMode(LED, OUTPUT);
   ros::NodeHandle n;
   ros::Subscriber sub = n.subscribe("led_blink",10,blink_
callback);
   ros::spin();
}
```

This code will subscribe to a topic called led_blink, which is a Boolean type. If we publish 1 to this topic, it will switch on the LED. If we publish 0, the LED will turn off.

A push button and a blinking LED using ROS on the Raspberry Pi 2

The next example is handling input from a button. When we press the button, the code will publish to the led_blink topic and blink the LED. When the switch is off, the LED will also be OFF. The LED is connected to the twelfth pin and GND, and the button is connected to the eleventh pin and GND. The following diagram shows the circuit of this example. The circuit is also the same for the Odroid:

Figure 9.29 – LED and push button on the Raspberry Pi 2

The code for interfacing the LED and button is given next. The code can be saved with the name `button.cpp` inside the `src` folder:

```
#include "ros/ros.h"
#include "std_msgs/Bool.h"

#include <iostream>
#include "wiringPi.h"

//Wiring PI 1
#define BUTTON 0
#define LED 1
```

The following code snippet is the `led_blink` ROS topic callback:

```
void blink_callback(const std_msgs::Bool::ConstPtr&amp; msg)
{

  if(msg->data == 1){

    digitalWrite (LED, HIGH) ;
   ROS_INFO("LED ON");
   }

  if(msg->data == 0){
    digitalWrite (LED, LOW) ;
   ROS_INFO("LED OFF");
   }

}
```

Initialize the ROS node and pins in the Raspberry Pi for output and input. The output pin is for the LED and the input pin is for interfacing a button. We also have to enable the pull-up resistor to handle input:

```
int main(int argc, char** argv)
{

   ros::init(argc, argv,"button_led");
```

```
ROS_INFO("Started Raspberry Button Blink Node");
wiringPiSetup ();

pinMode(LED, OUTPUT);
pinMode(BUTTON, INPUT);
  pullUpDnControl(BUTTON, PUD_UP); // Enable pull-up resistor
on button
```

Next, create the subscriber and publisher object for the led_blink topic. The publisher will publish when we press the button, and the subscriber of this topic will control the LED:

```
ros::NodeHandle n;
ros::Rate loop_rate(10);

ros::Subscriber sub = n.subscribe("led_blink",10,blink_
callback);
  ros::Publisher chatter_pub = n.advertise<std_
msgs::Bool>("led_blink", 10);


std_msgs::Bool button_press;
button_press.data = 1;

std_msgs::Bool button_release;
button_release.data = 0;

while (ros::ok())
  {
        if (!digitalRead(BUTTON)) // Return True if button
pressed
    {
      ROS_INFO("Button Pressed");
      chatter_pub.publish(button_press);
    }
    else
    {
      ROS_INFO("Button Released");
```

```
        chatter_pub.publish(button_release);
    }
    ros::spinOnce();
    loop_rate.sleep();
  }
}
```

CMakeLists.txt, for building these two examples, is given next. The WiringPi code needs to link with the WiringPi library. We have added this in the CMakeLists.txt file:

```
cmake_minimum_required(VERSION 2.8.3)
project(ros_wiring_examples)


find_package(catkin REQUIRED COMPONENTS
  roscpp
  std_msgs
)


find_package(Boost REQUIRED COMPONENTS system)

//Include directory of wiring Pi
set(wiringPi_include "/usr/local/include")


include_directories(
  ${catkin_INCLUDE_DIRS}
  ${wiringPi_include}
)

//Link directory of wiring Pi
LINK_DIRECTORIES("/usr/local/lib")


add_executable(blink_led src/blink.cpp)


add_executable(button_led src/button.cpp)
```

```
target_link_libraries(blink_led
   ${catkin_LIBRARIES} wiringPi
)
```

```
target_link_libraries(button_led
   ${catkin_LIBRARIES} wiringPi
)
```

Build the project using `catkin_make` and we can run each example. To execute the WiringPi-based code, we need root permission.

Running examples on the Raspberry Pi 4

Now that we have built the project, before running the examples, we should do the following setup for the Raspberry Pi. You can do this setup by logging in to the Raspberry Pi through SSH.

We need to add the following lines to the `.bashrc` file of the root user. Take the `.bashrc` file of the root user:

```
sudo -i
nano .bashrc
```

Add the following lines to the end of this file:

```
source /opt/ros/noetic/setup.sh
source /home/pi/catkin_ws/devel/setup.bash
export ROS_MASTER_URI=http://localhost:11311
```

We can now log in with a different terminal in our Raspberry Pi 4, and run the following commands to execute the `blink_demo` program.

Start `roscore` in one terminal:

```
roscore
```

Run the executable as the root in another terminal:

```
sudo -s
cd /home/pi/catkin_ws/build/ros_wiring_examples
./blink_led
```

After starting the `blink_led` node, publish 1 to the `led_blink` topic in another terminal:

- Here's the code to set the LED to the ON state:

```
rostopic pub /led_blink std_msgs/Bool 1
```

- Here's the code to set the LED to the OFF state:

```
rostopic pub /led_blink std_msgs/Bool 0
```

- Run the button LED node in another terminal:

```
sudo -s
cd  /home/pi/catkin_ws/build/ros_wiring_examples
./button_led
```

Press the button and we can see the LED blinking. We can also check the button state by echoing the topic `led_blink`:

```
rostopic echo /led_blink
```

Interfacing DYNAMIXEL actuators to ROS

One of the latest smart actuators available on the market is DYNAMIXEL, which is manufactured by a company called Robotis. The DYNAMIXEL servos are available in various versions, some of which are shown in the following figure:

Figure 9.30 – Different types of DYNAMIXEL servos

These smart actuators have complete support in ROS, and clear documentation is also available for them.

The official ROS wiki page of DYNAMIXEL is at `http://wiki.ros.org/dynamixel_controllers/Tutorials`.

Summary

This chapter was about interfacing I/O boards to ROS and adding sensors to them. We have discussed the interfacing of the popular I/O board called Arduino to ROS, and the interface's basic components, such as LEDs, buttons, accelerometers, ultrasonic sound sensors, and so on. After looking at the interfacing of Arduino, we discussed how to set up ROS on the Raspberry Pi 2 and Odroid-XU4. We also presented a few basic examples for Odroid and Raspberry Pi based on ROS and WiringPi. Finally, we looked at the interfacing of DYNAMIXEL smart actuators in ROS.

The chapter filled the void of interfacing robotic sensors and actuators to an I/O board or computer. Using this knowledge, you can choose a suitable I/O board for your robot and interface it with ROS.

The next chapter is about creating a differential drive robot from scratch and interfacing the robot with ROS.

Here are some questions based on what we covered in this chapter.

Questions

1. What are the different `rosserial` packages?
2. What is the main function of `rosserial_arduino`?
3. How does the rosserial protocol work?
4. What are the main differences between the Odroid and Raspberry Pi boards?

10
Programming Vision Sensors Using ROS, OpenCV, and PCL

In the previous chapter, we discussed how to interface sensors and actuators using I/O boards in ROS. In this chapter, we are going to discuss how to interface various vision sensors in ROS and program them using libraries such as **Open Source Computer Vision** (**OpenCV**) and **Point Cloud Library** (**PCL**). The robotic vision is an important aspect of any robot for manipulating objects and navigating the environment. There are lots of 2D/3D vision sensors available on the market, and most of these sensors have driver packages to interface with ROS. First, we will discuss how to interface vision sensors with ROS and how to program them using OpenCV and PCL. Finally, we will discuss how to use fiducial marker libraries to develop vision-based robotic applications.

We will cover the following topics in this chapter:

- Understanding ROS – OpenCV interfacing packages
- Understanding ROS – PCL interfacing packages
- Interfacing USB webcams with ROS
- Working with ROS camera calibration

- Interfacing Kinect and Asus Xtion Pro with ROS
- Interfacing the Intel RealSense camera with ROS
- Interfacing Hokuyo lasers with ROS
- Working with point cloud dat

Technical requirements

To follow this chapter, you will need the following software and hardware set up:

- **Hardware**: A good laptop, a webcam supported in Linux and, **optionally**, a depth camera and LIDAR.
- **Software**: Ubuntu **20.04** with ROS Noetic.

Let's start by configuring our system with the necessary ROS packages and libraries for working with robotic vision applications using ROS. We will provide a brief introduction to the OpenCV library and its interfacing package in ROS in the next section.

The reference code for this chapter can be downloaded from the following Git repository: `https://github.com/PacktPublishing/Mastering-ROS-for-Robotics-Programming-Third-edition/tree/main/Chapter10`

You can view this chapter's code in action here: `https://bit.ly/3yZYao1`.

Understanding ROS – OpenCV interfacing packages

OpenCV is one of the most popular open source, real-time computer vision libraries, and it is mainly written in C/C++. OpenCV comes with a BSD license and is free for both academic and commercial applications. OpenCV can be programmed using C/C++, Python, and Java, and it has multi-platform support, such as Windows, Linux, Mac OS X, Android, and iOS. OpenCV has tons of computer vision APIs that can be used for implementing computer vision applications. The web page of the OpenCV library can be found at `https://opencv.org/`.

The OpenCV library is interfaced with ROS via a ROS stack called `vision_opencv`. `vision_opencv` consists of two important packages for interfacing OpenCV with ROS, as follows:

- `cv_bridge`: The `cv_bridge` package contains a library that provides APIs for converting the OpenCV image data type, `cv::Mat`, into a ROS image message called `sensor_msgs/Image` and vice versa. In short, it can act as a bridge between OpenCV and ROS. We can use OpenCV APIs to process the image and convert it into ROS image messages whenever we want to send them to another node. We will discuss how to do this conversion in the upcoming sections.

- `image_geometry`: One of the first processes that we should do before working with cameras is calibration. The `image_geometry` package contains libraries written in C++ and Python, which helps to correct the geometry of the image using calibration parameters. The package uses a message type called `sensor_msgs/CameraInfo` for handling the calibration parameters and feeding the OpenCV image rectification function.

In this section, we will look at some of the important packages in ROS for interfacing the OpenCV library for 2D robotic vision applications. We will also learn how to interface ROS to PCL to perform 3D point cloud processing.

Understanding ROS – PCL interfacing packages

The point cloud is a group of 3D points in space that represent a 3D shape/object. Each point in the point cloud data is represented using X, Y, and Z values. Also, more than just a point in space, it can hold values such as RGB or HSV at each point (`https://en.wikipedia.org/wiki/Point_cloud`). The PCL library is an open source project for performing 3D point cloud processing.

Like OpenCV, it is under the BSD license, and free for academic and commercial purposes. It is also a cross-platform package that has support in Linux, Windows, macOS, and Android/iOS.

The library consists of standard algorithms for filtering, segmentation, feature estimation, and so on, which are required to implement different point cloud-based applications. The main web page of the point cloud library can be found at `http://pointclouds.org/`.

Point cloud data can be acquired by sensors such as Kinect, Asus Xtion Pro, Intel RealSense, and others. We can use this data for robotic applications, such as object detection, grasping, and manipulation. PCL is tightly integrated with ROS for handling point cloud data from various sensors. The `perception_pcl` stack is the ROS interface for the PCL library. It consists of packages for pumping the point cloud data from ROS to PCL data types and vice versa. `perception_pcl` consists of the following packages:

- `pcl_conversions`: This package provides APIs to convert PCL data types into ROS messages and vice versa.

  `pcl_msgs`: This package contains the definition of PCL-related messages in ROS. The PCL messages are `ModelCoefficients`, `PointIndices`, `PolygonMesh`, and `Vertices`.

- `pcl_ros`: This is the PCL bridge of ROS. This package contains the tools and nodes to bridge ROS messages to PCL data types and vice versa.

In the next section, we can discuss the installation of the ROS perception stack and can also see various functions of each package.

Installing ROS perception

In this section, we are going to install a single package called perception, which is a metapackage of ROS that contains all the perception-related packages, such as OpenCV, PCL, and so on:

```
sudo apt install ros-noetic-perception
```

The ROS perception stack contains the following ROS packages:

- `image_common`: This metapackage contains common functionalities for handling an image in ROS. The metapackage consists of the following list of packages (http://wiki.ros.org/image_common):

  - `image_transport`: This package helps compress the image during publishing and subscribes to the images to save bandwidth (http://wiki.ros.org/image_transport). The various compression methods we can use are JPEG/PNG compression and Theora for streaming videos. We can also add custom compression methods to `image_transport`.

  - `camera_calibration_parsers`: This package contains a routine for reading/writing camera calibration parameters from an XML file. This package is mainly used by camera drivers to access calibration parameters.

- `camera_info_manager`: This package consists of a routine that's used to save, restore, and load the calibration information. This is mainly used by camera drivers.

- `polled_camera`: This package contains the interface for requesting images from a polling camera driver (for example, `prosilica_camera`).

- `image_pipeline`: This metapackage contains packages to process the raw image from the camera driver. The processing that's done by this meta-package includes calibration, distortion removal, stereo vision processing, depth-image processing, and so on. The following packages are present in this metapackage for processing (`http://wiki.ros.org/image_pipeline`):

  - `camera_calibration`: One of the important tools for relating the 3D world to the 2D camera image is calibration. This package provides tools for doing monocular and stereo image calibration in ROS.

  - `image_proc`: The nodes in this package act between the camera driver and the vision processing nodes. It can handle the calibration parameters, correct camera distortion from the raw image, and convert images into different colour formats.

  - `depth_image_proc`: This package contains nodes and nodelets for handling depth images from Kinect and 3D vision sensors. Depth images can be processed by these nodelets to produce point cloud data.

  - `stereo_image_proc`: This package contains nodes to perform distortion removal for a pair of cameras. It is the same as the `image_proc` package, except that it handles two cameras – one for stereo vision and another for developing point cloud and disparity images.

  - `image_rotate`: This package contains nodes for rotating the input image.

  - `image_view`: This is a simple ROS tool for viewing ROS message topics. It can also view stereo and disparity images.

- `image_transport_plugins`: These plugins are used for ROS image transport in order to publish and subscribe to the ROS images in different compression levels or different video codecs. This helps reduce bandwidth and latency (`http://wiki.ros.org/image_transport_plugins`).

- `laser_pipeline`: This is a set of packages that can process laser data, such as filtering and converting it into 3D Cartesian points and assembling points to form a cloud (`https://wiki.ros.org/laser_pipeline`). The `laser_pipeline` stack contains the following packages:

  - `laser_filters`: This package contains nodes to filter the noise in the raw laser data, remove the laser points inside the robot footprint, and remove spurious values inside the laser data.

  - `laser_geometry`: After filtering the laser data, we must transform the laser ranges and angles into 3D Cartesian coordinates efficiently by taking into account the tilt and skew angle of the laser scanner.

  - `laser_assembler`: This package can assemble the laser scan into a 3D point cloud or 2.5D scan.

- `perception_pcl`: This is the stack of the PCL-ROS interface.

- `vision_opencv`: This is the stack of the OpenCV-ROS interface.

In this section, we learned how to install ROS perception packages and the list of ROS packages included in the ROS perception stack. In the next section, we will learn how to interface a USB webcam in ROS.

Interfacing USB webcams in ROS

We can interface with an ordinary webcam or a laptop cam in ROS. Overall, there are no ROS-specific packages we must install to use web cameras. If the camera is working in Ubuntu/Linux, it may be supported by the ROS driver too. After plugging in the camera, check whether a `/dev/videoX` device file has been created. You can also check this by using applications such as Cheese, VLC, and others. A guide for checking whether the webcam is supported on Ubuntu is available at `https://help.ubuntu.com/community/Webcam`.

We can find the video devices that are present on the system by using the following command:

```
ls /dev/ | grep video
```

If you get an output of `video0`, then this confirms that a USB camera is available for use.

After ensuring the webcam supports Ubuntu, we can install a ROS webcam driver called `usb_cam` using the following command:

```
sudo apt install ros-noetic-usb-cam
```

We can install the latest package of `usb_cam` from the source code. The driver is available on GitHub at `https://github.com/ros-drivers/usb_cam`.

The `usb_cam` package contains a node called `usb_cam_node`, which is the driver of USB cams. We must configure some ROS parameters before running this node. Let's run the ROS node along with its parameters. The `usb_cam-test.launch` file can launch the USB cam driver with the necessary parameters:

```
<launch>
  <node name="usb_cam" pkg="usb_cam" type="usb_cam_node"
output="screen" >
    <param name="video_device" value="/dev/video0" />
    <param name="image_width" value="640" />
    <param name="image_height" value="480" />
    <param name="pixel_format" value="yuyv" />
    <param name="camera_frame_id" value="usb_cam" />
    <param name="io_method" value="mmap"/>
  </node>
  <node name="image_view" pkg="image_view" type="image_view"
respawn="false" output="screen">
    <remap from="image" to="/usb_cam/image_raw"/>
    <param name="autosize" value="true" />
  </node>
</launch>
```

This launch file will start with `usb_cam_node`, contain the `device /dev/video0` video and have a resolution of 640 x 480. The pixel format here is **YUV** (`https://wiki.videolan.org/YUV`). After initiating `usb_cam_node`, it will start an `image_view` node for displaying the raw image from the driver. We can launch the previous file by using the following command:

```
roslaunch usb_cam usb_cam-test.launch
```

We will get the following message, along with an image preview:

```
[ INFO] [1509310151.685693448]: Using transport "raw"
[ INFO] [1509310151.851576979]: using default calibration URL
[ INFO] [1509310151.851731568]: camera calibration URL: file:///home/jcaca
ce/.ros/camera_info/head_camera.yaml
[ INFO] [1509310151.851937275]: Unable to open camera calibration file [/h
ome/jcacace/.ros/camera_info/head_camera.yaml]
[ WARN] [1509310151.852013709]: Camera calibration file /home/jcacace/.ros
/camera_info/head_camera.yaml not found.
[ INFO] [1509310151.852111773]: Starting 'head_camera' (/dev/video0) at 64
0x480 via mmap (yuyv) at 30 FPS
[ WARN] [1509310152.108112434]: unknown control 'focus_auto'
```

Figure 10.1 – USB camera view using the image view tool

The topics that are generated by the driver are shown in the following screenshot. These are all raw, compressed, and Theora codec topics:

```
/image_view/output
/image_view/parameter_descriptions
/image_view/parameter_updates
/rosout
/rosout_agg
/usb_cam/camera_info
/usb_cam/image_raw
/usb_cam/image_raw/compressed
/usb_cam/image_raw/compressed/parameter_descriptions
/usb_cam/image_raw/compressed/parameter_updates
/usb_cam/image_raw/compressedDepth
/usb_cam/image_raw/compressedDepth/parameter_descriptions
/usb_cam/image_raw/compressedDepth/parameter_updates
/usb_cam/image_raw/theora
/usb_cam/image_raw/theora/parameter_descriptions
/usb_cam/image_raw/theora/parameter_updates
```

Figure 10.2 – List of topics generated by the USB camera driver

We can visualize the image in another window by using the following command:

```
rosrun image_view image_view image:=/usb_cam/image_raw
```

As you can see from the topic list, since we installed the `image_trasport` package, images are published in multiple ways, both compressed and uncompressed. The latter format is useful for sending images to other ROS nodes over the network or to store the video data of the topic in bag files so that they occupy little space on the hard disk. To use the compressed image from a bag file on a remote machine or in the same machine, we must republish it in an uncompressed format by using the `republish` node of the `image_transport` package:

```
rosrun image_transport republish [input format] in:=<in_topic_
base> [output format] out:=<out_topic>
```

The following is an example of this:

```
rosrun image_transport republish compressed in:=/usb_cam/image_
raw [output format] out:=/usb_cam/image_raw/republished
```

Note that in the previous example, we used the topic base name as input (`/usb_cam/img_raw`), not its compressed version (`/usb_cam/image_raw/compressed`).

With that, we have learned how to acquire and process images from cameras. Now, let's look at camera calibration.

Working with ROS camera calibration

Like all sensors, cameras also need to be calibrated so that we can correct the distortions in the camera's images due to its internal parameters, as well as for finding the world coordinates from the camera coordinates.

The primary parameters that cause image distortions are radial distortions and tangential distortions. Using the camera calibration algorithm, we can model these parameters and also calculate the real-world coordinates from the camera coordinates by computing the camera calibration matrix, which contains the focal distance and the principal points.

Camera calibration can be done using a classic black-white chessboard, symmetrical circle pattern, or asymmetrical circle pattern. According to each pattern, we can use different equations to get the calibration parameters. Using certain calibration tools, we can detect these patterns, and each detected pattern is taken as a new equation. When the calibration tool detects enough patterns, it can compute the final parameters for the camera.

ROS provides a package named `camera_calibration` (http://wiki.ros.org/ camera_calibration/Tutorials/MonocularCalibration) to do camera calibration and is part of the image pipeline stack. We can calibrate monocular, stereo, and even 3D sensors, such as Kinect and Intel Realsense.

The first thing we must do before we perform calibration is download the chessboard pattern mentioned in the ROS Wiki page, and then print it and paste it onto some cardboard. This is the pattern we are going to use for calibration. This checkboard is 8 x 6 in size and has 108 mm squares.

Run the `usb_cam` launch file to start the camera driver. We are going to run the camera calibration node of ROS using the raw image from the `/usb_cam/image_raw` topic. The following command will run the calibration node with the necessary parameters:

```
rosrun camera_calibration cameracalibrator.py --size 8x6
--square 0.108 image:=/usb_cam/image_raw camera:=/usb_cam
```

A calibration window will pop up. When we show the calibration pattern to the camera and is it detected, we will see the following output:

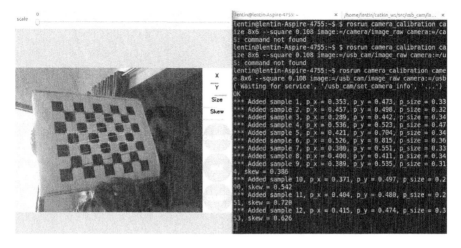

Figure 10.3 – ROS camera calibration

Move the calibration pattern in the **X** and **Y** directions. If the calibrator node gets a sufficient amount of samples, a **CALIBRATE** button will become active on the window. When we press this **CALIBRATE** button, it will compute the camera parameters using these samples. It will take some time to calculate them. After computation, two buttons, **SAVE** and **COMMIT**, will become active inside the window, as shown in the following image. If we press the **SAVE** button, it will save the calibration parameters to the `/tmp/calibrationdata.tar.gz` file. If we press the **COMMIT** button, the new calibration parameters will be updated in the camera driver using a service call. You can also find these calibration parameters are saved in `~/.ros/camera_info/<camera_name.yaml>`, where `camera_name` is the name assigned by the camera driver:

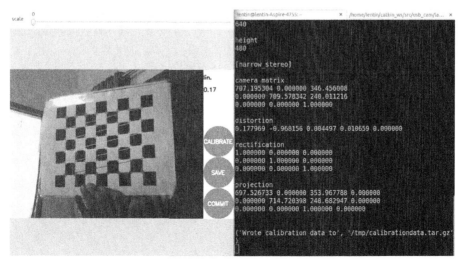

Figure 10.4 – Generating the camera calibration file

Now, if we restart the camera driver, we will see the YAML calibration file being loaded alongside the driver. The calibration file that we generated will look as follows:

```
image_width: 640
image_height: 480
camera_name: head_camera
camera_matrix:
rows: 3
cols: 3
data: [707.1953043273086, 0, 346.4560078627374, 0,
709.5783421541863, 240.0112155124814, 0, 0, 1]
distortion_model: plumb_bob
distortion_coefficients:
rows: 1
cols: 5
data: [0.1779688561999974, -0.9681558538432319,
0.004497434720139909, 0.0106588921249554, 0]
rectification_matrix:
rows: 3
cols: 3
data: [1, 0, 0, 0, 1, 0, 0, 0, 1]
projection_matrix:
  rows: 3
  cols: 4
  data: [697.5267333984375, 0, 353.9677879190494, 0, 0,
714.7203979492188, 240.6829465337159, 0, 0, 0, 1, 0]
```

Now that we have learned how to calibrate cameras using the ROS `camera_calibration` package, we will learn how to convert ROS image messages into OpenCV data types and vice versa. This will help us process ROS image message using the OpenCV library.

Converting images between ROS and OpenCV using cv_bridge

In this section, we will learn how to convert between the ROS image message (`sensor_msgs/Image`) and the OpenCV image data type (`cv::Mat`). The main ROS package that's used for this conversion is `cv_bridge`, which is part of the `vision_opencv` stack. The ROS library inside `cv_bridge`, called CvBridge, helps perform this conversion. We can use the CvBridge library inside our code and perform this conversion. The following diagram shows how the conversion is performed between ROS and OpenCV:

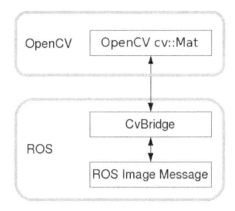

Figure 10.5 – Converting images using CvBridge

Here, the CvBridge library acts as a bridge for converting ROS messages into OpenCV images and vice versa. We will learn how the conversion between ROS and OpenCV is performed in the following example.

Image processing using ROS and OpenCV

In this section, we will look at an example of how to use `cv_bridge` to acquire images from a camera driver, as well as how to convert and process the images using OpenCV APIs. Let's look at how this example works:

- Subscribe the images from the camera driver from the `/usb_cam/image_raw` topic (`sensor_msgs/Image`).

- Convert the ROS images into the OpenCV image type using CvBridge.

- Process the OpenCV image using its APIs and find the edges on the image.

- Convert the OpenCV image type of the edge detection into ROS image messages and publish them to the `/edge_detector/processed_image` topic.

Follow these steps to build this example:

1. Create a ROS package for the experiment.

    You can get this package from the `Chapter 10` code folder. Alternatively, you can create a new package using the following command:

```
catkin_create_pkg cv_bridge_tutorial_pkg cv_bridge image_
transport roscpp sensor_msgs std_msgs
```

    This package is mainly dependent on `cv_bridge`, `image_transport`, and `sensor_msgs`.

2. Create the necessary source files.

    You can get the source code of the example `sample_cv_bridge_node.cpp` file from the `Chapter_10/cv_bridge_tutorial_pkg/src` folder.

3. Explain the code.

    Here is the explanation of the `cv_bridge node.cpp` source code.

```
#include <image_transport/image_transport.h>
```

4. Here, we are using the `image_transport` package to publish and subscribe to an image in ROS:

```
#include <cv_bridge/cv_bridge.h>
#include <sensor_msgs/image_encodings.h>
```

5. This header includes the `CvBridge` class and all the image encoding-related functions in the code:

```
#include <opencv2/imgproc/imgproc.hpp>
#include <opencv2/highgui/highgui.hpp>
```

6. These are the main OpenCV image processing modules and GUI modules, which provide image processing and GUI APIs in our code:

```
    image_transport::ImageTransport it_;
public:
  Edge_Detector()
    : it_(nh_)
  {
    // Subscribe to input video feed and publish output
video feed
```

```
    image_sub_ = it_.subscribe("/usb_cam/image_raw", 1,
        &ImageConverter::imageCb, this);


    image_pub_ = it_.advertise("/edge_detector/raw_
image", 1);
```

Let's look at the `image_transport::ImageTransport it_` line in more detail. This line creates an instance of `ImageTransport`, which is used to publish and subscribe to the ROS image messages. More information about the `ImageTransport` API will be provided in the next section.

Publishing and subscribing to images using image_transport

ROS `image_transport` is very similar to ROS publishers and subscribers, and it is used to publish or subscribe to the images, along with the camera information. We can publish the image data using `ros::Publisher`, but image transport is a more efficient way of sending image data.

The image transport APIs are provided by the `image_transport` package. Using these APIs, we can transport an image in different compression formats; for example, we can transport it as an uncompressed image, a JPEG/PNG compression, or as a **Theora** (https://www.theora.org/) compression in separate topics. We can also add different transport formats by adding plugins. By default, we can see the compressed and Theora transports:

```
    image_transport::ImageTransport it_;
```

```
In the following line, we are creating an instance of the
ImageTransport class:
    image_transport::Subscriber image_sub_;
    image_transport::Publisher image_pub_;
After that, we declare the subscriber and publisher objects
for subscribing and publishing the images, using the image_
transport object:
image_sub_ = it_.subscribe("/usb_cam/image_raw", 1,
        &ImageConverter::imageCb, this);
image_pub_ = it_.advertise("/edge_detector/processed_image",
1);
The following is how we subscribe and publish an image:
    cv::namedWindow(OPENCV_WINDOW);
}
```

```
~Edge_Detector()
{
    cv::destroyWindow(OPENCV_WINDOW);
}
```

This is how we subscribe and publish to an `image`. `cv::namedWindow()`, which is an OpenCV function that's used to create a GUI for displaying an image. The argument inside this function is the window's name. Inside the class destructor, we are destroying the named window.

Converting OpenCV into ROS images using cv_bridge

This is an image callback function, and it converts the ROS image messages into the OpenCV `cv::Mat` type using the `CvBridge` APIs. The following is how we can convert ROS into OpenCV, and vice versa:

```
void imageCb(const sensor_msgs::ImageConstPtr& msg)
{

    cv_bridge::CvImagePtr cv_ptr;
    namespace enc = sensor_msgs::image_encodings;

    try
    {
        cv_ptr = cv_bridge::toCvCopy(msg, sensor_msgs::image_
encodings::BGR8);
    }
    catch (cv_bridge::Exception& e)
    {
        ROS_ERROR("cv_bridge exception: %s", e.what());
        return;
    }
```

In terms of `CvBridge`, we should start by creating an instance of a `CvImage`. The following command creates the `CvImage` pointer:

```
cv_bridge::CvImagePtr cv_ptr;
```

The `CvImage` type is a class provided by `cv_bridge`, which consists of information such as an OpenCV image and its encoding, ROS header, and so on. Using this type, we can easily convert a ROS image into OpenCV, and vice versa:

```
cv_ptr = cv_bridge::toCvCopy(msg, sensor_msgs::image_
encodings::BGR8);
```

We can handle the ROS image message in two ways: we can make a copy of the image or we can share the image data. When we copy the image, we can process the image, but if we use a shared pointer, we can't modify the data. We can use `toCvCopy()` to create a copy of the ROS image; the `toCvShare()` function is used to get the pointer of the image. Inside these functions, we should mention the ROS message and the type of encoding:

```
if (cv_ptr->image.rows > 400 && cv_ptr->image.cols > 600){
  detect_edges(cv_ptr->image);
     image_pub_.publish(cv_ptr->toImageMsg());
  }
```

Here, we are extracting the image and its properties from the `CvImage` instance, and then accessing the `cv::Mat` object from this instance. This code simply checks whether the rows and columns of the image are in a particular range, and if this is true, it will call another method called `detect_edges(cv::Mat)`, which will process the image that was provided as an argument and display the edge-detected image:

```
image_pub_.publish(cv_ptr->toImageMsg());
```

The preceding line will publish the edge-detected image after converting it into the ROS image message. Here, we are using the `toImageMsg()` function to convert the `CvImage` instance into a ROS image message.

Finding edges on the image

After converting the ROS images into the OpenCV type, the `detect_edges(cv::Mat)` function must be called to find the edges on the image. We can do this using the following built-in OpenCV functions:

```
cv::cvtColor( img, src_gray, CV_BGR2GRAY );
cv::blur( src_gray, detected_edges, cv::Size(3,3) );
cv::Canny( detected_edges, detected_edges, lowThreshold,
lowThreshold*ratio, kernel_size );
```

Here, the cvtColor() function will convert an RGB image into a gray color space, and cv::blur() will add blurring to the image. After that, using the Canny edge detector, we can extract the edges of the image.

Visualizing raw and edge-detected images

Here, we are displaying the image data using the imshow() OpenCV function, which consists of the window name and the image name:

```
cv::imshow(OPENCV_WINDOW, img);
cv::imshow(OPENCV_WINDOW_1, dst);
cv::waitKey(3);
```

Now that we've looked at the code in detail, let's learn how to edit the CMakeLists.txt file to build the preceding code.

Editing the CMakeLists.txt file

The definition of the CMakeLists.txt file is as follows. In this example, we need OpenCV support, so we should include the OpenCV header path and also link the source code with the OpenCV libraries:

```
include_directories(
  ${catkin_INCLUDE_DIRS}
  ${OpenCV_INCLUDE_DIRS}
)

add_executable(sample_cv_bridge_node src/sample_cv_bridge_node.
cpp)

## Specify libraries to link a library or executable target
against
  target_link_libraries(sample_cv_bridge_node
    ${catkin_LIBRARIES}
    ${OpenCV_LIBRARIES}
  )
```

Now that we have edited the CMakeLists.txt file inside the ROS package, let's learn how to build the package and run the application.

Building and running an example

After building the package using `catkin_make`, we can run the node by performing the following steps:

1. Launch the webcam driver:

    ```
    roslaunch usb_cam usb_cam-test.launch
    ```

2. Run the `cv_bridge` sample node:

    ```
    rosrun cv_bridge_tutorial_pkg sample_cv_bridge_node
    ```

3. If everything works fine, we will get two windows, as shown in the following image. The first window shows the raw image, while the second shows the processed edge-detected image:

Figure 10.6 – Raw image and an edge-detected image

Now that we have learned how to run the ROS-OpenCV application, let's learn how to interface advanced depth sensors such as Kinect, Asus Xtion Pro, and Intel RealSense with ROS.

Interfacing Kinect and Asus Xtion Pro with ROS

The webcams that we have worked with until now can only provide 2D visual information of their surroundings. To get 3D information about our surroundings, we must use 3D vision sensors or range finders, such as laser finders. Some of the 3D vision sensors that we will be discussing in this chapter are Kinect, Asus Xtion Pro, Intel RealSense, and Hokuyo laser scanner:

Figure 10.7 – Top: Kinect; bottom: Asus Xtion Pro

The first two sensors we are going to discuss are Kinect and Asus Xtion Pro. Both of these devices need the **Open Source Natural Interaction (OpenNI)** driver library to operate in Linux. OpenNI acts as a middleware between the 3D vision devices and the application software. The OpenNI driver is integrated into ROS, and we can install these drivers by using the following commands. These packages help us interface OpenNI-supported devices such as Kinect and Asus Xtion Pro:

```
sudo apt install ros-noetic-openni2-launch ros-noetic-openni2-
camera
```

The preceding command will install the OpenNI drivers and launch files for starting the RGB/depth streams. After successfully installing these packages, we can launch the driver by using the following command:

```
roslaunch openni2_launch openni2.launch
```

This launch file will convert the raw data from the devices into usable data, such as 3D point clouds, disparity images, and depth, and the RGB images that use ROS nodelets.

Other than the OpenNI drivers, there is another driver available called `lib-freenect`. The common launch files of this driver are organized into a package called `rgbd_launch`. This package consists of common launch files that are used for the `freenect` and `openni` drivers.

We can visualize the point cloud that's generated by the OpenNI ROS driver using RViz.

You can run RViz using the following command:

```
rosrun RViz RViz
```

Set the fixed frame to `/camera_depth_optical_frame`, add a `PointCloud2` display, and set the topic to `/camera/depth/points`. This is the unregistered point cloud from the IR camera; that is, it may match the RGB camera and only use the depth camera to generate the point cloud:

Figure 10.8 – Unregistered point cloud view in RViz

We can enable the registered point cloud by using the **Dynamic Reconfigure** GUI. To do this, use the following command:

```
rosrun rqt_reconfigure rqt_reconfigure
```

You will get the following **Dynamic Reconfigure** plugin in `rqt`:

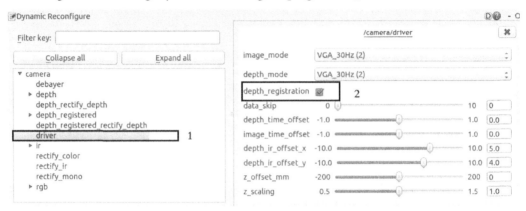

Figure 10.9 – Dynamic Reconfigure GUI

Click on **camera | driver** and tick `depth_registration`. Change the point cloud to `/camera/depth_registered/points` and **Color Transformer** to **RGB8** in RViz. The registered point cloud in RViz will look as follows. It takes information from the depth and the RGB camera to generate the point cloud:

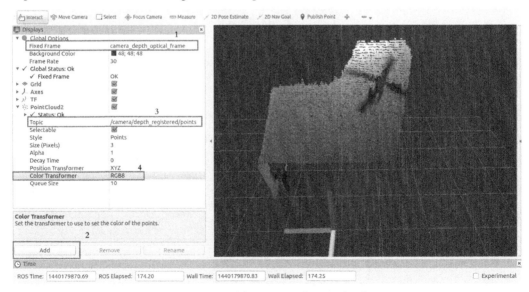

Figure 10.10 – The registered point cloud

With that, we have learned how to set up the interfaces of Kinect and Asus Xtion Pro in ROS. We also learned how to visualize the point cloud from these depth sensors. In the next section, we will learn how to interface another depth camera called **Intel RealSense** in ROS.

Interfacing the Intel RealSense camera with ROS

One of the new 3D depth sensors from Intel is RealSense. At the time of writing, different versions of this sensor have been released (LIDAR camera L515, D400 family, D435, T265, F200, R200, and SR30). To interface RealSense sensors with ROS, we must install the `librealsense` library.

You can install the `librealsense` library using the `apt` package manager. Detailed instructions for setting up this library can be found at `https://github.com/IntelRealSense/librealsense/blob/master/doc/distribution_linux.md`.

We can also build the `librealsense` library from source code manually. Let's learn how to install the library.

Download the RealSense SDK (`https://www.intelrealsense.com/sdk-2/`) from the following link: `https://github.com/IntelRealSense/librealsense/blob/master/doc/installation.md`.

After installing the RealSense library, we must install the ROS wrapper (`https://dev.intelrealsense.com/docs/ros-wrapper`) to start sensor data streaming. The binary installation and manual installation steps can be found in the following Github repository: `https://github.com/IntelRealSense/realsense-ros`.

Now, we can start the sensor using the example launch file and open RViz to visualize the color and depth data that's streamed by RealSense:

```
roslaunch realsense2_camera rs_camera.launch
```

The following image shows how the point cloud, depth image, RGB image, and IR image are visualized by the Intel RealSense sensor:

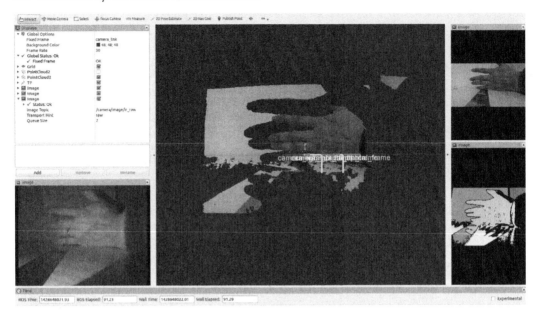

Figure 10.11 – Intel RealSense view in RViz

The following are the important topics that were generated by the RealSense driver:

sensor_msgs::PointCloud2	
/camera/depth/color/points	point cloud with RGB

sensor_msgs::Image	
/camera/image/image_raw sensor	raw image for RGB
/camera/depth/image_rect_raw sensor	raw image for depth
/camera/infra1/image_rect_raw infrared sensor	raw image for

With that, we have learned how to set up the Intel RealSense ROS package and visualized the different image data from the camera. In the next section, we will learn how to convert the point cloud and depth image data from the depth camera into laser scan data.

Converting point cloud to a laser scan

One of the most important applications of 3D vision sensors is mimicking the functionalities of a laser scanner. Most of the 2D/3D mapping and localization algorithms for robots use laser scan data as input. We can make a fake laser scanner using a 3D vision sensor by taking a slice of the point cloud data/depth image and converting it into laser range data. In ROS, we have a set of packages we can use to convert the point cloud data into laser scans:

- `depthimage_to_laserscan`: This package contains nodes that take the depth image from the vision sensor and generate a 2D laser scan based on the provided parameters. The inputs of the node are the depth image and camera info parameters, which include calibration parameters. After converting them into the laser scan data, it will publish laser scanner data in the `/scan` topic. The node parameters are `scan_height`, `scan_time`, `range_min`, `range_max`, and the output frame ID. The official ROS Wiki page for this package can be found at `http://wiki.ros.org/depthimage_to_laserscan`.

- `pointcloud_to_laserscan`: This package converts the real point cloud data into a 2D laser scan, instead of taking a depth image, as in the previous package. The official Wiki page for this package can be found at `http://wiki.ros.org/pointcloud_to_laserscan`.

The first package is suitable for normal applications; however, if the sensor has been placed at an angle, it is better to use the second package. Also, the first package takes less processing than the second one. Here, we are using the `depthimage_to_laserscan` package to convert a laser scan. We can install `depthimage_to_laserscan` and `pointcloud_to_laserscan` using the following command:

```
sudo apt install ros-noetic-depthimage-to-lasersca ROS-noetic-
pointcloud-to-laserscan
```

We can start converting from the depth image of the OpenNI device into the 2D laser scanner by creating a new ROS package.

We can use the following command to create a package for performing this conversion:

```
catkin_create_pkg fake_laser_pkg depthimage_to_laserscan
nodelet roscpp
```

Create a folder called `launch`. Then, inside this folder, create a launch file called `start_laser.launch`. You can get this package and file from the `fake_laser_pkg/launch` folder:

```
<launch>
  <!-- "camera" should uniquely identify the device. All topics
are pushed down
     into the "camera" namespace, and it is prepended to tf
frame ids. -->
  <arg name="camera"        default="camera"/>
  <arg name="publish_tf"    default="true"/>


. . .

. . .

  <group if="$(arg scan_processing)">
    <node pkg="nodelet" type="nodelet"      name="depthimage_
to_laserscan" args="load        depthimage_to_laserscan/
DepthImageToLaserScanNodelet $(arg        camera)/$(arg camera)_
nodelet_manager">
      <!-- Pixel rows to use to generate the laserscan. For
each       column, the scan willreturn the minimum value for
those         pixels centered vertically in the image. -->
      <param name="scan_height" value="10"/>
      <param name="output_frame_id" value="/$(arg
camera)_depth_frame"/>
      <param name="range_min" value="0.45"/>
      <remap from="image" to="$(arg camera)/$(arg          depth)/
image_raw"/>
      <remap from="scan" to="$(arg scan_topic)"/>


. . .

. . .

</launch>
```

The following code snippet will launch the nodelet in order to convert the depth image into a laser scanner:

```
<node pkg="nodelet" type="nodelet" name="depthimage_
to_laserscan" args="load depthimage_to_laserscan/
DepthImageToLaserScanNodelet $(arg camera)/$(arg camera)_
nodelet_manager">
```

Now, let's launch this file so that we can view the laser scanner in RViz.

You can launch the file using the following command:

```
roslaunch fake_laser_pkg start_laser.launch
```

Upon doing this, we will see the laser scanner data in RViz, as shown in the following screenshot:

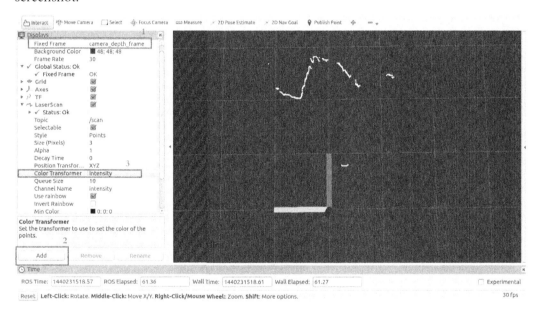

Figure 10.12 – Laser scan in RViz

As the steps are shown in the preceding figure, first, we can set **Fixed Frame** to `camera_depth_frame` and then press **Add** button to display a **LaserScan** data type in RViz. After loading the **LaserScan** display type in RViz, set the **Topic** to `/scan`. After setting the topic, change the **Color Transformer** to `Intensity`.

We can see the laser data in the viewport.

Interfacing Hokuyo lasers with ROS

We can interface with different ranges of laser scanners in ROS. One of the most popular laser scanners available in the market is the Hokuyo laser scanner (`http://www.robotshop.com/en/hokuyo-utm-03lx-laser-scanning-rangefinder.html`):

Figure 10.13 – Different series of Hokuyo laser scanners

One of the most commonly used Hokuyo laser scanner models is **UTM-30LX**. This sensor is fast and accurate and is suitable for robotic applications. The device has a USB 2.0 interface for communication and has a 30-meter range, along with a millimeter resolution. The arc range of the scan is about 270 degrees:

Figure 10.14 – Hokuyo UTM-30LX

There is already a driver available in ROS for interfacing with these scanners. One of the interfaces is called `urg_node` (`http://wiki.ros.org/urg_node`).

We can install this package using the following command:

```
sudo apt install ros-noetic-urg-node
```

When the device connects to the Ubuntu system, it will create a device called `ttyACMx`. Check the device's name by entering the `dmesg` command in the Terminal. You can change the USB device permissions using the following command:

```
sudo chmod a+rw /dev/ttyACMx
```

Start the laser scan device using the `hokuyo_start.launch` launch file:

```
<launch>
  <node name="urg_node" pkg="urg_node" type="urg_node"
output="screen">
          <param name="serial_port" value="/dev/ttyACM0"/>
      <param name="frame_id" value="laser"/>
      <param name="angle_min" value="-1.5707963"/>
          <param name="angle_max" value="1.5707963"/>
  </node>
    name="RViz" pkg="RViz" type="RViz" respawn="false"
output="screen" args="-d $(find hokuyo_node)/hokuyo_test.vcg"/>
</launch>
```

This launch file starts the node and gets the laser data from the `/dev/ttyACM0` device. The laser data can be viewed inside the RViz window, as shown in the following screenshot:

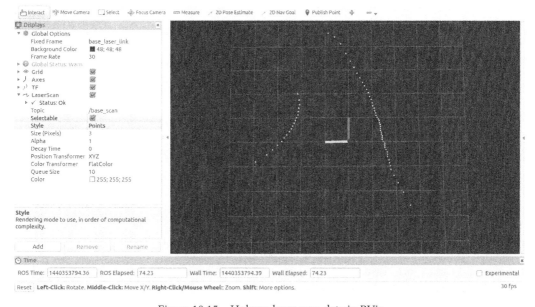

Figure 10.15 – Hokuyo laser scan data in RViz

With that, we have learned how to interface a Hokuyo laser scan with ROS and visualize the data in RViz. In the next section, we will learn how to interface **RPLIDAR** and **YDLIDAR** with ROS.

Interfacing RPLIDAR and YDLIDAR with ROS

If you are planning to work with a low-cost LIDAR for your hobby robot project, then there are a few solutions you can implement. RPLIDAR from SLAMTEC (`https://www.slamtec.com/en/`) and YDLIDAR (`https://www.ydlidar.com/`) are two cost-effective LIDAR solutions for your robot:

RPLIDAR   YDLIDAR

Figure 10.16 – RPLIDAR and YDLIDAR

There is a ROS driver available for both these models, both of which you can find at the following links:

- RPLIDAR ROS driver package: `https://github.com/slamtec/rplidar_ros`

- YDLIDAR ROS driver package: `https://github.com/YDLIDAR/ydlidar_ros`

In this section, we learned how to interface different LIDAR sensors in ROS. In the next section, we will learn how to work with point cloud data in ROS.

Working with point cloud data

We can handle the point cloud data from Kinect or other 3D sensors to perform a wide variety of tasks, such as 3D object detection and recognition, obstacle avoidance, 3D modeling, and so on. In this section, we will look at some basic functionalities; that is, using the PCL library and its ROS interface. We will discuss the following topics:

- How to publish a point cloud in ROS

- How to subscribe and process a point cloud

- How to write point cloud data to a PCD file
- How to read and publish a point cloud from a PCD file

Let's learn how to publish point cloud data as a ROS topic using a C++ example.

How to publish a point cloud

In this example, we will learn how to publish point cloud data using the `sensor_msgs/PointCloud2` message. The code will use PCL APIs to handle and create the point cloud, as well as to convert the PCL cloud data into the `PointCloud2` message type.

You can find the `pcl_publisher.cpp` example code file in the `pcl_ros_tutorial/src` folder. The important section of the code is explained here:

```
#include <ros/ros.h>


// point cloud headers
#include <pcl/point_cloud.h>
#include <pcl_conversions/pcl_conversions.h>
```

The preceding `headers` files contain the necessary functions for handling PCL data and converting between PCL and ROS:

```
#include <sensor_msgs/PointCloud2.h>
```

Here is the ROS message header for handling point cloud data. We must include this header to access the `PointCloud` message definition:

```
    ros::Publisher pcl_pub = nh.advertise<sensor_msgs::PointCloud2> ("pcl_output", 1);
```

Let's look at how to create the publisher object for publishing the point cloud. As you can see, the ROS message we are using here is `sensor_msgs::PointCloud2`, which we're getting by including the `sensor_msgs/PointCloud2.h` file:

```
pcl::PointCloud<pcl::PointXYZ> cloud;
```

Now, create a specific `pointcloud` type object to store the point cloud data:

```
    sensor_msgs::PointCloud2 output;
```

Then, create a point cloud ROS message instance to publish the point cloud data:

```
//Insert cloud data
cloud.width  = 50000;
cloud.height = 2;
cloud.points.resize(cloud.width * cloud.height);
for (size_t i = 0; i < cloud.points.size (); ++i)
{
    cloud.points[i].x = 512 * rand () / (RAND_MAX + 1.0f);
    cloud.points[i].y = 512 * rand () / (RAND_MAX + 1.0f);
    cloud.points[i].z = 512 * rand () / (RAND_MAX + 1.0f);
}
```

Now, let's learn how to insert points into a point cloud object message. Here, we are assigning a set of random points to the point cloud object:

```
pcl::toROSMsg(cloud, output);
output.header.frame_id = "point_cloud";
```

This is how we can convert the point cloud object into a ROS message:

```
ros::Rate loop_rate(1);
while (ros::ok())
{
    //publishing point cloud data
  pcl_pub.publish(output);
    ros::spinOnce();
    loop_rate.sleep();
}

    return 0;
}
```

In the preceding code, we are publishing the converted point cloud message to the /pcl_output topic.

In the next section, we will how to subscribe to and process the point cloud data from the /pcl_output topic.

How to subscribe and process a point cloud

In this section, we are going to look at a ROS C++ example that can subscribe to the topic: /pcl_output point cloud. After subscribing to this point cloud, we will apply a filter from the VoxelGrid class to PCL to downsample the subscribed cloud while keeping it the same shape as the original cloud. You can find the pcl_filter.cpp example code file in the src folder of pcl_ros_tutorial package. Now, let's look at the important sections of this code.

This code has a class called cloudHandler, which contains all the functions for subscribing the point cloud data from the /pcl_output topic:

```cpp
#include <ros/ros.h>
#include <pcl/point_cloud.h>
#include <pcl_conversions/pcl_conversions.h>
#include <sensor_msgs/PointCloud2.h>
//Vortex filter header
#include <pcl/filters/voxel_grid.h>
```

Let's look at the important header files that are required for subscribing to and processing the point cloud. The pcl/filters/voxel_grid.h header contains the definition of the VoxelGrid filter, which is used to downsample the point cloud:

```cpp
class cloudHandler
{
public:
    cloudHandler()
    {

//Subscribing pcl_output topics from the publisher
//This topic can change according to the source of point cloud

    pcl_sub = nh.subscribe("pcl_output", 10,
&cloudHandler::cloudCB, this);
//Creating publisher for filtered cloud data
        pcl_pub = nh.advertise<sensor_msgs::PointCloud2>("pcl_
filtered", 1);
    }
```

Next, we are creating a class called `cloudHandler`. This has a subscriber creation and callback function for the `pcl_output` topic and a `publisher` object for publishing the filtered point cloud:

```
//Creating cloud callback
    void cloudCB(const sensor_msgs::PointCloud2& input)
    {

        pcl::PointCloud<pcl::PointXYZ> cloud;
        pcl::PointCloud<pcl::PointXYZ> cloud_filtered;


        sensor_msgs::PointCloud2 output;
        pcl::fromROSMsg(input, cloud);

    //Creating VoxelGrid object
    pcl::VoxelGrid<pcl::PointXYZ> vox_obj;
    //Set input to voxel object
    vox_obj.setInputCloud (cloud.makeShared());

    //Setting parameters of filter such as leaf size
    vox_obj.setLeafSize (0.1f, 0.1f, 0.1f);

    //Performing filtering and copy to cloud_filtered variable
    vox_obj.filter(cloud_filtered);
        pcl::toROSMsg(cloud_filtered, output);
        output.header.frame_id = "point_cloud";
        pcl_pub.publish(output);
    }
```

Here is the callback function of the `pcl_output` topic. The callback function will convert the ROS PCL message into a PCL data type, then downsample the converted PCL data using the `VoxelGrid` filter, before publishing the filtered PCL to the `/pcl_filtered` topic after converting it into a ROS message:

```
int main(int argc, char** argv)
{
    ros::init(argc, argv, "pcl_filter");
```

```
    ROS_INFO("Started Filter Node");
    cloudHandler handler;
    ros::spin();
    return 0;
}
```

In the `main()` function, we created an object of the `cloudHandler` class and called the `ros::spin()` function to wait for the `/pcl_output` topic.

In the next section, we will learn how to store the point cloud data from `/pcl_output` in a file. `.PCD` files can be used to store point cloud data.

Writing data to a Point Cloud Data (PCD) file

We can save the point cloud data to a PCD file using the following code. Its filename is `pcl_write.cpp`, and it can be found inside the `src` folder:

```
#include <ros/ros.h>
#include <pcl/point_cloud.h>
#include <pcl_conversions/pcl_conversions.h>
#include <sensor_msgs/PointCloud2.h>
//Header file for writing PCD file
#include <pcl/io/pcd_io.h>
```

Here are the important header files that are required to handle the PCD and read/write it from a file:

```
void cloudCB(const sensor_msgs::PointCloud2 &input)
{

    pcl::PointCloud<pcl::PointXYZ> cloud;
    pcl::fromROSMsg(input, cloud);

//Save data as test.pcd file
    pcl::io::savePCDFileASCII ("test.pcd", cloud);
}
```

The preceding callback function, `cloudCB`, will execute whenever a point cloud message is available in the `/pcl_output` topic. The received point cloud ROS message must be converted into the PCL data type and saved as a PCD file using the `pcl::io::savePCDFileASCII()` function:

```
main (int argc, char **argv)
{
    ros::init (argc, argv, "pcl_write");

    ROS_INFO("Started PCL write node");

    ros::NodeHandle nh;
    ros::Subscriber bat_sub = nh.subscribe("pcl_output", 10,
cloudCB);

    ros::spin();

    return 0;
}
```

With that, we have learned how to write the point cloud data to a file. Now, let's learn how to read from the PCD file and publish the point cloud as a topic.

Reading and publishing a point cloud from a PCD file

This code can read a PCD file and publish the point cloud to the `/pcl_output` topic. The `pcl_read.cpp` file is available in the `src` folder:

```
#include <ros/ros.h>
#include <pcl/point_cloud.h>
#include <pcl_conversions/pcl_conversions.h>
#include <sensor_msgs/PointCloud2.h>
#include <pcl/io/pcd_io.h>
```

In this code, we are using the same header files that we used to write the point cloud:

```
main(int argc, char **argv)
{
    ros::init (argc, argv, "pcl_read");
```

```
    ROS_INFO("Started PCL read node");

    ros::NodeHandle nh;
    ros::Publisher pcl_pub = nh.advertise<sensor_
msgs::PointCloud2> ("pcl_output", 1);
```

In the `main()` function, we are creating a ROS publisher object to publish the point cloud that is being read from the PCD file:

```
    sensor_msgs::PointCloud2 output;
    pcl::PointCloud<pcl::PointXYZ> cloud;

//Load test.pcd file
    pcl::io::loadPCDFile ("test.pcd", cloud);

    pcl::toROSMsg(cloud, output);
    output.header.frame_id = "point_cloud";
```

In the preceding code, the PCL data is being read using the `pcl::io::loadPCDFile()` function. Then, it is being converted into a ROS-equivalent point cloud message via the `pcl::toROSMsg()` function:

```
    ros::Rate loop_rate(1);
    while (ros::ok())
    {
//Publishing the cloud inside pcd file
        pcl_pub.publish(output);
        ros::spinOnce();
        loop_rate.sleep();
    }

    return 0;
}
```

In the preceding loop, we are publishing the PCD to a topic at 1Hz.

We can create a ROS package called `pcl_ros_tutorial` to compile these examples:

```
catkin_create_pkg pcl_ros_tutorial pcl pcl_ros roscpp sensor_
msgs
```

Otherwise, we can use the existing package.

Create the preceding examples inside the `pcl_ros_tutorial/src` folder as `pcl_publisher.cpp`, `pcl_filter.cpp`, `pcl_write.cpp`, and `pcl_read.cpp`.

Create a `CMakeLists.txt` file for compiling all the sources:

```
## Declare a cpp executable
add_executable(pcl_publisher_node src/pcl_publisher.cpp)
add_executable(pcl_filter src/pcl_filter.cpp)
add_executable(pcl_write src/pcl_write.cpp)
add_executable(pcl_read src/pcl_read.cpp)


target_link_libraries(pcl_publisher_node
   ${catkin_LIBRARIES}
 )
target_link_libraries(pcl_filter
   ${catkin_LIBRARIES}
 )
target_link_libraries(pcl_write
   ${catkin_LIBRARIES}
 )
target_link_libraries(pcl_read
   ${catkin_LIBRARIES}
 )
```

Build this package using `catkin_make`. Now, we can run `pcl_publisher_node` and view the point cloud inside RViz using the following command:

```
rosrun RViz RViz -f point_cloud
```

The following is a screenshot of the point cloud from `pcl_output`:

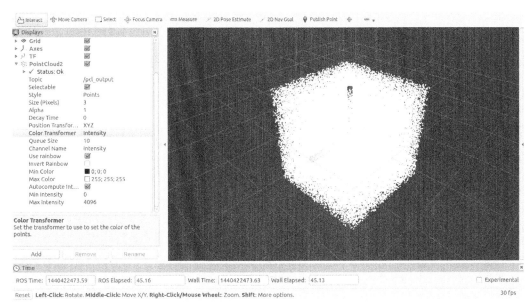

Figure 10.17 – Point cloud visualization

We can run the `pcl_filter` node to subscribe to this same cloud and do voxel grid filtering. The following screenshot shows the output of the `/pcl_filtered` topic, which is the resultant downsampled cloud:

Figure 10.18 - Filtered PCL cloud in RViz

We can write the `pcl_output` cloud by using the `pcl_write` node and read or publish it by using the `pcl_read` nodes.

This was the final topic in this chapter. In this section, we learned how to read, write, filter, and publish point cloud data in ROS. Now, let's summarize this chapter.

Summary

This chapter was about vision sensors and their programming in ROS. We looked at the interfacing packages that are used to interface the cameras and 3D vision sensors, such as `vision_opencv` and `perception_pcl`. We looked at each package and how they function on these stacks. We also looked at how to interface a basic webcam and processing image using ROS `cv_bridge`. After discussing `cv_bridge`, we looked at how to interface various 3D vision sensors and laser scanners with ROS. After this, we learned how to process the data from these sensors using the PCL library and ROS. In the next chapter, we will learn how to build an autonomous mobile robot using ROS.

Here are a few questions based on what we covered in this chapter.

Questions

- What are the packages in the `vision_opencv` stack?
- What are the packages in the `perception_pcl` stack?
- What are the functions of `cv_bridge`?
- How do we convert a PCL cloud into a ROS message?
- How do we do distributive computing using ROS?

11
Building and Interfacing Differential Drive Mobile Robot Hardware in ROS

In the previous chapter, we discussed robotic vision using ROS. In this chapter, we will see how to build autonomous mobile robot hardware with a differential drive configuration and how to interface it in ROS using ROS Control. We will see how to configure the ROS Navigation Stack for this robot and perform SLAM and AMCL to move the robot autonomously. This chapter aims to give you an idea about building a custom mobile robot and interfacing it with ROS. In this chapter, we are going to cover the following main topics:

- Introduction to the Remo robot – a DIY autonomous mobile robot

- Developing a low-level controller and a high-level ROS Control hardware interface for a differential drive robot

- Configuring and working with the Navigation Stack

The topics we are going to discuss in this chapter are how to build a **Do It Yourself** (**DIY**) autonomous mobile robot, called **Research Education Modular/Mobile Open** (**Remo**), develop its high-level software and low-level firmware, and interface it with ROS Control and the ROS Navigation Stack. The robot, called Remo, was built as part of the learning experience of Franz Pucher and received valuable input from the robotic books published by Packt Publishing (`http://learn-robotics.com`) and ROS courses by Joseph Lentin. The step-by-step procedure to build this robot is discussed in its online documentation published at `https://ros-mobile-robots.com`. In this chapter, we will learn more about how to implement a ROS Control `hardware_interface::RobotHW` C++ class and how to configure the ROS Navigation Stack to perform autonomous navigation using SLAM and AMCL. We have already discussed the ROS Navigation Stack in *Chapter 6, Using the ROS MoveIt! and Navigation Stack*, and we have simulated a differential robot using Gazebo and performed SLAM and AMCL. In the first part of the chapter, the Remo hardware is required to follow the tutorials. However, the concepts discussed in the first part of the chapter are then applied to a simulated robot.

Technical requirements

In the `https://github.com/ros-mobile-robots` organization on GitHub are the required ROS packages to set up a differential drive robot. One of the main software repositories is `https://github.com/ros-mobile-robots/diffbot`. It includes packages for simulation and the configurations and software to operate a real robot and interact with it from a development PC. For the hardware, you can build your own two-wheeled differential drive robot similar to the one present in the `diffbot_description` package or 3D print a more stable Remo robot with the `stl` files in `https://github.com/ros-mobile-robots/remo_description`. The next two sections describe the technical requirements for the software and hardware.

You can view this chapter's code in action here: `https://bit.ly/3xU9916`.

Software requirements

For the development PC, you should have ROS Noetic installed on *Ubuntu 20.04* (`https://releases.ubuntu.com/20.04/`). On the *Raspberry Pi 4 B* **Single-Board Computer** (**SBC**) that is mounted on Remo, we use *Ubuntu Mate 20.04* for `arm64` architecture (`https://ubuntu-mate.org/download/arm64/focal/`). To clone large `stl` files from the Git repository we use `git-lfs`. On both Ubuntu flavors it needs to be installed with the following:

```
sudo apt install git-lfs
```

On both the development PC and the SBC of the robot, you need a connection to the same local network and to enable the `ssh` protocol, to connect from the development PC (client) to the robot, which is running an `open-ssh` server. Install it on Ubuntu Mate 20.04 with the following:

```
sudo apt install openssh-server
```

Another interface setup that is needed to work with the microcontroller, is to add your user to the `dialout` group on both machines, the SBC and the development PC. This can be done with the following command, followed by a system reboot:

```
sudo adduser <username> dialout
```

When you clone the `diffbot` repository in a new catkin workspace, you will find two YAML files, `diffbot_dev.repos` and `remo-robot.repos`, that list required source dependencies together with their version control type, the repository address, and a relative path where these dependencies are cloned. `remo_robot.repos` is here to clone source dependencies on the real robot.

To make use of such YAML files and clone the listed dependencies, we use the command-line tools from `vcstool` (`http://wiki.ros.org/vcstool`), which replaces `wstool` (`http://wiki.ros.org/wstool`):

1. In a new catkin workspace, clone the `diffbot` repository inside the `src` folder:

    ```
    ros_ws/src$ git clone --depth 1 --branch 1.0.0 https://
    github.com/ros-mobile-robots/diffbot.git
    ```

2. Make sure to execute the `vcs import` command from the root of the catkin workspace and pipe in the `diffbot_dev.repos` or `remo_robot.repos` YAML file, depending on where you execute the command, either the development PC or the SBC of Remo to clone the listed dependencies:

    ```
    vcs import < src/diffbot/diffbot_dev.repos
    ```

3. Execute the next command on the SBC of the robot:

    ```
    vcs import < src/diffbot/remo_robot.repos
    ```

After obtaining the source dependencies with `vcstool`, we can compile the workspace. To successfully compile the packages of the repository, binary dependencies must be installed. As the required dependencies are specified in each ROS package's `package.xml`, the `rosdep` command can install the required ROS packages from the Ubuntu repositories:

```
rosdep install --from-paths src --ignore-src -r -y
```

Finally, the workspaces on the development machine and the SBC of the robot need to be built, either using `catkin_make` or `catkin tools`. The following uses `catkin_make` which comes pre-installed with ROS:

```
catkin_make
```

Network setup

ROS is a distributed computing environment. This allows running compute-expensive tasks such as visualization or path planning on machines with more performance and sending goals to robots that operate on less performant hardware such as Remo with its Raspberry Pi 4 B. For more details, see the pages on *ROS Network Setup* (`http://wiki.ros.org/ROS/NetworkSetup`) and *ROS Environment Variables* (`http://wiki.ros.org/ROS/EnvironmentVariables`).

The setup between the development machine that handles compute-heavy tasks and Remo is configured by setting the `ROS_MASTER_URI` environment variable to be the IP address of the development machine. To do this, add the `export ROS_MASTER_URI=http://{IP-OF-DEV-MACHINE}:11311/` line to your `bashrc` of the development machine and the SBC of the robot. This will make the development machine the ROS master and you need to execute `roscore` on this machine prior to executing the commands in this chapter.

Hardware requirements

The repository at `https://github.com/ros-mobile-robots/remo_description` contains the robot description of Remo. Remo is a modular mobile robot platform, which is based on NVIDIA's JetBot. The currently available parts can be 3D printed using the provided `stl` files in the `remo_description` repository. To do this, you either need a 3D printer with a recommended build volume of 15x15x15 cm or instruct a local or online 3D print service.

Introduction to the Remo robot – a DIY autonomous mobile robot

In *Chapter 6, Using the ROS MoveIt! and Navigation Stack*, we discussed some mandatory requirements for interfacing a mobile robot with the ROS Navigation Stack. These are recalled at `http://wiki.ros.org/navigation/Tutorials/RobotSetup`:

- **Odometry source**: The robot should publish its odometry/position data with respect to the starting position. The necessary hardware components that provide odometry information are wheel encoders and IMUs, The necessary hardware components that provide odometry information are wheel encoders or inertial measurement units (IMUs).

- **Sensor source**: There should be a laser scanner or a vision sensor. The laser scanner data is essential for the map-building process using SLAM.

- **Sensor transform using tf**: The robot should publish the transform of the sensors and other robot components using ROS transform.

- **Base controller**: A ROS node, which can convert a twist message from the Navigation Stack to the corresponding motor velocities.

We can check the components present in the **Remo** robot and determine whether they satisfy the Navigation Stack requirements.

Remo hardware components

The following figure shows a 3D-printed Remo robot together with its components that satisfy the requirements for the ROS Navigation Stack. These parts are introduced next:

Figure 11.1 – Remo prototype

- **Dagu DC Gear motor encoder** (https://www.sparkfun.com/products/16413): This motor operates in a voltage range between 3 V and 9 V, and provides 80 RPM at 4.5 V. The motor shaft is attached to a quadrature encoder, with a maximum of 542 ticks/rev of the gearbox output shaft. Encoders are one source of odometry.

- **Adafruit Feather motor driver** (https://www.adafruit.com/product/2927): This motor driver can control two stepper motors or four brushed DC motors. For Remo, two brushed DC motor terminals are used. It uses the I2C protocol and operates at 3.3 V for communication. To power the board and apply voltage to the motors, the supported voltages are between 4.5 V and 13.5 V and provide 1.2 A per bridge.

- **Teensy 3.2** (https://www.pjrc.com/teensy/): Remo has a Teensy microcontroller for interfacing with the motor driver and encoders. It can receive control commands from the SBC and can send appropriate signals to the motors, via the motor driver. Teensy 3.2 runs on 72 MHz, which is fast enough to handle reading the encoder ticks. An alternative is the Teensy 4.0 with its 600 MHz Cortex-M7 chip.

- **SLAMTEC RPLIDAR A2 M8** (`https://www.slamtec.com/en/Lidar/A2`): The laser scanner is the RPLIDAR A2 M8 from SLAMTEC with an angular range of 360 degrees. It has a 16 m range radius. Note that it is possible to use the SLAMTEC RPLIDAR A1 but due to its larger dimensions, it is required to adapt the lidar-platform `stl` file, found in the `remo_description/meshes/remo` folder.

- **Raspberry Pi Camera v2** (`https://www.raspberrypi.org/products/camera-module-v2/`): The official Raspberry Pi Camera Module with a Sony IMX219 8-megapixel sensor. It can be used for various tasks such as lane following.

- **Raspberry Pi 4 B**: This is an SBC from the Raspberry Pi Foundation where we install Ubuntu and ROS on its SD card. The SBC is connected to the RPLIDAR and Teensy MCU to retrieve sensor and odometry data. The nodes running on the SBC compute the `tf` transforms between the robot frames and run the ROS Control hardware interface. The Raspberry Pi SBC is placed on the exchangeable deck of Remo. Another deck is available for the Jetson Nano in the `remo_description` package.

- **Powerbank and battery pack**: The robot uses two power supplies. One power bank with 15,000 mAh is used to provide 5 V to the Raspberry Pi and its peripherals such as the Teensy MCU and the RPLIDAR. Another power supply is used to power the motors through the motor driver, which is a battery pack connected to the motor drivers' motor power input terminals. Remo uses a battery pack with eight rechargeable AA batteries (1.2 V, 2,000 mAh), that provides 9.6 V in total.

- **Wi-Fi dongle (optional, recommended)**: Although the Raspberry Pi has a built-in Wi-Fi module, its connectivity can be weak. Therefore, an external USB Wi-Fi dongle is recommended to get a reliable connection to the robot from the development PC.

- **MPU 6050 IMU (optional)**: The IMU used in this robot is the MPU 6050, which is a combination of an accelerometer, gyroscope, and **Digital Motion Processer (DMP)**. The values can be taken to calculate the odometry along with the wheel encoders.

- **OAK-1, OAK-D (optional)**: 4K Camera Modules with an IMX378 sensor and capable of running neural network inference thanks to its Movidius Myriad X chip. OAK-D is a stereo camera with two synchronized grayscale, global shutter cameras (OV9282 sensor) that provide depth information. 3D printable camera holder mounts are available for these cameras in the `remo_description` package.

We can check from the hardware list that all the requirements of the ROS Navigation Stack are satisfied. The following figure shows the block diagram of this robot:

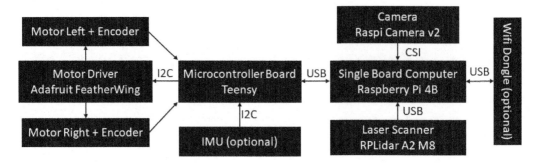

Figure 11.2 – Block diagram of Remo

The Teensy 3.2 microcontroller board is connected to the encoder and optional IMU sensors as well as the motor driver actuator. It communicates to the Raspberry Pi 4 B via USB over the `rosserial` protocol. The motor driver and the optional IMU exchange data over I2C with the microcontroller. The RPLIDAR has a serial-to-USB converter and is therefore connected to one of the USB ports of the SBC. The motor encoder sensors are interfaced through the GPIO pins of the microcontroller. The following shows the connection diagram of the components:

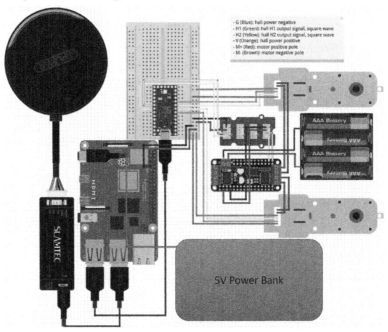

Figure 11.3 – Fritzing connection diagram of Remo

After having verified that the hardware requirements for the Navigation Stack are met, an overview of Remo's software follows.

Software requirements for the ROS Navigation Stack

The `diffbot` and `remo_description` repositories contain the following ROS packages:

- `diffbot_base`: This package contains the platform-specific code for the base controller component required by the ROS Navigation Stack. It consists of the firmware based on `rosserial` for the Teensy MCU and the C++ node running on the SBC that instantiates the ROS Control hardware interface including the `controller_manager` control loop for the real robot. The low-level `base_controller` component reads the encoder ticks from the hardware, calculates angular joint positions and velocities, and publishes them to the ROS Control hardware interface. Using this interface makes it possible to use the `diff_drive_controller` package from ROS Control (`http://wiki.ros.org/diff_drive_controller`). It provides a controller (`DiffDriveController`) for a differential drive mobile base that computes target joint velocities from commands received by either a teleop node or the ROS Navigation Stack. The computed target joint velocities are forwarded to the low-level base controller, where they are compared to the measured velocities to compute suitable motor PWM signals using two separate PID controllers, one for each motor.

- `diffbot_bringup`: Launch files to bring up the hardware driver nodes (camera, lidar, microcontroller, and so on) as well as the C++ nodes from the `diffbot_base` package for the real robot.

- `diffbot_control`: Configurations for `DiffDriveController` and `JointStateController` of ROS Control used in the Gazebo simulation and the real robot. The parameter configurations are loaded onto the parameter server with the help of the launch files inside this package.

- `remo_description`: This package contains the URDF description of Remo including its sensors. It allows you to pass arguments to visualize different camera and SBC types. It also defines the `gazebo_ros_control` plugin. Remo's description is based on the description at `https://github.com/ros-mobile-robots/mobile_robot_description`, which provides a modular URDF structure that makes it easier to model your own differential drive robot.

- `diffbot_gazebo`: Simulation-specific launch and configuration files for Remo and Diffbot, to be used in the Gazebo simulator.

- `diffbot_msgs`: Message definitions specific to Remo/Diffbot, for example, the message for encoder data is defined in this package.

- `diffbot_navigation`: This package contains all the required configuration and launch files for the ROS Navigation Stack to work.

- `diffbot_slam`: Configurations for simultaneous localization and mapping using implementations such as `gmapping` to create a map of the environment.

After this overview of the ROS packages of a differential robot that fulfill the requirements of the Navigation Stack, the next section implements the base controller component.

Developing a low-level controller and a high-level ROS Control hardware interface for a differential drive robot

In the following two sections, the base controller, mentioned in the Navigation Stack, will be developed. For Remo, this platform-specific node is split into two software components.

The first component is the high-level `diffbot::DiffBotHWInterface` that inherits from `hardware_interface::RobotHW`, acting as an interface between robot hardware and the packages of ROS Control that communicate with the Navigation Stack and provide `diff_drive_controller` (http://wiki.ros.org/diff_drive_controller) – one of many available controllers from ROS Control. With the `gazebo_ros_control` plugin, the same controller including its configuration can be used in the simulation and the real robot. An overview of ROS Control in a simulation and the real world is given in the following figure (http://gazebosim.org/tutorials/?tut=ros_control):

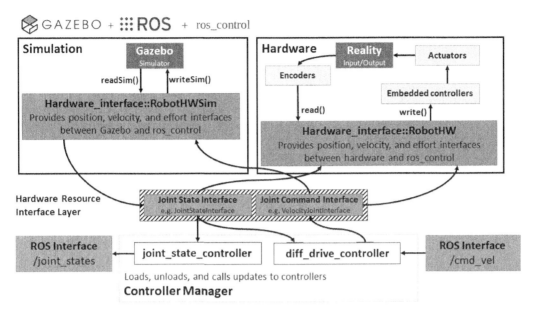

Figure 11.4 – ROS control in simulation and reality

The second component is the low-level base controller that measures angular wheel joint positions and velocities and applies the commands from the high-level interface to the wheel joints. The following figure shows the communication between the two components:

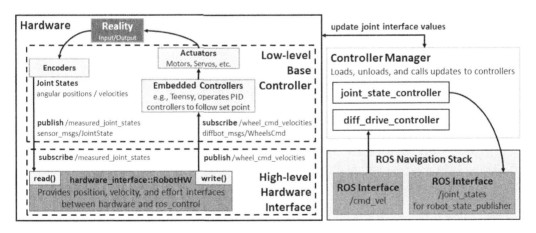

Figure 11.5 – Block diagram of the low-level controller and the high-level hardware interface (ROS Control)

The low-level base controller uses two PID controllers to compute PWM signals for each motor based on the error between measured and target wheel velocities.

`RobotHW` receives measured joint states (angular position (rad) and angular velocity (rad/s)) from which it updates its joint values. With these measured velocities and the desired command velocity (`geometry_msgs/Twist message` on the `cmd_vel` topic), from the Navigation Stack, the `diff_drive_controller` computes the target angular velocities for both wheel joints using the mathematical equations of a differential drive robot. This controller works with continuous wheel joints through a `VelocityJointInterface` class. The computed target commands are then published within the high-level hardware interface inside the robot's `RobotHW::write` method. Additionally, the controller computes and publishes the odometry on the `odom` topic (`nav_msgs/Odometry`) and the transform from `odom` to `base_footprint`.

Having explained the two components of the base controller, the low-level firmware is implemented first. The high-level hardware interface follows the next section.

Implementing the low-level base controller for Remo

The low-level base controller is implemented on the Teensy microcontroller using PlatformIO (`https://platformio.org/`). The programming language in PlatformIO is the same as Arduino (based on Wiring) and it is available as a plugin for the Visual Studio Code editor, which is covered in *Chapter 16, Troubleshooting and Best Practices in ROS*. On the development PC, we can flash the robot firmware to the board with this plugin. We will get the firmware code from the `diffbot_base` ROS package, located in the `scripts/base_controller` subfolder. Opening this folder in Visual Studio Code will recognize it as a PlatformIO workspace because it contains the `platformio.ini` file. This file defines the required dependencies and makes it straightforward to flash the firmware to the Teensy board after compilation. Inside this file, the used libraries are listed:

```
lib_deps = frankjoshua/Rosserial Arduino Library@^0.9.1
           adafruit/Adafruit Motor Shield V2 Library@^1.0.11
           Wire
```

As you can see, the firmware depends on `rosserial`, the `Adafruit Motor Shield V2` library, and `Wire`, an I2C library. PlatformIO allows using custom libraries defined in the local `./lib` folder, which are developed in this section.

The firmware is used to read from encoders and IMU sensor, and receive wheel velocity commands from the high-level `hardware_interface::RobotHW` class, discussed in the next section. The following code snippets are part of the low-level base controller's `main.cpp` file and show the used libraries, found in `diffbot_base/scripts/base_controller`, in the `lib` and `src` folders. `src` contains `main.cpp` consisting of the `setup()` and `loop()` functions, common to every Arduino sketch and starts off by including the following headers:

```
#include <ros.h>
#include "diffbot_base_config.h"
```

Besides the `ros` header file, it includes definitions specific to Remo, which are defined in the `diffbot_base_config.h` header. It contains constant parameter values such as the following:

- **Encoder pins**: Defines to which pins on the Teensy microcontroller the Hall effect sensors are connected.

- **Motor I2C address and pins**: The Adafruit motor driver can drive four DC motors. For good cable management, motor terminals M3 and M4 are used for the left and right motors, respectively.

- **PID**: The tuned constants for both PID controllers of `base_controller`.

- `PWM_MAX` and `PWM_MIN`: The minimum and maximum possible PWM values that can be sent to the motor driver.

- **Update rates**: Defines how often the functions of `base_controller` are executed. For example, the control portion of the low-level base controller code reads encoder values and writes motor commands at a specific rate.

After including Remo-specific definitions, next follows the custom libraries in the `lib` folder:

```
#include "base_controller.h"
#include "adafruit_feather_wing/adafruit_feather_wing.h"
```

These included headers and the libraries that get included with them and are introduced next:

- `base_controller`: Defines the `BaseController` template class, defined in the `base_controller.h` header, and acts as the main class to manage the two motors, including each motor's encoder, and communicate with the high-level hardware interface.

- `motor_controller_intf`: This library is indirectly included with `adafruit_feather_wing.h` and defines an abstract base class, named `MotorControllerIntf`. It is a generic interface used to operate a single motor using arbitrary motor drivers. It is meant to be implemented by other specific motor controller subclasses and therefore avoids changing code in classes that know the `MotorControllerIntf` interface and call its `setSpeed(int value)` method, such as with `BaseController`. The only requirement for this to work is for a subclass to inherit from this `MotorControllerIntf` interface and implement the `setSpeed(int value)` class method.

- `adafruit_feather_wing`: This library, in the `motor_controllers` folder, implements the `MotorControllerIntf` abstract interface class and defines a concrete motor controller. For Remo, the motor controller is defined in the `AdafruitMotorController` class. This class has access to the motor driver board and serves to operate the speed of a single motor, which is why two instances are created in the `main.cpp` file.

- `encoder`: This library is used in the `BaseController` class and is based on `Encoder.h` from `https://www.pjrc.com/teensy/td_libs_Encoder.html` that allows reading encoder tick counts from quadrature encoders, like the DG01D-E motors consist of. The `encoder` library also provides a method `jointState()` to directly obtain the joint state, which is returned by this method in the `JointState` struct, that consists of the measured angular position (rad) and angular velocity (rad/s) of the wheel joints:

```
diffbot::JointState diffbot::Encoder::jointState() {
long encoder_ticks = encoder.read();
ros::Time current_time = nh_.now();
ros::Duration dt = current_time - prev_update_time_;
double dts = dt.toSec();
double delta_ticks = encoder_ticks - prev_encoder_ticks_;
double delta_angle = ticksToAngle(delta_ticks);
joint_state_.angular_position_ += delta_angle;
joint_state_.angular_velocity_ = delta_angle / dts;
```

```
prev_update_time_ = current_time;
prev_encoder_ticks_ = encoder_ticks;
return joint_state_;
}
```

- `pid`: Defines a PID controller to compute PWM signals based on the velocity error between the measured and commanded angular wheel joint velocities.

With these libraries, we look at the `main.cpp` file. Inside it exist only a few global variables to keep the code organized and make it possible to test the individual components that get included. The main code is explained next:

1. First, we define the global ROS node handle, which is referenced in other classes, such as `BaseController`, where it is needed to publish, subscribe, or get the current time, using `ros::NodeHandle::now()`, to keep track of the update rates:

   ```
   ros::NodeHandle nh;
   ```

2. For convenience and to keep the code organized, we declare that we want to use the `diffbot` namespace, where the libraries of the base controller are declared:

   ```
   using namespace diffbot;
   ```

3. Next, we define two concrete motor controllers of type `AdafruitMotorController` found in the `motor_controllers` library:

   ```
   AdafruitMotorController motor_controller_right =
   AdafruitMotorController(3);
   AdafruitMotorController motor_controller_left =
   AdafruitMotorController(4);
   ```

   This class inherits from the abstract base class `MotorControllerIntf`, explained above. It knows how to connect to the Adafruit motor driver using its open source `Adafruit_MotorShield` library (`https://learn.adafruit.com/adafruit-stepper-dc-motor-featherwing/library-reference`) and how to get a C++ pointer to one of its DC motors (`getMotor(motor_num)`). Depending on the integer input value to `AdafruitMotorController::setSpeed(int value)`, the DC motor is commanded to rotate in a certain direction and at a specified speed. For Remo, the range is between –255 and 255, specified by the `PWM_MAX` and `PWM_MIN` identifiers.

4. The next class that is defined globally inside main is `BaseController`, which incorporates most of the main logic of this low-level base controller:

```
BaseController<AdafruitMotorController, Adafruit_
MotorShield> base_controller(nh, &motor_controller_left,
&motor_controller_right);
```

As you can see, it is a template class that accepts different kinds of motor controllers (`TMotorController`, which equals `AdafruitMotorController` in the case of Remo) that operate on different motor drivers (`TMotorDriver`, which equals `Adafruit_MotorShield`), using the `MotorControllerIntf` interface as explained previously. The `BaseController` constructor takes a reference to the globally defined ROS node handle and the two motor controllers to let it set the commanded speeds computed through two separate PID controllers, one for each wheel. In addition to setting up pointers to the motor controllers, the `BaseController` class initializes two instances of type `diffbot::Encoder`. Its measured joint state, returned from `diffbot::Encoder::jointState()`, is used together with the commanded wheel joint velocities in the `diffbot::PID` controllers to compute the velocity error and output an appropriate PWM signal for the motors.

After defining the global instances, the firmware's `setup()` function is discussed next.

The low-level `BaseController` class communicates with the high-level `DiffBotHWInterface` interface using ROS publishers and subscribers. These are set up in the `Basecontroller::setup()` method, which is called in the `setup()` function of `main.cpp`. In addition to that, the `BaseController::init()` method is here to read parameters stored on the ROS parameter server, such as the wheel radius and distance between the wheels. Beside initializing `BaseController`, the communication frequency of the motor driver is configured:

```
void setup() {
    base_controller.setup();
    base_controller.init();
    motor_controller_left.begin();
    motor_controller_right.begin();
}
```

The `begin(uint16_t freq)` method of the motor controllers has to be called explicitly in the main `setup()` function because `MotorControllerIntf` doesn't provide a `begin()` or `setup()` method. This is a design choice that, when added, will make the `MotorControllerIntf` less generic.

After the `setup()` function follows the `loop()` function, to read from sensors and write to actuators, which happens at specific rates, defined in the `diffbot_base_config.h` header. The bookkeeping of when these read/write functionalities occurred is kept in the `BaseController` class inside its `lastUpdateRates` struct. Reading from the encoders and writing motor commands happens in the same code block as the `control` rate:

```
void loop() {
ros::Duration command_dt = nh.now() - base_controller.
lastUpdateTime().control;
if (command_dt.toSec() >= ros::Duration(1.0 / base_controller.
publishRate().control_, 0).toSec()) {
   base_controller.read();
   base_controller.write();
   base_controller.lastUpdateTime().control = nh.now();
}
```

The following steps in this code block happen continuously at the control rate:

1. Encoder sensor values are read through the `BaseController::read()` method and the data is published inside this method for the high-level `DiffbotHWInterface` class, on the `measured_joint_states` topic of message type `sensor_msgs::JointState`.

2. The `BaseController` class subscribes to `DiffBotHWInterface` from which it receives the commanded wheel joint velocities (the `wheel_cmd_velocities`, type `diffbot_msgs::WheelsCmdStamped` topic) inside the `BaseController::commandCallback(const diffbot_msgs::WheelsCmdStamped&)` callback method. In `BaseController::read()`, the PID is called to compute the motor PWM signals from the velocity error and the motor speeds are set with the two motor controllers.

3. To keep calling this method at the desired control rate, the `lastUpdateTime().control` variable is updated with the current time.

After the control loop update block, if an IMU is used, its data could be read at the `imu` rate and published for a node that fuses the data with the encoder odometry to obtain more precise odometry. Finally, in the main `loop()`, all the callbacks waiting in the ROS callback queue are processed with a call to `nh.spinOnce()`.

This describes the low-level base controller. For more details and the complete library code, please refer to the `diffbot_base/scripts/base_controller` package. In the following section, the `diffbot::DiffBotHWInterface` class is described.

ROS Control high-level hardware interface for a differential drive robot

The `ros_control` (http://wiki.ros.org/ros_control) meta package contains the `hardware_interface::RobotHW` hardware interface class, which needs to be implemented to leverage many available controllers from the `ros_controllers` meta package. First, we'll look at the `diffbot_base` node that instantiates and uses the hardware interface:

1. The `diffbot_base` node includes the `diffbot_hw_interface.h` header, as well as the `controller_manager`, defined in `controller_manager.h`, to create the control loop (read, update, and write):

    ```
    #include <ros/ros.h>
    #include <diffbot_base/diffbot_hw_interface.h>
    #include <controller_manager/controller_manager.h>
    ```

2. Inside the main function of this `diffbot_base` node, we define the ROS node handle, the hardware interface (`diffbot_base::DiffBotHWInterface`), and pass it to the `controller_manager`, so that it has access to its resources:

    ```
    ros::NodeHandle nh;
    diffbot_base::DiffBotHWInterface diffBot(nh);
    controller_manager::ControllerManager cm(&diffBot);
    ```

3. Next, set up a separate thread that will be used to service ROS callbacks. This runs the ROS loop in a separate thread as service callbacks can block the control loop:

    ```
    ros::AsyncSpinner spinner(1);
    spinner.start();
    ```

4. Then define at which rate the control loop of the high-level hardware interface should run. For Remo, we choose 10 Hz:

    ```
    ros::Time prev_time = ros::Time::now();
    ros::Rate rate(10.0); rate.sleep(); // 10 Hz rate
    ```

5. Inside the blocking `while` loop of the `diffbot_base` node, we do basic bookkeeping to get the system time to compute the control period:

```
while (ros::ok()) {
    const ros::Time time = ros::Time::now();
    const ros::Duration period = time - prev_time;
    prev_time = time;
```

6. Next, we execute the control loop steps: read, update, and write. The `read()` method is here to get sensor values, while `write()` writes commands that were computed by `diff_drive_controller` during the `update()` step:

```
diffBot.read(time, period);
cm.update(time, period);
diffBot.write(time, period);
```

7. These steps keep getting repeated with the specified rate using `rate.sleep()`.

After having defined the code that runs the main control loop of the `diffbot_base` node, we'll take a look at the implementation of `diffbot::DiffBotHWInterface`, which is a child class of `hardware_interface::RobotHW`. With it, we register the hardware and implement the `read()` and `write()` methods.

The constructor of the `diffbot::DiffBotHWInterface` class is used to get parameters from the parameter server, such as the `diff_drive_controller` configuration from the `diffbot_control` package. Inside the constructor, the wheel command publisher and measured joint state subscriber are initialized. Another publisher is `pub_reset_encoders_`, which is used in the `isReceivingMeasuredJointStates` method to reset the encoder ticks to zero after receiving measured joint states from the low-level base controller.

After constructing `DiffBotHWInterface`, we create instances of `JointStateHandles` classes (used only for reading) and `JointHandle` classes (used for read, and write access) for each controllable joint and register them with the `JointStateInterface` and `VelocityJointInterface` interfaces, respectively. This enables the `controller_manager` to manage access for joint resources of multiple controllers. Remo uses `DiffDriveController` and `JointStateController`:

```
for (unsigned int i = 0; i < num_joints_; i++) {
 hardware_interface::JointStateHandle joint_state_handle(
    joint_names_[i], &joint_positions_[i],
    &joint_velocities_[i], &joint_efforts_[i]);
```

```
joint_state_interface_.registerHandle(joint_state_handle)
hardware_interface::JointHandle joint_handle(
  joint_state_handle, &joint_velocity_commands_[i]);
velocity_joint_interface_.registerHandle(joint_handle);
}
```

The last step that is needed to initialize the hardware resources is to register the
JointStateInterface and the VelocityJointInterface interfaces with the
robot hardware interface itself, thereby grouping the interfaces together to represent the
Remo robot in the software:

```
registerInterface(&joint_state_interface_);
registerInterface(&velocity_joint_interface_);
```

Now that the hardware joint resources are registered and the controller manager knows
about them, it's possible to call the read() and write() methods of the hardware
interface. The controller manager update happens in between the read and write steps.

Remo subscribes to the measured_joint_states topic, published by the low-level
base controller. The received messages on this topic are stored in the measured_
joint_states_ array of type diffbot_base::JointState using the
measuredJointStateCallback method, and are relevant in the read() method:

1. The read() method is here to update the measured joint values with the current
    sensor readings from the encoders – angular positions (rad) and velocities (rad/s):

```
void DiffBotHWInterface::read() {
for (std::size_t i = 0; i < num_joints_; ++i) {
joint_positions[i]=measured_joint_states[i].angular_position;
joint_velocity[i]=measured_joint_states[i].angular_velocity; }
```

2. The final step of the control loop is to call the `write()` method of the `DiffBotHWInterface` class to publish the angular wheel velocity commands of each joint, computed by `diff_drive_controller`:

```
void DiffBotHWInterface::write() {
  diffbot_msgs::WheelsCmdStamped wheel_cmd_msg;
  for (int i = 0; i < NUM_JOINTS; ++i) {
  wheel_cmd_msg.wheels_cmd.angular_velocities.joint.push_
  back(joint_velocity_commands_[i]); }
  pub_wheel_cmd_velocities_.publish(wheel_cmd_msg); }
```

In this method, it is possible to correct for steering offsets due to model imperfections and slight differences in the wheel radii.

This concludes the important parts of the `DiffBotHWInterface` class and enables Remo to satisfy the requirements to work with the ROS Navigation Stack. In the next section, we'll look at how to bring up the robot hardware and how the started nodes interact with each other.

Overview of ROS nodes and topics for the Remo robot

The following launch file will bring up the hardware nodes, load the robot description onto the parameter server, start `diff_drive_controller`, and begin to publish the transformations using `tf`. Run this launch file on the robot's SBC:

```
roslaunch diffbot_bringup bringup.launch model:=remo
```

On the development PC, you can use the `teleop` node to steer the robot. To do this, run the following:

```
roslaunch diffbot_bringup keyboard_teleop.launch
```

Issuing the `rosnode list` command shows the following list of started nodes:

```
/diffbot/controller_spawner
/diffbot/diffbot_base
/diffbot/robot_state_publisher
/diffbot/rosserial_base_controller
/diffbot_teleop_keyboard
/rosout
```

To launch the RPLIDAR laser scanner too, we use the `bringup_with_laser.launch` launch file from the `diffbot_bringup` package on the robot. This will publish the laser scans on the `/diffbot/rplidarNode` topic. The next figure shows the started nodes and topics:

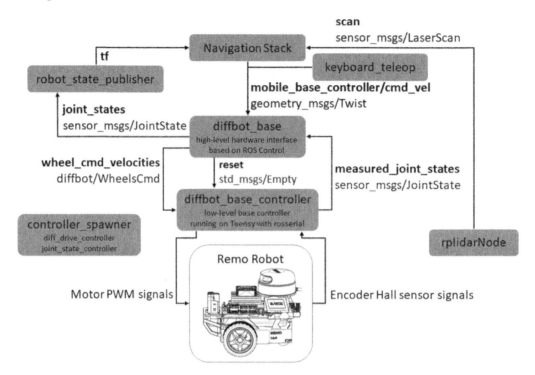

Figure 11.6 – The interconnection of each node in Remo

The nodes run by this launch file and their workings are described here:

- `rosserial_base_controller`: The Teensy MCU is interfaced with `rosserial` with the SBC. This acts as the ROS driver for the Teensy as well as a bridge between the robot hardware and the high-level hardware interface using ROS topics. This node reads sensor values from sensors connected to the Teensy and writes motor commands to the motors using two PID controllers. It publishes sensor data into topics (`measured_joint_states`) and subscribes to wheel commands on the `wheel_cmd_velocities` topic, published by the `diffbot_base` node.

- diffbot_base: Runs DiffBotHWInterface and controller_manager, which accesses the robot hardware and spawns diff_drive_controller with parameters from the diffbot_control package. Another spawned controller is JointStateController, which doesn't control anything but has access to the joint states and publishes them on the joint_states topic of type sensor_msgs/JointState. The node subscribes to the cmd_vel topic (geometry_msgs/Twist), either from a teleop node or the Navigation Stack and converts the message to angular wheel joint velocities (rad/s) and publishes it on the wheel_cmd_velocities topic (diffbot_msgs::WheelsCmdStamped), containing target angular velocities for each wheel. Furthermore, diff_drive_controller computes the odometry from the joint states.

- robot_state_publisher: Subscribes to the joint_states topic published by ROS Control's JointStateController and publishes tf transforms between all links for the Navigation Stack. The diff_drive_controller controller publishes only a single transform between odom and base_footprint.

The content of bringup.launch includes other launch files from packages, such as diffbot_base and remo_description. The following summarizes the content:

1. To load different robot descriptions into the ROS parameter server, this launch file, like some others, accepts the model argument, which is set to diffbot by default. For Remo, it is required to pass model:=remo to the launch command.

2. Run rosserial to connect with the Teensy MCU and start the base controller:

```
<node name="rosserial_base_controller" pkg="rosserial_
python" type="serial_node.py" respawn="false"
output="screen" args="_port:=/dev/ttyACM0 _
baud:=115200"/>
```

3. Run the diffbot_base node with its high-level hardware interface:

```
<node name="diffbot_base" pkg="diffbot_base"
type="diffbot_base" output="screen"/>
```

4. Load the controller and base configs to the parameter server:

```
<rosparam command="load" file="$(find diffbot_control)/
config/diffbot_control.yaml"/>
```
```
<rosparam command="load" file="$(find diffbot_base)/
config/base.yaml"/>
```

5. After having loaded the controller config, load the controller itself:

```
<node name="controller_spawner" pkg="controller_
manager" type="spawner" respawn="false" output="screen"
args="joint_state_controller mobile_base_controller"/>
```

6. Run the robot_state_publisher node to read joint states published by ROS Control's joint_state_controller and publish tf transforms:

```
<node name="robot_state_publisher" pkg="robot_state_
publisher" type="robot_state_publisher" output="screen"
ns="diffbot" />
```

After running bringup.launch, we can visualize the robot in RViz, with this command:

```
roslaunch diffbot_bringup view_diffbot.launch model:=remo
```

This will open RViz and we will see the robot model. Next, launch the keyboard teleop node:

```
roslaunch diffbot_bringup keyboard_teleop.launch
```

Using the keys displayed in the terminal moves the robot and we can observe the movement and odometry in RViz:

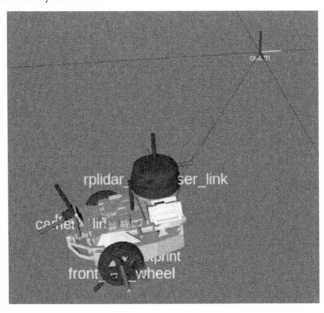

Figure 11.7 – Visualizing robot odometry

Until now, we have discussed Remo interfacing in ROS. The C++ code is kept modular, and a lot of available official ROS packages were used, mostly from ROS Control. These provide the differential drive kinematics out of the box and support the requirements to interface with the ROS Navigation Stack. All that we have left to do is to write the high- and low-level code.

Configuring and working with the Navigation Stack

After creating the hardware interface and low-level controller, we need to configure the Navigation Stack to perform SLAM and **Adaptive Monte Carlo Localization** (**AMCL**) to build the map, localize the robot, and perform autonomous navigation. In *Chapter 6, Using the ROS MoveIt! and Navigation Stack*, we saw the basic packages in the Navigation Stack. To build the map of the environment, we will configure gmapping and move_base, together with the global and local planners and global and local cost maps. To perform localization, we will configure the amcl node. We start with the gmapping node.

Configuring the gmapping node and creating a map

gmapping is the package to perform SLAM (http://wiki.ros.org/gmapping). Remo's gmapping node parameters are in diffbot_slam/config/gmapping_params.yaml and loaded with diffbot_slam/launch/diffbot_gmapping.launch. By fine-tuning the parameters, we improve the accuracy of the gmapping node. For example, reduce delta to get a better map resolution. For more details, refer to *Chapter 6, Using the ROS MoveIt! and Navigation Stack*.

Working with the gmapping node

To work with gmapping, the robot hardware needs to run first. To do this, launch the following launch file on the SBC of the real robot:

```
roslaunch diffbot_bringup bringup_with_laser.launch model:=remo
```

This will initialize the hardware interface and the low-level base controller and run the rplidar node, and the laser will start to rotate and stream laser scans on the diffbot/scan topic. Then, on your development PC, start the gmapping node using the following command:

```
roslaunch diffbot_slam diffbot_slam.launch
```

It launches the `gmapping` node together with its configuration and opens RViz, where we see the map building process:

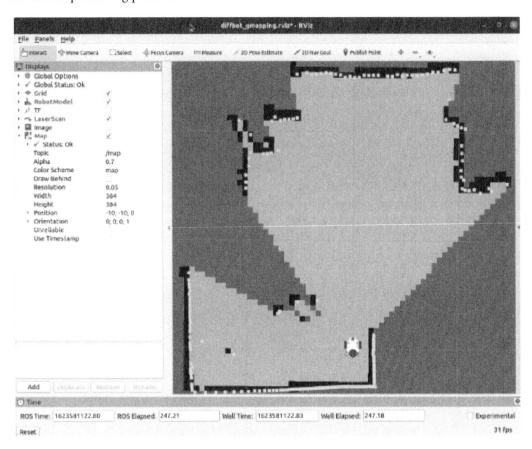

Figure 11.8 – Creating a map using gmapping shown in RViz

We can now launch a `teleop` node for moving the robot to build the map of the environment. The following will launch the `teleop` node to move the robot around:

```
roslaunch diffbot_bringup keyboard_teleop.launch
```

After completing the mapping process, we save the map using this command:

```
rosrun map_server map_saver -f ~/room
```

The `map_server` package in ROS contains the `map_server` node, which provides the current map data as a ROS service. It provides a command utility called `map_saver`, which helps to save the map. The current map is saved as two files in the user's home folder: `room.pgm` and `room.yaml`. The first one is the map data and the next is its metadata, which contains the map file's name and its parameters. For more details, see `http://wiki.ros.org/map_server`.

After building a map of the environment, the next step is to implement localization and navigation. Before starting the AMCL node, we will look at `move_base` in the next section.

Configuring the move_base node

Along with the `move_base` node, we need to configure the global and the local planners, and also the global and the local cost maps. To load all these configuration parameters, the launch file `diffbot_navigation/launch/move_base.launch` is used.

Next, we will briefly outline each configuration file and its parameters.

Common configurations for the local_costmap and global_costmap nodes

The costmap is created using the obstacles present around the robot. Fine-tuning the parameters can increase the accuracy of map generation. The customized file `costmap_common_params.yaml` in the `diffbot_navigation/config` folder contains the common parameters of both the global and the local cost maps, such as the `obstacle_range`, the `raytrace_range`, and the `inflation_radius` parameters of obstacles and the footprint of the robot. It also specifies the `observation_sources` parameter. To get a working local costmap, it is required to set the correct laser scan topic. For all parameters, see `http://wiki.ros.org/costmap_2d/flat`.

The following are the main configurations required for building global and local costmaps. The definitions of the parameters are found in `diffbot_navigation/config/costmap_global_params.yaml` and `costmap_local_params.yaml`. The `global_frame` parameter for both costmaps is map. The `robot_base_frame` parameter is `base_footprint`; it is the coordinate frame in which the costmap is referenced around the robot base. The `update_frequency` parameter is the frequency at which the costmap runs its main update loop, whereas `publishing_frequency` is set to 10 Hz to publish display information. If we are using an existing map, we set `static_map` as true, otherwise we set it as false. For `global_costmap`, it's set to true, and false for the local costmap. The `transform_tolerance` parameter is the rate at which the transform is performed. The robot will stop if the transforms are not updated at this rate.

The `rolling_window` parameter of the local costmap is set to true to center it around the robot. The `width`, `height`, and `resolution` parameters are the width, height, and resolution of the costmap. The next step will be to configure the base local planner.

Configuring the base local planner and DWA local planner parameters

The base local planner and DWA local planner are similar, with almost the same parameters. We can either use the base local planner or the DWA local planner for our robot using the `local_planner` argument of the `diffbot_navigation/launch/diffbot_navigation.launch` launch file. The functionality of these planners is to compute the velocity commands from a goal sent from a ROS node. The base local planner configuration of Remo is in `diffbot_navigation/config/base_local_planner_params.yaml`, along with the DWA config in `dwa_local_planner_params.yaml`. These files contain parameters related to limits of velocity and acceleration and specify the differential drive robot configuration with `holonomic_robot`. For Remo, it is set to false because it is a *non-holonomic* robot. We can also set a goal tolerance, specifying when a goal is reached.

Configuring move_base node parameters

The `move_base` node configuration is defined in the `move_base_params.yaml` file, defining parameters such as `controller_frequency`, which defines the rate at which the `move_base` node runs the update loop and sends velocity commands. We also define `planner_patience`. That is the planner's wait time for finding a valid path before the space-clearing operations take place. For more details, refer to *Chapter 6, Using the ROS MoveIt! and Navigation Stack*, and `http://wiki.ros.org/move_base`.

Configuring the AMCL node

In this section, we will cover the available `amcl` launch files of Remo. The AMCL algorithm uses particle filters for tracking the pose of the robot with respect to a map. The algorithm is implemented in the AMCL ROS package (`http://wiki.ros.org/amcl`), which has a node that receives laser scan messages, `tf` transforms, the initial pose, and the occupancy grid map. After processing the sensor data, it publishes `amcl_pose`, `particlecloud`, and `tf`.

The main launch file for starting `amcl` is called `diffbot_navigation.launch` in the `diffbot_navigation` package. It launches the `amcl` related nodes, the map server for providing the map data, the `amcl` node for performing localization, and the `move_base` node to move the robot from the commands received from the Navigation Stack.

The complete `amcl` launch parameters are set inside another file called `amcl.launch`. The arguments accepted by this launch file are `scan_topic` and the initial pose. If the initial pose of the robot is not mentioned, the particles will be near the origin. Other parameters such as `laser_max_range` are set to the specifications of the RPLIDAR. Most other parameters are close to the defaults found in the ROS wiki, `http://wiki.ros.org/amcl`.

We have discussed the parameters used in the Navigation Stack, the `gmapping` and `move_base` nodes. Now we will see how to localize and navigate Remo around an existing map.

AMCL planning

Launch the robot hardware nodes by using the following command:

```
roslaunch diffbot_bringup bringup_with_laser.launch model:=remo
```

Then, on your development PC, run the `navigation` launch file with the previously stored map file from your user's home folder, using the following command:

```
roslaunch diffbot_navigation diffbot_hw.lauch map_file:=/
home/<username>/room.yaml
```

This will launch RViz to command the robot to move to a particular pose on the map:

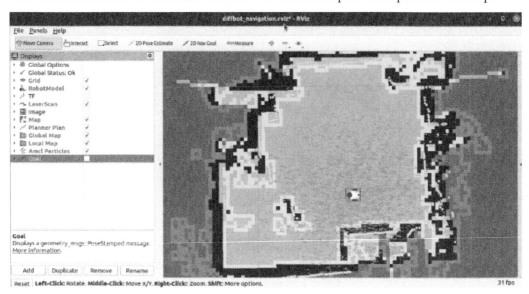

Figure 11.9 – Robot autonomous navigation using AMCL

Next, we will see more options in RViz and how to command the robot on the map.

2D pose estimate and 2D nav goal buttons

The first step in RViz is to set the initial position of the robot on the map. If the robot can localize itself on the map, there is no need to set the initial position. Otherwise, we set the position using the **2D Pose Estimate** button in RViz, as shown in the following screenshot:

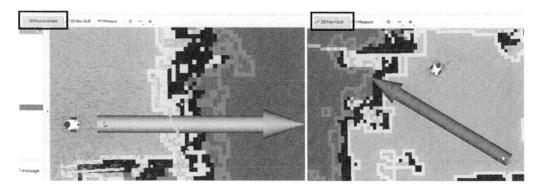

Figure 11.10 – RViz 2D Pose Estimate (left) and 2D Nav Goal (right) buttons

The green color cloud around the robot is the particle cloud of amcl. The spread of particles describes the uncertainty of the position. Low spread means low uncertainty and the robot is almost sure about its position. After setting the pose, we can start to plan a path.

The **2D Nav Goal** button is used to give a goal position to the move_base node through RViz and move the robot to that location. We can select this button from the top panel of RViz and place the goal position inside the map by left-clicking inside it.

Obstacle avoidance using the Navigation Stack

The Navigation Stack enables the robot to avoid random obstacles during its motion. The following is a scenario where a dynamic obstacle is placed in the planned path of the robot. In particular, the left part of the following figure shows path planning without obstacles on the path. When a dynamic obstacle is placed on the robot path, a path avoiding the obstacle is planned:

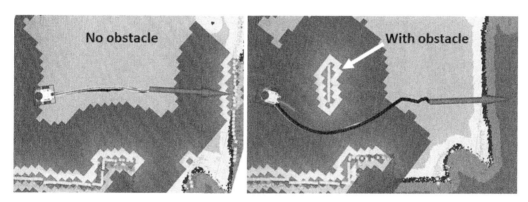

Figure 11.11 – Visualizing obstacle avoidance capabilities in RViz

The preceding figures show the local and global cost maps, the real obstacles detected by the laser scans (represent by the dots), and the inflated obstacles. To avoid collision with the real obstacles, they are inflated to some distance from the real obstacles, called inflated obstacles, as per the values in the configuration files. The robot only plans a path beyond the inflated obstacle; inflation is a technique to avoid a collision with real obstacles.

In the following figure, we can see the global, local, and planner plans:

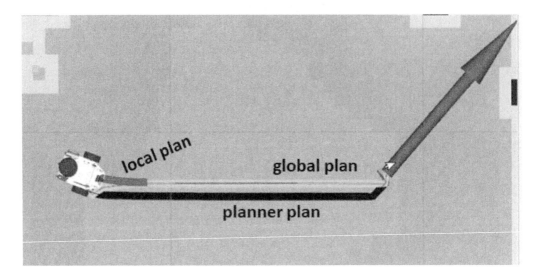

Figure 11.12 – Visualizing the global, local, and planner plans in RViz

The planner and the global plans represent the complete plan to reach the goal. The local plan represents a short-term plan to follow global planning. The global plan and the planner plan can be changed if there are any obstacles. The plans can be displayed using the RViz path display type.

So far, we have worked with Remo in the real world. Next, we will look at available simulations.

Working with Remo robot in simulation

The diffbot_gazebo simulator package is available in the diffbot repository. With it, we can simulate the robot in Gazebo. Instead of launching bringup.launch from diffbot_bringup for the hardware, we can start examples to get a more complex simulated environment for the robot using the diffbot world:

```
roslaunch diffbot_navigation diffbot.launch model:=remo
```

This will load a previously stored map from the diffbot_navigation/maps folder, open the Gazebo simulator, which loads the db_world.world world from the diffbot_gazeb/worlds folder, and a robot_rqt_steering window will appear too. With that, you can steer Remo manually. The launch command also opens Rviz, shown in the following figure, where you can use the navigation tools from the toolbar to let the robot navigate autonomously, as we did for the real robot:

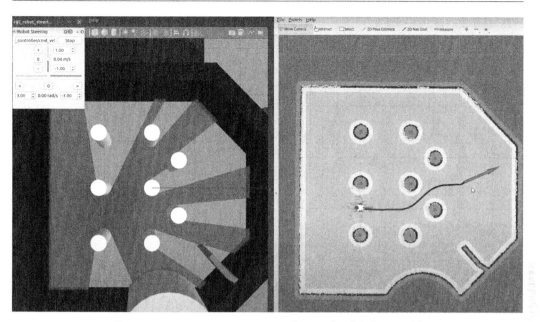

Figure 11.13 – Navigating Remo in the simulated diffbot world

Other operations, such as SLAM and AMCL, have the same procedure that we followed for the hardware. The following launch files are used to perform SLAM and AMCL in the simulation:

1. To run SLAM in the simulation, we first launch Gazebo and the diffbot world:

    ```
    roslaunch diffbot_gazebo diffbot.launch model:=remo
    ```

2. In a second terminal, run SLAM `gmapping`:

    ```
    roslaunch diffbot_slam diffbot_slam.launch slam_
    method:=gmapping
    ```

3. Then steer the robot around manually with the already opened `rqt_robot_
    steering` window or run the keyboard `teleop` node and start moving the robot with the keys:

    ```
    roslaunch diffbot_bringup keyboard_teleop.launch
    ```

4. After moving the robot around, we can save the generated map as done before:

    ```
    rosrun map_server map_saver -f /tmp/db_world
    ```

The created map can then be used in the simulation. For this, we just need to pass the map file and the world file to the `diffbot_navigation/launch/difbot.launch` launch file. An example of a complete command is the following:

```
roslaunch diffbot_navigation diffbot.launch model:=remo
world_name:='$(find diffbot_gazebo)/worlds /turtlebot3_
world.world'
map_file:='$(find diffbot_navigation)/maps/map.yaml'
```

This will launch the turtlebot3 world together with its previously stored map.

This concludes the simulation of Remo in Gazebo, where we made use of launch files to navigate autonomously in an existing map of the diffbot world. We also saw how the mapping of the diffbot world is done. This procedure can be used to map new simulated environments and drive the Remo robot autonomously afterward using the launch files from the `diffbot_navigation` package.

Summary

In this chapter, we covered interfacing a DIY autonomous mobile robot with ROS and the Navigation Stack. After introducing the robot and the necessary components and connection diagrams, we looked at the robot firmware and saw how to flash it into the real robot. After that, we learned how to interface it with ROS using ROS Control packages by developing a hardware interface. With `diff_drive_controller` it is easy to convert twist messages to motor velocities and encoder ticks to `odom` and `tf`. ROS Control also enables simulation with the `gazebo_ros_control` plugin. After discussing these nodes, we looked at configurations of the ROS Navigation Stack. We also did `gmapping` and AMCL and looked at how to use RViz with the Navigation Stack. We also covered obstacle avoidance using the Navigation Stack and worked with Remo in a simulation. The next chapter introduces `pluginlib`, `nodelets`, and Gazebo plugins.

Here are some questions based on what we covered in this chapter.

Questions

- What are the basic requirements for working with the ROS Navigation Stack?
- What benefits does ROS Control provide?
- What are the steps to implement the ROS Control hardware interface?
- What are the main configuration files for working with the ROS Navigation Stack?
- What are the methods to send a goal pose to the Navigation Stack?

Section 4 – Advanced ROS Programming

In this section, we will deal with advanced concepts in ROS. These chapters will be helpful in prototyping advanced concepts such as controllers, plugins, and the interfacing of ROS to third-party applications such as MATLAB.

This section comprises the following chapters:

- *Chapter 12, Working with pluginlib, Nodelets, and Gazebo Plugins*
- *Chapter 13, Writing ROS Controllers and Visualization Plugins*
- *Chapter 14, Using ROS in MATLAB and Simulink*
- *Chapter 15, ROS for Industrial Robots*
- *Chapter 16, Troubleshooting and Best Practices in ROS*

12

Working with pluginlib, nodelets, and Gazebo Plugins

In the previous chapter, we discussed the interfacing and simulation of a mobile robot to the **Robot Operating System** (**ROS**) Navigation Stack. In this chapter, we will look at some advanced concepts in ROS, such as the ROS `pluginlib`, `nodelets`, and `Gazebo` plugins. We will discuss the functionalities and applications of each concept and will look at an example to demonstrate its working. We have used `Gazebo` plugins in the previous chapters to get the sensor and robot behavior inside the Gazebo simulator. In this chapter, we're going to see how to create it. We will also discuss a different form of ROS node, called ROS `nodelets`. These features in ROS are implemented using a plugin architecture called `pluginlib`.

In this chapter, we will discuss the following topics:

- Understanding `pluginlib`
- Understanding ROS `nodelets`
- Understanding and creating a `Gazebo` plugin

Technical requirements

To follow along with this chapter, you should have the following set up on your computer:

- Ubuntu 20.04 **Long-Term Support** (**LTS**)
- ROS Noetic Desktop full installation

The reference code for this chapter can be downloaded from the following Git repository: `https://github.com/PacktPublishing/Mastering-ROS-for-Robotics-Programming-Third-edition/tree/main/Chapter12`
You can view this chapter's code in action here: `https://bit.ly/3AZxg0p`.

Understanding pluginlib

Plugins are a commonly used term in the computer world. They are modular pieces of software that can add a new feature to an existing software application. An advantage of plugins is that we don't need to write all the features in the main software; instead, we can create an infrastructure on the main software to accept new plugins to it. Using this method, we can extend the capabilities of the software to any level.

We need plugins for our robotics applications too. When we are building a complex ROS-based application for a robot, plugins are a good choice to extend the capabilities of the application.

The ROS system provides a plugin framework called `pluginlib` to dynamically load/unload plugins, which can be a library or a class. `pluginlib` is basically a C++ library that helps to write plugins and load/unload them whenever we need to.

Plugin files are runtime libraries—such as **shared objects** (`.so`) or **dynamic-link libraries** (`.dll`)—that are built without linking to the main application code. Plugins are separate entities that do not have any dependencies with the main software.

The main advantage of plugins is that we can expand the application capabilities without making changes to the main application code. We can also load/unload these capabilities dynamically at runtime.

We can create a simple plugin using `pluginlib` and see all the procedures involved in creating a plugin using ROS `pluginlib`.

Here, we are going to create a simple calculator application using `pluginlib`. We are adding each functionality of the calculator using plugins.

Implementing a calculator plugin using pluginlib

Creating a calculator application using plugins is a slightly tedious task compared to writing a single piece of code. The aim of this example, however, is to show how to add new features to a calculator without modifying the main application code.

In this example, we will see a ROS application that loads plugins to perform each operation. Here, we only implement the main operations, such as addition, subtraction, multiplication, and division. We can expand to any level by writing individual plugins for each operation.

Before going on to create a plugin definition, we can access the calculator code from the `pluginlib_calculator` folder for reference.

We are going to create a ROS package called `pluginlib_calculator` to build these plugins and the main calculator application.

The following diagram shows how the calculator plugins and applications are organized inside the `pluginlib_calculator` ROS package:

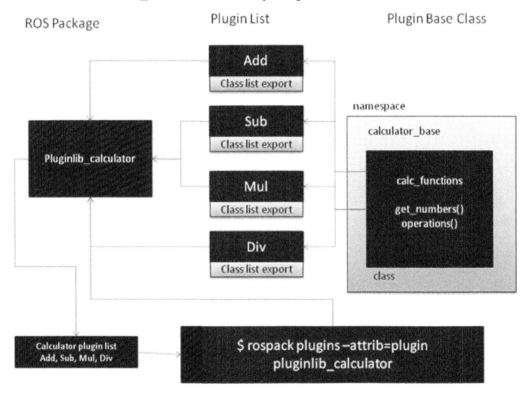

Figure 12.1 – Organization of plugins in the calculator application

We can see a list of calculator plugins and a plugin base class called `CalcFunctions`. The plugin base class implements the common functionalities that are required by these plugins.

This is how we can create a ROS package and start developing plugins for the main calculator application.

Working with the pluginlib_calculator package

For a quick start, we can use the existing `pluginlib_calculator` ROS plugin package.

If we want to create this package from scratch, we can use the following command:

```
catkin_create_pkg pluginlib_calculator pluginlib roscpp std_
msgs
```

The main dependency of this package is `pluginlib`. We can discuss the main source files in this package to build plugins. However, you can get the plugin code from the `Chapter 12/plugins calculator` folder.

After cloning the repository, you can copy each file from the repository to the new package, or you can go through the following steps to understand the function of each file inside the plugin calculator package.

Step 1 – Creating a calculator_base header file

The `calculator_base.h` file is present in the `pluginlib_calculator/include/pluginlib_calculator` folder, and the main purpose of this file is to declare functions/methods that are commonly used by the plugins. Have a look at the following code snippet:

```
namespace calculator_base
{
class CalcFunctions
{
```

Inside the preceding code, we declare an abstract base class called `CalcFunctions` that encapsulates methods used by the plugins. This class is included in a namespace called `calculator_base`. Have a look at the following code snippet:

```
virtual void get_numbers(double number1, double number2) = 0;
virtual double operation() = 0;
```

These are the main methods implemented inside the `CalcFunctions` class. The `get_number()` function can retrieve two numbers as input to the calculator, and the `operation()` function defines the mathematical operation we want to perform.

Step 2 – Creating a calculator_plugins header file

A `calculator_plugins.h` file is present in the `pluginlib_calculator/include/pluginlib_calculator` folder, and the main purpose of this file is to define complete functions of the calculator plugins, which are named `Add`, `Sub`, `Mul`, and `Div`. Here is an illustration of the code in this file:

```
#include <pluginlib_calculator/calculator_base.h>
#include <iostream>
#include <cmath>


namespace calculator_plugins
{
  class Add : public calculator_base::CalcFunctions
  {
```

This header file includes a `calculator_base.h` file for accessing the basic functionalities of a calculator. Each plugin is defined as a class, and it inherits the `CalcFunctions` class from the `calculator_base.h` class, as illustrated in the following code snippet:

```
class Add : public calculator_base::CalcFunctions
{
  public:
Add()
{
  number1_ = 0;
  number2_ = 0;
}
```

The following function is a definition of the `get_numbers()` function that is overriding from the base class. It retrieves two numbers as input:

```
  void get_numbers(double number1, double number2)
  {
```

```
try
{
    number1_ = number1;
    number2_ = number2;
}
catch(int e)
{
    std::cerr<<"Exception while inputting
numbers"<<std::endl;
}
}
```

The `operation()` function performs the desired math operation. In this case, it performs an additional operation, as illustrated in the following code snippet:

```
double operation()
{
    return(number1_+number2_);
}

private:
    double number1_;
    double number2_;
};

};
```

In the next step, we have to export the plugin we have created. The plugin can be loaded at runtime if it is properly exported.

Step 3 – Exporting plugins using the calculator_plugins.cpp file

To load the class of plugins dynamically, we must export each class using a special `PLUGINLIB_EXPORT_CLASS` macro. This macro must be present in any `.cpp` file that consists of plugin classes. We have already defined the plugin class, and, in this file, we are going to define a macro statement only.

Locate the `calculator_plugins.cpp` file from the `pluginlib_calculator/` `src` folder. This is how we export each plugin:

```
#include <pluginlib/class_list_macros.h>
#include <pluginlib_calculator/calculator_base.h>
#include <pluginlib_calculator/calculator_plugins.h>


PLUGINLIB_EXPORT_CLASS(calculator_plugins::Add, calculator_
base::CalcFunctions);
```

Inside `PLUGINLIB_EXPORT_CLASS`, we need to provide the class name of the plugin and the base class.

Step 4 – Implementing a plugin loader using the calculator_loader.cpp file

This plugin loader node loads each plugin, inputs a number to each plugin, and fetches the result from the plugin. We can locate the `calculator_loader.cpp` file from the `pluginlib_calculator/src` folder.

Here is an illustration of the code in this file:

```
#include <boost/shared_ptr.hpp>
#include <pluginlib/class_loader.h>
#include <pluginlib_calculator/calculator_base.h>
```

These are the necessary header files to load the plugins:

```
pluginlib::ClassLoader<calculator_base::CalcFunctions>
calc_loader("pluginlib_calculator", "calculator_
base::CalcFunctions");
```

The `pluginlib` plugin provides the `ClassLoader` class, which is inside `class_loader.h`, to load classes at runtime. We need to provide a name for the loader and the calculator base class as arguments, as follows:

```
    boost::shared_ptr<calculator_base::CalcFunctions> add =
 calc_loader.createInstance("pluginlib_calculator/Add");
```

This will create an instance of the `add` class using the `ClassLoader` object, as illustrated in the following code snippet:

```
    add->get_numbers(10.0,10.0);
    double result = add->operation();
```

These lines give input and perform the operations in the plugin instance.

Step 5 – Creating a plugin description file: calculator_plugins.xml

After creating the calculator loader code, we must next describe a list of plugins inside this package in an **Extensible Markup Language** (**XML**) file called a plugin description file. The plugin description file contains all the information about the plugins inside a package, such as the name of the classes, types of classes, base class, and so on.

The plugin description file is an important file for plugin-based packages because it helps the ROS system to automatically discover, load, and reason about the plugin. It also holds information such as a description of the plugin.

The following code snippet shows the `calculator_plugins.xml` plugin description file of our package, which is stored along with the `CMakeLists.txt` and `package.xml` files. You can get this file from the package folder.

Here is an illustration of the code in this file:

```
<library path="lib/libpluginlib_calculator">
    <class name="pluginlib_calculator/Add" type="calculator_
plugins::Add" base_class_type="calculator_base::CalcFunctions">
    <description>This is a add plugin.</description>
    </class>
```

This code is for the `Add` plugin and it defines the library path of the plugin, the class name, the class type, the base class, and the description.

Step 6 – Registering a plugin with the ROS package system

For `pluginlib` to find all plugin-based packages in the ROS system, we should export the plugin description file inside `package.xml`. If we do not include this plugin, the ROS system won't find the plugins inside the package.

Here, we add the `export` tag to `package.xml`, as follows:

```
<export>
  <pluginlib_calculator plugin="${prefix}/calculator_plugins.
xml" />
</export>
```

We are done with exporting the plugin description file. Next, we can edit the `CMakeLists.txt` file to build the plugin.

Step 7 – Editing the CMakeLists.txt file

Another difference with respect to a common ROS node regards the compilation directives included in the CMakeLists.txt file. To build the calculator plugins and loader nodes, we should add the following lines to CMakeLists.txt:

```
## pluginlib_tutorials library
add_library(pluginlib_calculator src/calculator_plugins.cpp)
target_link_libraries(pluginlib_calculator ${catkin_LIBRARIES})
## calculator_loader executable
add_executable(calculator_loader src/calculator_loader.cpp)
target_link_libraries(calculator_loader ${catkin_LIBRARIES})
```

We are almost done with all the settings, and it's now time to build the package using the catkin_make command.

Step 8 – Querying a list of plugins in the package

If the package is built properly, we can execute the loader. The following command will query the plugins inside the package:

```
rospack plugins --attrib=plugin pluginlib_calculator
```

We will get the following result if everything is built properly:

```
pluginlib_calculator /home/robot/master_ros_ws/src/plugin_
calculator/calculator_plugins.xml
```

In the next step, we can see how to load all these plugins.

Step 9 – Running the plugin loader

After launching the roscore, we can execute the calculator_loader executable using the following command:

```
rosrun pluginlib_calculator calculator_loader
```

The following code block shows the output of this command, to check whether everything is working fine. The loader gives both inputs as 10.0, and we are getting a proper result:

```
[ INFO] [1609673718.399514348]: Sum result: 20.00
[ INFO] [1609673718.399737057]: Substracted result: 0.00
[ INFO] [1609673718.399838030]: Multiplied result: 100.00
[ INFO] [1609673718.399916915]: Division result: 1.00
```

In the next section, we will look at a new concept called **nodelets** and discuss how to implement them.

Understanding ROS nodelets

Nodelets are specific ROS nodes designed to run multiple algorithms within the same process in an efficient way, executing each process as threads. The threaded nodes can communicate with each other efficiently without overloading the network, with zero-copy transport between two nodes. These threaded nodes can communicate with external nodes too.

Each `nodelet` can dynamically load like a `plugin` that has a separate namespace. Each nodelet can act as a separate node, but on a single process.

Nodelets is used when the volume of data transferred between nodes is very high; for example, in transferring data from **three-dimensional** (**3D**) sensors or cameras. The disadvantage of using `nodelets` is they can't be run in a separate process, so they don't parallelize well.

Next, we will look at how to create a `nodelet`.

Implementing a sample nodelet

In this section, we are going to create a basic `nodelet` that can subscribe to a string topic called `/msg_in` and publish the same string (`std_msgs/String`) on a `/msg_out` topic.

Step 1 – Creating a package for a nodelet

We can create a package called `nodelet_hello_world`, using the following command to create our `nodelet`:

```
catkin_create_pkg nodelet_hello_world nodelet roscpp std_msgs
```

Otherwise, we can use the existing `nodelet_hello_world` package, which you can find in the `Chapter 12/ nodelet_hello_world` folder in the code repository.

Here, the main dependency of this package is the `nodelet` package, which provides **application programming interfaces** (**APIs**) to build a ROS `nodelet`.

Step 2 – Creating a hello_world.cpp nodelet

Now, we are going to create the `nodelet` code. Create a folder called `src` inside the `nodelet_hello_world` package and create a file called `hello_world.cpp`.

You will get the existing code from the `nodelet_hello_world/src` folder.

Step 3 – Explanation of hello_world.cpp

Here is an illustration of the code in the `hello_world.cpp` file:

```
#include <pluginlib/class_list_macros.h>
#include <nodelet/nodelet.h>
#include <ros/ros.h>
#include <std_msgs/String.h>
#include <stdio.h>
```

These are the header files inclueded in this code file. We should include `class_list_macro.h` and `nodelet.h` to access the `pluginlib` APIs and nodelet APIs. Have a look at the following code snippet:

```
namespace nodelet_hello_world
{
  class Hello : public nodelet::Nodelet
  {
```

Here, we create a `nodelet` class called `Hello` that inherits a standard `nodelet` base class. All `nodelet` classes should inherit from the `nodelet` base class and be dynamically loadable using `pluginlib`. Here, the `Hello` class is going to be used for dynamic loading. The code is illustrated in the following snippet:

```
virtual void onInit()
{
  ros::NodeHandle& private_nh = getPrivateNodeHandle();
  NODELET_DEBUG("Initialized the Nodelet");
  pub = private_nh.advertise<std_msgs::String>("msg_out",5);
  sub = private_nh.subscribe("msg_in",5, &Hello::callback, this);
}
```

This is the initialization function of a `nodelet`. This function should not block or do significant work. Inside the function, we are creating a `NodeHandle` object, topic publisher, and subscriber on the `msg_out` and `msg_in` topics, respectively. There are macros to print debug messages while executing a `nodelet`. Here, we use `NODELET_DEBUG` to print debug messages in the console. The subscriber is tied up with a `callback()` callback function, which is inside the `Hello` class. The code is illustrated in the following snippet:

```
void callback(const std_msgs::StringConstPtr input)
{
    std_msgs::String output;
    output.data = input->data;
    NODELET_DEBUG("Message data = %s",output.data.c_str());
    ROS_INFO("Message data = %s",output.data.c_str());
    pub.publish(output);
}
```

In the `callback()` function, it will print the messages from the `/msg_in` topic and publish them to the `/msg_out` topic, as illustrated in the following code snippet:

```
PLUGINLIB_EXPORT_CLASS(nodelet_hello_
world::Hello,nodelet::Nodelet);
```

Here, we are exporting `Hello` as a plugin for the dynamic loading.

Step 4 – Creating a plugin description file

As with the `pluginlib` example, we have to create a plugin description file inside the `nodelet_hello_world` package. The `hello_world.xml` plugin description file is illustrated in the following code snippet:

```
<library path="libnodelet_hello_world">
    <class name="nodelet_hello_world/Hello" type="nodelet_hello_
world::Hello" base_class_type="nodelet::Nodelet">
        <description>
        A node to republish a message
        </description>
    </class>
</library>
```

After adding the plugin description file, we can see in the next step how to add the path of the plugin description file to `package.xml`.

Step 5 – Adding the export tag to package.xml

We need to add the `export` tag to `package.xml` and add build and run dependencies, as follows:

```
<export>
    <nodelet plugin="${prefix}/hello_world.xml"/>
</export>
```

After editing the `package.xml` file, we can see how to edit the `CMakeLists.txt` file to compile the `nodelets`.

Step 6 – Editing CMakeLists.txt

We need to add additional lines of code in `CMakeLists.txt` to build a nodelet package. Here are the extra lines. You will get the complete `CMakeLists.txt` file from the existing package:

```
## Declare a cpp library
 add_library(nodelet_hello_world
   src/hello_world.cpp
 )


## Specify libraries to link a library or executable target
against
 target_link_libraries(nodelet_hello_world
   ${catkin_LIBRARIES}
 )
```

After editing the `CMakeLists.txt` file, let's see how to build the `nodelet` ROS package.

Step 7 – Building and running nodelets

After following this procedure, we can build the package using `catkin_make` and, if the build is successful, we can generate a `libnodelet_hello_world.so` shared object file, which represents the plugin.

The first step in running `nodelets` is to start a **nodelet manager**. A `nodelet` manager is a C++ executable program that will listen to the ROS services and dynamically load `nodelets`. We can run a standalone manager or embed it within a running node.

The following commands can start the `nodelet` manager:

1. Start `roscore`, as follows:

   ```
   roscore
   ```

2. Start the `nodelet` manager, using the following command:

   ```
   rosrun nodelet nodelet manager __name:=nodelet_manager
   ```

3. If the `nodelet` manager runs successfully, we will get the following message:

   ```
   [ INFO] [1609674707.691565050]: Initializing nodelet with
   6 worker threads.
   ```

4. After launching the `nodelet` manager, we can start the `nodelet` by using the following command:

   ```
   rosrun nodelet nodelet load nodelet_hello_world/Hello
   nodelet_manager __name:=nodelet1
   ```

5. When we execute the preceding command, the `nodelet` contacts the `nodelet` manager to instantiate an instance of `nodelet_hello_world/Hello` `nodelet` with the name of `nodelet1`. The following code block shows the message we receive when we load the `nodelet`:

   ```
   [ INFO] [1609674752.075787641]: Loading nodelet /nodelet1
   of type nodelet_hello_world/Hello to manager nodelet_
   manager with the following remappings:
   ```

6. The topics generated after running this `nodelet` and a list of nodes are shown here:

   ```
   rostopic list
   /nodelet1/msg_in
   /nodelet1/msg_out
   /nodelet_manager/bond
   /rosout
   /rosout_agg
   ```

We can test the node by publishing a string to the `/nodelet1/msg_in` topic and check whether we receive the same message in `nodelet1/msg_out`.

7. The following command publishes a string to `/nodelet1/msg_in`:

```
rostopic pub /nodelet1/msg_in std_msgs/String "Hello" -r
1
```

8. You will get the same data that we have given as input from the `/nodelet1/msg_out` topic, as illustrated in the following code snippet:

```
rostopic echo /nodelet1/msg_out
data: "Hello"
---
```

We can echo the `msg_out` topic and confirm whether the code is working properly.

Here, we have seen that a single instance of the `Hello()` class is created as a node. We can create multiple instances of the `Hello()` class with different node names inside this `nodelet`.

Step 8 – Creating launch files for nodelets

We can also write launch files to load more than one instance of the `nodelet` class. The following launch file will load two `nodelets` with the names `test1` and `test2`, and we can save it as `launch/hello_world.launch`:

```
<launch>

<!-- Started nodelet manager -->

    <node pkg="nodelet" type="nodelet" name="standalone_nodelet"
args="manager" output="screen"/>

<!-- Starting first nodelet -->

    <node pkg="nodelet" type="nodelet" name="test1" args="load
nodelet_hello_world/Hello standalone_nodelet" output="screen">
    </node>

<!-- Starting second nodelet -->
```

```
    <node pkg="nodelet" type="nodelet" name="test2" args="load
nodelet_hello_world/Hello standalone_nodelet" output="screen">
    </node>

</launch>
```

The preceding launch file can be launched with the following command:

```
roslaunch nodelet_hello_world hello_world.launch
```

The following message will show up on the terminal if it is launched successfully:

```
[ INFO] [1609675205.643405707]: Loading nodelet /test1 of type
nodelet_hello_world/Hello to manager standalone_nodelet with
the following remappings:
[ INFO] [1609675205.645714262]: waitForService: Service [/
standalone_nodelet/load_nodelet] has not been advertised,
waiting...
[ INFO] [1609675205.652567416]: Loading nodelet /test2 of type
nodelet_hello_world/Hello to manager standalone_nodelet with
the following remappings:
[ INFO] [1609675205.655896332]: waitForService: Service [/
standalone_nodelet/load_nodelet] has not been advertised,
waiting...
[ INFO] [1609675205.707828044]: Initializing nodelet with 6
worker threads.
[ INFO] [1609675205.711686663]: waitForService: Service [/
standalone_nodelet/load_nodelet] is now available.
[ INFO] [1609675205.719831856]: waitForService: Service [/
standalone_nodelet/load_nodelet] is now available.
```

A list of topics and nodes is shown in the following code snippet. We can see two
nodelets instantiated, as well as their topics:

```
rostopic list
```

```
/rosout_agg
/standalone_nodelet/bond
/test1/msg_in
/test1/msg_out
/test2/msg_in
/test2/msg_out
```

Topics are generated by multiple instances of the `Hello()` class. We can see the interconnection between these `nodelets` using the `rqt_graph` tool. Open `rqt` by running the following command:

```
rqt
```

Load the Node Graph plugin from the **Plugins->Introspection->Node Graph** option, and you will get a graph like the one shown in the following diagram:

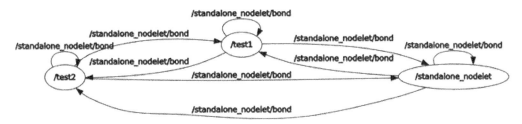

Figure 12.2 – A two-node instance of a nodelet

Alternatively, you can directly load the `rqt_graph` plugin, as follows:

```
rqt_graph
```

In this preceding section, we have seen how to work with ROS `nodelets`. In the next section, we will see how to create plugins for the Gazebo simulator.

Understanding and creating a Gazebo plugin

`Gazebo` plugins help us to control the robot models, sensors, world properties, and even the way `Gazebo` runs. As with `pluginlib` and `nodelets`, `Gazebo` plugins are a set of C++ code that can be dynamically loaded/unloaded from the Gazebo simulator.

Using plugins, we can access all the components of `Gazebo`, which are independent of ROS so that they can be shared with people who are not using ROS (that is, the components). We can mainly classify the plugins as follows:

- **The world plugin**: Using the world plugin, we can control the properties of a specific world in `Gazebo`. We can change the physics engine, the lighting, and other world properties using this plugin.

- **The model plugin**: The model plugin is attached to a specific model in `Gazebo` and controls its properties. The parameters, such as the joint state of the model, control of the joints, and so on, can be controlled using this plugin.

- **The sensor plugin**: The sensor plugins are for modeling sensors—such as camera, **inertial measurement unit (IMU)**, and so on—in `Gazebo`.

- **The system plugin**: The system plugin is started along with the Gazebo startup. A user can control a system-related function in Gazebo using this plugin.

- **The visual plugin**: The visual property of any Gazebo component can be accessed and controlled using the visual plugin.

- **The GUI plugin**: The **graphical user interface (GUI)** plugin can be used to create a custom GUI widget on Gazebo and can change the existing GUI parameters of Gazebo.

Before starting development with `Gazebo` plugins, we might need to install some packages. The `Gazebo` version installed along with ROS Noetic is 11.0, so you might need to install its development package in Ubuntu using the following command:

```
sudo apt install libgazebo11-dev
```

The `Gazebo` plugins are independent of ROS and we don't need ROS libraries to build a plugin.

Creating a basic world plugin

We will look at a basic `Gazebo` world plugin and try to build and load it in `Gazebo`.

This project is also included in the `Chapter 12/gazebo_ros_hello_world` folder provided with this book.

Create a folder called `gazebo_basic_world_plugin` in the desired folder and create a CPP file called `hello_world.cc`, as follows:

```
mkdir gazebo_basic_world_plugin && cd gazebo_basic_world_plugin
```

You can open the following code using a text editor. Here, I am using `gedit`:

```
gedit hello_world.cc
```

The definition of `hello_world.cc` is shown in the following code snippet:

```
#include <gazebo/gazebo.hh>
namespace gazebo
{
  class WorldPluginTutorial : public WorldPlugin
  {
```

```
    public: WorldPluginTutorial() : WorldPlugin()
            {
                printf("Hello World!\n");
            }
    public: void Load(physics::WorldPtr _world, sdf::ElementPtr
_sdf)
            {
            }
  };
  GZ_REGISTER_WORLD_PLUGIN(WorldPluginTutorial)
}
```

The header file used in this code is `<gazebo/gazebo.hh>`. The header contains the core functionalities of `Gazebo`. Other headers are listed here:

- `gazebo/physics/physics.hh`: This is a `Gazebo` header for accessing the physics engine parameters.

- `gazebo/rendering/rendering.hh`: This is a `Gazebo` header for handling rendering parameters.

- `gazebo/sensors/sensors.hh`: This is a `Gazebo` header for handling sensors.

At the end of the code, we must export the plugin using the following statements.

The `GZ_REGISTER_WORLD_PLUGIN(WorldPluginTutorial)` macro will register and export the plugin as a world plugin. The following macros are used to register for sensors, models, and so on:

- `GZ_REGISTER_MODEL_PLUGIN`: This is an export macro for the `Gazebo` robot model.

- `GZ_REGISTER_SENSOR_PLUGIN`: This is an export macro for the `Gazebo` sensor model.

- `GZ_REGISTER_SYSTEM_PLUGIN`: This is an export macro for the `Gazebo` system.

- `GZ_REGISTER_VISUAL_PLUGIN`: This is an export macro for `Gazebo` visuals.

After setting the code, we can make a CMakeLists.txt file for compiling the source code. Here is the source code of CMakeLists.txt:

```
gedit gazebo_basic_world_plugin/CMakeLists.txt
```

```
cmake_minimum_required(VERSION 2.8 FATAL_ERROR)
find_package(gazebo REQUIRED)
include_directories(${GAZEBO_INCLUDE_DIRS})
link_directories(${GAZEBO_LIBRARY_DIRS})
list(APPEND CMAKE_CXX_FLAGS "${GAZEBO_CXX_FLAGS}")
add_library(hello_world SHARED hello_world.cc)
target_link_libraries(hello_world ${GAZEBO_LIBRARIES})
```

Create a build folder for storing the shared object, as follows:

```
mkdir build && cd build
```

After switching to the build folder, execute the following command to compile and build the source code:

```
cmake ../
make
```

After building the code, we will get a shared object called libhello_world.so, and we have to export the path of this shared object in GAZEBO_PLUGIN_PATH and add it to the .bashrc file.

Make sure you have edited the path to the build folder before exporting GAZEBO_PLUGIN_PATH, as follows:

```
export GAZEBO_PLUGIN_PATH=${GAZEBO_PLUGIN_PATH}:/path/to/
gazebo_basic_world_plugin/build
```

After setting the Gazebo plugin path and reloading the `.bashrc` file, we can use it inside the **Unified Robot Description Format** (**URDF**) file or the **Simulation Description Format** (**SDF**) file. The following is a sample world file called `hello.world`, which includes this plugin:

```
gedit gazebo_basic_world_plugin/hello.world
```

```xml
<?xml version="1.0"?>
<sdf version="1.4">
  <world name="default">
    <plugin name="hello_world" filename="libhello_world.so"/>
  </world>
</sdf>
```

Run the `Gazebo` server and load this world file, as follows:

```
cd gazebo_basic_world_plugin
gzserver hello.world --verbose
```

Here is the output from the preceding command:

```
Gazebo multi-robot simulator, version 11.1.0
Copyright (C) 2012 Open Source Robotics Foundation.
Released under the Apache 2 License.
http://gazebosim.org
[Msg] Waiting for master.
[Msg] Connected to gazebo master @ http://127.0.0.1:11345
[Msg] Publicized address: 192.168.47.131
Hello World!
```

The `Gazebo` world plugin prints `Hello World!`. We can also launch the plugin using a launch file as well. Here is the command to start from a launch file

```
gzserver hello.world --verbose
```

We will source the code for various `Gazebo` plugins from the `Gazebo` repository.

We can check `https://github.com/osrf/gazebo`, browse for the source code, and take the `examples` folder and then the plugins, as shown in the following screenshot:

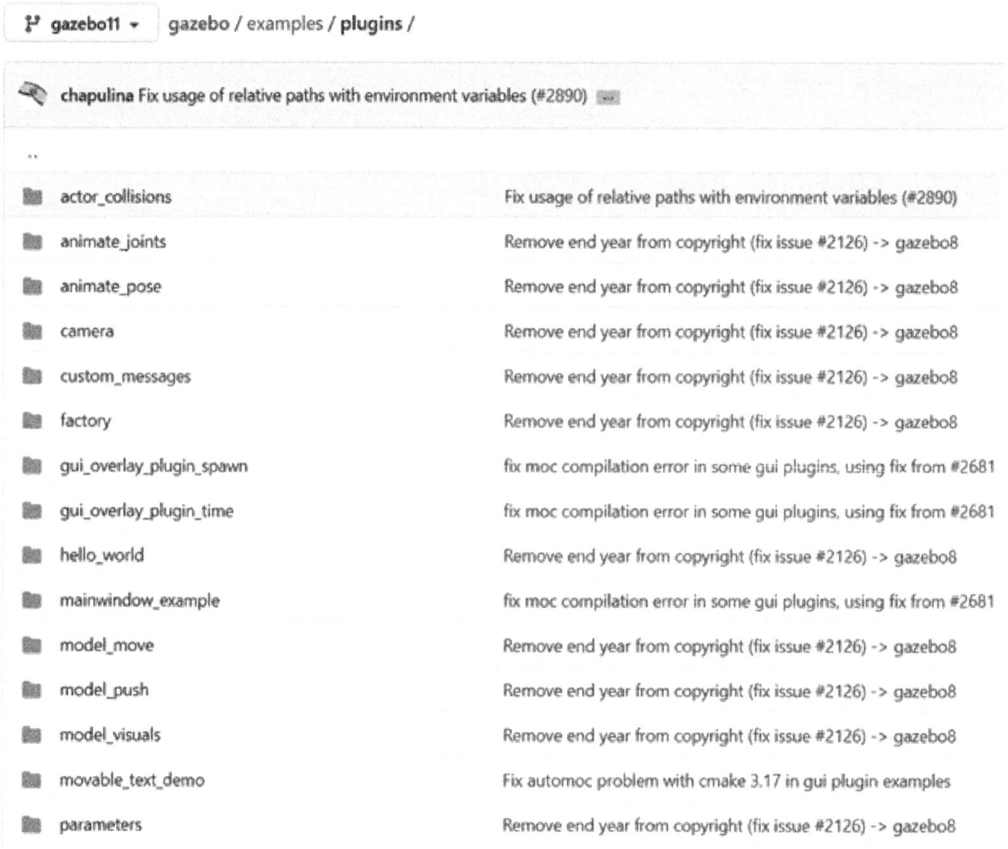

Figure 12.3 – List of sample Gazebo plugins

We can clone this repository and build the selected `Gazebo` plugin based on our simulation. We can follow the same build instructions to build the preceding list of plugins, as we did for the basic `hello world Gazebo` plugin.

Summary

In this chapter, we covered some advanced concepts—such as the `pluginlib`, `nodelets`, and `Gazebo` plugins—that can be used to add more functionalities to a complex ROS application. We discussed the basics of `pluginlib` and saw an example of using it. After covering `pluginlib`, we looked at ROS `nodelets`, which are widely used in high-performance applications. We also looked at an example using ROS `nodelets`. Finally, we came to the `Gazebo` plugins that are used to add functionalities to Gazebo simulators.

This chapter will have given you a clear idea of how to write plugins and `nodelets` in ROS. Nodelets will be very useful when working with computer vision and 3D point-cloud applications. The `Gazebo` plugins will give you a good understanding of how to create custom plugins for your robots.

In the next chapter, we will discuss the **ROS Visualization** (**RViz**) plugin and ROS controllers in more detail.

Here are some questions based on what we learned in this chapter.

Questions

- What is `pluginlib` and what are its main applications?
- What is the main application of `nodelets`?
- What are the different types of `Gazebo` plugins?
- What is the function of the model plugin in `Gazebo`?

13
Writing ROS Controllers and Visualization Plugins

In the previous chapter, we discussed `pluginlib`, `nodelets`, and Gazebo plugins. The base library for making plugins in ROS is `pluginlib`, and the same library can be used in `nodelets`. In this chapter, we will continue with `pluginlib`-based concepts, such as ROS controllers and **ROS visualization (RViz)** plugins. We have already worked with ROS controllers and have reused some standard controllers, such as joint state, position, and trajectory controllers, in *Chapter 4, Simulating Robots Using ROS and Gazebo*.

In this chapter, we will see how to write a basic ROS controller for a generic robot. We will implement the desired controller for our seven-**Degree of Freedom (DOF)** arm robot, developed in previous chapters, executing it in the Gazebo simulator. RViz plugins can add more functionality to RViz, and in this chapter, we will look at how to create a basic RViz plugin. The detailed topics that we are going to discuss in this chapter are as follows:

- Understanding `ros_control` packages
- Writing a basic joint controller in ROS

- Understanding the RViz tool and its plugins

- Writing an RViz plugin for teleoperation

Technical requirements

To follow this chapter, you should have the following setup on your computer:

- Ubuntu 20.04 LTS

- ROS Noetic desktop full installation

The reference code for this chapter can be downloaded from the following Git repository: `https://github.com/PacktPublishing/Mastering-ROS-for-Robotics-Programming-Third-edition/tree/main/Chapter13`
You can view this chapter's code in action here: `https://bit.ly/3k51SGW`.

Understanding ros_control packages

Let's see how to develop a ROS controller. The first step is to understand the dependency packages required to start building custom controllers.

The main set of packages used to develop a controller generic to all robots is contained in the `ros_control` stack. This is a rewritten version of `pr2_mechanism`, containing useful libraries to write low-level controllers for PR2 robots (`http://wiki.ros.org/Robots/PR2`) used in the past version of ROS. In ROS Kinetic, `pr2_mechanism` has been substituted with the `ros_control` stack (`http://wiki.ros.org/ros_control`). The following is a description of some useful packages that help us to write robot controllers:

- **ros_control**: This package takes as input the joint state data directly from the robot's actuators and the desired set point, generating the output to send to its motors. The output is usually represented by the join position, velocity, or effort.

- **controller_manager**: The controller manager can load and manage multiple controllers and can work them in a real-time compatible loop.

- **controller_interface**: This is the controller base class package from which all custom controllers should inherit the controller base class.

- **hardware_interface**: This package represents the interface between the implemented controller and the hardware of the robot. Using this interface, controllers can directly access the hardware components cyclically.

- **joint_limits_interface**: This package allows us to set joint limits to safely work with our robot. Joint limits are also included in the **Unified Robotic Description Format (URDF)** of the robot. This package is different than the URDF because it allows us to additionally specify acceleration and jerk limits. Also, the position, velocity, and effort values contained within the URDF model can be overridden using this package. Commands sent to the hardware are filtered according to the specified joint limits.

- **realtime_tools**: This contains a set of tools that can be used from a hard real-time thread if the operating system supports real-time behavior. The tools currently only provide the real-time publisher, which makes it possible to publish messages to a ROS topic in real time.

Since we have already worked with `ros_control` in *Chapter 4*, *Simulating Robots Using ROS and Gazebo*, everything should already be installed on our system. Otherwise, to operate this package, we should install the following ROS packages from the Ubuntu/Debian repositories:

```
sudo apt install ros-noetic-ros-control ros-noetic-ros-
controllers
```

Before writing the ROS controller, it would be good to understand the use of each package of the `ros_control` stack.

The `ros_control` stack contains packages for using ready-made controllers as well as libraries for creating our own custom ROS controllers for a simulated or real robot. The main packages include controller interfaces, controller managers, hardware interfaces, and transmissions. The first package that we are going to discuss is the `controller_interface` package.

The controller_interface package

The basic ROS low-level controller that we want to implement must inherit a base class called `controller_interface::Controller`. We also have to mention `hardware_interface` (https://github.com/ros-controls/ros_control/wiki/hardware_interface), which is going to be used by this controller. In order to create our controller, basically, we have to override four important functions: `init()`, `starting()`, `update()`, and `stopping()`. The controller class should be in a custom namespace. A basic code snippet of a custom ROS `Controller` class is as follows:

```
namespace our_controller_ns
{
```

```
class Controller: public controller_interface::Controller<Th
type of hardware interface>
    {
public:
    virtual bool init(hardware_interface *robotHW,
                      ros::NodeHandle &nh);
    virtual void starting(const ros::Time& time);
    virtual void update(const ros::Time& time, const
ros::Duration& period);
    virtual void stopping(const ros::Time& time);
    };
}
```

The workflow of a ROS controller class is as follows:

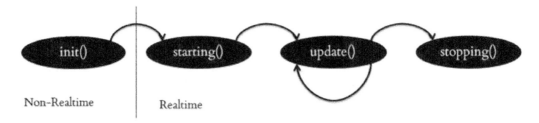

Figure 13.1 – Workflow of the ROS controller

In the next section, we will see how each part of the controller works.

Initializing the controller

The first function that executes when a controller is loaded is init(). The init() function will not start running the controller; it will just initialize it. The initialization can take any amount of time before starting the controllers. The declaration of the init function is as follows:

```
virtual bool init(harware_interface *robotHW, ros::NodeHandle
&nh);
```

The function arguments are as follows:

- `hardware_interface *robotHW`: This pointer represents the specific hardware interface used by the controller. ROS contains a list of already-implemented hardware interfaces, such as the following:

  A. Joint command interfaces (effort, velocity, and position)

  B. Joint state interfaces

  C. Actuator state interfaces

- `ros::NodeHandle &nh`: The controller can read the robot configuration and even advertise topics using this `NodeHandle` object nh.

The `init()` method only executes once while the controller is loaded by the controller manager. If the `init()` method is not successful, it will unload from the controller manager. We can write a custom message if any error occurs inside the `init()` method.

Starting the ROS controller

This method will only execute once before updating and running the controller. The `starting()` method declaration is as follows:

```
virtual void starting(const ros::Time& time);
```

The controller can also call the `starting()` method when it restarts the controller without unloading it.

Updating the ROS controller

The `update()` function is the most important method that makes the controller alive. The `update()` method, by default, executes the code inside it at a rate of 1,000 Hz. This means the controller completes one execution within 1 millisecond:

```
virtual void update(const ros::Time& time, const ros::Duration&
period);
```

Whenever we wish to stop the controller, we will execute the function described in the following section.

Stopping the controller

This method will call when a controller is stopped. The stopping() method will execute as the last update() call and only executes once. The stopping() method will not fail and it does not return any value either. The following is the declaration of the stopping() method:

```
virtual void stopping(const ros::Time& time);
```

We have seen basic functions present inside a controller. In the following section, we will discuss the ROS controller manager.

controller_manager

The controller_manager package can load and unload the desired controller. The controller manager also ensures that the controller will not set a goal value that is less than or greater than the safety limits of the joint. The controller manager also publishes the states of the joint in the /joint_state (sensor_msgs/JointState) topic at a default rate of 100 Hz. The following figure shows the basic workflow of a controller manager:

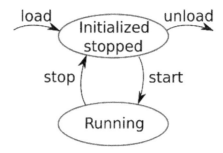

Figure 13.2 – Workflow of the ROS control manager

The controller manager can load and unload a plugin. When a controller is loaded by the controller manager, it will first initialize it, but the controller will not start running.

After loading the controller inside the controller manager, we can individually start and stop the controller. When we start the controller, the controller starts working, and when we stop it, it will simply stop. Stopping doesn't mean it is unloaded. But if the controller is unloaded from the controller manager, we can't access the controller.

In this section, we have seen the important functions inside the Controller class. In the next section, we will see how to create a new controller based on the Controller class. We will see how to test the controller we have developed using the seven-DOF arm simulation package.

Writing a basic joint controller in ROS

The basic prerequisites for writing a ROS controller are already installed. We have discussed the underlying concepts of controllers. Now, we can start creating a package for our controller.

We are going to develop a controller that can access a joint of the robot and move the robot in a sinusoidal fashion. In particular, the first joint of the seven-DOF arm will follow a sinusoidal motion.

The procedure for building a controller is similar to other plugin development that we have seen earlier. The procedure to create a ROS controller is as follows:

1. Create a ROS package with the necessary dependencies.
2. Write controller code in C++.
3. Register or export the C++ class as a plugin.
4. Define the plugin definition in an XML file.
5. Edit the `CMakeLists.txt` and `package.xml` files for exporting the plugin.
6. Write the configuration for our controller.
7. Load the controller using the controller manager.

Let's discuss each of these steps in detail.

Step 1 – creating the controller package

The first step is to create a controller package with all its dependencies. The following command can create a package for the controller called `my_controller`:

```
catkin_create_pkg my_controller roscpp pluginlib controller_
interface
```

We will get the existing package from the `Chapter13/my_controller` folder of the code provided with this book's code.

After getting the package, you can copy each file from the repository to the new package, or you can go through the following steps to understand the function of each file inside the `my_controller` package.

Step 2 – creating the controller header file

We will get the my_controller.h header file from the my_controller/include/ my_controller folder. Given in the following code block is the header file definition of my_controller.h. As already stated, in this header, we are going to implement the functions contained in the controller_interface::Controller class:

```cpp
#include <controller_interface/controller.h>
#include <hardware_interface/joint_command_interface.h>
#include <pluginlib/class_list_macros.h>


namespace my_controller_ns {

    class MyControllerClass: public
controller_interface::Controller<hardware_
interface::PositionJointInterface>
    {
    public:
        bool init(hardware_interface::PositionJointInterface*
hw, ros::NodeHandle &n);
        void update(const ros::Time& time, const
ros::Duration& period);
        void starting(const ros::Time& time);
        void stopping(const ros::Time& time);

    private:
        hardware_interface::JointHandle joint_;
        double init_pos_;
    };
}
```

In the preceding code, we can see the controller class, MyControllerClass, and we are inheriting the base class, controller_interface::Controller. We can see that each function inside the Controller class is overridden in our MyControllerClass class.

Step 3 – creating the controller source file

Create a folder called `src` inside the package and create a C++ file called `my_controller_file.cpp`, which is the class definition of the preceding header.

The following is an explanation of `my_controller_file.cpp`, which has to be saved inside the `src` folder.

First, you can include `my_controller.h`, which has the class declaration of `my_controller_ns::MyControllerClass`:

```
#include "my_controller.h"
namespace my_controller_ns {
```

Here is the function to initialize the controller. The `init()` function will execute only once when the controller is loaded. Inside `init()`, we are trying to get the joint handle of `elbow_pitch_joint` to control that specific joint. The `joint_name` parameter is set in `my_controller.yaml`, which is inside the package:

```
bool MyControllerClass::init(hardware_
interface::PositionJointInterface* hw, ros::NodeHandle &n)
{
//Retrieve the joint object to control
    std::string joint_name;
    if( !nh.getParam( "joint_name", joint_name ) ) {
        ROS_ERROR("No joint_name specified");
        return false;
    }
    joint_ = hw->getHandle(joint_name);
    return true;
}
```

The following function is the definition of the `starting()` function of the controller. Inside this function, we are just getting the initial position of `elbow_pitch_joint`:

```
void MyControllerClass::starting(const ros::Time& time) {
        init_pos_ = joint_.getPosition();
    }
```

The following function is the definition of update(), which will keep on running when the controller is running. The time argument in update() gives the current time and the period argument gives the time passed since the last call to update(). Inside the function, we are continuously updating elbow_pitch_joint to get a sinusoid motion:

```
void MyControllerClass::update(const ros::Time& time, const
ros::Duration& period)
{
//---Perform a sinusoidal motion for joint shoulder_pan_joint
double dpos = init_pos_ + 10 * sin(ros::Time::now().toSec());
        double cpos = joint_.getPosition();
     joint_.setCommand( -10*(cpos-dpos)); //Apply command to
the selected joint
        //---
}
```

The following stopping() function will execute when the controller stops. Currently, we haven't added anything to the function:

```
//Controller exiting
void MyControllerClass::stopping(const ros::Time& time) { }
}
```

The following code exports the controller class as a plugin, which helps to find this controller in ROS:

```
PLUGINLIB_EXPORT_CLASS(my_controller_ns::MyControllerClass,
controller_interface::ControllerBase);
```

In the next section, we will see a detailed explanation of each section of the code.

Step 4 – detailed explanation of the controller source file

In this section, we will see a greater explanation of each section of the code:

```
/// Controller initialization in non-real-time
bool MyControllerClass::init(hardware_
interface::PositionJointInterface* hw, ros::NodeHandle &n)
{
```

The preceding code is the definition of the init() function in the controller. This will be called when a controller is loaded by the controller manager. Inside the init() function, we are creating an instance of the state of the robot (hw) and NodeHandle, and we also get the manager of the joint interacting with the controller. In our example, we defined the joint to control in the my_controller.yaml file, loading the joint name into the ROS parameter server. This function returns the success or the failure in the controller initialization:

```
std::string joint_name;
if( !nh.getParam( "joint_name", joint_name ) )
{
        ROS_ERROR("No joint_name specified");
        return false;
}
joint_ = hw->getHandle(joint_name);
return true;
```

This preceding code will initialize a hardware_interface::JointHandle object called joint_. We can able to control the desired joint using this object. The hw is an instance of the hardware_interface class. joint_name is the desired joint to which we are attaching the controller:

```
/// Controller startup in realtime
void MyControllerClass::starting(const ros::Time& time)
{
init_pos_ = joint_.getPosition();
}
```

After the controller is loaded, the next step is to start it. The preceding function will execute when we start a controller. In this function, it will retrieve the current position of the joint, storing its value in the `init_pos_` variable:

```
/// Controller update loop in real-time
void MyControllerClass::update(const ros::Time& time, const
ros::Duration& period)
{
//---Perform a sinusoidal motion for joint shoulder_pan_joint
double dpos = init_pos_ + 10 * sin(ros::Time::now().toSec());
double cpos = joint_.getPosition();
joint_.setCommand( -10*(cpos-dpos)); //Apply command to the
selected joint
}
```

The preceding code is the definition of the `update()` function in the controller. This function will be continuously called whenever the controller starts working. Inside the `update()` function, one of the joints defined in the `my_controller.yaml` controller configuration file will be continuously moving in a sinusoidal fashion.

Step 5 – creating the plugin description file

In this section, we will see how to define the plugin definition file for our controller. The plugin file is saved inside the package folder under the name of `controller_plugins.xml`:

```xml
<library path="lib/libmy_controller_lib">
    <class name="my_controller_ns/MyControllerClass" type="my_
controller_ns::MyControllerClass"
base_class_type="controller_interface::ControllerBase" />
</library>
```

The controller description file consists of the name of the controller class. In our controller, the name of the class is `my_controller_ns/MyControllerClass`.

The next step is to update `package.xml` to export the plugin description file.

Step 6 – updating package.xml

We need to update `package.xml` to point the `controller_plugins.xml` file:

```
    <export>
      <controller_interface plugin="${prefix}/controller_plugins.
xml" />
    </export>
```

The `<export>` tag in `package.xml` helps to find the plugins/controllers inside a package.

Step 7 – updating CMakeLists.txt

After doing all these things, we can compose `CMakeLists.txt` of the package:

```
 ## my_controller_file library
 add_library(my_controller_lib src/my_controller.cpp)
 target_link_libraries(my_controller_lib ${catkin_LIBRARIES})
```

We have to compile and build the controller as a ROS library rather than an executable. The ROS controller uses `pluginlib` as the backend, which can be loaded at runtime.

Step 8 – building the controller

After completing `CMakeLists.txt`, we can build our controller using the `catkin_make` command. After building, check that the controller is configured as a plugin using the `rospack` command, as shown here:

```
 rospack plugins --attrib=plugin controller_interface
```

With this command, all the controllers related to `controller_interface` will be listed.

If everything has been performed correctly, the output may look like the following:

```
velocity_controllers /opt/ros/noetic/share/velocity_
controllers/velocity_controllers_plugins.xml
```

```
diff_drive_controller /opt/ros/noetic/share/diff_drive_
controller/diff_drive_controller_plugins.xml
```

```
joint_state_controller /opt/ros/noetic/share/joint_state_
controller/joint_state_plugin.xml
```

```
my_controller /home/robot/master_ros_ws/src/my_controller/
controller_plugins.xml
```

We will see how to write a controller configuration file in the next section.

Step 9 – writing the controller configuration file

After proper installation of the controller, we can configure and run it. The first procedure is to create a configuration file of the controller that consists of the controller type, joint name, joint limits, and so on. The configuration file is saved as a YAML file that must be saved inside the package.

We are creating a YAML file with the name my_controller.yaml, and the definition is as follows:

```
#File loaded during Gazebo startup
my_controller_name:
   type: my_controller_ns/MyControllerClass
   joint_name: elbow_pitch_joint
```

This file is the configuration of the controller. In particular, this file contains the type of the controller represented by the name of the class compiled with the controller source code and the set of parameters to pass to the controller. In our case, this is the name of the joint to control.

Step 10 – writing the launch file for the controller

The joint assigned for showing the working of this controller is elbow_pitch_joint of the seven_dof_arm robot. After creating the YAML file, we can create a launch file inside the launch folder, which can load the controller configuration file and run the controller. The launch file is called my_controller.launch, which is given as follows:

```
<?xml version="1.0" ?>
<launch>
```

```
   <include file="$(find my_controller)/launch/seven_dof_arm_
world.launch" />
   <rosparam file="$(find my_controller)/my_controller.yaml"
command="load"/>
   <node name="my_controller_spawner" pkg="controller_manager"
type="spawner" respawn="false"
   output="screen" args="my_controller_name"/>
</launch>
```

In the following code, we explain the launch file:

```
<launch>
   <include file="$(find my_controller)/launch/seven_dof_arm_
world.launch" />
```

Here, we run the Gazebo simulator, launching a modified version of `seven_dof_arm`:

```
<rosparam file="$(find my_controller)/my_controller.yaml"
command="load"/>
```

Then, we load the developed controller.

Finally, we spawn the controller:

```
   <node name="my_controller_spawner" pkg="controller_manager"
type="spawner" respawn="false"
   output="screen" args="my_controller_name"/>
```

In this way, `controller_manager` will run the controller specified in the `args` list. In our case, only `my_controller_name` is executed through `init()`, `start()`, and the `update()` functions implemented by the controller.

Step 11 – running the controller along with the seven-DOF arm in Gazebo

After creating the controller launch files, we should test them on our robot. We can launch the Gazebo simulation using the following command:

```
roslaunch my_controller my_controller.launch
```

When we launch the simulation, all of the controllers associated with the robot also get started. The objective of our ROS controller is to move the `elbow_pitch_joint` of `seven_dof_arm`, as defined in the controller configuration file. If everything is properly working, the elbow of the robot should start to move in a sinusoidal way:

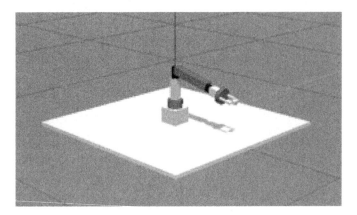

Figure 13.3 – Working of my_controller in the Gazebo simulation

If existing controllers are handling this same joint, our controller can't work properly. To avoid this situation, we need to stop the controller that is handling the same joint of the robot. A set of services are exposed by `controller_manager` to manage the controllers of the robot.

For example, we can use the following command to check the state of the controllers loaded in the system:

```
rosservice call /controller_manager/list_controllers
```

The output of this command is as follows:

```
controller:
  -
    name: "my_controller_name"
    state: "running"
    type: "my_controller_ns/MyControllerClass"
    claimed_resources:
      -
        hardware_interface: "hardware_
interface::PositionJointInterface"
        resources:
          - elbow_pitch_joint
```

In the previous screenshot, you can see that our controller (`my_controller_name`) is running. We can stop it using the `/controller_manager/switch_controller` service, as shown in the following command:

```
rosservice call /controller_manager/switch_controller "start_
controllers: ['']
stop_controllers: ['my_controller_name']
strictness: 0
start_asap: true
timeout: 0.0"
```

You will get the following output if the operation is successful:

```
ok: True
```

You can check the list of controllers running using the following command:

```
rosservice call /controller_manager/list_controllers
```

You will get the list of the controllers like this:

```
controller:
  -
    name: "my_controller_name"
    state: "stopped"
    type: "my_controller_ns/MyControllerClass"
    claimed_resources:
      -
        hardware_interface: "hardware_
interface::PositionJointInterface"
        resources:
          - elbow_pitch_joint
```

Consider that in this example, we are exploiting the `gazebo_ros_control` plugin to run our controller. This plugin represents the hardware interface of our robot in the simulated scene. In the case of a real robot, we should write our hardware interface to apply control data to robot actuators.

In conclusion, `ros_control` implements a standard set of generic controllers, such as `effort_controllers`, `joint_state_controllers`, `position_controllers`, and velocity controllers for any kind of robot. We used these ROS controllers in *Chapter 3, Working with ROS for 3D Modeling*.

Here, we used `ros_control` to develop a simple dedicated position controller for our `seven_dof_arm` robot. You can check the availability of new controllers through the wiki page of `ros_control` at `https://github.com/ros-controls/ros_control/wiki`.

In the next section, we will see more about RViz and how to extend the capabilities of RViz by writing plugins.

Understanding the RViz tool and its plugins

The RViz tool is an official 3D visualization tool of ROS. Almost all kinds of data from sensors can be viewed through this tool. RViz will be installed along with the full ROS desktop installation. Let's launch RViz and see the basic components present in RViz. Make sure you are executing these commands in separate terminals (or tabs).

Start `roscore`:

```
roscore
```

Start `rviz`:

```
rviz
```

The important sections of the RViz GUI are marked, and the uses of each section are shown in the following screenshot:

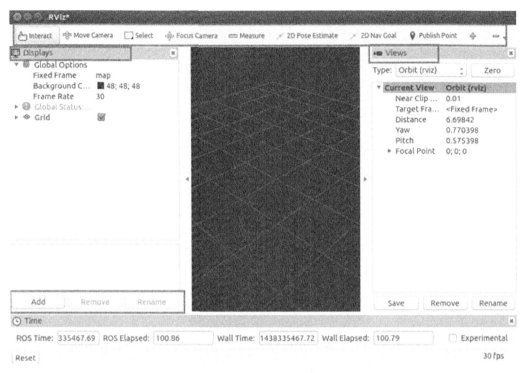

Figure 13.4 – Sections of RViz

We have seen how to work with RViz in ROS, and have seen different sections in RViz. In the following sections, we will provide a detailed explanation of each section of RViz.

The Displays panel

The panel on the left side of RViz is called the **Displays** panel. The **Displays** panel contains a list of the display plugins of RViz and its properties. The main use of display plugins is to visualize different types of ROS messages, mainly sensor data in the RViz 3D viewport. There are lots of display plugins already present in RViz for viewing images from the camera, and for viewing the 3D point cloud, LaserScan, robot model, TF, and so on. Plugins can be added by pressing the **Add** button on the left panel. We can also write our display plugin and add it there.

The RViz toolbar

There is a set of tools present in the RViz toolbar for manipulating the 3D viewport. The toolbar is present at the top of RViz. There are tools present for interacting with the robot model, modifying the camera view, giving navigation goals, and giving the robot 2D pose estimations. We can add our custom tools to the toolbar in the form of plugins.

The Views panel

The **Views** panel is placed on the right side of RViz. Using the **Views** panel, we can save different views of the 3D viewport and switch to each view by loading the saved configuration.

The Time panel

The **Time** panel displays the ROS time and wall time (`http://wiki.ros.org/roscpp/Overview/Time`), which are useful while working with Gazebo simulation. It is also helpful for seeing the simulated time when playing ROS bag files. We can also reset the RViz initial setting using this panel.

Dockable panels

The preceding toolbar and panels belong to dockable panels. We can create our dockable panels as an RViz plugin. We are going to create a dockable panel that has an RViz plugin for robot teleoperation.

Writing an RViz plugin for teleoperation

In this section, we will see how to create an RViz plugin from scratch. The objective of this plugin is to teleoperate the robot from RViz. Normally, we use separate teleoperation nodes for controlling the robot, but using this plugin, we can mention the `teleop` topic and the linear and angular velocity, as shown in the following screenshot:

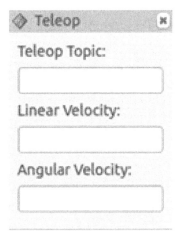

Figure 13.5 – RViz Teleop plugin

In the following section, we discuss the detailed procedure of building this plugin.

The methodology of building a RViz plugin

Before starting to build the teleoperation plugin, we should understand how to write a RViz plugin in general. The standard method to build a ROS plugin is applicable for this plugin too. The difference is that the RViz plugin is GUI-based. RViz is written using a GUI framework called **Qt**, so we need to create a GUI in Qt and, using Qt APIs, we have to get the GUI values and send them to the ROS system.

The following steps describe how this teleoperation RViz plugin is going to work:

1. The dockable panel will have a Qt GUI interface, and the user can input the topic, linear velocity, and angular velocity of teleoperation from the GUI.

2. Collect the user input from GUI using Qt signals and slots, and publish the values using the ROS subscribe-and-publish method. (The Qt signals and slots are a trigger-invoke technique available in Qt. When a signal/trigger is generated by a GUI field, it can invoke a slot or function, such as a callback mechanism.)

3. Here also, we build the RViz plugin in the same way we have built other ROS plugins in this and previous chapters.

Now we will see the step-by-step procedure to build this plugin. You can also find the complete package from `Chapter13/rviz_teleop_commander`.

Step 1 – creating the RViz plugin package

Let's create a new package for creating the `teleop` plugin:

```
catkin_create_pkg rviz_telop_commander roscpp rviz std_msgs
```

The package is mainly dependent on the `rviz` package. RViz is built using Qt libraries, so we don't need to include additional Qt libraries in the package. In the **Ubuntu 20.04** version, we need to use **Qt5** libraries.

Step 2 – creating the RViz plugin header file

Let's create a new header inside the `src` folder called `teleop_pad.h`. You will get this source code from the existing package. This header file consists of the class and methods of declaration for the plugin.

The following is the explanation of this header file:

```
#ifndef Q_MOC_RUN
    #include <ros/ros.h>
    #include <rviz/panel.h>
#endif
```

The preceding code is from the header file required to build this plugin. We need ROS headers for publishing the teleop topic and <rviz/panel.h> for getting the base class of the RViz panel for creating a new RViz panel. The #ifndef Q_MOC_RUN macro is to skip the ROS header from the **Meta-Object Compiler (moc)**. If you want to know about moc, you can check out this link (https://doc.qt.io/archives/4.6/moc.html):

```
class TeleopPanel: public rviz::Panel
{
```

TeleopPanel is a RViz plugin class and it is inherited from the rviz::Panel base class.

```
Q_OBJECT
public:
```

The TeleopPanel class is using the Qt signals and slots(https://doc.qt.io/qt-5/signalsandslots.html), and it's also a subclass of Q_Object in Qt. In that case, we should use the Q_OBJECT macro.

```
TeleopPanel( QWidget* parent = 0 );
```

This is the constructor of the TeleopPanel() class, and we are initializing a QWidget class to 0. We are using the QWidget instance inside the TeleopPanel class for implementing the GUI of the teleop plugin.

```
virtual void load( const rviz::Config& config );
virtual void save( rviz::Config config ) const;
```

The preceding code shows how to override the rviz::Panel functions for saving and loading the RViz config file.

```
public Q_SLOTS:
```

After the preceding line, we can declare some public Qt slots required for the `TeleopPanel` plugin.

```
void setTopic( const QString& topic );
```

When we enter the topic name in the GUI and press *Enter*, the `setTopic()` slot will be called and will initialize the ROS topic publisher with the topic name given in the GUI.

```
protected Q_SLOTS:
  void sendVel();
  void update_Linear_Velocity();
  void update_Angular_Velocity();
  void updateTopic();
```

The preceding lines of code are the protected slots for sending the velocity, updating the linear velocity and angular velocity, and updating the topic name when we change the name of the existing topic.

```
QLineEdit* output_topic_editor_;
QLineEdit* output_topic_editor_1;
QLineEdit* output_topic_editor_2;
```

We are now creating the Qt `QLineEdit` object to create three text fields in the plugin to receive the topic name, linear velocity, and angular velocity.

```
ros::Publisher velocity_publisher_;
ros::NodeHandle nh_;
```

These are the publisher object and the `NodeHandle` object for publishing topics and handling a ROS node.

Step 3 – creating the RViz plugin definition

In this step, we will create the main C++ file that contains the definition of the plugin. The file is `teleop_pad.cpp`, and you will get it from the `src` package folder.

The main responsibilities of this file are as follows:

- It acts as a container for a Qt GUI element, such as `QLineEdit`, to accept text entries.
- It publishes the command velocity using the ROS publisher.
- It saves and restores the RViz config files.

The following is the explanation for each section of the code:

```
TeleopPanel::TeleopPanel( QWidget* parent )
  : rviz::Panel( parent )
  , linear_velocity_( 0 )
  , angular_velocity_( 0 ) {
```

The preceding code is the constructor of `TeleopPanel::TeleopPanel` RViz plugin class. It also initializes `rviz::Panel` with `QWidget`, setting the linear and angular velocity as 0.

```
QVBoxLayout* topic_layout = new QVBoxLayout;
topic_layout->addWidget( new QLabel( "Teleop Topic:" ));
output_topic_editor_ = new QLineEdit;
topic_layout->addWidget( output_topic_editor_ );
```

This preceding code will add a new `QLineEdit` widget on the panel for handling the topic name. Similarly, two other `QLineEdit` widgets handle the linear velocity and angular velocity.

```
QTimer* output_timer = new QTimer( this );
```

This will create a `QTimer` object for updating a function that is publishing the velocity topic.

```
connect( output_topic_editor_, SIGNAL( editingFinished() ),
this, SLOT( updateTopic() ));
connect( output_topic_editor_, SIGNAL( editingFinished() ),
this, SLOT( updateTopic() ));
connect( output_topic_editor_1, SIGNAL( editingFinished() ),
this, SLOT( update_Linear_Velocity() ));
connect( output_topic_editor_2, SIGNAL( editingFinished() ),
this, SLOT( update_Angular_Velocity() ));
```

This will connect a Qt signal to the slots. Here, the signal is triggered when `editingFinished()` returns `true`, and the `slot` here is `updateTopic()`. When the editing inside a `QLineEdit` widget is finished by pressing the *Enter* key, the signal will trigger, and the corresponding slot will execute.

Here, this slot will set the topic name, angular velocity, and linear velocity value from the text field of the plugin:

```
    connect( output_timer, SIGNAL( timeout() ), this, SLOT(
sendVel() ));
    output_timer->start( 100 );
```

These lines generate a signal when the QTimer object output_timer times out. The timer will time out after every 100 ms and execute a slot called sendVel(), which will publish the velocity topic.

We can see the definition of each slot after this section. This code is self-explanatory and, finally, we can see the following code to export it as a plugin:

```
#include <pluginlib/class_list_macros.h>
PLUGINLIB_EXPORT_CLASS(rviz_telop_commander::TeleopPanel,
rviz::Panel )
```

We have gone through the important sections of the RViz plugin code. Now, we can see how to write the plugin description file of the RViz plugin.

Step 4 – creating the plugin description file

The definition of plugin_description.xml is as follows:

```
<library path="lib/librviz_telop_commander">
   <class name="rviz_telop_commander/Teleop"
          type="rviz_telop_commander::TeleopPanel"
          base_class_type="rviz::Panel">
     <description>
        A panel widget allowing simple diff-drive style robot
base control.
     </description>
   </class>
</library>
```

After creating the plugin description file, we can add the path of this file to the package. xml file. This will help ROS nodes to find the RViz plugin and load the appropriate plugin files.

Step 5 – adding the export tags in package.xml

We have to update the package.xml file to include the plugin description. The following is the update of package.xml:

```
<export>
    <rviz plugin="${prefix}/plugin_description.xml"/>
</export>
```

After updating the `<export>` tag in package.xml, let's update CMakeLists.txt in order to build the plugin source code.

Step 6 – editing CMakeLists.txt

We need to add extra lines to the CMakeLists.txt definition, as given in the following code:

```
find_package(Qt5 COMPONENTS Core Widgets REQUIRED)
set(QT_LIBRARIES Qt5::Widgets)
catkin_package(
    LIBRARIES ${PROJECT_NAME}
    CATKIN_DEPENDS roscpp
                    rviz
)
include_directories(include
      ${catkin_INCLUDE_DIRS}
      ${Boost_INCLUDE_DIRS}
)
link_directories(
      ${catkin_LIBRARY_DIRS}
      ${Boost_LIBRARY_DIRS}
)
add_definitions(-DQT_NO_KEYWORDS)
QT5_WRAP_CPP(MOC_FILES
  src/teleop_pad.h
  OPTIONS -DBOOST_TT_HAS_OPERATOR_HPP_INCLUDED -DBOOST_
LEXICAL_CAST_INCLUDED
)

set(SOURCE_FILES
```

```
    src/teleop_pad.cpp
    ${MOC_FILES}
 )
   add_library(${PROJECT_NAME} ${SOURCE_FILES})
   target_link_libraries(${PROJECT_NAME} ${QT_LIBRARIES}
${catkin_LIBRARIES})
```

You will get the complete CMakeLists.txt source code from the rviz_telop_
commander package from Chapter13/rviz_teleop_commander.

After building the RViz plugin in the catkin workspace, we can load the plugin in RViz
using the following steps.

Step 7 – building and loading plugins

After creating these files, build a package using catkin_make. If the build is successful,
we can load the plugin in RViz. Open RViz and load the panel by going to the **Menu** panel
| **Add New Panel**. We will get a panel such as the following:

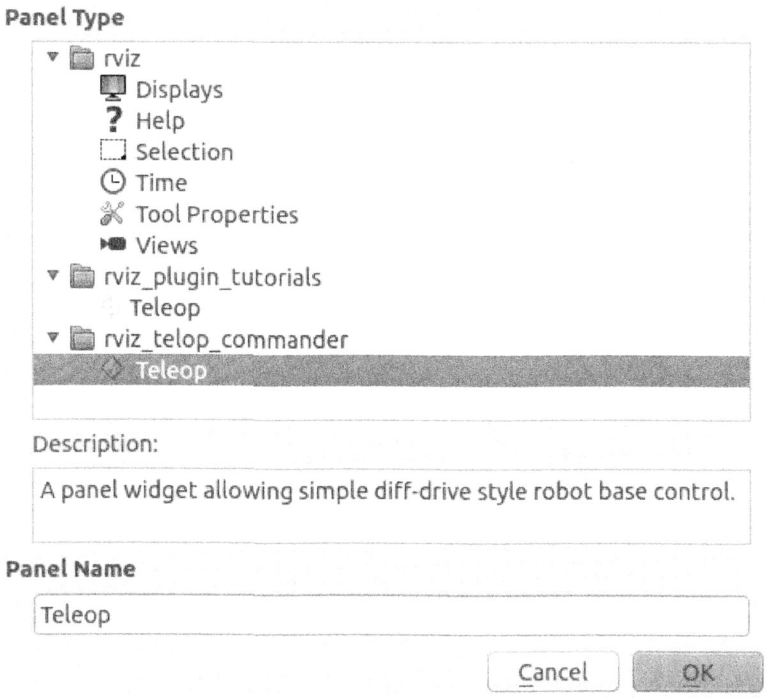

Figure 13.6 – Choosing the RViz Teleop plugin

If we load the **Teleop** plugin from the list, we will get a panel such as the following:

Figure 13.7 – RViz Teleop plugin

We can choose the **Teleop Topic** name and add values for **Linear Velocity** and **Angular Velocity**, and we can print the **Teleop Topic** values using the following command:

```
robot@ubuntu:~$ rostopic echo /cmd_vel
linear:
  x: 1.0
  y: 0.0
  z: 0.0
angular:
  x: 0.0
  y: 0.0
  z: 2.0
---
linear:
  x: 1.0
  y: 0.0
  z: 0.0
angular:
  x: 0.0
  y: 0.0
  z: 2.0
```

Figure 13.8 – Printing velocity command in the terminal

This plugin can help to drive a wheeled robot from RViz. We can also easily customize this plugin to add more control to the GUI.

Summary

In this chapter, we discussed creating plugins for RViz and writing basic ROS controllers. We have already worked with default controllers in ROS, and in this chapter, we developed a custom controller for moving joints. After building and testing the controller, we looked at RViz plugins. We created a new RViz panel for teleoperation. We can manually enter the topic name and linear and angular velocity in the panel. This panel is useful for controlling robots without starting another teleoperation node.

In the next chapter, we will discuss using ROS with **MATLAB**. MATLAB is a powerful numeric computing environment developed by **MathWorks**. The next chapter discusses how to interface this tool with ROS to create robot applications.

Here are some questions based on what we covered in this chapter.

Questions

- What is the list of packages needed for writing a low-level controller in ROS?

- What are the different processes happening inside a ROS controller?

- What are the main packages of the `ros_control` stack?

- What are the different types of RViz plugins?

14

Using ROS in MATLAB and Simulink

In previous chapters, we discussed how to simulate and control robots implementing ROS nodes in C++. In this chapter, we will learn how to create ROS nodes using **MATrix LABoratory** (**MATLAB**), a powerful piece of software that provides several toolboxes with algorithms and hardware connectivity to develop autonomous robotic applications for ground vehicles, manipulators, and humanoid robots. Also, MATLAB integrates Simulink: a block diagram environment for model-based design, allowing the implementation of our control programs through a graphical editor. In this chapter, we will also discuss how to implement robotic applications using Simulink.

The first part of this chapter is dedicated to a brief introduction to MATLAB and Robotics System Toolbox. After we have learned how to exchange data between ROS and MATLAB, we will implement an obstacle avoidance system for the differential drive mobile robot **TurtleBot**, showing how simple it is to use components already available in Robotics System Toolbox and to minimize the number of elements to develop in the system. In the second part of the chapter, we will introduce Simulink, showing an initial model as an example, and then discuss a publisher-and-subscriber model to demonstrate the Simulink and ROS communication interface. Finally, a control system to regulate the orientation of the TurtleBot robot will be developed in Simulink and tested in the **Gazebo simulator**.

The following are the main topics discussed in this chapter:

- Getting started with MATLAB

- Getting started with ROS Toolbox and MATLAB

- Developing a robotic application using MATLAB and Gazebo

- Getting started with ROS and Simulink

- Developing a simple control system in Simulink

Technical requirements

To follow this chapter, you need a standard laptop running **Ubuntu 20.04** with ROS Noetic installed and properly configured. Also, a version of **MATLAB 2020b** must be installed, selecting **ROS Toolbox**, **Robotics System Toolbox**, and **Navigation Toolbox**.

The reference code for this chapter can be downloaded from the following Git repository: `https://github.com/PacktPublishing/Mastering-ROS-for-Robotics-Programming-Third-edition/tree/main/Chapter14/ros_matlab_test`

You can view this chapter's code in action here: `https://bit.ly/37WE0zy`.

Getting started with MATLAB

MATLAB is a multi-platform numerical computing environment widely used by industries, universities, and research centers. MATLAB was born as a mathematical software, but now it offers a lot of additional packages for different areas, such as control design, plotting, image processing, and robotics. Every year, two new versions of MATLAB are released. The first one is called *XXXXa* (where *XXXX* is the year of the release) and it is released in March, while the second one is called *XXXXb* and it is released in September. In this chapter, we assume the installation of the MATLAB 2020b version. MATLAB is a proprietary product of MathWorks, and it is not free software. Usually, free licenses are distributed to students and academic institutions. You can use MATLAB on Windows, GNU/Linux, and macOS. After you have launched it, the main window of MATLAB will appear with its default layout, as shown in the following screenshot:

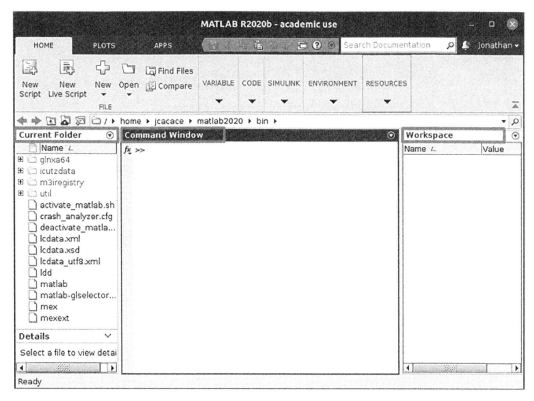

Figure 14.1 – The main window of MATLAB in its default layout

This window includes three main panels:

- **Current Folder**: This shows local files.

- **Command Window**: This is a command line to enter MATLAB commands or run MATLAB scripts.

- **Workspace**: This shows data created from the Command Window or in MATLAB scripts.

Using the Command Window, you can issue mathematical commands and create variables that will be shown in the workspace. The same window can be used to view MATLAB function documentation. In fact, all the built-in MATLAB functions have supporting documentation, including examples and descriptions of the function inputs, outputs, and calling syntax. You can access the documentation using the doc or help command. The first one will open an external window containing the documentation, while the second one will display the documentation in the Command Window. Let's see how to get the documentation about the mean function:

```
>> doc mean
```

You could also use this command to obtain the same result:

```
>> help mean
```

After this very brief introduction to MATLAB, we will discuss in the next section how to connect it with the ROS network to use ROS functions.

Getting started with ROS Toolbox and MATLAB

Beyond the standard functions provided by the default installation of MATLAB, several external toolboxes give you access to other utilities and libraries. To use ROS with MATLAB, you need to install ROS Toolbox (`https://it.mathworks.com/products/ros.html`). This toolbox implements an interface between MATLAB and ROS that enables developers to test and port their applications on real robots and robotic simulators. To implement robotic applications, it is also useful to install Robotics System Toolbox (`https://it.mathworks.com/products/robotics.html`) and Navigation Toolbox (`https://it.mathworks.com/products/navigation.html`), providing several algorithms that help us to develop autonomous robot applications, such as path planners, obstacle avoidance methods, state estimations, kinematics, and dynamics algorithms.

You can add ROS Toolbox, Robotics System Toolbox, and Navigation Toolbox from the package list during the MATLAB installation, or download them from the MATLAB website:

Figure 14.2 – ROS Toolbox selection during MATLAB installation

Using ROS Toolbox, we can transform MATLAB into a ROS node that will be able to exchange information with other nodes of the system and directly control simulated or real ROS-enabled robots using topics and services. After connecting MATLAB to a ROS master node, it can fetch data to process from the robot or other ROS nodes. MATLAB could itself initialize a ROS master node to manage the communication with the nodes of the network, or it could be connected to another remote ROS master, like any other element of the ROS network. In addition, in the final version of the application, we are not forced to run MATLAB on our computer to execute it, but we can deploy the developed application as a typical C++ node. The following block diagram depicts the connection between MATLAB and ROS:

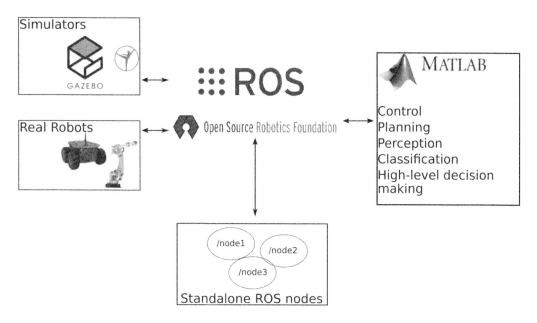

Figure 14.3 – ROS-MATLAB interface schema

With the installation of Robotics System Toolbox, we will have access to several ROS commands equivalent to the ones used under Linux. To list these commands, you can enter the following line in the Command Window:

```
>> help ros
```

The output of this command is shown in the following figure:

```
ros Toolbox
Version 1.2 (R2020b) 29-Jul-2020

Network Connection and Exploration
    rosinit           - Initialize the ros system
    rosshutdown       - Shut down the ros system
    rosaction         - Get information about actions in the ros network
    rosmsg            - Get information about messages and message types
    rosnode           - Get information about nodes in the ros network
    rosservice        - Get information about services in the ros network
    rostopic          - Get information about topics in the ros network
    rosparam          - Get and set values on the parameter server
    rosdevice         - Connect to remote ros device

    ros2              - Retrieve information about ros 2 network

Publishers and Subscribers
    rosmessage        - Create a ros message
    rostype           - View available ros message types
    rospublisher      - Create a ros publisher
    rossubscriber     - Create a ros subscriber
```

Figure 14.4 – ROS-MATLAB interface commands

To initialize the ROS-MATLAB interface, we can use the rosinit command, while rosshutdown is used to stop it. By default, rosinit creates a ROS master node in MATLAB, starting matlab_global_node to communicate with the ROS network. We can see the active ROS nodes after initializing roscore using the rosnode list command:

```
>> rosinit
Initializing ROS master on http://DESKTOP-40TG18P:11311/.
Initializing global node /matlab_global_node_16208 with NodeURI http://DESKTOP-40TG18P:61762/
>> rosnode list
/matlab_global_node_16208
```

Figure 14.5 – Default initialization of the ROS-MATLAB interface

Using the default configuration of the ROS-MATLAB interface, we must set the ROS_ MASTER_URI environmental variable on the other node of the ROS network with the IP address of the computer running MATLAB. If you are running MATLAB on Windows, you can easily get the IP address of your computer by using the following command:

```
>> !ipconfig
```

Or, you can use the following command if you are running MATLAB on Linux:

```
>> !ifconfig
```

The output of this command in Windows is shown in the following screenshot:

```
wlp4s0: flags=4163<UP,BROADCAST,RUNNING,MULTICAST>  mtu 1500
        inet 100.102.1.236  netmask 255.255.0.0  broadcast 100.102.255.255
        inet6 fe80::63e0:7643:8c30:b6b  prefixlen 64  scopeid 0x20<link>
        ether 08:5b:d6:dc:09:6f  txqueuelen 1000  (Ethernet)
        RX packets 729463  bytes 909652975 (909.6 MB)
        RX errors 0  dropped 13  overruns 0  frame 0
        TX packets 261822  bytes 70550108 (70.5 MB)
        TX errors 0  dropped 0 overruns 0  carrier 0  collisions 0
```

Figure 14.6 – The ifconfig command on MATLAB, running on Linux

Otherwise, we can directly connect MATLAB to an active ROS network. In this case, we must inform the ROS-MATLAB interface about the address of the computer/robot where the ROS master is running. This is done with the following commands:

```
>> setenv('ROS_MASTER_URI', 'http://192.168.1.131:11311');
>> rosinit
The value of the ROS_MASTER_URI environment variable, http://192.168.1.131:11311, will be used to connect
Initializing global node /matlab_global_node_75920 with NodeURI http://192.168.1.130:61991/
>> rosnode list
/matlab_global_node_75920
/rosout
```

Figure 14.7 – Initializing the ROS-MATLAB interface on an external ROS network

In the next section, we will start to work with topic callbacks, initializing the ROS-MATLAB interface and adding data directly from MATLAB scripts.

Starting with ROS topics and MATLAB callback functions

In this section, we will discuss how to publish and subscribe ROS messages using MATLAB scripts. The first script that we will analyze defines a typical template to develop the control loop of our robot. Firstly, we will subscribe to an input topic, and, then we will republish its value on an output topic for a certain amount of time. The complete source code is contained in `talker.m`, in the code provided with the book, in the `ros_matlab_test` package.

Let's see the content of the `talker.m` script:

```matlab
rosinit
pause(2)
talker_sub = rossubscriber( '/talker' );
[chatter_pub, chatter_msg] = rospublisher('/chatter','std_msgs/String');
r = rosrate(2); % 2 Hz loop rate
pause(2) % wait a bit the roscore initialization
for i = 1:20
      %Get data from the input topic
      data = talker_sub.LatestMessage;
      chatter_msg.Data = data.Data;
      %Publish data on the output topic
      send(chatter_pub, chatter_msg);
      %Wait for the control loop rate
      waitfor(r);
end
%Shutdown ROS connection
rosshutdown
```

Let's see how the script works. The first thing to do is to initialize the MATLAB-ROS node. In this example, we want to connect MATLAB to the local ROS network and make it able to both read and write data on topics. It could be convenient to include a pause after the `init` command before continuing with the MATLAB script to wait for the completion of the initialization:

```matlab
rosinit
pause(2)
```

Then, we subscribe to the `/talker` topic while initializing the advertiser to the `/chatter` topic of the `std_msgs/String` type:

```
talker_sub = rossubscriber( '/talker' );
[chatter_pub, chatter_msg] = rospublisher('/chatter','std_msgs/
String');
```

Finally, we use the `LatestMessage` function to get the last message on the input topic, while publishing the message on the `/chatter` topic:

```
data = talker_sub.LatestMessage;
send(chatter_pub, chatter_msg);
```

At this point, you can publish the desired message on the `/talker` topic, using the command line from one of the computers running Linux in the same network as the MATLAB computer, and visualize the message published on the `/chatter` topic.

Now, you can run the script by typing its name in the Command Window:

```
>> talker
```

If everything has been correctly set, the output on the Linux machine should appear as in the following screenshot:

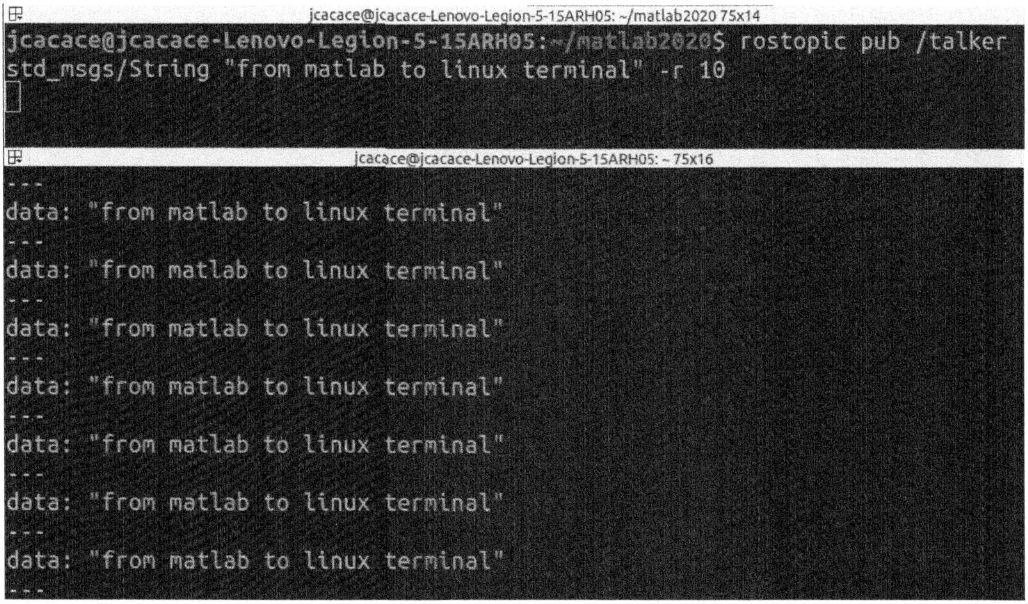

Figure 14.8 – Communication between MATLAB and ROS

The previous script defines a typical template to implement the control loop of an autonomous robot. Instead of continuously asking for the last message received on the topics, we can define a callback function that is called every time that a new message is received. In this way, we could write more complex control loops to handle the robot behavior, asynchronously receiving multiple information from ROS topics. In the next example, we will start to connect ROS-MATLAB to Gazebo, simulating the TurtleBot robot and plotting the value of its laser sensor using MATLAB.

To run the Gazebo simulation, we will use the turtlebot3_gazebo package. Note that the turtlebot3 package has configuration and source files for three different turtlebot3 models. We will use the simulation with the burger model, so we set it before launching the Gazebo scene:

```
export TURTLEBOT3_MODEL=burger
roslaunch turtlebot3_gazebo turtlebot3_world.launch
```

If you have not installed turtlebot3 packages yet, you can install them with the following command:

```
sudo apt-get install ros-noetic-turtlebot3*
```

After starting Gazebo, different topics are published, among which is /scan. In this example, we need the following MATLAB functions:

- plot_laser.m: This initializes the ROS-MATLAB interface subscribing to the desired laser scanner topic and plots the laser data at the desired frame rate.

- get_laser.m: This receives and stores the value of the laser scanner data.

Let's look at the code of the plot_laser script:

```
function plot_laser()
    global laser_msg;
    %ROS_MASTER_URI
    rosinit
    pause(2)
    laser_sub = rossubscriber( '/scan', @get_laser );
    r = rosrate(2); % 2 Hz loop rate
    for i=1:50
    plot(laser_msg    ); %Plot laser_msg
    waitfor(r);
    end
```

```
        rosshutdown
        close all
 end
```

After setting up the ROS-MATLAB interface, we initialize the subscriber to the laser scan topic:

```
 laser_sub = rossubscriber('/scan', @get_laser );
```

With this line, we demand that the `get_laser` function handles the data contained in the `/scan` topic. To exchange data between different MATLAB scripts, we use a global variable:

```
        global laser_msg;
```

Finally, we plot the laser scanner data of the laser data for 25 seconds:

```
        plot(laser_msg);
```

Let's now look at the code of the `get_laser` function:

```
 function get_laser(~, message)
 global laser_msg;
 laser_msg = message;
 End
```

In this function, we just save the value of the laser scanner data. After launching the Gazebo simulation, we can run the MATLAB script:

```
 >> plot_laser
```

The output of the default placement of the scene objects is shown in the following screenshot:

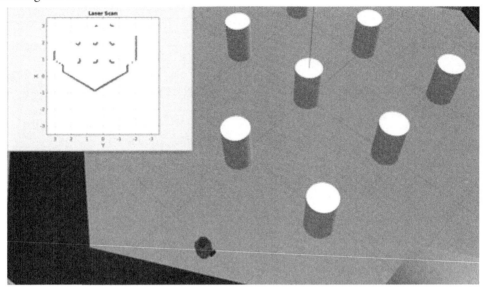

Figure 14.9 – Gazebo laser scanner data plotted in MATLAB

In the previous examples, we just showed how to get data from the ROS network. In the next section, we will implement a motion algorithm that drives the TurtleBot robot into its environment using laser scanner data to avoid obstacles.

Developing a robotic application using MATLAB and Gazebo

Until now, we have used MATLAB only to exchange data using ROS topics. In this section, we are going to demonstrate how easy it is to create a robotic application for a mobile robot using MATLAB and Navigation Toolbox. We will design an obstacle avoidance system for a differential mobile robot that allows the TurtleBot robot to navigate a crowded environment without colliding with any obstacles. We will present a MATLAB script that will set the control velocities of the robot to generate a random movement. At the same time, the laser scanner data of the sensor of the robot will be used to avoid obstacles. To implement this behavior, we will rely on the **Vector Field Histogram** (**VFH**) algorithm to compute the obstacle-free steering directions of the robot, based on range sensor data. This algorithm is already provided by Navigation Toolbox in the `controllerVFH` class. Finally, after some navigation time, some log data will be plotted, using the MATLAB function. This could help developers to debug our application.

The complete source code of the script that we are going to discuss can be found in the `vfh_obstacle_avoidance.m` source file and its content is explained.

We include the source code in a function called `vfh_obstacle_avoidance`. As usual, at the start, we initialize the ROS interface:

```
function vfh_obstacle_avoidance()
      rosinit
pause(2)
```

Then, we subscribe to the laser scan message and declare variables to advertise the commands to control the robot. The ROS publisher function returns both the instantiated publisher, `velPub`, and the type of the message to send via the publisher, `velMsg`. In addition, we subscribe to the odometry of the robot to track its velocity during the motion:

```
      laserSub = rossubscriber('/scan');
      odomSub =  rossubscriber('/odom');
       [velPub, velMsg] = rospublisher('/cmd_vel');
```

We are now ready to instantiate the VFH object to implement our obstacle avoidance system:

```
      vfh = controllerVFH;
```

Some parameters are needed for the VFH algorithm. These are as follows:

- `DistanceLimits`: The limits for laser readings, specified with a two-dimensional vector continuing the minimum and maximum ranges to consider a valid laser measure
- `RobotRadius`: The dimension of the robot specified in meters
- `MinTurningRadius`: The minimum turning radius, in meters, of the robot
- `SafetyDistance`: The maximum space to allow between the robot and the obstacles

We set these values in the following way:

```
vfh.DistanceLimits = [0.05 1];
      vfh.RobotRadius = 0.1;
      vfh.MinTurningRadius = 0.2;
      vfh.SafetyDistance = 0.1;
```

We are now ready to start the control loop that allows the motion of the robot. Firstly, we define the control loop rate:

```
rate = robotics.Rate(10);
```

In the following, the motion control loop is described. We want to perform the control loop for a desired amount of time. We can use `rate.TotalElapsedTime` to track the elapsed time. This function returns the elapsed time in seconds from the creation of the `rate` object. Inside the control loop, we will read the sensor data from the laser scanner topic:

```
while rate.TotalElapsedTime < 25
        laserScan = receive(laserSub);
        odom = receive(odomSub);
        ranges = double(laserScan.Ranges);
angles = double(laserScan.readScanAngles);
```

`targetDir` specifies the angle direction of the robot movement. Its value must be expressed in radians, and the robot's forward direction is considered as 0 radians. As already stated, the target direction in our example is randomly calculated at each control loop:

```
targetDir = (r_max-r_min).*rand();
```

Then, we can call the field histogram method to calculate an obstacle-free steering direction on the base of the input laser scanner data and the actual desired direction of the movement:

```
steerDir= vfh(ranges, angles, targetDir);
```

If a valid steering direction exists, we need to calculate the rotation velocity to send to the robot to actuate it. To do this, we will use the following function:

```
w = exampleHelperComputeAngularVelocity(steerDir, 1);
```

This function returns the angular velocity for a differential drive robot expressed in `rad/s`, given a steering direction in the robot's frame, like in our case. In addition, the second parameter of the function represents a maximum velocity value to saturate the calculated one. Finally, we plot the minimum distance of the robot from the detected obstacles during its motion, the performed path, and the actuated angular and forward velocities:

```
figure(1);
plot( ob_dist, 'red-' );
figure(2);
```

```
plot( odom_vel_x, 'red' );
figure(3);
plot( odom_vel_z, 'blue' );
figure(4)
plot( odom_pos_x, odom_pos_y, 'red');
```

To test this example, first we need to launch the TurtleBot simulation scene on the computer where we want to run `roscore`:

```
roslaunch turtlebot3_gazebo turtlebot_world.launch
```

Then we must invoke the MATLAB script:

```
>> vfh_obstacle_avoidance
```

While the robot will navigate the same environment depicted in *Figure 14.9*, an example of the output of the MATLAB script is shown in the following screenshot:

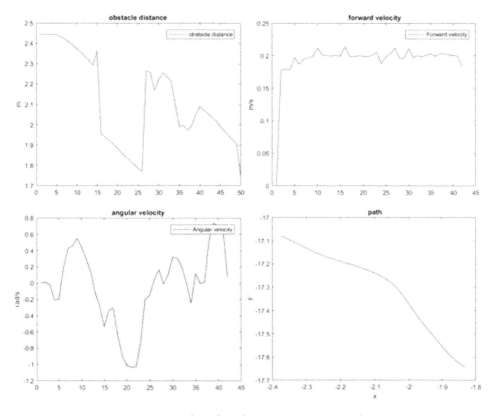

Figure 14.10 – Log data plotted using MATLAB print functions

In this screenshot, we have different data retrieved by the simulation. In particular, at the upper left, the minimum obstacle distance is reported, at the upper right, the linear forward velocity is reported, and at the bottom left and bottom right, the angular velocity and executed path are depicted.

The previous plots can be used to check the performance of the obstacle avoidance algorithm.

Another useful tool of MATLAB software is the possibility to use, create, and model control systems with a graphical tool called Simulink. Simulink can be connected with the ROS network and can use ROS functions, as discussed in the next section.

Getting started with ROS and Simulink

In the previous sections, we discussed how to interact with ROS using MATLAB. In this section, we are going to use another powerful tool of MATLAB: **Simulink**. Simulink is a graphical programming environment for modeling, simulating, and analyzing dynamical systems. We can use Simulink to create a model of a system and simulate its behavior over time. In this section, we will start creating our first simple system from the ROS framework. We will also discuss how to develop a ROS application using Simulink.

Creating a wave signal integrator in Simulink

To model a new system, let's start by opening Simulink. We can open it by typing the following command in the Command Window:

```
>> Simulink
```

Then, you should choose to create a new blank model. To create a new system, we must import the desired Simulink blocks that will compose it. These blocks can be directly dragged and dropped into the model window from the Library Browser. To open the Library Browser, select **View | Library** from the model pane toolbar. For our first system, we need four blocks:

- **Sine wave**: This generates a sinusoidal signal that will represent the input of our system.

- **Integrator**: This integrates an input signal.

- **Bus creator**: This combines multiple signals in one signal.

- **Scope**: This graphically visualizes the input signal.

After importing these blocks, your model pane should appear as in the following figure:

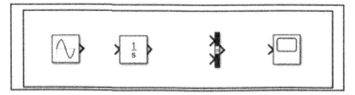

Figure 14.11 – The sine wave, integrator, bus creator, and scope Simulink blocks

Some blocks must be properly configured with some parameters. For example, the sine wave block requires the amplitude and the frequency sinusoidal signal to generate. To set these values, we can explore block parameters with a double-click on the desired block. To make the system work, we need to properly connect the Simulink blocks, as shown in this model:

Figure 14.12 – Sinusoidal signal integrator

Now that the model components have been connected, we can simulate the behavior of our system. First, we should configure the duration of the simulation by setting the start and stop simulation times. Open the **Simulation | Model Configuration Parameters** window and insert the desired value. In our example, we are considering a start time of 0 and a stop time of 10.0:

Figure 14.13 – Simulation time for our system

Now, we can press the play button in the model pane toolbar, while we check the output by exploring the content of the scope block, with a double-click on it:

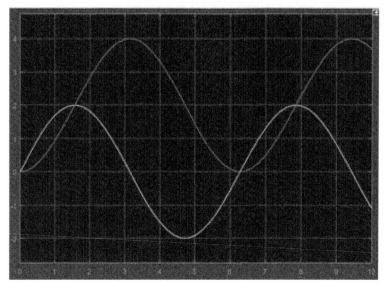

Figure 14.14 – Sinusoidal and integrated signal

Note that even if we inserted 10 seconds of simulation time, Simulink would not work in real time but would only simulate the increment of the time steps in the simulation. In this way, the effective elapsed time during the simulation will be very short. The model proposed in this example can be found in the book's *source code* in the `ros_matlab_test/staring_example.mdl` model file.

Working with ROS messages in Simulink

The Simulink interface for ROS allows us to model systems that can be linked to other nodes of the ROS network. This support includes a library of Simulink blocks for sending and receiving messages via topics. When we start the simulation of the developed model, Simulink will try to connect to a ROS network, which can be running on the same computer where Simulink is or on another remote machine. Once this connection is established, Simulink exchanges messages with the ROS network until the simulation is terminated. As we did in the previous section, we will start by showing how to read and write data, using ROS topics, and then we will discuss how to create a more complex system to control the TurtleBot robot simulated in Gazebo. Let's start to create two different Simulink models. In one model, we are going to develop a message publisher while in the other one, we will implement a simple subscriber. These models can be found in the source code directory, `ros_matlab_test`, called `publisher.mdl` and `subscriber.mdl`, respectively.

Publishing a ROS message in Simulink

To publish a ROS message in Simulink, we mainly need two blocks:

- **Publish**: This block sends a message on the ROS network. Using block parameters, we can specify the topic name and the message type.

- **Blank message**: This block creates a blank message with the specified message type.

Let's see how to connect these blocks to publish a `geometry_msgs/Twist` message on a new topic, called `/position`. Get started by importing the blank message block from the Library Browser and configuring the type of message by double-clicking on it. From the block parameters pane, we can press the **Select** button to select the ROS message type from a list, as shown in the following screenshot:

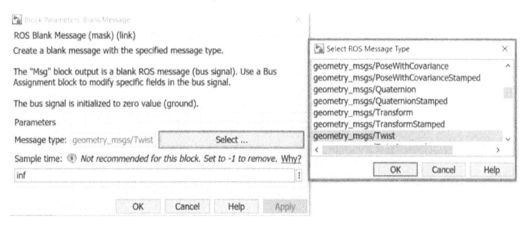

Figure 14.15 – Parameter configuration for a Simulink ROS blank message block

Now we are ready to import the ROS publish block: drag and drop the block to the model and double-click on it to configure the topic source and the message type. Select **Specify your own** for the topic source field to enter the desired topic name. Enter /position in the **Topic** field. As we have already seen, we can select the type of the message to publish:

Figure 14.16 – Parameter configuration for a Simulink ROS publish block

Now, we must fill in the fields of the ROS message to publish before sending it into the ROS network. We will use two other Simulink components to do this work. The first is the *sine wave*, the sinusoidal signal generation already used in the first Simulink example. The second one is a signal bus assignment. In fact, a ROS message is represented as a bus signal in the Simulink environment, allowing us to manage its field using the bus signal block. Connect the output port of the blank message block to the bus input port of the **BusAssignment** block. Connect the output port of the **BusAssignment** block to the input port of the ROS publish block. Then, configure the bus signal parameters: double-click on the **BusAssignment** block. You should see **X**, **Y**, and **Z** (the signals comprising a geometry_msgs/Twist message) listed on the left. Remove the element in the right list and select both the **X** and **Y** signals of the linear part of the message in the left list, click **Select >>**, and then click **OK** to close the block mask. In this case, we will assign only the first two components of the linear part of the Twist message:

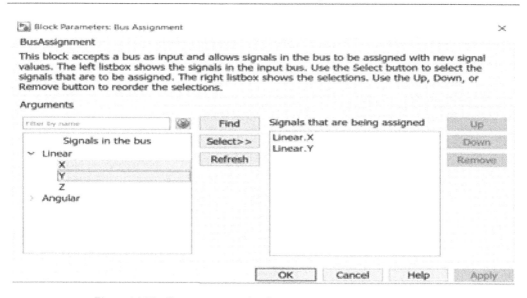

Figure 14.17 – Bus assignment for the geometry_msgs/Twist message

After completing the parameter configuration of the bus assignment module, the shape of the block will change, accepting the value of the selected input signals. Now, we should assign the desired value to publish to these components. We can do this by using the sine wave block, as we did in the previous example. Drag and drop two sinusoidal signal generators, linking them to the bus assignment block. The final model will look as follows:

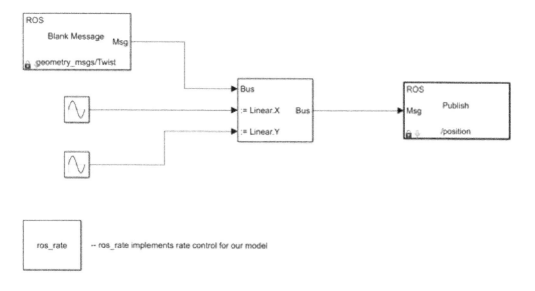

Figure 14.18 – The publisher Simulink model

An additional block has been included in our publisher Simulink model: ros_rate. This block is needed to simulate real-time behavior during the execution of our model, implementing the ROS rate mechanism. Without this module, in fact, the execution rate of this node will be very high, publishing ROS messages at maximum frequency. The ros_rate block is a special module called the MATLAB System block and allows us to instantiate and invoke a MATLAB class object. After importing this block into the system model, we should select the system object name to invoke, or create a new one:

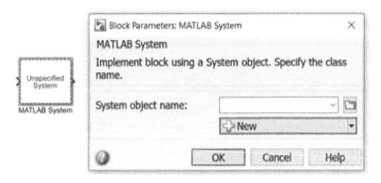

Figure 14.19 – MATLAB System block

The code of the ros_rate block is in the ros_rate.m source file and it is reported and discussed. In this code, we defined the ros_rate class, which has two objects: the rate specifying the loop frequency and rateObj, which implements the rate mechanism. The most important methods of this class are the setupImpl(obj) method, which is called at the start of the simulation and is used to initialize the class stuff, and the stepImpl(obj) method, which is invoked at each step time to regulate the execution time of the simulation:

```
classdef ros_rate < matlab.System
    properties
        RATE;
end
    methods(Access = protected)
    function setupImpl(obj)
            obj.rateObj = robotics.Rate(obj.RATE);
        end
    function stepImpl(obj)
            obj.rateObj.waitfor();
        end
end
```

Now that our model is complete, we require a never-ending duration for our simulation setting to `inf` value the stop time of the simulation. In this way, we can terminate the simulation when desired by using the **Stop** button. Now, we can play the simulation and read the content published on the `/position` topic. In the next section, we will discuss the subscriber implementation.

Subscribing to a ROS topic in Simulink

To subscribe to a ROS topic, we only need the `Subscribe` block. Even in this case, we must configure the type of the message to read and the topic name. Let's select the `/position` topic in order to read the data sent to the ROS network by the publisher Simulink model. The `Subscribe` block has two outputs: `IsNew`, a Boolean signal that defines whether a new message is received, and `Msg`, which contains the received message:

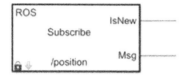

Figure 14.20 – Simulink subscriber block

In the publisher model, if we have used a bus creator to aggregate multiple data in one message, then we need to split the data of the message. For this, we will use a **BusSelector** block with one input and two outputs: the **X** and **Y** fields of the linear part of the `Twist` message. To create this block, configure it to have, as the selected signals, only the **Linear.X** and **Linear.Y** parts of the `Twist` message:

Figure 14.21 – BusSelector block

In our implementation, we include the bus selector in a subsystem, another type of block that can be enabled/disabled with the use of an enable port. In this way, we can link the IsNew field of the subscriber block to the subsystem and enable its output only if a new message is received. To explore the content of a subsystem, it is enough to double-click on it, like any other block. Finally, we can add two scope blocks to plot the output of the subsystem. The final linked model is shown in the following figure:

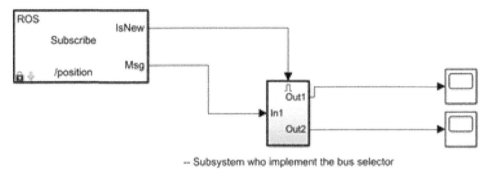

-- Subsystem who implement the bus selector

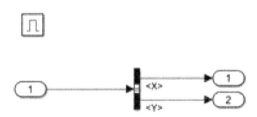

Figure 14.22 – Subscriber system model

We can now run both the publisher and subscriber systems and check the output on the scope blocks. Note that `roscore` must be running on your machine before starting the publisher and subscriber models.

Before concluding this chapter, we will discuss how to implement a control system using Simulink.

Developing a simple control system in Simulink

Now that we have learned how to interface Simulink and ROS, we can try to implement a more complex system that is able to control a real or simulated robot. We will continue to work with the TurtleBot robot simulated in Gazebo, and we will see how to control its orientation to bring it to the desired value. In other words, we will implement a control system that will measure the orientation of the robot using its odometry, comparing this value with the desired orientation and obtaining the orientation error. We will use a PID controller to calculate the velocity to actuate the robot to reach the final desired orientation, setting the orientation error to 0. This controller is already available in Simulink, so we don't need to implement it by ourselves. Let's start to discuss all the elements of our model:

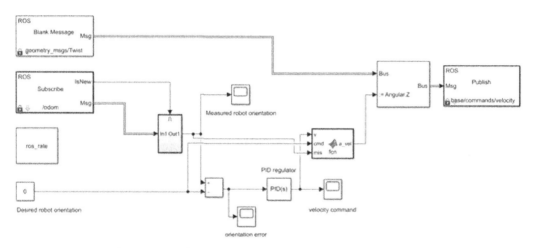

Figure 14.23 – TurtleBot orientation control model in Simulink

The input of the system is represented by the /odom message, which contains information about the actual pose of the robot and its velocity, and the constant block, which specifies the desired orientation of TurtleBot. The first thing that our model does is to estimate the orientation from the /odom message. The orientation is estimated by considering the angular velocity of the robot, integrating it at each time step. We use a MATLAB function block to threshold the velocity value of the /odom message to discard noise measurements. To integrate the velocity data, we use the **Integrator** block provided by Simulink. Again, we include this part in a subsystem:

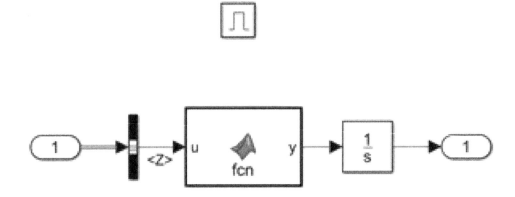

Figure 14.24 – MATLAB function block

The MATLAB function block allows developers to translate their own MATLAB functions into Simulink blocks. In this case, the code function is as follows:

```
function y = fcn(u)
y = 0.0;
if abs( u ) > 0.01
        y = u;
end
end
```

We extract the Angular.z value from the received Twist message that specifies the angular velocity with respect to the z axis, representing which direction is rotating the robot. We consider as noise any values below 0.01 rad/s. Now that we know how to rotate the robot, we can calculate the orientation error by considering the desired orientation (which is constant) using the Simulink **Sum** block. To change the desired orientation, we can double-click on the **Constant** block and configure its parameters.

Finally, we can implement our robot controller. For this scope, we will use a PID controller, one of the most used control loop mechanisms with feedback. This kind of controller is widely used both in industry and university settings for a variety of applications. It continuously tries to minimize the input error, applying a control output based on proportional, integral, and derivative terms, which gives the controller its name. After dragging and dropping this controller in the model, its response to the input data will depend on *P*, *I*, and *D* terms (called gains) that can be properly tuned from the block properties. Finally, we must publish the data generated by the PID controller on the / cmd_vel topic to actuate the robot in the Gazebo simulation. As usual, we can check on the scope block how the orientation error decreases after starting the simulation. Before applying the calculated velocity, we use another MATLAB function block to set the sign of the velocity. In fact, considering the sign of the velocity, the robot will rotate in two different directions: a negative velocity will make the robot rotate in a clockwise direction, while a positive velocity will make the robot rotate in a counterclockwise direction. In our case, we want to choose the direction that will bring the robot more quickly to its direction:

```
function a_vel = fcn(v, cmd, mis)
a_vel = 0;
if (mis < cmd )
    a_vel = abs(v);
elseif ( mis > cmd )
    a_vel = -abs(v);
end
end
```

This function block receives as input the calculated velocity, the commanded orientation, and the actual orientation of the robot. When the measured orientation is lower than the commanded one, the robot must rotate in a clockwise direction, or otherwise in a counterclockwise direction.

Configuring the Simulink model

Now that our model is fully connected, we only need to configure and simulate it. Firstly, we need to import the `ros_rate` module to synchronize the Simulink simulation. In this case, a higher frame rate assures a better behavior, so you can double-click on the **ros_rate** block and set the rate to `100` Hz. Then, open the model configuration parameters by clicking on **Simulation | Model Configuration Parameters** from the main menu bar of the model window, or just press *Ctrl + E*. A suggested configuration is to use a fixed-step size solver, specifying the desired step size (we can use `0.01` seconds):

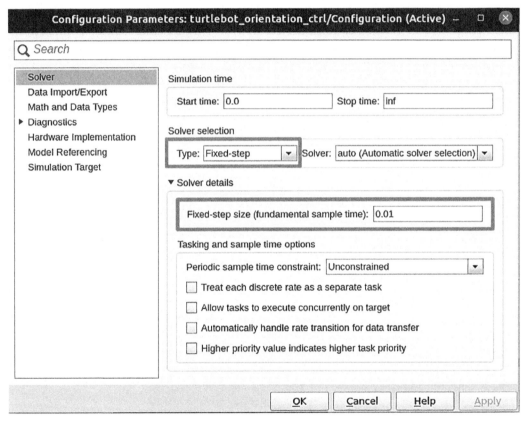

Figure 14.25 – Model configuration parameters

Now that the model has been configured, we can simulate it. As in the last example, launch the TurtleBot simulation:

```
roslaunch turtlebot3_gazebo turtlebot_world.launch
```

Then, push the **Play** button to start the Simulink simulation. On Gazebo, you should see the robot tries to reach the desired orientation, while on Simulink, you can use the scope panels to monitor the orientation error and the generated velocity command:

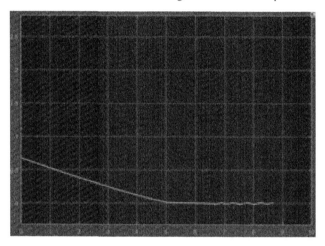

Figure 14.26 – turtlebot3 orientation error evolution

You can also check the Gazebo simulator to see that the robot is reaching the desired orientation.

Summary

In this chapter, we learned how to use MATLAB to develop simple or complex robotic applications and how to connect MATLAB with the other ROS nodes running on the same computer or in other nodes of the ROS network. We discussed how to handle topics in MATLAB and how to develop a simple obstacle avoidance system for a differential driver robot, reusing functions already available in the MATLAB toolboxes. Then, we introduced Simulink, a graphically based program editor that allows developers to implement, simulate, and validate their dynamic system models. We learned how to get and set data into the ROS network and how to develop a simple control system that controls the orientation of the TurtleBot robot. In the next chapter, we will present ROS-Industrial, a ROS package to interface industrial robot manipulators to ROS, and how to control it using the power of ROS, such as MoveIt!, Gazebo, and RViz.

Here are some questions based on what we covered in this chapter.

Questions

- What is MATLAB and Robotics System Toolbox?
- How can we connect MATLAB with the ROS network?
- Why is MATLAB useful for developing robotic applications?
- What is Simulink?
- What is a PID controller and how can we implement it using Simulink?

15
ROS for Industrial Robots

Until now, we have been mainly discussing interfacing personal and research robots with ROS, but some of the main areas where robots are extensively used are in industries such as manufacturing, the automotive industry, and packaging. Does ROS support industrial robots? Are there any companies that use ROS to handle manufacturing processes? **ROS-Industrial** comes with a solution to interface industrial robot manipulators to ROS and control them using its powerful tools, such as **MoveIt**, **Gazebo**, and **RViz**.

In this chapter, we will discuss the following topics:

- Understanding and getting started with ROS-Industrial packages
- Creating a URDF for an industrial robot and interfacing it with MoveIt
- Working with the MoveIt configuration for a Universal Robots arm and ABB robots
- Understanding ROS-Industrial robot support packages
- Understanding ROS-Industrial robot client and driver packages
- Working with IKFast algorithms and the MoveIt IKFast plugin

Let's start with a brief overview of ROS-Industrial.

Technical requirements

To follow this chapter, you need a standard laptop running Ubuntu 20.04 with ROS Noetic installed. The reference code for this chapter can be downloaded from the following Git repository: `https://github.com/PacktPublishing/Mastering-ROS-for-Robotics-Programming-Third-edition.git`. The code is contained in the `Chapter15/ abb_irb6640_moveit_plugins` and `Chapter15/ikfast_demo` folders.

Understanding ROS-Industrial packages

ROS-Industrial basically extends the advanced capabilities of ROS software to industrial robots employed in manufacturing processes. ROS-Industrial consists of many software packages, which help us to control industrial robots. These packages are **BSD** (legacy)/ **Apache 2.0** (preferred) licensed programs, which contain libraries, drivers, and tools with a standard solution for industrial hardware. ROS-Industrial is now guided by the **ROS-Industrial Consortium**. The official website of **ROS-Industrial (ROS-I)** can be found at `http://rosindustrial.org/`.

Goals of ROS-Industrial

The main goals behind ROS-Industrial development are as follows:

- Combining the strength of ROS with existing industrial technologies to explore the advanced capabilities of ROS in the manufacturing process

- Developing reliable and robust software for industrial robot applications

- Providing an easy way to do research and development in industrial robotics

- Creating a wide community supported by researchers and professionals for industrial robotics

- Providing industrial-grade ROS applications and becoming a one-stop location for industry-related applications

Before exploring the capabilities of ROS-Industrial with a set of industrial robots, let's briefly introduce it, discussing its history, architecture, and installation.

ROS-Industrial – a brief history

In 2012, the ROS-Industrial open source project started as a collaboration of **Yaskawa Motoman Robotics** (http://www.motoman.com/), **Willow Garage** (https://www.willowgarage.com/), and the **Southwest Research Institute (SwRI)** (http://www.swri.org/) for using ROS in industrial manufacturing. ROS-I was founded by *Shaun Edwards* in *January 2012*.

In *March 2013*, the **ROS-I Consortium Americas and Europe** were launched, led by SwRI in Texas and *Fraunhofer IPA* in Germany, respectively. In the following list, a set of benefits that ROS-I provides to the community are detailed:

- **Explores the features in ROS**: The ROS-Industrial packages are tied to the ROS framework so that we can use all the ROS features in industrial robots too. Using ROS, we can create custom inverse kinematic solvers for each robot and implement object manipulation, using 2D/3D perception.

- **Out-of-the-box applications**: The ROS interface enables advanced perception in robots for working with picking up and placing complex objects.

- **Simplifies robotic programming**: ROS-I eliminates teaching and planning the paths of robots and instead, automatically calculates a collision-free optimal path for the given points.

- **Open source**: ROS-I is open source software that allows commercial use without any restrictions.

Installing ROS-Industrial packages

The main repository of ROS-Industrial packages can be found at the following link: https://github.com/ros-industrial. In this repository, developers can find different packages used to interface their ROS system with typical industrial tools and devices, such as **Programmable Logic Controller** (**PLC**), or directly communicate with the hardware driver of popular industrial manipulators such as **Kuka**, **abb**, or **Fanuc**. Apart from this, the main repository for ROS-Industrial resources is the industrial_ core stack, which can be downloaded from the following Git repository:

```
git clone https://github.com/ros-industrial/industrial_core
```

This repository is still under development to assure full compatibility with ROS Noetic. However, the `industrial-core` stack includes the following set of ROS packages:

- `industrial-core`: This stack contains packages and libraries for supporting industrial robotic systems. The package consists of nodes for communicating with industrial robot controllers and industrial robot simulators and also provides ROS controllers for industrial robots.

- `industrial_deprecated`: This package contains nodes, launch files, and so on that are going to be deprecated. The files inside this package could be deleted from the repository in the next ROS versions, so we should look for the replacements of these files before the content is deleted.

- `industrial_msgs`: This package contains message definitions that are specific to the ROS-Industrial packages.

- `simple_message`: This is a part of ROS-Industrial and is a standard message protocol containing a simple messaging framework for communicating with industrial robot controllers.

- `industrial_robot_client`: This package contains a generic robot client for connecting to industrial robot controllers, which runs an industrial robot server and can communicate using a simple message protocol.

- `industrial_robot_simulator`: This package simulates the industrial robot controller, which follows the ROS-Industrial driver standard. Using this simulator, we can simulate and visualize the industrial robot.

- `industrial_trajectory_filters`: This package contains libraries and plugins for filtering the trajectories that are sent to the robot controller.

ROS-I implements a multilayer high-level architecture to implement an application for industrial manipulators, as discussed in the next section.

Block diagram of ROS-Industrial packages

The following diagram is a simple block diagram representation of ROS-I packages that are organized on top of ROS. We can see the ROS-I layers on top of the ROS layers.

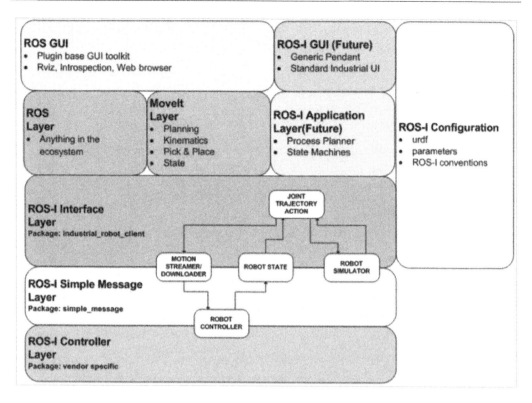

Figure 15.1 – The high-level system architecture of ROS-Industrial

We can look at a brief description of each of the layers for a better understanding:

- **The ROS GUI**: This layer includes the ROS plugin-based GUI tools layer, which consists of tools such as RViz, `rqt_gui`, and so on.

- **The ROS-I GUI**: These GUIs are standard industrial UIs for working with industrial robots that may be implemented in the future.

- **The ROS Layer**: This is the base layer in which all communications take place.

- **The MoveIt Layer**: The MoveIt layer provides a direct solution to industrial manipulators in planning, kinematics, and picking and placing.

- **The ROS-I Application Layer**: This layer consists of an industrial process planner, which is used to plan what is to be manufactured, how it will be manufactured, and what resources are needed for the manufacturing process.

- **The ROS-I Interface Layer**: This layer consists of the industrial robot client, which can be connected to the industrial robot controller using the simple message protocol.

- **The ROS-I Simple Message Layer**: This is the communication layer of the industrial robot, which is a standard set of protocols that will send data from the robot client to the controller and vice versa.

- **The ROS-I Controller Layer**: This layer consists of vendor-specific industrial robot controllers.

After discussing the basic concepts, we will start to interface an industrial robot to ROS using ROS-Industrial. First, we will show how to create a URDF model of an industrial robot and how to create a proper MoveIt configuration for it. Then, we will discuss how to control real and simulated Universal Robots and Abb industrial manipulators, analyzing all the necessary elements of a ROS-I package. Finally, we will work with the `Ikfast` algorithm and plugin to speed up kinematic calculations with MoveIt.

Creating a URDF for an industrial robot

Creating the URDF file for an ordinary robot and an industrial robot are the same, but industrial robots require some standards that should be strictly followed during their URDF modeling, which are as follows:

- **Simplify the URDF design**: The URDF file should be simple and readable and only need the important tags.

- **Develop a common design**: Develop a common design formula for all industrial robots by various vendors.

- **Modularize the URDF**: The URDF needs to be modularized using **XACRO** macros and it can be included in a large URDF file without much hassle.

The following points are the main differences in the URDF design followed by ROS-I:

- **Collision-aware**: Industrial robot IK planners are collision-aware, so the URDF should contain an accurate collision 3D mesh for each link. Every link in the robot should export to STL or DAE with a proper coordinate system. The coordinate system that ROS-I is following is the *x* axis pointing forward and the *z* axis pointing up when each joint is in the zero position. It is also to be noted that, if the joint's origin coincides with the base of the robot, the transformation will be simpler. It will be good if we put robot-based joints in the zero position (origin), which can simplify the robot design. In ROS-I, the mesh file used for visual purposes is highly detailed, but the mesh file used for collision will not be detailed, because it takes more time to perform collision checking. In order to remove the mesh details, we can use tools such as MeshLab (http://meshlab.sourceforge.net/), using its option from the top bar menu (**Filters | Remeshing, Simplification and Reconstruction | Convex Hull**).

- **URDF joint conventions**: The orientation value of each robot joint is limited to a single rotation; that is, out of the three orientation (roll, pitch, and yaw) values, only one value will be there.

- **xacro macros**: In ROS-I, the entire manipulator section is written as a macro using xacro. We can add an instance of this macro in another macro file, which can be used for generating a URDF file. We can also include additional end-effector definitions in this same file.

- **Standard frames**: In ROS-I, the base_link frame should be the first link and tool0 (tool-zero) should be the end-effector link. Also, the base frame should match the base instance of the robot controller. In most cases, the transform from base to base_link is treated as fixed.

After building the xacro file for the industrial robot, we can convert to URDF and verify it using the following command:

```
rosrun xacro xacro -o <output_urdf_file> <input_xacro_file>
check_urdf <urdf_file>
```

Next, we will discuss the differences in creating the MoveIt configuration for an industrial robot.

Creating the MoveIt configuration for an industrial robot

The procedure for creating the MoveIt interface for industrial robots is the same as the other ordinary robot manipulators, except for some standard conventions. The following procedure gives a clear idea about these standard conventions:

1. Launch the MoveIt setup assistant by using the following command:

```
roslaunch moveit_setup_assistant setup_assistant.launch
```

2. Load the URDF from the robot description folder or convert xacro to URDF and load the setup assistant.

3. Create a self-collision matrix with **Sampling Density** of ~ 80,000. This value can increase the accuracy of collision checking in the arm.

4. Add a virtual joint, as shown in the following screenshot. Here, the virtual and parent frame names are arbitrary:

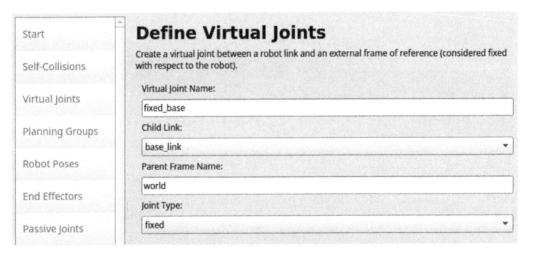

Figure 15.2 – Adding MoveIt – virtual joints

5. In the next step, we are adding planning groups for the manipulator and end effectors. Here, also, the group names are arbitrary. The default plugin is KDL; we can change it even after creating the MoveIt configuration for the manipulator.

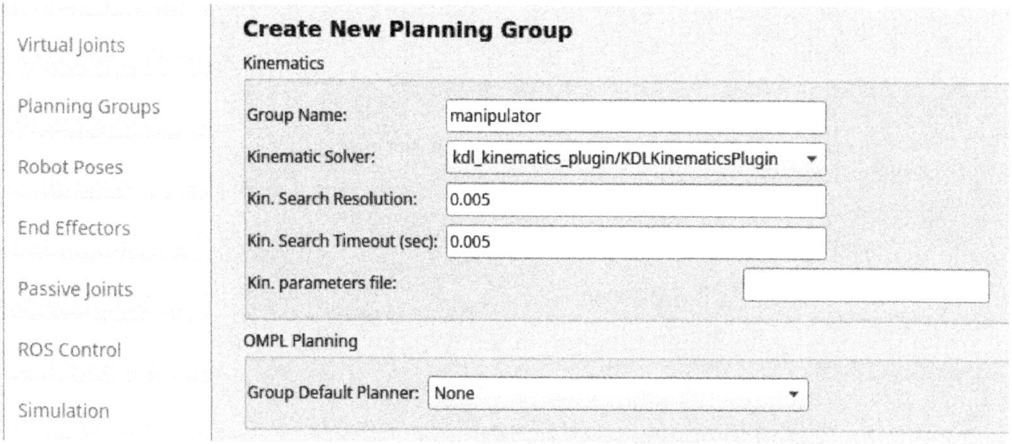

Figure 15.3 – Creating a manipulator planning group in MoveIt

6. Then, we can create the planning group for the end effector as well:

Figure 15.4 – Creating an endeffector planning group in MoveIt

7. The planning groups, that is, the **manipulator** plus the **endeffector** configuration, will be shown like this:

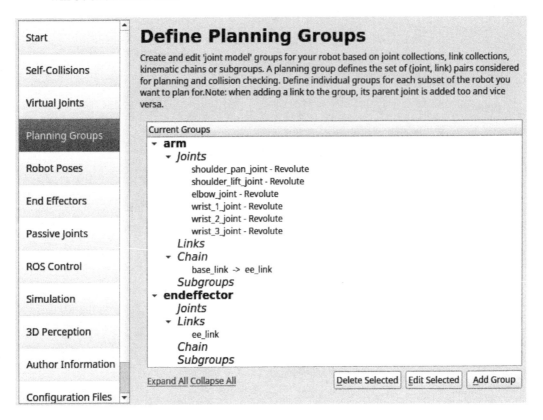

Figure 15.5 – Planning groups of manipulators and end effectors in MoveIt

8. We can assign robot poses, such as the **home** position, the **up** position, and so on. This setting is an optional one.

9. We can assign end effectors, as shown in the following screenshot; this is also an optional setting:

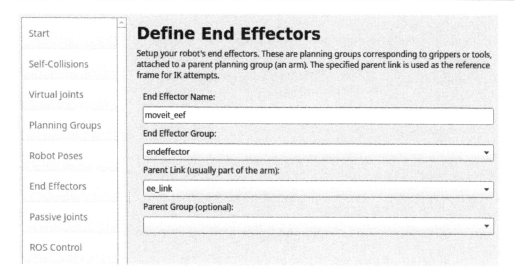

Figure 15.6 – Setting end effectors in the MoveIt setup assistant

10. Configure the ROS controllers to actuate a simulated or real robotic arm. This can be done using the **Auto Add FollowjointsTrajectory Controllers** button, as shown in the following screenshot:

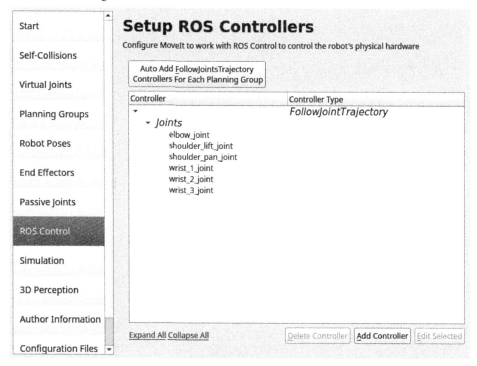

Figure 15.7 – Generate ROS controller configuration

11. After setting the end effector, we can directly generate the configuration files. It should be noted that the `moveit-config` package should be named `<robot_name>_config`, where `robot_name` is the name of the URDF file. Also, if we want to move this generated `config` package to another PC, we need to edit the `.setup_assistant` file, which is inside the package generated by the `setup_assistant` tool and it is a hidden file. We should change the absolute path to the relative path. Here is an example of the `abb_irb2400` robot. We should mention the relative path of URDF and SRDF in this file, as follows:

```
moveit_setup_assistant_config:
  URDF:
    package: abb_irb2400_support
    relative_path: urdf/irb2400.urdf
  SRDF:
    relative_path: config/abb_irb2400.srdf
  CONFIG:
    generated_timestamp: 1402076252
```

The configuration of the MoveIt package for our robot is now complete. We should only modify the ROS controller's configuration to properly stream the generated position trajectory robot joints, as discussed in the next section.

Updating the MoveIt configuration files

After creating the MoveIt configuration, we should update the `ros_controllers.yaml` file inside the `config` folder of the MoveIt package. Here is an example of `ros_controllers.yaml`:

```
controller_list:
  - name: ""
    action_ns: follow_joint_trajectory
    type: FollowJointTrajectory
    joints:
      - shoulder_pan_joint
      - shoulder_lift_joint
      - elbow_joint
      - wrist_1_joint
      - wrist_2_joint
      - wrist_3_joint
```

In the previous file, we have to pay attention to the `action_ns` field. This field represents the name of the action server used to send the trajectory to the simulated or real robotic platform. We will discuss in the next section how to configure it.

We should also update `joint_limits.yaml` with the joint information. Here is a code snippet of `joint_limits.yaml`:

```
joint_limits:
  shoulder_pan_joint:
    has_velocity_limits: true
    max_velocity: 2.16
    has_acceleration_limits: true
    max_acceleration: 2.16
```

We can also change the kinematic solver plugin by editing the `kinematics.yaml` file. After editing all the configuration files, we need to edit the controller manager launch file (`<robot>_config/launch/<robot>_moveit_controller_manager.launch.xml`).

Here is an example of the `controller_manager.launch.xml manager.launch` file:

```
<launch>
    <arg name="moveit_controller_manager" default="moveit_simple_
controller_manager/MoveItSimpleControllerManager" />
    <param name="moveit_controller_manager" value="$(arg moveit_
controller_manager)"/>
    <!-- loads ros_controllers to the param server -->
    <rosparam file="$(find ur10_config)/config/ros_controllers.
yaml"/>
</launch>
```

Finally, we should configure the `demo.launch` file to start all necessary configuration and additional launch files needed for the execution of a motion trajectory. In particular, the `demo.launch` file includes the `move_group.launch` file, which is responsible for running all the main MoveIt executables with and without a real trajectory execution. Here is an example of the `move_group` inclusion:

```
<include file="$(find ur10_config)/launch/move_group.launch">
        <arg name="allow_trajectory_execution" value="false"/>
        <arg name="fake_execution" value="true"/>
```

```
        <arg name="info" value="true"/>
        <arg name="debug" value="$(arg debug)"/>
        <arg name="pipeline" value="$(arg pipeline)"/>
    </include>
```

In the previous example, the `allow_trajectory_execution` parameter is set to false. This means that we can check the resulting planned trajectory in the RViz window, without relying on a real or a simulated robot. In the following section, we will discuss how to connect the `move_group` node to a robot simulated in Gazebo.

Installing ROS-Industrial packages for Universal Robots arms

Universal Robots (`http://www.universal-robots.com/`) is an industrial robot manufacturer based in Denmark. The company mainly produces three arms: **UR3**, **UR5**, and **UR10**. The robots are shown in the following figure:

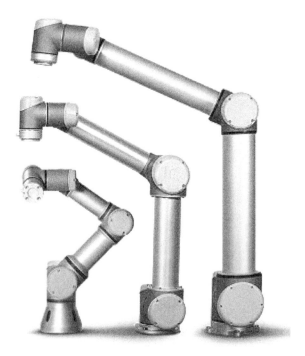

Figure 15.8 – UR3, UR5, and UR10 robots

The specifications of these robots are given in the following table:

Robot	UR-3	UR-5	UR-10
Working radius	500 mm	850 mm	1300 mm
Payload	3 Kg	5 Kg	10 Kg
Weight	11 Kg	18.4 Kg	28.9 Kg
Footprint	118 mm	149 mm	190 mm

Figure 15.9 – Universal Robots robot properties

In the next section, we will install the Universal Robots packages and work with the MovetIt interface to simulate industrial robots in Gazebo.

Installing the ROS interface for Universal Robots

We get the **Universal Robots ROS-I** packages by downloading them from the following repository:

```
git clone https://github.com/ros-industrial/universal_robot.git
```

The Universal Robots packages are as follows:

- `ur_description`: This package consists of the robot description and Gazebo description of UR-3, UR-5, and UR-1.

- `ur_driver`: This package contains client nodes, which can communicate with the UR-3, UR-5, and UR-10 robot hardware controllers.

- `ur_bringup`: This package consists of launch files to start communication with the robot hardware controllers to start working with the real robot.

- `ur_gazebo`: This package consists of Gazebo simulations of UR-3, UR-5, and UR-10.

- `ur_msgs`: This package contains ROS messages used for communication between various UR nodes.

- `urXX_moveit_config`: These are the `moveit` config files of Universal Robots manipulators. One different package exists for each type of arm (`ur3_moveit_config`, `ur5_moveit_config` and `ur10_moveit_config`).

- `ur_kinematics`: This package contains kinematic solver plugins for UR-3, UR-5, and UR-10. We can use this solver plugin in MoveIt.

After installing or compiling the Universal Robots packages, we can launch the simulation in Gazebo of the UR-10 robot by using the following command:

```
roslaunch ur_gazebo ur10.launch
```

After running this command, a Gazebo scene with a UR10 robot will open.

Figure 15.10 – Universal Robots UR-10 model simulation in Gazebo

We can see the robot controller configuration file for interfacing with the MoveIt package. The following YAML file defines the `JointTrajectory` controller. It is placed in the `ur_gazebo/controller` folder with the name `arm_controller_ur10.yaml`:

```
arm_controller:
  type: position_controllers/JointTrajectoryController
  joints:
     - elbow_joint
     - shoulder_lift_joint
     - shoulder_pan_joint
     - wrist_1_joint
     - wrist_2_joint
     - wrist_3_joint
  constraints:
     goal_time: 0.6
     stopped_velocity_tolerance: 0.05
     elbow_joint: {trajectory: 0.1, goal: 0.1}
     shoulder_lift_joint: {trajectory: 0.1, goal: 0.1}
```

```
    shoulder_pan_joint: {trajectory: 0.1, goal: 0.1}
    wrist_1_joint: {trajectory: 0.1, goal: 0.1}
    wrist_2_joint: {trajectory: 0.1, goal: 0.1}
    wrist_3_joint: {trajectory: 0.1, goal: 0.1}
  stop_trajectory_duration: 0.5
  state_publish_rate:  25
  action_monitor_rate: 10
```

After starting the simulation, the robot will accept trajectory commands on the `/arm_controller/follow_joint_trajectory` server. We are now ready to configure the MoveIt package to plan and execute a motion trajectory.

Understanding the MoveIt configuration of a Universal Robots arm

The MoveIt configuration for Universal Robots arms is in the `config` directory of each `moveit_config` package (`ur10_moveit_config` for the UR-10 configuration).

Here is the default content of the `controller.yaml` file of UR-10:

```
controller_list:
  - name: ""
    action_ns: follow_joint_trajectory
    type: FollowJointTrajectory
    joints:
      - shoulder_pan_joint
      - shoulder_lift_joint
      - elbow_joint
      - wrist_1_joint
      - wrist_2_joint

      - wrist_3_joint
```

To properly connect the MoveIt side, we must set the correct `action_ns` element. Let's change this file in the following way:

```
controller_list:
  - name: ""
    action_ns: /arm_controller/follow_joint_trajectory
```

```
  type: FollowJointTrajectory
  joints:
    - shoulder_pan_joint
    - shoulder_lift_joint
    - elbow_joint
    - wrist_1_joint
    - wrist_2_joint

    - wrist_3_joint
```

In the same directory, we can find the kinematic configuration: `kinematics.yaml`. This file specifies the IK solvers used for the robotic arm. For the UR-10 robot, the content of the kinematic configuration file is shown here:

```
#manipulator:
#   kinematics_solver: ur_kinematics/UR10KinematicsPlugin
#   kinematics_solver_search_resolution: 0.005
#   kinematics_solver_timeout: 0.005
#   kinematics_solver_attempts: 3
manipulator:
  kinematics_solver: kdl_kinematics_plugin/KDLKinematicsPlugin
  kinematics_solver_search_resolution: 0.005
  kinematics_solver_timeout: 0.005
  kinematics_solver_attempts: 3
```

The definition of `ur10_moveit_controller_manager.launch` inside the `launch` folder is given as follows. This launch file loads the trajectory controller configuration and starts the trajectory controller manager:

```
<launch>
  <rosparam file="$(find ur10_moveit_config)/config/
controllers.yaml"/>
  <param name="use_controller_manager" value="false"/>
  <param name="trajectory_execution/execution_duration_
monitoring" value="false"/>
  <param name="moveit_controller_manager" value="moveit_simple_
controller_manager/MoveItSimpleControllerManager"/>
</launch>
```

After editing the configuration and launch files in the MoveIt configuration, we can start running the robot simulation and can check whether the MoveIt configuration is working well or not. Here are the steps to test an industrial robot:

1. First, start the robot simulator. We will use the `ur_gazebo` package:

```
roslaunch ur_gazebo ur10.launch
```

2. Then, start the MoveIt planner using the `demo.launch` file of the `ur10_moveit_config` package, changing the `allow_trajectory_execution` and `fake_execution` parameter values, setting them to `true` and `false` respectively:

```
roslaunch ur10_moveit_config demo.launch
```

3. This launch file starts RViz as well. From its interface, we can set the desired target point of the robotic end effector and then use the **Plan and Execute** button. If MoveIt is able to find a feasible trajectory, it will also be executed in the Gazebo simulator, as shown in the following figure:

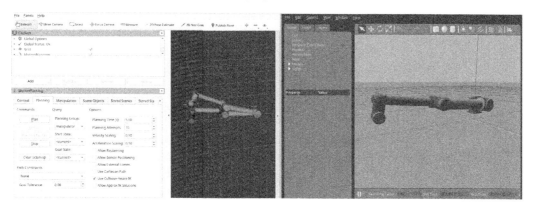

Figure 15.11 – Motion planning in the UR-10 model in Gazebo and RViz

In addition, we can move the end-effector position of the robot and plan the path by using the **Plan** button. When we click the **Execute** button or the **Plan and Execute** button, the trajectory should be sent to the simulated robot, performing the motion in the Gazebo environment.

Getting started with real Universal Robots hardware and ROS-I

After testing our control algorithms in simulation using Gazebo, we can start to perform manipulation tasks with a real Universal Robots arm. The main difference between performing a trajectory simulating the robot and using real hardware is that we need to start the driver that will contact the arm controller to set the desired joint positions.

The default driver of Universal Robots arms is released with the `ur_driver` package of ROS-I. This driver has been successfully tested with system versions ranging from `v1.5.7` to `v1.8.2`. The last version of Universal Robots controllers is `v3.2`, so the default version of the ROS-I driver might not be fully compatible. For the newer versions of these systems (`v3.x` and up), it is recommended to use the unofficial `ur_modern_driver` package:

1. To download `ur_modern_driver`, use the following Git repository:

   ```
   git clone https://github.com/ros-industrial/ur_modern_
   driver.git
   ```

2. After downloading this package, we need to compile the workspace to be able to use the driver.

3. The next step is to configure Universal Robots hardware to control it from our computer. Firstly, we must enable the networking capabilities of the Universal Robots hardware, using the teach pendant. Navigate into the **Robot | Setup Network** menu in order to select a proper configuration compatible with our network. If you prefer to have a fixed internet address for the robot, you must select the **Static Address** option and manually input the desired address information.

4. You can also rely on the automatic address assignment selecting the DHCP option, and then apply the configuration. After setting the IP address, it could be useful to check the connection status by pinging the robot controller:

   ```
   ping IP_OF_THE_ROBOT
   ```

5. If the controller replies to the `ping` command, the connection is successfully established, and we can start to control the manipulator.

6. If your Universal Robots system has a version lower than v3.x, we can bring it up by running the following command:

```
roslaunch ur_bringup ur10_bringup.launch robot_ip:=IP_OF_
THE_ROBOT [reverse_port:=REVERSE_PORT]
```

7. Replace IP_OF_THE_ROBOT with the IP address assigned to the robot controller. Then, we can test the motion of the robot by using the following script:

```
rosrun ur_driver IP_OF_THE_ROBOT [reverse_port:=REVERSE_
PORT]
```

8. To operate with systems greater than v3.x, we can use launch files provided by the ur_modern_driver package:

```
roslaunch ur_modern_driver ur10_bringup.launch robot_
ip:=IP_OF_THE_ROBOT [reverse_port:=REVERSE_PORT]
```

9. The next step is to use MoveIt to control the robot:

```
roslaunch ur10_moveit_config ur5_moveit_planning_
execution.launch
```

```
roslaunch ur10_moveit_config moveit_rviz.launch
config:=true
```

10. Note that for some desired robot configurations, MoveIt could have difficulties with finding plans with full joint limits. There is another version with lower restrictions for the joint limits. This operating mode can be started simply by using the argument limited in the launch command:

```
roslaunch ur10_moveit_config ur5_moveit_planning_
execution.launch limited:=true
```

We have seen how to simulate and control a Universal Robots arm. In the next section, we will work with ABB robots.

Working with MoveIt configuration for ABB robots

We will work with two of the most popular ABB industrial robot models: **IRB 2400** and **IRB 6640**. The following are photographs of these two robots and their specifications:

ABB IRB 2400   ABB IRB 6640

Figure 15.12 – ABB IRB 2400 and IRB 6640

The specifications of these robotic arms are given in the following table:

Robot	IRB 2400-10	IRB 6640-130
Working radius	1.55 m	3.2 m
Payload	12 Kg	130 Kg
Weight	380 Kg	1310 Kg
Footprint	723x600 mm	1107x720 mm

Figure 15.13 – ABB IRB robot properties

To work with ABB packages, clone the ROS packages of the robot into the `catkin` workspace. We can use the following command to do this task:

```
git clone https://github.com/ros-industrial/abb
```

Then, build the source packages using `catkin_make`. Actually, this package mainly contains configuration files, so nothing related to C++ code needs to be compiled. However, in the `abb` folder, we have a particular package defining kinematic plugins to speed up the inverse kinematic calculation. More details on this topic will be provided in the next section.

To launch the ABB IRB 6640 in RViz for motion planning, use the following command:

```
roslaunch abb_irb6640_moveit_config demo.launch
```

The RViz window will open, and we can start motion planning the robot in RViz:

Figure 15.14 – Motion planning of ABB IRB 6640

One of the other popular ABB robot models is the IRB 2400. We can launch the robot in RViz by using the following command:

```
roslaunch abb_irb2400_moveit_config demo.launch
```

As after the previous command, a new RViz window will show the ABB IRB 2400 robot:

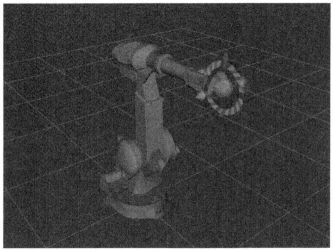

Figure 15.15 – Motion planning of ABB IRB 2400

This last model is slightly different with respect to the other robots present in the ABB package. In fact, this model uses a particular plugin to solve the inverse kinematic problem. This plugin is implemented in the `abb_irb2400_moveit_plugins` ROS package, which can be selected as the default kinematic solver, as shown in the following figure:

Figure 15.16 – Kinematic solver for the ABB IRB 2400 robot

In particular, when the MoveIt configuration package for this robot has been created, the **Kinematic Solver** field will be filled with the `IKFastKinematicsPlugin` solver, differently from the default `KDL` solver previously used. In this way, we will use a specific plugin to plan the motion trajectory that will provide better and faster solutions.

Understanding the ROS-Industrial robot support packages

The ROS-I robot support packages are a new convention followed for industrial robots. The aim of these support packages is to standardize the ways of maintaining ROS packages for a wide variety of industrial robot types of different vendors. Because of the standardized way of keeping files inside support packages, we don't have any confusion in accessing the files inside them. We can demonstrate a support package of an ABB robot and can see the folders and files and their uses.

We have already cloned the ABB robot packages, and inside this folder, we can see three support packages that support three varieties of ABB robots. Here, we are taking the ABB IRB 2400 model support package: `abb_irb2400_support`. The following list shows the folders and files inside this package:

- `config`: As the name of the folder, this contains the configuration files of joint names, RViz configuration, and robot model-specific configuration.

- `joint_names_irb2400`: Inside the `config` folder, there is a configuration file, which contains the joint names of the robot that is used by the ROS controller.

- `launch`: This folder contains the launch file definitions of this robot. These files follow a common convention for all industrial robots.

- `load_irb2400.launch`: This file simply loads `robot_description` on the parameter server. According to the complexity of the robot, the number of `xacro` files can be increased. This file loads all `xacro` files in a single launch file. Instead of writing separate code for adding `robot_description` in other launch files, we can simply include this launch file.

- `test_irb2400.launch`: This launch file can visualize the loaded URDF. We can inspect and verify the URDF in RViz. This launch file includes the preceding launch files and starts the `joint_state_publisher` and `robot_state_publisher` nodes, which help to interact with the user on RViz. This will work without the need for real hardware.

- `robot_state_visualize_irb2400.launch`: This launch file visualizes the current state of the real robot by running nodes from the ROS-Industrial driver package with appropriate parameters. The current state of the robot is visualized by running RViz and the `robot_state_publisher` node. This launch file needs a real robot or simulation interface. One of the main arguments provided along with this launch file is the IP address of the industrial controller. Also, note that the controller should run a ROS-Industrial server node.

- `robot_interface_download_irb2400.launch`: This launch file starts bi-directional communication with the industrial robot controller to ROS and vice versa. There are industrial robot client nodes for reporting the state of the robot (`robot_state node`) and subscribing the joint command topic and issuing the joint position to the controller (`joint_trajectory node`). This launch file also requires access to the simulation or real robot controller and needs to mention the IP address of the industrial controllers. The controller should run the ROS-Industrial server programs too.

- `urdf`: This folder contains the set of standardized `xacro` files of the robot model.

- `irb2400_macro.xacro`: This is the `xacro` definition of a specific robot. It is not a complete URDF, but it's a macro definition of the manipulator section. We can include this file inside another file and create an instance of this macro.

- `irb2400.xacro`: This is the top-level `xacro` file, which creates an instance of the macro that was discussed in the preceding section. This file doesn't include any other files other than the macro of the robot. This `xacro` file will load inside the `load_irb2400.launch` file that we have already discussed.

- `irb2400.urdf`: This is the URDF generated from the preceding `xacro` file, using the `xacro` tool. This file is used when tools or packages can't load `xacro` directly. This is the top-level URDF for this robot.

- `meshes`: This contains meshes for visualization and collision checking.

- `irb2400`: This folder contains mesh files for a specific robot.

- `visual`: This folder contains STL files used for visualization.

- `collision`: This folder contains STL files used for collision checking.

- `tests`: This folder contains the test launch file to test all the preceding launch files.

- `roslaunch_test.xml`: This launch file tests all the launch files.

Among all the configuration files, the real node that enables the communication between the robot and MoveIt is the robot client package. In the next section, we will discuss how this client is programmed.

The ROS-Industrial robot client package

The industrial robot client nodes are responsible for sending robot position/trajectory data from ROS MoveIt to the industrial robot controller. The industrial robot client converts the trajectory data to `simple_message` and communicates to the robot controller using the `simple_message` protocol. The industrial robot controller runs a server and industrial robot client nodes connect to this server and start communicating with it.

Designing industrial robot client nodes

The `industrial_robot_client` package contains various classes to implement industrial robot client nodes. The main functionalities that a client should have include updating the robot's current state from the robot controller, and also sending joint position messages to the controller. There are two main nodes that are responsible for getting the robot state and sending joint position values:

- The `robot_state` node: This node is responsible for publishing the robot's current position, status, and so on.

- The `joint_trajectory` node: This node subscribes to the robot's command topic and sends the joint position commands to the robot controller via the simple message protocol.

The following figure gives the list of APIs provided by the industrial robot client:

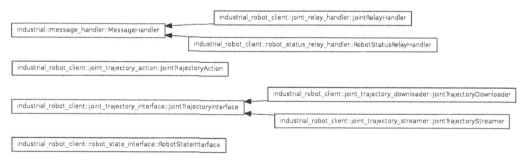

Figure 15.17 – A list of the industrial robot client APIs

We can briefly go through these APIs and their functionalities, as follows:

- `RobotStateInterface`: This class contains methods to publish the current robot position and status at regular intervals after receiving the position data from the robot controller.

- `JointRelayHandler`: The `RobotStateInterface` class is a wrapper around a class called `MessageManager`. What it does is it listens to the `simple_message` robot connection and processes each message handling process, using `Messagehandlersnode`. The `JointRelayHandler` functionality is a message handler program, and its function is to publish the joint position in the `joint_states` topic.

- `RobotStatusRelayHandler`: This is another `MessageHandler`, which can publish the current robot status info in the `robot_status` topic.

- `JointTrajectoryInterface`: This class contains methods to send the robot's joint position to the controller when it receives a ROS trajectory command.

- `JointTrajectoryDownloader`: This class is derived from the `JointTrajectoryInterface` class, and it implements a method called `send_to_robot()`. This method sends an entire trajectory as a sequence of messages to the robot controller. The robot controller will execute the trajectory in the robot only after getting all sequences sent from the client.

- `JointTrajectoryStreamer`: This class is the same as the preceding class except in the implementation of the `send_to_robot()` method. This method sends independent joint values to the controller in separate threads. Each position command is sent only after the execution of the existing command. On the robot side, there will be a small buffer for receiving the position to make the motion smoother.

The list of nodes inside the industrial robot client is as follows:

- `robot_state`: This node runs based on `RobotStateInterface`, which can publish the current robot states.

- `motion_download_interface`: This node runs `JointTrajectoryDownloader`, which will download the trajectory in sequence with the controller.

- `motion_streaming_interface`: This node runs `JointTrajectoryStreamer`, which will send the joint position in parallel using threading.

- `joint_trajectory_action`: This node provides a basic `actionlib` interface.

Finally, to connect the client package with the hardware of the robot, a proper driver package must be used. This package is specific for each robot controller and in the next section, we will discuss the ABB robot driver package.

The ROS-Industrial robot driver package

In this section, we will discuss the industrial robot driver package. If we take the ABB robot as an example, it has a package called `abb_driver`. This package is responsible for communicating with the industrial robot controller. This package contains industrial robot clients and launches the file to start communicating with the controller. We can check what is inside the `abb_driver/launch` folder. The following is a definition of a launch file called `robot_interface.launch`:

```
<launch>
  <!-- robot_ip: IP-address of the robot's socket-messaging
server -->
  <arg name="robot_ip" />
  <!-- J23_coupled: set TRUE to apply correction for J2/J3
parallel linkage -->
  <arg name="J23_coupled" default="false" />


  <!-- copy the specified arguments to the Parameter Server,
for use by nodes below -->
  <param name="robot_ip_address" type="str" value="$(arg robot_
ip)"/>
  <param name="J23_coupled" type="bool" value="$(arg J23_
coupled)"/>


  <node pkg="abb_driver" type="robot_state" name="robot_
state"/>
```

After the configuration of the robot using the preceding instructions, we are ready to start the driver of the robot as well:

```
<!-- motion_download_interface: sends robot motion commands
by DOWNLOADING path to robot

                                    (using socket connection to
robot) -->


<node pkg="abb_driver" type="motion_download_interface"
name="motion_download_interface"/>


<!-- joint_trajectory_action: provides actionlib interface
for high-level robot control -->
<node pkg="industrial_robot_client" type="joint_trajectory_
action" name="joint_trajectory_action"/>
</launch>
```

This launch file provides a socket-based connection to ABB robots using the standard ROS-Industrial `simple_message` protocol. Several nodes are started to supply both low-level robot communication and high-level `actionlib` support:

- `robot_state`: This publishes the current joint positions and robot state data.
- `motion_download_interface`: This commands the robot motion by sending motion points to the robot.
- `joint_trajectory_action`: This is the `actionlib` interface to control the robot motion.

Their typical usage is as follows:

```
roslaunch [robot_interface.launch] robot_ip:=IP_OF_THE_ROBOT
```

We can see the `abb_irb6600_support/launch/ robot_interface_download_irb6640.launch` file, and this is the driver for the ABB IRB 6640 model. This definition of `launch` is given in the following code. The preceding driver launch file is included in this `launch` file. In other support packages of other ABB models, use the same driver with different joint configuration parameter files:

```
<launch>
  <arg name="robot_ip" />
  <arg name="J23_coupled" default="true" />

  <rosparam command="load" file="$(find abb_irb2400_support)/
config/joint_names_irb2400.yaml" />

  <include file="$(find abb_driver)/launch/robot_interface.
launch">
    <arg name="robot_ip"    value="$(arg robot_ip)" />
    <arg name="J23_coupled" value="$(arg J23_coupled)" />
  </include>
</launch>
```

The preceding file is the manipulator-specific version of `robot_interface.launch` (of `abb_driver`):

- Defaults provided for IRB 2400: - `J23_coupled = true`
- Usage: `robot_interface_download_irb2400.launch robot_ip:=<value>`

We should run the driver launch file to start communicating with the real robot controller. For the ABB robot IRB 2400, we can use the following command to start bi-directional communication with the robot controller and the ROS client:

```
roslaunch abb_irb2400_support robot_interface_download_irb2400.
launch robot_ip:=IP_OF_THE_ROBOT
```

After launching the driver, we can start planning by using the MoveIt interface. It should also be noted that the ABB robot should be configured, and the IP of the robot controller should be found before starting the robot driver.

Understanding the MoveIt IKFast plugin

One of the default numerical IK solvers in ROS is KDL. This library is used to calculate the direct and inverse kinematics of a robot using the URDF. KDL mainly uses DOF > 6. In DOF <= 6 robots, we can use analytic solvers, which are much faster than numerical solvers, such as KDL. Most industrial arms have DOF <= 6, so it will be good if we make an analytical solver plugin for each arm. The robot will work on the KDL solver too, but if we want a fast IK solution, we can choose something such as the IKFast module to generate analytical solver-based plugins for MoveIt. We can check which are the IKFast plugin packages present in the robot (for example, universal robots and ABB):

- ur_kinematics: This package contains IKFast solver plugins of UR-5 and UR-10 robots from Universal Robotics.
- abb_irb2400_moveit_plugins/irb2400_kinematics: This package contains IKFast solver plugins for the ABB robot model IRB 2400.

We can go through the procedures to build an IKFast plugin for MoveIt. It will be useful when we create an IK solver plugin for a custom industrial robotics arm. Let's see how to create a MoveIt IKFast plugin for the industrial robot ABB IRB 6640.

Creating the MoveIt IKFast plugin for the ABB IRB 6640 robot

We have seen the MoveIt package for the ABB robot IRB 6640 model. This robot works with a default numerical solver. In this section, we will discuss how to generate an IK solver plugin using IKFast, a powerful inverse kinematics solver provided within Rosen Diankov's OpenRAVE motion planning software. At the end of this section, we will be able to run the MoveIt demo of this robot, using our custom inverse kinematic plugin.

In short, we will build an IKFast MoveIt plugin for the robot ABB IRB 66400. This plugin can be selected during the MoveIt setup wizard or we can mention it in the config/kinematics.yaml file of the moveit-config package.

Prerequisites for developing the MoveIt IKFast plugin

The following is the configuration we have used for developing the MoveIt IKFast plugin:

- Ubuntu 20.04 LTS
- ROS Noetic desktop, full installation
- OpenRave

The OpenRave and IKFast modules

OpenRave is a set of command lines and GUI tools for developing, testing, and deploying motion planning algorithms in real-world applications. One of the OpenRave modules is IKFast, which is a robot kinematics compiler. OpenRave was created by a robotic researcher called *Rosen Diankov*. The IKFast compiler analytically solves the inverse kinematics of a robot and generates optimized and independent C++ files, which can be deployed in our code for solving IK. The IKFast compiler generates analytic solutions of IK, which is much faster than numerical solutions provided by KDL. The IKFast compiler can handle any number of DOFs, but practically it is well suited for DOF <= 6. IKFast is a Python script that takes arguments such as IK types, robot model, the joint position of the base link, and end effectors.

The following are the main IK types supported by IKFast:

- Transform 6D: This end effector should calculate the commanded 6D transformation.
- Rotation 3D: This end effector should calculate the commanded 3D rotation.
- Translation 3D: This end effector origin should reach the desired 3D translation.

MoveIt IKFast

The ikfast package for MoveIt contains tools to generate a kinematic solver plugin using the OpenRave source files. We will use this tool to generate an IKFast plugin for MoveIt.

Installing the MoveIt IKFast package

The following command will install the moveit-ikfast package in ROS Indigo:

```
sudo apt-get install ros-noetic-moveit-kinematics
```

Let's discuss how to install and use OpenRave.

Installing OpenRave on Ubuntu 20.04

Installing OpenRave on the latest Ubuntu (Ubuntu 20.04) is an easy task. We will install OpenRave from a set of convenient scripts used to also install its dependencies. To install OpenRave, follow these steps:

1. The first step is to download these scripts from the following Git repository:

```
git clone https://github.com/crigroup/openrave-
installation
```

2. You can download it whenever you prefer. Now, we are ready to install the OpenRave dependencies. Always pay attention to prompts for sudo and insert the administrator password:

```
cd openrave-installation
```

3. Install a set of library dependencies:

```
./install-dependencies.sh
```

4. Install OpenSceneGraph:

```
./install-osg.sh
```

5. Install the Flexible Collision Library:

```
./install-fcl.sh
```

6. Finally, we can install OpenRave:

```
./install-openrave.sh
```

7. After installing OpenRave, execute the following command to check that OpenRave is working:

```
openrave
```

If everything works fine, it will open a 3D view window. In the next section, we will use OpenRave to create a plugin to solve the inverse kinematic problem of our manipulator.

Creating the COLLADA file of a robot to work with OpenRave

In this section, we will discuss how to use URDF robot models with OpenRave. Firstly, we will see how to convert a URDF in a `collada` file (`.dae`) format; this file will then be used to generate the `IKFast` source file. To convert a URDF model into a `collada` file, we can use a ROS package called `collada_urdf`. This can be installed with the following command:

```
sudo apt-get install ros-noetic-collada-urdf
```

We will work with the ABB IRB 6640 robot model, which can be found in the `abb_irb6600_support` package in the `/urdf` folder named `irb6640.urdf`. Alternatively, you can take this file from the `ikfast_demo` folder released with the book's source code. Copy this file into your working folder and run the following command for the conversion:

```
roscore && rosrun collada_urdf urdf_to_collada irb6640.urdf
irb6640.dae
```

The output of the previous command is the robotic model in the `collada` file format.

In most cases, this command fails because most of the URDF file contains STL meshes and it may not convert into DAE as we expected. If the robot meshes in the DAE format, it will work fine. If the command fails, follow this procedure:

Install the `meshlab` tool for viewing and editing meshes, using the following command:

```
sudo apt-get install meshlab
```

Open meshes present at `abb_irb6600_support/meshes/irb6640/visual` in MeshLab and export the file into DAE with the same name. Edit the `irb6640.urdf` file and change the visual meshes in the STL extension to DAE. This tool only processes meshes for visual purposes, so we will get a final DAE model.

We can open the `irb6640.dae` file using OpenRave with the following command:

```
openrave irb6640.dae
```

We will get the model in OpenRave, as shown in the following screenshot:

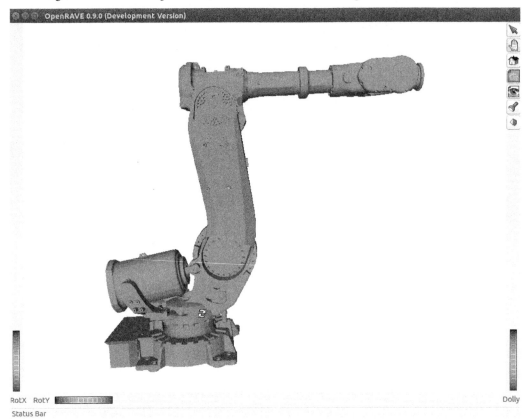

Figure 15.18 – Viewing the ABB IRB 6640 model on OpenRave

We can check the link information of the robot by using the following command:

```
openrave-robot.py irb6640.dae --info links
```

We can get the link info about the robot in the following format:

name	index	parents
base_link	0	
base	1	base_link
link_1	2	base_link
link_2	3	link_1
link_4	5	link_3
link_5	6	link_4

link_6	7	link_5
tool0	8	link_6
link_cylinder	9	link_1
link_piston	10	link_cylinder
---------------------------		--

Now that we have prepared the .dae file, we can generate the IKFast source file for this robot.

Generating the IKFast CPP file for the IRB 6640 robot

After getting the link information, we can start to generate the inverse kinematic solver source file for handling the IK of this robot. All the files needed to follow the tutorial of this section are available in the source code folder, ikfast_demo, provided with this book. Alternatively, you can download this code by cloning the following Git repository:

```
git clone https://github.com/jocacace/ikfast_demo.git
```

Use the following command to generate the IK solver for the ABB IRB 6640 robot:

```
python `openrave-config --python-dir`/openravepy/_openravepy_/
ikfast.py --robot=irb6640.dae --iktype=transform6d --baselink=1
--eelink=8 --savefile=ikfast61.cpp
```

The preceding command generates a CPP file called ikfast61.cpp, in which the IK type is transform6d, the position of the baselink link is 1, and the end effector link is 8. We need to mention the robot DAE file as the robot argument.

Before using this code with MoveIt, we can test it with the ikfastdemo.cpp demo source. This ikfastdemo.cpp source code has been modified to include the ikfast61.cpp source code, as you can see from the header file list:

```
#define IK_VERSION 61
#include "output_ikfast61.cpp"
```

Compile the demo source files:

```
g++ ikfastdemo.cpp -lstdc++ -llapack -o compute -lrt
```

The previous command generates an executable called `compute`. If you run it without input arguments, the program displays the usage menu. To get the forward kinematic solution, given a set of joint angle values, use the following command:

```
./compute fk j0 j1 j2 j3 j4 j5
```

Here, `j0 j1 j2 j3 j4 j5` represents the joint angle values in radians. To measure the average time taken by the IKFast algorithm for a set of random joint angles, use the following command:

```
./compute iktiming
```

Now that we have successfully created the inverse kinematic solver CPP file, we can create a MoveIt `IKFast` plugin by using this source code.

Creating the MoveIt IKFast plugin

Creating a MoveIt `IKFast` plugin is quite easy. There is no need to write code; everything can be generated using some tools. The only thing we need to do is to create an empty ROS package. The following is the procedure to create a plugin:

1. Create an empty package in which the name should contain the robot name and model number. This package is going to convert into the final plugin package, using the plugin generation tool:

    ```
    catkin_create_pkg abb_irb6640_moveit_plugins
    ```

2. Then, build the workspace by using the `catkin_make` command.
3. After building the workspace, copy `ikfast.h` to `abb_irb6640_moveit_plugins/include`.
4. Copy the switch `ikfast61.cpp`, previously created in the package folder, renaming it `abb_irb6640_manipulator_ikfast_solver.cpp`. This filename consists of the robot's name, model number, type of robot, and so on. This kind of naming is necessary for the generating tool.

After performing these steps, open two terminals in the current path where the IK solver CPP file exists. In one terminal, start the `roscore` command. In the next terminal, move into the `create` package and enter the plugin creation command, as follows:

```
rosrun moveit_kinematics create_ikfast_moveit_plugin.py abb_
irb6640 manipulator abb_irb6640_moveit_plugins abb_irb6640_
manipulator_ikfast_solver.cpp
```

This command could fail due to a mismatch of the robot name specified in the URDF and SRDF files. To work around this error, we need to change the name of the robot in the SRDF file, placed in the `abb_irb6640_mveit_config/config` folder. You change line seven of this file from `<robot name="abb_irb6640_185_280">` to `<robot name="abb_irb6640">`. Or simply replace this file with the one contained in the `ikfast_demo` folder.

The `moveit_ikfast` ROS package includes the `create_ikfast_moveit_plugin.py` script for plugin generation. The first parameter is the robot name with the model number, the second argument is the type of robot, the third argument is the package name we created earlier, and the fourth argument is the name of the IK solver CPP file. This tool needs the `abb_irb6640_moveit_config` package in order to work. It will search this package using the given name of the robot. So, if the name of the robot is wrong, the tool for raising an error will say that it couldn't find the robot `moveit` package.

If the creation is successful, the following messages will be displayed in the terminal:

```
IKFast Plugin Generator
Loading robot from 'abb_irb6640_moveit_config' package ...
Creating plugin in 'abb_irb6640_moveit_plugins' package ...
  found 1 planning groups: manipulator
  found group 'manipulator'
  found source code generated by IKFast version 268435529

Created plugin file at '/home/jcacace/ros_ws/src/MASTERING_ROS/ch13/abb_irb6640_moveit_plugins/src/abb_irb6640_manipulator_ikfa
st_moveit_plugin.cpp'

Created plugin definition at: '/home/jcacace/ros_ws/src/MASTERING_ROS/ch13/abb_irb6640_moveit_plugins/abb_irb6640_manipulator_m
oveit_ikfast_plugin_description.xml'

Overwrote CMakeLists file at '/home/jcacace/ros_ws/src/MASTERING_ROS/ch13/abb_irb6640_moveit_plugins/CMakeLists.txt'

Modified package.xml at '/home/jcacace/ros_ws/src/MASTERING_ROS/ch13/abb_irb6640_moveit_plugins/package.xml'

Modified kinematics.yaml at /home/jcacace/ros_ws/src/abb_irb6640_moveit_config/config/kinematics.yaml

Created update plugin script at /home/jcacace/ros_ws/src/MASTERING_ROS/ch13/abb_irb6640_moveit_plugins/update_ikfast_plugin.sh
```

Figure 15.19 – Terminal messages on the successful creation of the IKFast plugin for MoveIt

As you can see from these messages, after creating the plugin, the `abb_irb6640_moveit_config/config/kinematics.yaml` file has been updated, specifying `abb_irb6640_manipulator_kinematics/IKFastKinematicsPlugin` as the kinematics solver. The updated version of the file is shown in the following code:

```
manipulator:
  kinematics_solver:      abb_irb6640_manipulator_kinematics/
  IKFastKinematicsPlugin
  kinematics_solver_search_resolution: 0.005
  kinematics_solver_timeout: 0.005
  kinematics_solver_attempts: 3
```

Now you can build the workspace again in order to install the plugin and start to operate with the robot and the new IKFast plugin, using the demo.launch file from the abb_irb6640_moveit_config package. At this point, this plugin will be used every time that a motion trajectory is requested by MoveIt.

Summary

In this chapter, we discussed a new interface of ROS for industrial robots called ROS-Industrial. We looked at the basic concepts of developing industrial packages and installing them in Ubuntu. After installation, we looked at the block diagram of this stack, and discussed developing the URDF model for industrial robots and also creating the MoveIt interface for an industrial robot.

After covering these topics in detail, we installed the industrial robot packages for Universal Robots and ABB. We learned the structure of the MoveIt package and then shifted to the ROS-Industrial support packages. We discussed them in detail and switched to concepts such as the industrial robot client and how to create the MoveIt IKFast plugin. Finally, we used the developed plugin in the ABB robot.

In the next chapter, we will look at troubleshooting and best practices in ROS software development.

Here are some questions that will help you better understand this chapter.

Questions

- What are the main benefits of using ROS-Industrial packages?
- What are the conventions followed by ROS-I in designing a URDF for industrial robots?
- What is the purpose of ROS' support packages?
- What is the purpose of ROS' driver packages?
- Why do we need the IKFast plugin for our industrial robot, rather than the default KDL plugin?

16
Troubleshooting and Best Practices in ROS

In this chapter, we will discuss how to set up an **Integrated Development Environment (IDE)** with ROS, best practices in ROS, and troubleshooting tips for ROS. This is the last chapter of this book, so before we start development in ROS, it would be good to know the standard methods for writing code. The following are the topics that we are going to discuss in this chapter:

- Setting up Visual Studio Code IDE with ROS

- Best practices in ROS

- Best coding practices for ROS packages

- Important troubleshooting tips for ROS

Before we start coding in ROS, we should set up a ROS development environment in an IDE.

Setting up an IDE for coding and, in particular, for ROS is not mandatory, but it can save developers time. IDEs can provide auto-completion features, as well as build and debugging tools that can make programming easy. We can use any editor, such as **Sublime Text** or **Vim**, or simply **Gedit** for coding in ROS, but it's good if you choose certain IDEs when you are planning a big project in ROS. For this reason, in this chapter, we will focus on **Visual Studio Code**, an IDE that can be easily configured for ROS development.

Visual Studio Code can be used with any kind of programming language. In theory, it is only a code editor. Besides, several extensions are available to support additional functionalities, transforming it into a powerful IDE. Among them, a proper extension makes ROS development visual, simple, and manageable. In addition, Visual Studio Code offers useful tools to manage the ROS workspace, how ROS nodes are created, handled, and compiled, and the support-running ROS tools.

Setting up Visual Studio Code with ROS

Several IDEs are available in Linux – such as **NetBeans** (`https://netbeans.org`), **Eclipse** (`www.eclipse.org`), and **QtCreator** (`https://wiki.qt.io/Qt_Creator`) – and they are suitable for different programming languages. To build and run ROS programs from IDEs, the ROS environment must be set up. Some IDEs might have a configuration file for that, but running your IDE from your ROS-sourced shell should be the easiest way to avoid any inconsistencies. In this section, we will discuss how to use the **Visual Studio Code** IDE with ROS. A comprehensive list of other IDEs that can be configured with ROS can be found at `http://wiki.ros.org/IDEs`.

Visual Studio Code (`https://code.visualstudio.com/`) is a multi-platform IDE that's available for Linux, Windows, and macOS. It is a powerful source code editor but at the same time, it is very lightweight. It comes with a set of functionalities that support web-based programming languages such as JavaScript, TypeScript, and Node.js. However, it also provides a rich ecosystem of extensions for other languages (such as C++, C#, Java, Python, and similar). Before starting with Visual Studio Code and ROS, let's learn how to install it on an Ubuntu system and describe its basic usage.

Installing/uninstalling Visual Studio Code

The easiest way to install Visual Studio Code on Ubuntu 20.04 is by using the official
.deb file, which is available on Visual Studio Code's official website. You can download it
using the following command:

```
wget https://go.microsoft.com/fwlink/?LinkID=760868 -O  vscode.
deb
```

At this point, you can install the .deb package using the dpkg command:

```
cd /path/to/the/deb/file/
sudo dpkg -i vscode.deb
```

To remove the software, you can use the following command:

```
sudo apt-get remove code
```

Now that Visual Studio Code has been installed on your system, you can start using its
functionalities.

Getting started with Visual Studio Code

Once you have installed **vscode**, you can start it from the command line or the program
launcher of your system:

```
code
```

After launching this command, the main window of vscode will open, as shown in the following screenshot:

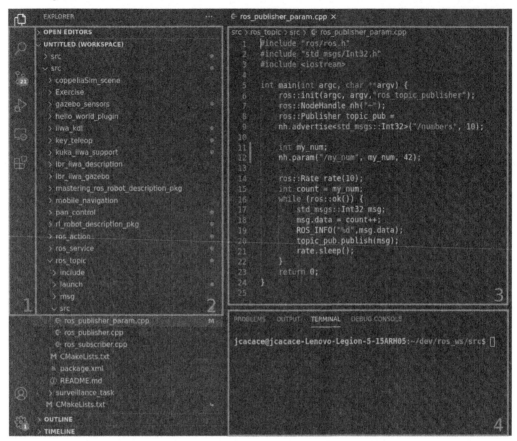

Figure 16.1 – Visual Studio Code user interface

The main elements of the window are as follows:

1. **ACTIVITY BAR**: This panel allows you to switch between the different functionalities and plugins of vscode. To see the code, the **Explorer** window must be selected. Using the other buttons, you can explore the available extensions, an interface for the versioning system, and more.

2. **EXPLORER** window: This panel shows the content of your code workspace. From this panel, you can navigate through all the ROS packages that have been installed in your ROS workspace.

3. **EDITOR**: In this panel, you can edit the source code of the packages.

4. **TERMINAL** and **OUTPUT**: These panels allow developers to use the Linux Terminal that's integrated with the IDE and check for possible errors during compilation.

The main features of vscode are integrated into the term **IntelliSense**. This term is quite general and consists of different code editing features such as code completion, function parameter information, the class member list, and many others. By default, Python and C++ are not configured to be supported by the IntelliSense system of vscode, so we need to configure them by installing the necessary extensions. Moreover, the first time you start vscode, the explorer windows will be empty, since no workspaces will have been configured. Later in this chapter, we will learn how to add source code directories to Visual Studio Code. For now, let's learn how to install a set of additional extensions for programming robots.

Installing new Visual Studio Code extensions

A new extension can be installed in two ways. One way is by using the extension panel to open the extension marketplace, in which you can search for the desired extension and install it, as shown in the following screenshot:

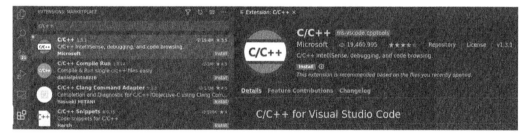

Figure 16.2 – Visual Studio Code extension marketplace

Using the search panel, you can also discover new extensions. Another way to install extensions is by using the vscode Quick Open bar, which you can open by pressing *CTRL + P*. For example, to install the C/C++ IntelliSense support shown in the preceding screenshot using the Quick Open bar, press *CTRL + P* in the editor window and paste the following command:

```
>> ext install ms-vscode.cpptools
```

Of course, in this case, you should already know the correct command for the extension.

By executing this command, you will have added the C/C++ language support to Visual Studio Code, including IntelliSense and debugging features.

Before installing the ROS extension, you may find the following plugins useful:

- **CMake**: This extension installs the IntelliSense support in `CMakeLists.txt` files. To install this plugin, use the `ext install twxs.cmake` command.

- **CMake Tools**: This extension provides the native developer with a full-featured, convenient, and powerful workflow for CMake-based projects in Visual Studio Code. To install this plugin, use the `ext install ms-vscode.cmake-tools` command.

- **GitLens**: This extension installs additional functionalities built into Visual Studio Code so that you can use Git features. To install this plugin, use the `ext install eamodio.gitlens-insiders` command.

- **Python**: This extension installs IntelliSense support for Python. To install this plugin, use the `ext install ms-python.python` command.

Finally, an add-on that is very useful when you are programming real robots is the `Remote - SSH` extension. This extension lets you use any remote machine with an SSH server as your development environment. After establishing a connection with the remote host, you can use the vscode Terminal to run commands on the remote machine and also inspect its source files. The `Remote - SSH` extension can be installed with the following command:

```
>> ext install ms-vscode-remote.remote-ssh
```

Now that we've installed all these plugins, let's learn how to install the ROS extension for vscode and configure the ROS environment.

Getting started with the Visual Studio Code ROS extension

To install the ROS extension, you can use the following command after pressing *CTRL + P* in the vscode interface:

```
>> ext install ms-iot.vscode-ros
```

Let's discuss the main features of this plugin. The ROS environment is automatically configured, and the ROS version is detected once you've installed this extension. However, this extension can only be used once a ROS workspace has been loaded. To load a workspace, you can use the main bar of the vscode window and go to **File | Open Folder**, and then select the desired workspace.

At this point, a new icon containing information about ROS and its version should appear in the bottom status bar, as shown in the following screenshot:

Figure 16.3 – ROS status icon in the bottom bar of VSCode

In this case, vscode finds that the Noetic version of ROS has been installed. The cross icon on the left-hand side of the ROS version is the ROS indicator and indicates that `roscore` is not active yet. At this point, a new set of commands can be used to create, compile, and manage your ROS nodes and the overall system. In this context, a new command can be inserted into vscode using the *CTRL + Shift + P* shortcut. For example, to start `roscore` directly from vscode, you should use the following command:

```
>> ROS: Start Core
```

To check the effect of the command, you can directly click on the ROS icon shown in the preceding screenshot to open a new page inside vscode. This page can be seen in the following screenshot and shows the status of our `roscore`, as well as the active topics and services:

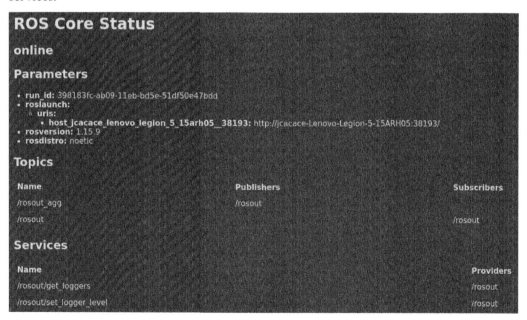

Figure 16.4 – ROS status page in VSCode

The same result can be obtained using the `Show Core Status` command:

```
>> ROS: Show Core Status
```

Similarly, to stop roscore, you can use the following command:

```
>> ROS: Stop Core
```

However, roscore can be also controlled externally from the classic Linux Terminal. As part of the IntelliSense section of vscode, with the ROS extension, we can enable syntax highlighting for common ROS files, such as the message, service, action, and URDF files.

Inspecting and building the ROS workspace

After loading the ROS workspace in vscode, you can quickly open source files using the *CTRL + P* shortcut to make the **Quick Open** bar appear. From this panel, you can search for any source file just by typing in part of its name, as shown in the following screenshot:

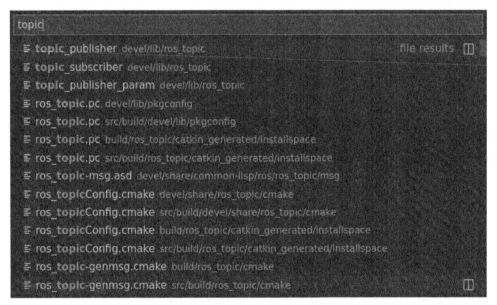

Figure 16.5 – Quick Open bar of Visual Studio Code

Now, you can start compiling the workspace using a vscode command. This can be done with the *CTRL + Shift + B* shortcut command, which lets you select the build task to run. In particular, ROS is compiled with the **catkin** compilation tool. To use this tool, the following compilation task must be inserted:

```
>> catkin_make: build
```

The compilation output will be shown in the Terminal window. In this window, eventual compilation errors are shown. You can use the *CTRL + Click* shortcut to directly open the line of code that produced this error in the editor, as shown in the following screenshot:

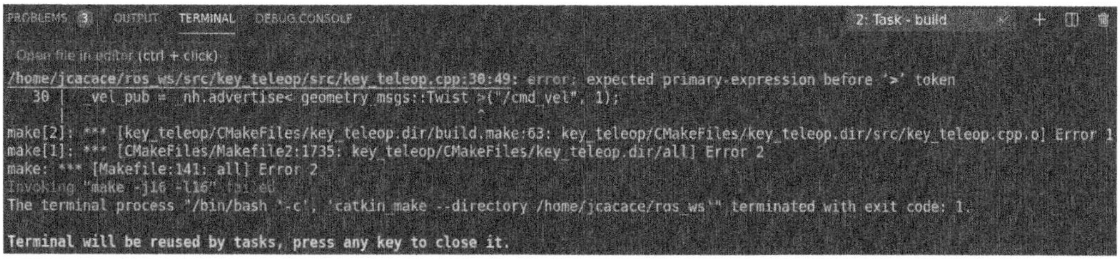

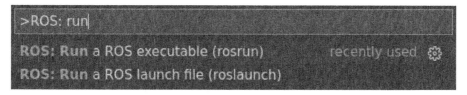

Figure 16.6 – Compilation error in the vscode terminal window

Additional commands can be used to manage the ROS packages and its nodes, as discussed in the next section.

Managing ROS packages using Visual Studio Code

To create a new ROS package, you can use the following command:

```
>> ROS: Create Catkin Package
```

The vscode editor will ask you to insert the name of the package and its dependencies, as shown in the following screenshot:

```
package_name
Package name (Press 'Enter' to confirm or 'Escape' to cancel)
```

```
roscpp std_msgs geometry_msgs
Dependencies (Press 'Enter' to confirm or 'Escape' to cancel)
```

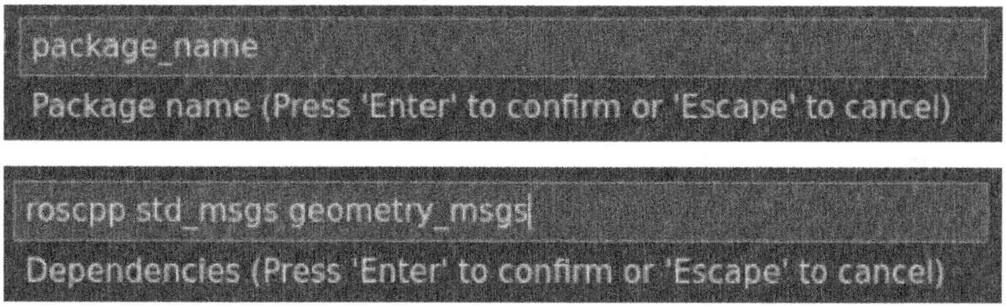

Figure 16.7 – Creating a ROS package using vscode

After creating and compiling the new package, you can manage the execution of its nodes directly from vscode. To start a new node, we can use both the `rosrun` and `roslaunch` commands. After opening the command window and typing the `run` keyword, vscode helps you choose the desired action, as shown in the following screenshot

```
>ROS: run
ROS: Run a ROS executable (rosrun)              recently used  ⚙
ROS: Run a ROS launch file (roslaunch)
```

Figure 16.8 – Running a node from vscode

Of course, to start the desired node properly, we must insert the name of the package that it is contained in, the name of the executable, and a list of eventual arguments for the node. When this occurs, a set of suggestions are provided in the vscode window. In the same way, you can select a launch file as part of a given package to start multiple nodes at the same time.

Visualizing the preview of a URDF file

Among the different functionalities provided by the ROS extension for Visual Studio Code, a useful feature is the URDF preview command. This command opens a vscode window in which the result of a URDF file is shown in real time. In this way, developers can see the results of the modifications they've made to a robot model file. To preview the URDF file, open a robot model file in the editor window; for example, the pan-tilt model we developed in *Chapter 3, Working with ROS for 3D Modeling*. You can use the **Quick Open** bar (*CTRL + P*) and type in the pan_tilt keyword to quickly find it. At this point, use the following command to visualize this preview:

```
>> ROS: Preview URDF
```

The result of this command is displayed in the following screenshot:

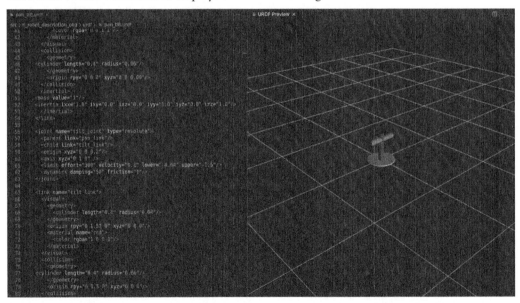

Figure 16.9 – URDF preview command used on the pan_tilt.urdf file in vscode

At this point, you can also try to change the parameters and elements of this URDF file to see the change in the visualized model, in the URDF **Preview** window. It is quite clear that working with this IDE allows developers to speed up how they design and code their robotic applications. In the next section, a brief overview of the best practices in ROS development will be discussed.

Best practices in ROS

This section will give you a brief idea of the best practices that can be followed when developing something with ROS. ROS provides detailed tutorials about its **Quality Assurance (QA)** process. A QA process is a detailed developer guide that includes C++ and Python code style guides, naming conventions, and so on. First, we will discuss the ROS C++ coding styles.

ROS C++ coding style guide

ROS C++ nodes follow a coding style to make the code more readable, debuggable, and maintainable. If the code is styled properly, it will be very easy to reuse and contribute to the current code. In this section, we will quickly go through some commonly used coding styles.

Standard naming conventions used in ROS

Here, we are using the text `HelloWorld` to demonstrate the naming patterns we use in ROS:

- `HelloWorld`: This name starts with an uppercase letter, and each new word starts with an uppercase letter with no spaces or underscores.

- `helloWorld`: In this naming convention, the first letter will be lowercase, but new words will be in uppercase without spaces.

- `hello_world`: This only contains lowercase letters. Words are separated by underscores.

- `HELLO_WORLD`: All letters are uppercase letters. Words are separated by SPACEunderscores.

The following are the naming conventions that are followed by each component in ROS:

- **Packages, topics/services, files, and libraries**: These ROS components follow the `hello_world` pattern.

- **Classes/types**: These classes follow the `HelloWorld` naming convention – for example, `class ExampleClass`.

- **Functions/methods**: Functions follow the `helloWorld` naming convention, while function arguments follow the `hello_world` pattern – for example, `void exampleMethod(int sample_arg);`.

- **Variables**: Generally, variables follow the `hello_world` pattern.

- **Constants**: Constants follow the `HELLO_WORLD` pattern.

- **Member variables**: The member variable inside a class follows the `hello_world` pattern with a trailing underscore added – for example, `int sample_int_`.

- **Global variables**: Global variables follow the `hello_world` convention with a leading `g_` – for example, `int g_samplevar;`.

- **Namespace**: Namespaces follow the `hello_world` naming pattern.

Now, let's take a look at code license agreement.

Code license agreement

We should add a license statement at the top of our code. ROS is an open source software framework, and it's in the BSD license. The following is a code snippet of a license, which must be inserted at the top of the code. You can get a license agreement from any of the ROS nodes in this book's GitHub repository. You can check out the source code for the ROS tutorial at `https://github.com/ros/ros_tutorials`:

```
/***************************************************************
********
* Software License Agreement (BSD License)
*
* Copyright (c) 2012, Willow Garage, Inc.
* All rights reserved.
*
* Redistribution and use in source and binary forms, with or
without
* modification, are permitted provided that the following
conditions
```

```
 * are met:
 *************************************************************
 *******/
```

For more information about the various licensing schemes in ROS, refer to `http://wiki.ros.org/DevelopersGuide#Licensing`.

ROS code formatting

One thing that needs to be taken care of while developing code is its formatting. One of the basic things to remember about formatting is that each code block in ROS is separated by two spaces. The following is a code snippet showing this kind of formatting:

```
if(a < b)
{
  // do stuff
}
else
{
  // do other stuff
}
```

The following is an example code snippet in the ROS standard formatting style. It starts with the inclusion of header files and the definition of a constant:

```
#include <boost/tokenizer.hpp>
#include <moveit/macros/console_colors.h>
#include <moveit/move_group/node_name.h>

static const std::string ROBOT_DESCRIPTION = "robot_
description";    // name of the robot description (a param
name, so it can be changed externally)
```

Then, a namespace is defined:

```
namespace move_group
{
```

Finally, the definition of a class and its members is reported:

```
class MoveGroupExe
{
public:

  MoveGroupExe(const planning_scene_
monitor::PlanningSceneMonitorPtr& psm, bool debug) :
    node_handle_("~")
  {
    // if the user wants to be able to disable execution of
paths, they can just set this ROS param to false
    bool allow_trajectory_execution;
    node_handle_.param("allow_trajectory_execution", allow_
trajectory_execution, true);

    context_.reset(new MoveGroupContext(psm, allow_trajectory_
execution, debug));

    // start the capabilities
    configureCapabilities();
  }

  ~MoveGroupExe()
  {
```

Now, let's learn how the code's output should be presented in a Linux Terminal.

Console output information

Try to avoid printf or cout statements when printing debug messages inside ROS nodes.

We can use rosconsole (http://wiki.ros.org/rosconsole) to print debug messages from ROS nodes, instead of the printf or cout functions. rosconsole offers timestamped output messages, automatically logs the printed messages, and provides five different levels of verbosity. For more details about these coding styles, please refer to http://wiki.ros.org/CppStyleGuide.

In this section, we mainly focused on how to correctly write the source code inside ROS nodes. In the following section, we will discuss how to maintain the ROS package, as well as some important tips for solving typical problems that occur when compiling the ROS package and executing its nodes.

Best coding practices for the ROS package

The following are the key points to bear in mind while creating and maintaining a package:

- **Version control**: ROS supports version control using Git, Mercurial, and Subversion. We can host our code in GitHub and Bitbucket. Most of the ROS packages are in GitHub.

- **Packaging**: Inside a ROS catkin package, there will be a `package.xml` file. This file should contain the author's name, a description of its content, and its license.

    The following is an example of a `package.xml` file:

```
<?xml version="1.0"?>
<package>
   <name>roscpp_tutorials</name>

   <version>0.6.1</version>

   <description>
     This package attempts to show the features of ROS
step-by-step,
     including using messages, servers, parameters, etc.
   </description>

   <maintainer email="dthomas@osrfoundation.org">Dirk
Thomas</maintainer>

   <license>BSD</license>

   <url type="website">http://www.ros.org/wiki/roscpp_
tutorials</url>
   <url type="bugtracker">https://github.com/ros/ros_
tutorials/issues</url>
   <url type="repository">https://github.com/ros/ros_
```

```
tutorials</url>
    <author>Morgan Quigley</author>
```

In the next section, we will look at some common errors and mistakes that are made by developers when they create ROS nodes.

Important troubleshooting tips in ROS

In this section, we'll look at some of the common issues that are experienced when working with ROS, as well as tips on how to solve them.

One of ROS's in-built tools for finding issues in a ROS system is `roswtf`. `roswtf` is a command-line tool that checks for issues in the following areas of ROS:

- Environment variables and configuration
- Packages or metapackages configuration
- Launch files
- Online graphs

Now, let's take a look at using `roswtf`.

Using roswtf

We can check the issues inside a ROS package by simply going into the package and entering `roswtf`. We can also check for issues in our ROS system by entering the following command:

```
roswtf
```

This command generates a report about the health of the system – for example, in the case of an incorrect ROS hostname and master configuration, we will have the following report:

```
Loaded plugin tf.tfwtf
==============================================================================
Static checks summary:

Found 1 warning(s).
Warnings are things that may be just fine, but are sometimes at fault

WARNING ROS_HOSTNAME may be incorrect: ROS_HOSTNAME [192.168.2.23] resolves to [192.168.2.23], which does
not appear to be a local IP address ['127.0.0.1', '192.168.1.7'].

==============================================================================

ROS Master does not appear to be running.
Online graph checks will not be run.
ROS_MASTER_URI is [http://192.168.2.2:11311]
```

Figure 16.10 – roswtf output in the case of a wrong ROS hostname configuration

We can also run `roswtf` on launch files to search for potential issues:

```
roswtf <file_name>.launch
```

Additional information on the `roswtf` command can be found at `http://wiki.ros.org/roswtf`.

The following are some of the common issues that you may face when working with ROS:

- **Issue 1**: An error message stating `Failed to contact master at [localhost:11311]. Retrying...`:

```
jcacace@jcacace-Inspiron-7570:~$ rosrun roscpp_tutorials talker
[ERROR] [1515175271.173829991]: [registerPublisher] Failed to contact ma
ster at [localhost:11311]. Retrying...
```

Figure 16.11 – Failed to contact master error message

- **Solution**: This message appears when the ROS node executes without running the `roscore` command or checking the ROS master configuration.

- **Issue 2**: An error message stating `Could not process inbound connection: topic types do not match`:

```
jcacace@jcacace-Inspiron-7570:~$ rostopic pub /chatter std_msgs/Int32 "data: 1"
publishing and latching message. Press ctrl-C to terminate
[WARN] [1515176143.614150]: Could not process inbound connection: topic types do not
match: [std_msgs/String] vs. [std_msgs/Int32]{'topic': '/chatter', 'tcp_nodelay': '0'
, 'md5sum': '992ce8a1687cec8c8bd883ec73ca41d1', 'type': 'std_msgs/String', 'callerid'
: '/listener'}
```

Figure 16.12 – Inbound connection warning messages

- **Solution**: This occurs when there is a topic message mismatch, where we publish and subscribe to a topic with a different ROS message type.

- **Issue 3**: An error message stating `Couldn't find executables`:

```
jcacace@jcacace-Inspiron-7570:~$ rosrun roscpp_tutorials taker
[rosrun] Couldn't find executable named taker below /opt/ros/kinetic/sha
re/roscpp_tutorials
```

Figure 16.13 – Couldn't find executables

- **Solution**: This error could occur for different reasons. One error could be the wrong executable name being specified in the command line or the missing name of the executable in the ROS package. In this case, we should check its name inside the `CMakeLists.txt` file. In the case of nodes written in Python, this error can be solved by changing the execute permissions of the related script using the `chmod` command.

- **Issue 4**: An error message stating `roscore command is not working`:

```
jcacace@jcacace-Inspiron-7570:~$ roscore
^C... logging to /home/jcacace/.ros/log/5a62571a-f2d2-11e7-9514-9cda3ea0
e939/roslaunch-jcacace-Inspiron-7570-6141.log
Checking log directory for disk usage. This may take awhile.
Press Ctrl-C to interrupt
Done checking log file disk usage. Usage is <1GB.
```

Figure 16.14 – roscore command is not running properly

- **Solution**: One of the reasons that can hang the `roscore` command is the definitions of `ROS_IP` and `ROS_MASTER_URI`. When we run ROS on multiple computers, each computer has to assign its own IP as `ROS_IP`, and then use `ROS_MASTER_URI` as the IP of the computer that is running `roscore`. If this IP is incorrect, `roscore` will not run. This error can be generated by assigning an incorrect IP to these variables.

- **Issue 5**: An error message stating `Compiling and linking errors`:

```
Base path: /home/jcacace/ros_ws
Source space: /home/jcacace/ros_ws/src
Build space: /home/jcacace/ros_ws/build
Devel space: /home/jcacace/ros_ws/devel
Install space: /home/jcacace/ros_ws/install
####
#### Running command: "make cmake_check_build_system" in "/home/jcacace/ros_ws/build"
####
####
#### Running command: "make -j8 -l8" in "/home/jcacace/ros_ws/build"
####
[ 50%] Linking CXX executable /home/jcacace/ros_ws/devel/lib/linking_error_test/linking_error
CMakeFiles/linking_error.dir/src/linking_error.cpp.o: In function 'main':
/home/jcacace/ros_ws/src/linking_error_test/src/linking_error.cpp:7: undefined reference to 'ros::init(int&, char**, std::__cxx
11::basic_string<char, std::char_traits<char>, std::allocator<char> > const&, unsigned int)'
collect2: error: ld returned 1 exit status
linking_error_test/CMakeFiles/linking_error.dir/build.make:104: recipe for target '/home/jcacace/ros_ws/devel/lib/linking_error
_test/linking_error' failed
make[2]: *** [/home/jcacace/ros_ws/devel/lib/linking_error_test/linking_error] Error 1
CMakeFiles/Makefile2:493: recipe for target 'linking_error_test/CMakeFiles/linking_error.dir/all' failed
make[1]: *** [linking_error_test/CMakeFiles/linking_error.dir/all] Error 2
Makefile:138: recipe for target 'all' failed
make: *** [all] Error 2
Invoking "make -j8 -l8" failed
```

Figure 16.15 – Compiling and linking errors

- **Solution**: If the `CMakeLists.txt` file contains no dependencies, which are required to compile the ROS nodes, this error may appear. Here, we have to check the package dependencies in the `package.xml` and `CMakeLists.txt` files. Here, we are generating this error by commenting on the `roscpp` dependencies:

```
cmake_minimum_required(VERSION 2.8.3)
project(linking_error_test)

find_package(catkin REQUIRED COMPONENTS
  #roscpp
  std_msgs
)
```

Figure 16.16 – CMakeLists.txt without a package dependency

The preceding list covers a set of common mistakes that developers commit at the start of their programming experience in ROS. Additional tips can be found on the ROS wiki page: `http://wiki.ros.org/ROS/Troubleshooting`.

Summary

In this chapter, we learned how to work with the Visual Studio Code IDE, how to set up the ROS development environment inside the IDE, how to create nodes and packages, and how to manage ROS data. Then, we discussed some of the best practices in ROS while looking at naming conventions, coding styles, best practices while creating a ROS package, and so on. After discussing these best practices, we looked at ROS troubleshooting. There, we discussed various troubleshooting tips that we need to bear in mind when we work with ROS.

With this chapter, we conclude the Mastering ROS for Robotics Programming book. We hope you enjoyed reading this book and are satisfied with your learning path. Thank you for reading this book.

Here are some questions based on what we covered in this chapter.

Questions

- Why do we need an IDE to work with ROS?
- What are the common naming conventions that are used in ROS?
- Why is documentation important when we create a package?
- What is the use of the `roswtf` command?

Other Books You May Enjoy

If you enjoyed this book, you may be interested in these other books by Packt:

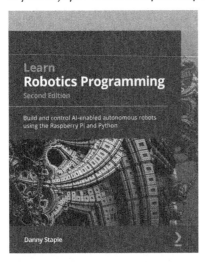

Learn Robotics Programming - Second Edition

Danny Staple

ISBN: 978-1-83921-880-4

- Leverage the features of the Raspberry Pi OS
- Discover how to configure a Raspberry Pi to build an AI-enabled robot
- Interface motors and sensors with a Raspberry Pi
- Code your robot to develop engaging and intelligent robot behavior
- Explore AI behavior such as speech recognition and visual processing
- Find out how you can control AI robots with a mobile phone over Wi-Fi
- Understand how to choose the right parts and assemble your robot

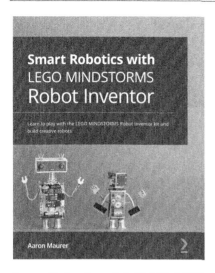

Smart Robotics with LEGO MINDSTORMS Robot Inventor

Aaron Maurer

ISBN: 978-1-80056-840-2

- Discover how the Robot Inventor kit works, and explore its parts and the elements inside them
- Delve into the block coding language used to build robots
- Find out how to create interactive robots with the help of sensors
- Understand the importance of real-world robots in today's landscape
- Recognize different ways to build new ideas based on existing solutions
- Design basic to advanced level robots using the Robot Inventor kit

Packt is searching for authors like you

If you're interested in becoming an author for Packt, please visit `authors.packtpub.com` and apply today. We have worked with thousands of developers and tech professionals, just like you, to help them share their insight with the global tech community. You can make a general application, apply for a specific hot topic that we are recruiting an author for, or submit your own idea.

Share Your Thoughts

Now you've finished *Mastering ROS for Robotics Programming, Third edition*, we'd love to hear your thoughts! Scan the QR code below to go straight to the Amazon review page for this book and share your feedback or leave a review on the site that you purchased it from.

`https://packt.link/r/1-801-07102-0`

Your review is important to us and the tech community and will help us make sure we're delivering excellent quality content.

Index

Y